CHINA LIVE

TWO DECADES IN THE HEART OF THE DRAGON

CHINA LIVE

TWO DECADES IN THE HEART OF THE DRAGON

MIKE CHINOY

CNN HONG KONG BUREAU CHIEF

Turner Publishing, Inc.

ATLANTA

ISBN 1-57036-360-9 (hardcover)
ISBN 1-57036-404-4 (paper)

Library of Congress Cataloging-in-Publication Data

Chinoy, Mike.
    China live : two decades in the heart of the dragon / by Mike Chinoy.
    p.   cm.
    ISBN 1-57036-360-9 (alk. paper)
    1. China—History—1976-   2. China—History—Tiananmen Square
    Incident, 1989.   I. Title
    DS779.2.C465   1997
    951.05'7—dc21   96-6606
                                                           CIP

Editor: Alan Axelrod
Copy Editor: Patrice Silverstein
Copy Chief: Jim Davis
Editorial Assistance: Michon Wise and Lisa Lewis
Design: Steven Acklin
Production Manager: Anne Murdoch

Published by Turner Publishing, Inc.
1050 Techwood Drive, NW
Atlanta, Georgia 30318

Distributed by Andrews and McMeel
A Universal Press Syndicate Company
4520 Main Street
Kansas City, Missouri 64111-7701

First Edition   10 9 8 7 6 5 4 3 2 1

Printed in the United States of America

Photo Credits:
BGEA/Russ Busby—Interior photo of Mike Chinoy with Billy Graham, back cover photo of cameraman at North Korea airport.
Victoria Yokota/*Washington Times Photo Agency*—Interior photo of Mike Chinoy broadcasting from Kim Il Sung Square, back cover photo of Kim Il Sung.
All other photos—collection of Mike Chinoy.

To my mother and the

memory of my father,

and to

Lynne, Daniel, and Benjamin

Once Zhuangzi dreamt that he was a butterfly. He did not know that he had ever been anything but a butterfly and was content to hover from flower to flower.

Suddenly he awoke and discovered to his astonishment that he was Zhuangzi. But it was hard to be sure whether he really was Zhuangzi and had only dreamt that he was a butterfly, or really was a butterfly and only dreaming that he was Zhuangzi.

—ZHUANGZI
The Realm of Nothing

TABLE OF CONTENTS

Preface

This book is the story of my personal journey, the education of a foreign correspondent caught up in some of the most momentous events of the twentieth century. China's turbulent transformation from Maoist poverty and isolation to rising superpower, wrought by the greatest economic boom of modern times but stained by the blood of Tiananmen Square, plays a central role in my narrative. However, the China story shares top billing with a profoundly important development of a different kind— the emergence of global satellite TV news, with its power to transmit human experience in real time across vast distances, crucially influencing political decisions, economic relationships, and social trends. For most of my adult life, I have been in the unusual and sometimes uncomfortable position of straddling both these powerful forces, watching as they interacted and sometimes collided. My experiences in the television revolution and the Chinese revolution—eight years as a Hong Kong–based China-watcher, nearly five years as a London-based roving reporter, and another eight years as CNN's Beijing bureau chief—form the heart of this book.

As an idealistic sixties student radical, I was drawn to Chairman Mao's China because I believed it might offer some answers to our own troubled American society. Before long and in the face of grim reality, my youthful political enthusiasm faded. It was replaced, however, by a deeper and more enduring fascination, both with China—a country as vast, complex, and compulsively interesting as it is difficult to figure out—and with the broader dynamic of revolutionary social and political change, as "people power" challenged, frightened, and sometimes toppled dictatorial governments around the world.

My China obsession led me to seek a career in broadcast journalism. At a time when the People's Republic remained largely off-limits to Americans, being a foreign correspondent, I thought, offered the best chance for a ticket to Beijing and a more extensive firsthand look at the Chinese revolution. My career did provide this—eventually—but, in the process, it also drew me into a revolution of a different kind. This one was led not by Mao Zedong but by Ted Turner. It took me not only to China but to countries from North Korea to Northern Ireland, from Pakistan to the Philippines, and introduced me to a brave new world of electronic news gathering, microwave uplinks, Inmarsat phones, and portable satellite dishes.

In this book, I have not tried to write a definitive history of CNN or an in-depth study of post-Mao China. Rather, I have sought to convey what it was like, professionally, intellectually, and, equally important, personally, to witness events I covered around the world, such as the opening of China in the mid-1970s, the bombing of the U.S. embassy in Lebanon in 1983, and the crackdown in Tiananmen Square. Along with a colorful cast of presidents, protestors, diplomats, soldiers, bar girls, and fellow reporters, the medium in which I work is itself a central character in my story. My narrative covers the years when CNN was transformed from "Chicken Noodle News," the fledgling operation I joined in 1983, to an immensely influential media colossus. CNN became not just a network but an idea of how we see the world—transcending traditional means of delivering information, confounding authoritarian rulers, allowing tens of millions of people to share the experience of watching historic events unfiltered, as they happen. Today, live television reports from distant corners of the globe are taken almost for granted. Viewers have come to expect to see revolutions, wars, and summits in real time, as if they were so many football games or tennis tournaments. But the technology is astonishingly new, as are the techniques for exploiting it. I was fortunate enough to be one of the foot soldiers in the vanguard of this revolution. *China Live* is an attempt to paint a picture of the process and some of the people involved in making it a reality.

The triumph of this new form of communication has created a host of tough questions. Thanks to satellite technology, the housewife in Des Moines, the mullah in Karachi, the business executive in Tokyo, the tourist in Paris, the Politburo member in Beijing, the hotel proprietor in Buenos Aires, and the president of the United States can all watch—and react to—the same report at the same time. Indeed, global television has become not simply a purveyor of news but, through its extraordinary impact and reach, a player in international politics and diplomacy. With the whole world watching, the pressure on those of us gathering the news in the field—to get it right, to be fair, and to tell the truth—is unrelenting.

Nowhere is such pressure more acute than in China. The People's Republic is a paradox—arguably both the best and worst country in the world in which to be a TV reporter. China's colorful people, breathtaking landscape, and rich history are a cameraperson's dream. Its historic changes make the People's Republic during the last quarter of the twentieth century one of the most compelling news stories ever. Yet its politics remain steeped in secrecy, its leaders hostile to reporters with cameras, and its entire culture imbued with a deep suspicion of foreigners. Deciphering its complexities and contradictions—let alone translating them into a medium that favors action, drama, and confrontation over ideas, subtlety, and contemplation—proved to be a daunting, at times overpowering, task. How ironic, then, that it was China during the Tiananmen Square crisis of 1989 that provided the setting for one of the defining moments of the Information Age: the first time a popular uprising in an authoritarian state was broadcast live around the world. The images from that time—the Goddess of Democracy and the man who stopped the tank—have taken their place as enduring symbols of protest. Even today they retain the power to stir emotions, so much so that they have somewhat distorted international understanding of the dramatic changes in China since Tiananmen. By the early 1990s, there was a vast gap between conventional Western perceptions of China as a one-dimensional police state, and the reality of a booming, vibrant, increasingly open and more loosely controlled society. I found myself in the curious position of feeling compelled to try, in my own reporting, to undo the impact of images I had helped to broadcast in 1989.

That the portrayal of one Chinese reality obscured another was typical of the ambiguities and paradoxes I repeatedly encountered. Senior Chinese leader Deng Xiaoping may have admonished his people to "seek truth from facts," but the long personal journey recounted in this book has left me with a sobering awareness of how hard it is to discern truth from lies and to separate fact from fiction. In an age of global television, with its power both to report and to distort reality, those of us in front of and behind the camera face a formidable challenge: to keep alive the search for a comprehensive, fair-minded understanding of the epic events we cover.

The personal narrative of *China Live* is drawn not only from my memories but also from a rich store of material dating back decades. In reconstructing events, I was able to rely on letters, diaries, journals, notebooks, copies of almost all my stories, and a huge collection of audiotapes and videotapes, the result of my inability to throw anything out. I have kept every single reporter's notebook from the earliest days of my career, including a 100-page, single-spaced, typed account of my first China trip in 1973, and equally detailed descriptions of other journeys. I retained every telex and every fax to and from the CNN Beijing bureau, from the day it opened. For eight years, I kept every script, as well as edited copies of all my TV spots, and had access to hundreds of raw videotapes that never went on the air. Many colleagues, friends, and family members generously shared their own letters, journals, diaries, and memories, and often consented to long and detailed interviews. I was able to recheck dates and other facts with the vast collection of articles and clippings from scores of newspapers and magazines I accumulated over the years. In the attic where I wrote, I was able to refer to everything from the *People's Daily* at the time of Chairman Mao's death to the *Indian Express* on the day Indian prime minister Indira Gandhi was murdered, to a remarkable compilation prepared by democracy activists in Hong Kong of the front pages of every leading newspaper from Hong Kong and Beijing for the entire tumultuous spring of 1989. In addition, I was able to take advantage of the rich resources of Smith College, with its outstanding library and research facilities. As a visiting scholar in the Government Department for the 1995–96 academic year, Smith not only gave me a base from which to work on this book, but offered the kind of support that made the entire project possible.

Because of the complex political situation in China, I have been concerned in writing this book not to jeopardize the safety of many of those I encountered over the years. To protect them, I have altered the names of some of those I mention. When I use a Chinese name in full—like President Jiang Zemin—it has not been changed. If I use only a surname—like my friend Yang from the *China Daily*—then it has been disguised to shield someone's identity. Equally, of my many Chinese friends and associates, there are some I cannot thank publicly for their help. But they know who they are.

Television is a collective endeavor, and, like the broadcast reports I did during the many years covered in this book, *China Live* could not have been written without the help of my colleagues. Above all, I want to thank my comrades in the CNN Beijing bureau: Cynde Strand, Mitch Farkas, Tim Schwarz, Rebecca MacKinnon, Wenchun Fan, Jessica Smith, Miranda Kuo, Tan Yadong, David Spindler, Wang Yuhang, and Li Aimin, plus the small army of researchers and interns, too numerous to name, who offered their help over the years. Thanks are due as well to the many others at CNN who shared in my adventures: John Lewis, Donna Liu, Tom Mintier, Alec Miran, Dick Blystone, Mick Deane, Phil Turner, Jeff Martino, John Towriss, Doug Habersin, Kit Swartz, Ken Jautz, Jane Maxwell, Joyce Fraser, Peter Vesey, Jim Schiffman, Parisa Khosravi, Jiro Mishina, Joe Manguno, Bernard Shaw, Peter Arnett, Steve Hurst, Ralph Begleiter, Larry Register, Will King, Françoise Husson, Jeanee Von Essen, Annie Steeper Morita, and Mei Yan. I owe a special debt to Ted Turner and to CNN's management, above all to Burt Reinhardt, Tom Johnson, Ed Turner, and Eason Jordan. They hired me, sent me to Beijing, had the confidence to keep me there for so many years, supported me when the going got tough, and then graciously agreed to grant me a year off to write.

There are many others who helped along the way: Brian Ellis, Mike Lam, Joe Yue, Nayan Chanda, Mark Mohr, Chris Szymanski, James Lilley, J. Stapleton Roy, Steven Young, Zorana Bakovic, the late Dave Schweisberg, Charlene Fu, Robert Benjamin, Andrew Halper, Danny Russel, Tsang Tak-sing, Carma Hinton, Richard Gordon, Yang Weiguang, Sheng Yilai, Susie Brown, Suzanne Phan, Marcia Burick, the late James Aronson, Betty Friedan, Steven Linton, Josette Shiner, Michael Breen, Charles McLaughlin, Lisa Prestwich, Grace Wong, and Adam Williams.

At Smith College, special thanks to presidents Mary Maples Dunn and Ruth J. Simmons; deans Robert Merritt and John

Connolly; professors Steven Goldstein, Peter Rose, Susan Bourque, and Donna Divine; and Phoebe Lewis, Lea Ahlen, Beth Muramoto, and Marlene Wong.

Michael Reagan of Turner Publishing initially encouraged me to write this book, and his enthusiastic support for the project never wavered. My editor at Turner Publishing, Alan Axelrod, was a constant source of guidance and help.

Steven Goldstein, Danny Russel, Ann Kraybill, Robert Benjamin, John Lewis, Donna Liu, Jordan Ryan, John Krich, Ada Mei, Robert Ross, and Betsy Glaser read all or substantial portions of the manuscript. I thank them for their always incisive comments and criticism.

I owe a special debt to my family. My sister, Claire, who has pursued her own international career as a professional flamenco dancer, and my cousin, the writer John Krich offered valuable suggestions, advice, and encouragement. My wife, Lynne, not only lived through most of the experiences recounted here but patiently read the manuscript and tolerated my constant mood swings and preoccupations as I struggled to bring this book to life. I had never really appreciated the meaning of the words so often found in book acknowledgments about how it couldn't have been done without the help of the author's family. Now I understand.

My biggest debt is to my mother, Helen Krich Chinoy. Despite the tragic death of my father in 1975, she unfailingly supported what must have often seemed to her to be my eccentric, if not downright reckless, ambition to be a foreign correspondent. With grace and unfailing good humor, she coped with the anxieties of watching me repeatedly risk my neck in distant corners of the globe On this project, she has been both my biggest fan and most relentless critic. She literally read every word of every draft: without her suggestions and advice, this book would not have been completed.

Finally, I want to thank Daniel and Benjamin, who had to do without the devoted attention of their father for so many months. When they are old enough to read this book, I hope it will help them not only to understand their family a little better, but to make sense of some of the major forces that have shaped not only my life but theirs as well.

CHINA LIVE

TWO DECADES IN THE HEART OF THE DRAGON

CHAPTER ONE

The Whole World Is Watching

T he walkie-talkie strapped to my belt crackled to life. It was nine o'clock Saturday morning, May 20, 1989. Producer Alec Miran was speaking from CNN's makeshift production studio at Beijing's Great Wall Sheraton Hotel, four miles from Tiananmen Square.

"Mike, get over here right away," he said, his voice tense. "The Chinese have just ordered us off the air. In an hour, they're pulling the plug."

I had been in Tiananmen Square day and night for most of the spring of 1989. This symbolic heart of China, where Chairman Mao Zedong had proclaimed the establishment of the People's Republic forty years earlier, was occupied by a new generation of rebels. Young and fresh-faced, the best and brightest of China's leading universities had poured into the square, chanting, "We demand dialogue," "Down with corruption," and "Long live democracy." For the past week, several thousand had gone without food to dramatize their call for political change. The hunger strikers were camped out in tents at the center of the hundred-acre expanse, next to the Monument to the Heroes of the Revolution erected by the Communists decades earlier. Now it was the nerve center of the student movement, where its leaders cranked out pamphlets, made announcements over a makeshift loudspeaker system, and held endless, acrimonious strategy sessions.

Bedecked with slogan-bearing headbands, sweating in the heat of the humid Beijing spring, many so weak that they lay prostrate on filthy pallets on the ground, the hunger strikers became the catalyst for a display of public disaffection that was shaking the Chinese Communist Party to its foundations. They were supported by what the Chinese called the *laobaixing*, "old hundred names," the ordinary citizens of Beijing: office assistants, rickshaw drivers, workers in still-grimy overalls, private entrepreneurs on shiny new motorcycles, all of them pressing toward the heart of the square in an endless drumbeating, flag-waving, singing procession.

In the past twelve hours, however, the bitter internal struggle between Communist Party moderates and old-guard conservatives sparked by the democracy demonstrations had reached a climax. Those sympathetic to the students had lost. A crackdown, possibly a military assault on Tiananmen, appeared imminent. The young people in the square readied themselves for the worst.

Through an accident of history, my colleagues and I were conveying this extraordinary drama to millions of people around the world. Eager for publicity about the summit meeting that week between paramount leader Deng Xiaoping and Soviet president Mikhail Gorbachev, the Chinese government, normally suspicious of the foreign media, had allowed CNN and other Western broadcasters to provide unprecedented live television coverage from Beijing. In the days before the summit, CNN had imported tons of TV equipment to the People's Republic, setting up a portable satellite dish in the Sheraton Hotel garden. From this uplink, our signal was beamed to a satellite orbiting the earth, down to CNN headquarters in Atlanta, and then, almost instantaneously, transmitted by satellite to viewers across the world.

Instead of a Chinese diplomatic triumph, however, our audience was witnessing day after day—live—a political drama of protest that soon captured the imagination of the world. But now, the hopes and dreams of China's democracy movement were colliding with a harsh reality. A few hours earlier, CNN had relayed a Chinese television broadcast in which hard-line Premier Li Peng, grim-faced in a black Mao suit, declared that the situation was out of control. Punching the air with his fist for emphasis, Li announced in his midnight television address that tough measures would be introduced to end what he called a "counterrevolutionary rebellion." As the premier's speech was relayed on giant loudspeakers, catcalls, curses, boos, and chants of "Down with Li Peng" echoed through the darkened square. The entire scene was beamed around the world on CNN, as were the astonishing moments that followed, when the People's Liberation Army (PLA) convoys deployed to crush the protests were blocked in the suburbs of Beijing by a series of human barricades. With CNN cameramen following the huge crowds that filled the streets throughout the night, the citizens of Beijing clambered over the armored vehicles and trucks carrying the estimated 150,000 troops who had been ordered into action. Offering the soldiers food, water, and cigarettes, the *laobaixing* begged, pleaded, and argued with them not to turn on their own people. Confused and visibly upset, the youthful recruits, largely unaware of the scale or nature of the democracy movement, stopped in their tracks.

Outraged by word of the crackdown, yet emboldened by the news that the "people's army" had so far heeded the demands of the people, more citizens began making their way toward Tiananmen, at a dawn hour promising a warm, sunny spring day after the downpours and gray skies of the past forty-eight hours. On foot, on bicycles, in three-wheeled carts, in buses, trucks, and cars, they had surged into the square.

But how long would they stay? That was the question on everyone's mind when Alec Miran issued his urgent summons. The government had given CNN sixty minutes to get off the air. At ten A.M., Li Peng's declaration of martial law would take effect. The Chinese media were already setting forth the contents of Martial Law Edicts One, Two, and Three: all demonstrations, gatherings, and speeches not approved by the government were banned. The security forces were authorized to take whatever action was deemed necessary to restore order. Foreign journalists were barred from reporting or filming any activities by those demanding political change in China.

With CNN's live camera in Tiananmen Square operating on borrowed time, I drove to the Great Wall Sheraton through a city in open revolt against the government. Normal life was at a standstill: stores were closed and public transport had come to a halt, but the streets were packed. At most key intersections, I was forced to make my way past barricades of fencing, tires, and trash cans that had been erected to keep the army away. Agitated, shouting crowds swarmed around my car. "Who are you?" they demanded. "Where are you coming from? Where are you going?"

"I am an American reporter," I replied. "I am on my way to broadcast about the democracy demonstrations in Tiananmen Square."

Abruptly the protestors burst into applause. Some of them shook my hand. "Go ahead," they said. "And tell the truth!"

I raced into the Sheraton, a luxurious Sino-American joint venture symbolizing the reform process in Deng Xiaoping's China that now seemed to have gone dreadfully wrong. It was here that my colleagues and I had gathered in quieter days during the past two years for ice cream, hamburgers, and satellite TV broadcasts of American football games. The bar in the lobby was the official headquarters of the Beijing Foreign Correspondents' Club. For what was intended to be live reporting of the Deng-Gorbachev summit, CNN had created a temporary TV studio at the front of a traditional Chinese-style building in the hotel garden. During the past week, it had been used as a backdrop for anchor Bernard Shaw to preside over the network's coverage of the events unfolding on the streets outside.

Now I joined Shaw and two other colleagues. A cynical, sardonic Asia hand, Tokyo bureau chief John Lewis was hollow-eyed and unshaven after spending virtually every night for two weeks in the square. Always smooth and polished, whatever the occasion, Moscow bureau chief Steve Hurst, who had been with me all night in Tiananmen, was somehow still presentable, even though the diplomatic story he had come to China to cover had abruptly turned into a drama of rebellion and growing fears of bloodshed. I hastily applied a layer of pancake to my own night's growth of beard, although the makeup did little to disguise the bags under my eyes. Then we were on the air, live, the four of us attempting to make sense of what we were witnessing—for our viewers as well as for ourselves.

"It is unbelievable to me that we were allowed to continue broadcasting for so long," Lewis mused. "They can stop us, but I don't know how they're going to stop these hundreds of thousands or million or so people in the streets right now."

"There is a tremendous risk now in this situation," I added, "and tremendous possibility of confrontation, if the government actually moves to carry out martial law. I think there is a great danger of bloodshed."

While we spoke, we remained acutely aware that at any moment the Chinese could pull the plug, taking us off the air. With so much armed might massed in the outskirts of the city, I worried that much worse might be in store for us. I was swept by a wave of anxiety for my wife, Lynne, and my two-year-old son, Daniel.

At ten o'clock, martial law formally came into force. Over Tiananmen, helicopters swooped low, dropping leaflets warning the protesters to disperse. But our live satellite link was still up. In the square, our crew panned their camera along the front of the Gate of Heavenly Peace, dominated by the thirty-foot-high portrait of Chairman Mao, perhaps the single most famous image of Communist rule in China. Below the chairman's stern visage, the camera captured truckloads of protestors waving antigovernment banners and flags, flashing V-for-victory signs, or shaking their clenched fists in the air. One truck carried a placard identifying its occupants as workers from the Capital Iron and Steel Works, Beijing's biggest factory. Several dozen medics, dressed in white gowns and caps, suddenly raced into view. Its siren blaring, an ambulance sped by on its way to a nearby hospital. Inside was yet another fasting student, weakened to the point of collapse by the hunger strike.

A moment later, producer Miran radioed down to us new details of the crackdown. "The government is announcing the city of Beijing is closed," Bernie said, repeating what he heard in his earpiece. "Foreign journalists can no longer report any news and information from this capital."

"I think that is a clear sign," I told our worldwide audience, "that we are going to have bloodshed here, and that all of us are now at some risk."

As we spoke, a new drama began to unfold in Miran's office nine floors above us. Two scowling Chinese officials from the Ministry of Posts and Telecommunications entered the hotel suite that CNN had used as a control room to cover the Gorbachev visit. They ordered an immediate end to our transmissions and threatened to confiscate our satellite dish and other equipment if we did not comply. But Miran, who had coordinated CNN's coverage throughout the tumultuous summit week, refused to obey. A tall, swarthy man with a bushy mustache who had handled big stories for the CNN Special Events unit all over the world, he demanded an explanation for the Chinese ultimatum, pointing out that it violated an earlier agreement under which CNN's permission to broadcast live did not expire until the following day. Unsure how to respond to Miran's defiance, they kept repeating, "You are here to report on Gorbachev. Gorbachev is gone. Your task is over. Your task is over." Moments later, Miran phoned a Chinese Foreign Ministry official. "You're saying we are only allowed to cover the Gorbachev visit?" he argued. "How about all the other stories we did in China that didn't concern Mr. Gorbachev? That has nothing to do with you? Then why does *this* have anything to do with you? What is the government afraid of?"

With mounting apprehension, Shaw, Hurst, Lewis, and I, standing on the set in the garden, listened through our earpieces to the confrontation upstairs. Then Miran told us it was being seen on TV sets around the world. In a gesture of journalistic cooperation appropriate to the nature of this threat to press freedom, an ABC News crew had hooked a camera to our feed equipment, enabling CNN to broadcast the control-room drama live. As the two officials kept repeating their instructions, our audience got a chilling insight into the workings of a totalitarian system unused to having its orders defied. Among the viewers, Alec said, was President George Bush.

Now Miran tried to stall for time by demanding that the Chinese give him something in writing instructing the network to end its transmissions. On the phone to CNN vice president Jane Maxwell in Atlanta, he said, "I am trying to make it clear to them that we require a letter. That is company policy, correct?"

Minutes before eleven, with martial law an hour old, defiant crowds still in the square, and confused troops still blocked in the suburbs, the exasperated Chinese finally put the injunction in writing. As the ABC cameraman zoomed in for a close-up of an official scribbling in Chinese on a yellow legal pad, Jane Maxwell in Atlanta reluctantly conceded that the game was up. Flanked by CNN president Burt Reinhardt, both of them visible on a split screen, she said, "The government has ordered us to shut down our facility. We'll have to shut down." A moment later, with our camera in the square, framing truckloads of banner-waving protestors in front of the giant Mao portrait, CNN ceased its live transmissions from Beijing.

"We came to cover a summit," mused Bernie Shaw a few minutes before the plug was pulled. "We walked into a revolution."

This was not the revolution I thought I was walking into when, as a youthful sixties radical, I was first drawn to China. A product of the baby boom, I was the only son of liberal-minded professors at Smith College in Northampton, Massachusetts, who had been left-wing activists themselves during the Great Depression of the 1930s. My father, Ely, a gentle man with curly hair and a quick smile, was a sociologist and a student of history. The child of Russian Jewish emigrants who ran a candy store in Newark, New Jersey, for most of their lives, my father became a well-known specialist on the experiences, dreams, and frustrations of industrial workers in America. My mother, Helen, whose parents had also fled the anti-Semitic pogroms of czarist Russia for a new life in the United States, had more artistic interests. Her father became an automobile dealer in Newark, her mother a volunteer for many community causes; but Helen wanted to be an actress, performing first in workers' theater troupes and, later, in summer-stock companies, before eventually becoming a distinguished theater historian.

During my childhood, interesting people—professors, students, performers, and publishers—always filled our house, exposing my little sister, Claire, and me to constant discussion and debate about political, cultural, and social issues. Watching the evening news on television every night was a family ritual, and to me, that half hour with Walter Cronkite, Chet Huntley, and David Brinkley was the highlight of the day. Already hooked on history—as a child, I had been able to recite the gory details of which king engaged in what battle when my parents took me to visit the famous castles of Europe—I now became obsessed with current affairs. My transformation into a teenage news junkie coincided with the massive American involvement in Vietnam. Obsessively glued to the radio and TV for the latest news from the battlefront, I made myself a walking encyclopedia on Indochina. For a high school student, I was precocious, and no doubt obnoxious—more interested in talking about the 1954 battle of Dien Bien Phu or the coup against South Vietnamese president Ngo Dinh Diem in 1963 than the fate of my school football team.

The televised images of death and destruction convinced me something was terribly wrong with U.S. policy in Vietnam. Like many of my contemporaries, I joined the antiwar movement, writing editorials in my high school newspaper, participating in a weekly "peace vigil" on the main street of my hometown, and demonstrating outside my local draft board. Eventually I applied for and was granted conscientious-objector status. I rang doorbells on behalf of Senator Eugene McCarthy's quixotic 1968 presidential campaign, then watched TV images of the tumultuous Democratic Convention in Chicago, Mayor Richard Daley's police beating and teargassing antiwar protestors on the streets outside. It was a lesson in the power of television. I couldn't get the demonstrators' words out of my head: "The whole world is watching!" they chanted. "The whole world is watching!"

I marched on Washington, participating in the Moratorium, a weekend of demonstrations in November 1969 that marked the peak of public protest against the war. On a raw, rainy night, I carried a candle in one hand and a placard with the name of an American serviceman killed in Vietnam in the other, walking in the March Against Death, single-file, from Arlington National Cemetery to the Capitol. There were 43,000 placards. The next evening, I stumbled into my first riot. With my cousin and political mentor John Krich, I tagged along as a group of flag-waving pro–Viet Cong radicals stormed the South Vietnamese Embassy. Police fired canister after canister of tear gas, scattering us through the elegant streets of Dupont Circle. The following day, I joined half a million people marching past the White House to the Washington Monument, where we cheered Mrs. Martin Luther King, Senator George McGovern, Dr. Benjamin Spock, and a host of other activists, singing "We Shall Overcome" and "Where Have All the Flowers Gone?" with folk trio Peter, Paul and Mary.

As I prepared to graduate from high school in the spring of 1970, President Nixon ordered American troops into Cambodia, drawing that neutral nation into the carnage of Vietnam and triggering campus protests all across the United States. On my TV set, I watched National Guardsmen gun down four student demonstrators at Kent State University, an act of brutality that set off a national student strike. At the center of the action was Yale University, to which I had just been admitted as a member of the next fall's freshman class. Ignoring my remaining high school papers and tests, I hurried to join the action in New Haven. In contrast to the relatively mainstream Moratorium, the speakers on the New Haven green in front of the university campus came from the extreme fringes of what was known as "the movement." They were supporters of the Black Panthers, whose leader, Bobby Seale, had been charged with murder, and of Abbie Hoffman and Jerry Rubin, who had organized the Chicago convention demonstrations and admonished us not to "trust anyone over thirty."

Anger boiled over as the youthful crowds of protestors battled riot police. Clouds of tear gas wafted past the dormitory where I would take up residence four months later. The sonorous tones of the poet Allen Ginsberg, chanting the Buddhist incantation *Om*, mingled in the huge Yale quadrangle with cries, antiwar slogans, exploding tear-gas canisters, and rock 'n' roll blaring from nearby dorm rooms. The revolution was coming to America, or so we thought—as did the police trying to disperse us.

I became a full-fledged foot soldier in my generation's rebellion against the status quo, with shoulder-length hair, a droopy mustache, a taste for pot, and a yearning for utopian change. While many of my friends turned to community activism, communes, or LSD, the intellectual and political ferment of the time drew me to China. The catalyst may have been a fellow demonstrator emulating the Red Guards by waving a copy of Mao's *Little Red Book* at an antiwar rally, or simply a feeling that if the U.S. government said it was fighting in Vietnam to contain Chinese communism, then Mao must be doing something right. The People's Republic of China, in the midst of a "Cultural Revolution," seemed to offer lessons for my own troubled society. I had read about the success of Chinese Communists in eliminating crime, venereal disease, inflation, corruption, and hopelessness; how they had liberated peasants from the oppression of the landlords, given work to beggars and the unemployed, reeducated the prostitutes, and rebuilt the cities. Education and literacy campaigns, "barefoot doctors" who took medical care to the most remote areas, new rights for women, social justice, and equality—these seemed to be the watchwords of the new China that Mao had created. Even more intriguing was that the Chinese revolution stressed spiritual and ethical values as well as more mundane political and economic issues—trying to build a new "Maoist man" dedicated not to selfish individualism but to selfless service for the collective good. With the enthusiasm of an eager young convert, I threw myself into the study of this ancient, distant nation, which seemed to have found answers to the problems of modern society.

It says something about China's remoteness from ordinary Americans that in my first year at Yale, my Chinese language class consisted of only two students, myself and the son of a Nobel Prize–winning Chinese-American physicist who sought to rediscover his Chinese roots. Most people had little interest in learning the language of a country that for a generation had been completely shut off from the United States.

My teacher at Yale University was a slight, soft-spoken man with graying hair and a round face named Zhao Haosheng, or, as he called himself in America, Howard Zhao. Every week we sat together as I struggled to master the four tones and complex written characters of Mandarin Chinese. With the bearing of a classical Chinese scholar, he corrected the strange sounds coming from my throat, in which a slight difference in inflection determined whether I had said the number "four" or the verb "to die." I was as captivated as I was incompetent.

But more compelling to me than the language was Howard's own story. A journalist in China's World War II capital of Chongqing (Chungking), he had come to know Zhou Enlai, then the Chinese Communist Party's front man and later premier of the People's Republic. When the Communists triumphed in 1949, however, Howard fled with the Nationalist forces of Chiang Kai-shek to Taiwan, later emigrating to the United States, where he became a leading anticommunist writer and commentator, as well as the author of the Chinese-language textbook that I found so difficult.

His tales of the correspondent's life in wartime Chongqing entranced me, but I argued with him all the time. "Professor Zhao," I would object, "Chairman Mao's revolution created a new, more egalitarian society, liberating millions of peasants and freeing China from Western influence. Chiang Kai-shek and his government were only puppets of the American imperialists."

"Mike," Howard would reply with a weary, knowing expression, "the Communists killed and imprisoned millions of people. They destroyed an ancient culture. Educated people like myself were forced to flee." Howard undoubtedly was convinced I was a naive Communist dupe. Caught up in my revolutionary enthusiasm, I thought he was a hopeless reactionary. Nevertheless, we forged a traditionally Chinese bond between student and teacher despite our endless disagreements.

The summer of my graduation in 1973, my bitterly anticommunist Chinese teacher suddenly showed up in Beijing, becoming one of the first prominent pro-Taiwan figures to break with the Chinese Nationalists and reach out to the Chinese Communists. Received by his old friend Premier Zhou Enlai, he was taken to visit his ancestral village and reunited with his mother, whom he hadn't seen since 1949. He quickly became a regular and honored guest in the Chinese capital, an important trophy for Beijing in the battle with nationalist Taiwan for the loyalty of the overseas Chinese community. I often wondered if our endless campus debates had anything to do with his dramatic change of heart.

As Howard Zhao was exchanging reminiscences with Zhou Enlai, I was trying to figure out what to do with the rest of my life. Out of college with no job prospects, I was armed only with what seemed to be a useless degree in Chinese Studies, an overwhelming desire to go to the People's Republic, and vague notions that the way to get there might be to become a foreign correspondent. My ambitions had been fueled by reading the exploits of Edgar Snow, the American journalist who had braved blockades, bandits, and warlords to become the first Westerner to make contact with Mao and the Chinese Communists in the 1930s. Snow had traveled to China in 1928 at the age of twenty-two, found work as a journalist in Shanghai and then Beijing, wandered the country in search of news and adventure, and eventually immersed himself in the world of student and peasant activists who propelled China on the road to revolution. I wished I had been born fifty years earlier.

As my interest in China had deepened, the country itself remained almost entirely inaccessible. It looked as if I might never see the land that had captured my imagination. In April 1971, the Chinese government invited an American Ping-Pong team to Beijing. Soon after came the earthshaking news that President Richard Nixon himself would travel to China the following year. On February 21, 1972, I had sat transfixed in my living room, watching an American president set foot on the frozen tarmac at Beijing airport to shake the hand of Premier Zhou Enlai. My fascination at what I was seeing overcame my discomfort that the country I viewed as a shining symbol of revolutionary virtue was welcoming the right-wing president I loved to hate. How I envied the TV correspondents sending back their daily reports from the Great Wall, the Forbidden

City, and the Great Hall of the People, even as I mocked some of the harsh, silly, and uninformed comments they made.

Although the Nixon trip marked the beginning of a Sino-U.S. rapprochement, access to a China still consumed by the legacy of the Cultural Revolution remained extremely difficult. The door was still closed to all but a handful of prominent American politicians or distinguished journalists. The only broader exceptions were "political tours" by small groups of American radicals sympathetic to Beijing. An organization of antiwar, pro-China academics called the Committee of Concerned Asian Scholars had sent two delegations. As a member of the Yale chapter, I applied to join a third CCAS trip planned for 1973, but my youth, inexperience, and lack of ideological sophistication ruled me out.

A month after my graduation in June 1973, sitting on the deck of my family's summer home in Martha's Vineyard, writing job application letters to every news organization I could think of, I got a call from Frank Kehl. A good friend, Frank was a bearded, dyed-in-the-wool Maoist and Columbia University graduate student who had visited China with the first CCAS China delegation in 1971

"Hi, Mike," he said. "Do you want to go to China?"

I was so excited I could barely speak.

My ticket to Beijing was to come courtesy of the *Guardian*, a left-wing newspaper in New York founded in the late 1940s by two radical journalists, Cedric Belfrage and James Aronson, which for decades had written sympathetically about the People's Republic. Anna Louise Strong, an old-time Communist who lived in Beijing and knew Mao well, and Australian Wilfred Burchett, who covered the Korean and Vietnam wars from the Communist side, were among the *Guardian*'s regular contributors. With many American radicals now turning toward China, the paper was taking advantage of its unique and long-standing relationship with Beijing to organize tours for the politically committed.

Borrowing the $1,400 fare from my parents, I boarded Japan Airlines flight 731 in San Francisco a month later and headed for Hong Kong. No holiday tour, the *Guardian* trip featured visits to factories, communes, schools, universities, hospitals, revolutionary cultural performances, giant pandas at the zoo, and political briefings from peasants, workers, and Red Guards. For three weeks, I was exposed to a world both utterly alien and totally compelling, a society convulsed by the politics of revolutionary transformation. The experience would change my life.

CHAPTER TWO

We Have Friends
All Over the World

Iset foot in China for the first
time on a steaming hot day in August 1973. I had started out an hour
earlier, boarding a crowded train in the prosperous, bustling British
colony of Hong Kong. The towering office blocks and teeming tenements of what had once been described by legendary Asia hand
Richard Hughes as "an impudent capitalist pimple on the derrière
of Communist China" soon gave way to placid fields and rolling
hills. The train, now almost empty, lurched to a halt at its final stop,
a border post on the Hong Kong side of a muddy stream called the
Shenzhen River.

Beyond the rickety wooden covered bridge that marked the
gateway to China, I could see the village of Shenzhen. Bordered by
brilliant green rice paddies shimmering in the tropical sun, with
water buffalo lolling in the streams by the side of the road, it was little more than a few muddy streets baking in the summer heat.
Peasants in conical hats, carrying bundles precariously balanced on
wooden poles, trod carefully past naked, dark-skinned youngsters
playing boisterously in nearby ponds. A ridge of low mountains,
thick with green vegetation, loomed in the distance. The air was
heavy and still. A half dozen soldiers of the People's Liberation
Army, dressed in baggy green uniforms with red stars on their caps,
guarded the Chinese side of the bridge. Sweating in the tropical
heat, they stood listlessly in front of an immense billboard that

trumpeted the slogan WE HAVE FRIENDS ALL OVER THE WORLD.

It took barely a minute for me to walk across the bridge from Hong Kong to China. In 1973, those few steps represented a leap into the unknown.

"Warmly welcome our American friends," announced beaming Zhu Baochen and Yin Tianfu as they escorted me and my twenty-one-member group swiftly from the bridge, through customs and immigration formalities. "Your visit will promote friendship and understanding between the Chinese and American peoples." Both men, in their mid-thirties, wearing white short-sleeved shirts and baggy gray trousers, were official guides from the China International Travel Service. They would accompany us on our three-week journey, handling the logistics and, even more important, indoctrinating us in the virtues of Chairman Mao's revolution.

"The East is red, the sun rises. China has produced Mao Zedong." With the words of the Maoist anthem *The East Is Red* blaring from loudspeakers in each compartment, our train pulled out of Shenzhen's tiny station for Canton, capital of Guangdong province. As we headed north, I sat in my spotless, air-conditioned car, sipping a covered mug of green tea, the first of hundreds I was to be offered in the coming weeks, and peered out at the gleaming rice paddies speeding by. We raced past small villages, the gray brick walls of their little houses brightened with red painted slogans, LONG LIVE THE CHINESE COMMUNIST PARTY, WE WILL CERTAINLY LIBERATE TAIWAN, and, above all, LONG LIVE CHAIRMAN MAO. I was really in China.

When the train pulled into Canton, what struck me most was what was missing. There were no advertisements, no neon lights, virtually no cars, very little color, apart from the gray drabness of buildings whose paint had long ago peeled away in the moist south China air, and absolutely no foreigners. Wearing green or gray trousers, black cloth shoes, and white shirts, the local people stared at my group—fair-skinned, long-haired, dressed in bell-bottoms and psychedelic T-shirts—as if we had dropped from another planet. But many broke into smiles in response to our enthusiastic waves and greetings. In the streets, tens of thousands of bicyclists made their way through what before the revolution had been a busy commercial hub and a hotbed of corruption and political intrigue. Now this metropolis of three million seemed to be moving in slow motion, with the only sound the occasional honking of trucks and the perpetual tinkle of bicycle bells. In my naiveté, I attributed the languorous pace to the enervating heat and humidity, not a quarter century of communism.

Our visit began at a time of intense behind-the-scenes political conflict in China. In the preceding seven years, the country had been swept by the Great Proletarian Cultural Revolution. Originally conceived by Chairman Mao as a way of toppling his political opponents and reviving a spirit of struggle and sacrifice he believed was being suffocated by an entrenched Communist Party bureaucracy, the Cultural Revolution had quickly plunged the whole nation into chaos. Encouraged by "The Great Helmsman" and his wife, Jiang Qing, bands of youthful Red Guards had swarmed through the country, engaging in an orgy of destruction, attacking, humiliating, and often killing those who got in their way. Within the party leadership, factional strife led to a series of purges and counterpurges. Among the many victims were Liu Shaoqi, for many years China's head of state and one of Mao's oldest comrades-in-arms, and Deng Xiaoping, the Party's former secretary-general.

Eventually the country teetered on the brink of anarchy. As rival worker and Red Guards organizations with names like the "Struggle Until Death to Defend Chairman Mao Combat Corps," the "Million Heroes," and "The Scarlet Guard for the Defense of Mao Zedong Thought" fought on the streets and campuses, the People's Liberation Army was called in to restore order. The casualties were immense. In Guangdong province alone, one estimate put the number killed at 40,000. The national death toll ran at least into the hundreds of thousands.

With army intervention, Chinese society gradually regained a more orderly rhythm. During the early 1970s, some of those purged and disgraced during the preceding years were restored to their positions, while the government sought a cautious rapprochement with the United States in order to strengthen its position against its chief enemy and ideological nemesis, the "social imperialists" of the Soviet Union.

But daily life remained dominated by Mao's long-standing dictum to "put politics in command." And the power struggle between radical leaders of the Cultural Revolution period and those advocating a more moderate course continued to seethe within the top ranks of the Chinese Communist Party.

On the train to the border on the day of my arrival, I had read in a Hong Kong newspaper a dispatch from the French News Agency AFP, reporting that Beijing was awash in rumors that the Chinese Communist Party's Tenth Congress, long delayed by purges and infighting, might soon be held. However, in a telling illustration of the paucity of information available to Western observers, AFP noted that "there is nothing to show clearly whether it will in fact open tomorrow, in a month's time, or a year."

Back home, my group and I had read stories of mass violence, purges, and crude political skullduggery, but we dismissed them as the exaggerations of a biased and uninformed bourgeois Western press whose reporters were missing the real news about China. To us, the People's Republic was creating a society in which the driving force was not selfishness and greed but revolutionary spirit and consciousness. Youthful and idealistic, we wanted to learn how the Chinese had restructured their society for the benefit of the common people. We hoped that what we would learn would inspire our own activism for social justice at home. We felt privileged to see the revolution for ourselves, and we were willing to give the Chinese the benefit of the doubt.

For all my excitement, the next morning I was having trouble staying awake, and it wasn't simply the jet lag or the humidity. Comrade Zhuang, the "responsible cadre" of the Guangdong Hongmian Textile Mill in Foshan, a town outside Canton, was delivering our first *jieshao*, or "brief introduction," the ritual mind-numbing recitation of facts, figures, and propaganda that we had to endure at every stop. As I pinched myself, chewed on my pencil, and desperately refilled my tiny porcelain teacup, Comrade Zhuang harangued us about the Cultural Revolution, accusing Mao's now-disgraced heir Liu Shaoqi and other "capitalist-roaders" of corrupting the workers by offering them material incentives, betraying Mao's call to put ideology first.

We had driven to Foshan in a dilapidated bus through teeming rain along a deeply rutted rural road, passing a large sign in Chinese and English reading OUT OF BOUNDS FOR FOREIGNERS WITHOUT SPECIAL PERMISSION. Sitting next to me at the back of the bus was Xiao Yan, a second-year English student at a Canton college and one of our local interpreters. As the only member of our group who could speak some Chinese, I bravely engaged her in conversation.

"What do you study?" I asked in Mandarin.

"Apart from English, I'm studying history, philosophy, and politics," she replied. "But every year, we students have to work in the countryside for several months to learn from the peasants."

"What would you like to do after you graduate?" I inquired.

"I will do whatever the party asks me to do to serve the people."

"You must have been in high school during the Cultural Revolution," I said with a certain amount of envy. "Tell me, what was it like? Were you a Red Guard?"

"And how do you like our country?" she replied, a faint smile crossing her face as she sought, like most of the other Chinese I would meet, to avoid any personal questions.

The textile mill in Foshan evoked images of Victorian England, with its rows of ancient, noisy spinning machines throwing up clouds of fine dust and young female workers, dressed in blue, methodically checking the operation by the light of a single bulb. "Last year, we filled our production quota ahead of schedule," Comrade Zhuang proudly shouted through the din as we walked across the shop floor. "Twelve hundred workers on three eight-hour shifts producing thirty varieties of silk. This year, production will be 61 percent higher than before the Cultural Revolution."

And what was it then, we inquired.

"I'm not too clear about that," he answered with a smile.

The Soviet-built Air China Ilyushin-62 that was to take us from Canton to Beijing featured, for in-flight service, candy, gum, an apple, an air-sick bag, and the propaganda magazine *China Reconstructs*. After two extremely bumpy hours, we were surprised to land abruptly in Shanghai, China's largest city, which was not on our initial schedule. Bad weather made it impossible to continue to the capital, and we were told we would have to spend the night. I was ecstatic. Shanghai was where Edgar Snow got his start, not to mention the place where the Chinese Communist Party was founded in 1921. The name alone evoked mystery, intrigue, romance, and revolution.

As I settled into my room at the Peace Hotel, I could see why. With its Art Deco architecture, high ceilings, elaborate chandeliers,

37

and unique green pyramid roof, the hotel, known as the Cathay before the revolution, was once the most elegant address in Asia. It dominated the Bund, the waterfront along the Huangpu River where the great Western banks and trading houses had been located. It was at the Cathay that the adventurers, socialites, diplomats, tycoons, journalists, gangsters, White Russian ladies of the evening, and assorted other characters who made up Shanghai's colorful pre-revolutionary foreign community had mingled. Here, Noel Coward wrote his famous play *Private Lives,* and the Westerners who controlled Shanghai's banks, shipping companies, insurance firms, and textile mills dined and danced in restaurants and suites overlooking the river while millions of impoverished Chinese provided the labor that kept the factories and ports operating.

Despite the faded carpets and rusty, chipped bathtub, the ghosts of that earlier time were almost palpable in my huge suite. At dawn the next day, however, when I ventured out to the Bund, it became clear how distant those ghosts were from Shanghai's present reality.

The river was shrouded in a mist through which the outlines of freighters and fantailed junks were faintly visible, their tooting horns and clanging bells breaking the early morning silence. In the gardens along the Bund, off-limits to most Chinese during the colonial era, thousands of people were twisting, turning, whirling, and leaping, practicing *taiji quan* and traditional martial arts. It was a breathtaking sight. Strolling down a nearby side street, I heard a child's voice shout "hello" in English. As I walked over, a crowd of giggling children and curious adults gathered around me, inquisitive rather than unfriendly, excited to see such a rare sight as a visiting foreigner. "I'm an American friend," I said in my horribly accented Chinese. "I am visiting your country with a delegation of students. We hope to build friendship between our two peoples." The people smiled and clapped, and for a half an hour I chatted with them about such bland topics as the weather and mutual friendship.

For me it was a thrilling moment. Even to a student of Chinese history, language, culture, and politics, the country still seemed remote and unfathomable, almost unreal. This first unsupervised, spontaneous encounter with ordinary people, however superficial, left a deep impression on me. Despite the decades of hostility, I felt the Chinese were displaying a genuine warmth and a clear desire to reach out to me as an American.

Suddenly two men in police uniforms arrived.

"Who are you?" they demanded sternly as they shooed everyone away.

I launched into my Chinese set speech about being a *meiguo pengyou*, an "American friend." The cops became less suspicious but insisted my presence on the streets might disrupt traffic. Appropriately chastised, I walked back to the Peace Hotel.

Serving the capital of a country with almost a billion people, the airport in Beijing was curiously quiet. Only a handful of planes, mostly Russian models with an occasional British-made Trident, were parked on the tarmac next to our Ilyushin. A huge white plaster statue of Chairman Mao towered over the almost deserted main lobby. The buzz of cicadas provided a sharp counterpoint to the silence and absence of activity.

The narrow, tree-lined airport road gradually gave way to clusters of gray, rectangular low-rise buildings and numerous construction sites. Gnarled peasants in their horse-drawn carts jostled for space with bicycles, buses, and the occasional car. It was the height of summer, and stands packed with watermelons, cucumbers, eggplants, and tomatoes clogged the streets and alleys. In the old, gray-walled *hutongs*, or lanes, near the city center, I could see grandparents pushing infants in bamboo prams while children played nearby, darting in and out of courtyards guarded by ornate red gates. Suddenly we turned onto Changan Street, the Avenue of Eternal Peace, which runs for miles from east to west through the heart of the capital. The Western Hills, purple in the afternoon light, loomed in the distance. Moments later, we were in Tiananmen Square.

I was giddy with excitement. At the northern end of the square, in front of the vermilion walls of the Forbidden City, which had long been home to China's emperors, was the rostrum, the Gate of Heavenly Peace, draped with a huge image of Chairman Mao. The portrait was flanked by two slogans: LONG LIVE THE PEOPLE'S REPUBLIC OF CHINA, and LONG LIVE THE UNITY OF THE PEOPLES OF THE WORLD. It was here that Mao proclaimed the founding of the People's Republic in 1949, and, at the height of the Cultural Revolution, bestowed his endorsement on millions of wildly cheering Red Guards. On the western side of the square was the immense, solid rectangular form of the Great Hall of the People, with its 5,000-seat banquet room and 10,000-seat auditorium. On the east was the cavernous Museum of the Revolution. In the middle was a tall granite obelisk honoring the country's revolutionary martyrs.

I had reached the heart of the revolution. The sensation was overwhelming.

"I am sorry, comrades," guide Zhu Baochen announced that evening over dinner in the Minzu Hotel, located to the west of Tiananmen Square, "but we must leave Beijing tomorrow. We will spend the next two weeks in the Northeast."

This was exciting news, but I was also puzzled. The three provinces of *Dongbei* ("Northeast"), as the area known as Manchuria is called in Chinese, had been almost entirely off-limits to Westerners since the revolution. We would be among the first Americans to see it in a quarter of a century. A region of broad, windswept prairies and heavily industrialized cities adjacent to the Soviet Far East, Manchuria was rich in history. In this century alone, it had been occupied by the Japanese, the Russians, the KMT (Chinese Nationalists), and, finally, Mao's Communists. It was along its frigid frontiers with the Soviet Union that the Sino-Soviet border clashes of 1969 had threatened to draw the two nations into all-out war.

But Zhu's announcement left me wondering. Why were we leaving Beijing so soon after we arrived? We had seen so little. Apart from the Summer Palace, we had only visited an elementary school, where fresh-faced youngsters serenaded us with "Try to Be a Good Party Member When I Grow Up," and the home of a model worker, who sang the praises of the revolution. Then it dawned on me. Perhaps a leadership shake-up was imminent. Maybe the historic Party Congress the press was speculating about was going to be held soon, and all unnecessary foreigners were being escorted out of the capital. Not surprisingly, I learned nothing from our guides.

On the long train trip from Beijing to Jilin, deep in the heart of Manchuria, we passed small villages with square brick buildings, muddy roads, and fields of wheat and sorghum, or *gaoliang*. We also noticed another familiar plant growing by the side of the tracks. The guides could not understand why we were all laughing. We could not figure out a politically appropriate way to explain our delight in seeing so much unharvested marijuana!

The food on the train was exceptionally good. We enjoyed multi-course meals washed down by vast quantities of beer and a super potent sorghum-based liquor, *maotai*, accompanied by numerous toasts to "friendship" between the Chinese and American peoples. So we were bleary-eyed and stiff when we stumbled off the train in Jilin, an industrial town of 800,000 people, surrounded on three sides by mountains and on the fourth by the Sungari River. As our bus bounced from the train station, I was astonished to find the broad streets lined with thousands of cheering, clapping, waving people. My initial thought was that they were waiting for somebody important and that we had simply happened to arrive shortly before the visiting VIP.

"But you must understand," Yin said, "you are the VIPs! You are the first Americans to visit this city since liberation. The masses are waiting, and they are very happy to welcome you."

Each time we entered or left the hotel, even on visits to such prosaic sites as an industrial waste-products factory, a chemical-fertilizer plant, or an electric power station, the masses packed the streets. But for all their talk of "friendship," the guides were wary of unsupervised contact between foreigners and Chinese. They actively discouraged us from leaving the hotel on our own and mingling, promoting abstract friendships between "peoples" rather than between individuals. But our frustration faded as we marveled at the huge crowd, numbering in the thousands, that gathered at the train station to bid us an emotional farewell. We had never experienced anything like it. But as we were to discover, this was just a foretaste of the sensation we were to cause in Shenyang.

Shenyang, once known as Mukden, was a grimy industrial center, its skyline dotted with smokestacks belching black, yellow, and gray clouds into the moist summer air, its streets clogged with rickety buses, horse-drawn carts, and bicycle rickshaws. There was a toughness about the city and its people that I did not find elsewhere in China, produced, I supposed, by years of living in the harsh and frozen Manchurian climate and by working in the primitive, dangerous, and grossly polluting factories that dominated the landscape.

I noticed the statue initially from ten blocks away as we drove toward the city center. First I glimpsed an enormous head, then an outstretched arm, and then to my astonishment, an entire statue. It was Mao, 100 feet high, wearing a trench coat, staring resolutely ahead and flanked at the base by carvings of adoring workers, peasants, and soldiers—the most extraordinary manifestation of the chairman's personality cult I saw anywhere in China. The statue was directly across from our hotel in Zhongshan Square, where, one balmy evening, a few of us managed to create a near riot by playing Frisbee in the shadow of the Great Helmsman.

It took just a few moments for word to spread. Barbarians at play! What a spectacle! Throngs of people began to arrive. Quickly the road surrounding the square was jammed with vehicles. Buses, trucks, rickshaws, cars, bicyclists, and pedestrians stopped and gawked, gasping in amazement. Soon we couldn't turn around, let alone toss a Frisbee. I tried to explain to the crowd in Chinese both who we were and what we were playing. "Just step back a few feet, folks," I said, "and we'll give you a free lesson." This merely created more tumult. Older children pushed smaller ones out of the way to get a better view. We were actually in danger of being crushed. Faintly through the hubbub I heard the voices of our two guides, Zhu and Yin, calling from the steps of the hotel. "Please come back!" they appealed. "You are disrupting public order."

I tried to move forward, offering my hand to anyone who would shake it. Dozens of hands were thrust out in return, and I soon discovered a way out of the teeming crowd, which I worked like a politician, pressing the flesh as I made my way from the center of the square. As in Jilin, for all their intense curiosity, the people were friendly. Small children clung to me, grinning, while their parents beamed. I stumbled ahead saying *ni hao* ("hello") again and again.

Sweating, disheveled, and exhausted, we all found our way back to the hotel. I was elated by my contact with the people. I mounted the steps, and as my guides looked on aghast, I turned around, raised my arms, and shouted in Chinese at the top of my lungs, "Long live the friendship between the Chinese and American peoples." The masses roared their approval as I waved goodbye. "This is a much bigger crowd," I noted triumphantly to one of my fellow travelers, "than we got for most antiwar demonstrations at school!"

As I walked back inside the hotel, the guides said, "Now we will have a meeting." They scolded us, but nothing could dampen our youthful enthusiasm. The following morning, awakened at six o'clock by the chimes of *The East Is Red*, several of us strolled into a People's Liberation Army barracks down the street and started a pickup basketball game. It ended with the guides, mortified that we'd entered a military installation, hustling us back to the hotel.

Promising to stay away from all military locations, I ventured out on my own. A few blocks away, I came upon a glass-enclosed display case featuring the *People's Daily*, the provincial newspaper *Liaoning Daily*, and the *Shenyang Daily*. It was an unexpected find. Provincial and local newspapers were restricted to domestic consumption. For a foreigner to get even a glimpse was so rare an occurrence that the U.S. Consulate in Hong Kong regularly offered small sums of cash to any traveler able to secure such a paper. I was trying to make sense of an article denouncing Confucius, but before I got very far, a plump woman with cropped hair and a blue jacket made her way through the crowd and unlocked the glass case, taking the *People's Daily* and carefully tacking it over the provincial paper I was reading before relocking the window and walking away without saying a word.

Back at the hotel, Comrade Shi from the Shenyang branch of the China International Travel Service marched into my room. "It is absolutely forbidden for foreigners to look at provincial and local newspapers," he lectured sternly. "This is a serious problem. Please do not do this again." Somewhat taken aback, I apologized.

Our continuing escapades finally forced Zhu and Yin to schedule another group meeting to complain about our attitude and behavior, especially our "lack of discipline" and respect for Chinese rules and regulations. As the sole Chinese speaker in the group, I tried to explain our perhaps excessive exuberance. While pledging political solidarity, I pleaded for more contact with ordinary people and fewer factory tours where "responsible cadres" dodged our questions by inundating us with often irrelevant statistics. The air cleared, the meeting ended with renewed dedications to "friendship" and with promises from us to improve our behavior and from Zhu and Yin to revamp our schedule.

A day with Yu Kexin was the first noticeable change.

Feeling faintly absurd, I bent low in the fields of the Wusan People's Commune near Shenyang, my back aching. Next to me was a model Maoist peasant who looked like he had just stepped from the pages of *China Reconstructs*. Yu Kexin had a broad, weatherbeaten face, thick, calloused hands, and wore a green Mao cap, a white short-sleeved shirt, and faded blue trousers. Together we had spent the past two hours harvesting tomatoes and cucumbers. Responding to our complaints, the guides had arranged for us to "engage in manual labor." Participating in ordinary peasant life was a welcome respite from endless *jieshao*, "brief introductions," and turned out to be one of the most memorable moments of my trip. But my intentions were better than my skills. I left the fields full of squashed, trampled, and mashed bits of vegetable as Yu Kexin struggled to contain both his annoyance at the waste and his mirth at my clumsiness.

While instructing me in the subtleties of vegetable picking, Yu told me about himself. Married in 1957, he had four children, three young sons and a sixteen-year-old daughter. He earned 174 yuan a year, slightly less than seventy-five dollars, though he hastened to tell me this was double the average peasant income in the village at the time of the revolution. "Before liberation," he said, "most of the villagers here toiled in the fields for the landlord. Many were beggars. There was never enough food. Children died or were sold. Now everyone has enough to eat, and we can all lead healthy lives."

The Wusan Commune was one of about 70,000 collective farms in China. Home to eight out of every ten Chinese, the People's Communes represented one of Mao's most remarkable endeavors. When he established the communes during the Great Leap Forward in 1958, he sought to reshape China's landscape, both literally and politically, by mobilizing the peasant masses in a spirit of self-reliance, austerity, and ideological dedication to create pure communism in the Chinese countryside. Initially the process was a disaster, leading to economic catastrophe and widespread famine. The peasants resisted, reluctant to see their fields, tools, and animals turned over to a Party-controlled collective. By the time of my visit, however, the commune system was well-entrenched, forming the core of Mao's vision of socialism for China. At Wusan, officials regaled us with statistics to prove their success. Vegetable output was up four times from liberation in 1949; there were five times as many pigs as before the Cultural Revolution, twice as many cows. And Yu Kexin was presented as a shining example of how the communes had transformed the lives of ordinary peasants.

Yu, however, was less interested in statistics than in serving what turned out to be the best meal I had in China. From the vegetable fields, he took me to his home, a small three-room brick dwelling with a dusty courtyard. A modest table and two *kangs* dominated the main room. These brick platforms, raised off the floor so a fire could be lit under them for heating in the winter, functioned as the typical peasant bed in north China. Yu's wife, Li Lianfang, round-faced with cropped hair, and his daughter, wearing long braids and baggy white shirt and blue trousers, awaited us.

"They have been cooking for you all morning." Yu laughed as he ushered me inside. As I sat on the *kang*, the Yu family brought out an extraordinarily lavish spread. Dish after dish appeared—stir-fried eggs with scallions, chicken, vegetables, whole-wheat noodles with black bean sauce, endless portions of rice, melons, and the biggest corn on the cob I had ever seen. The portions were so large I was unable to finish. As we ate, scrawny chickens kept running in from the courtyard, forcing his daughter to interrupt the meal to chase them away.

Our conversation was a bit stilted at first. Yu and his family had never met an American before and were only vaguely aware of the United States. Even though I spoke Chinese, they still seemed to regard me like a creature from outer space—friendly, but an alien nonetheless. For my part, coming as I did from a rather sheltered middle-class background, I had hardly ever been on a farm in the U.S., let alone met a peasant from a country as distant, rural, and underdeveloped as China. Once we finished the ritualized expressions of friendship, the gap between us seemed much greater than the table on which the Yu family had laid our extraordinary feast. Slowly and haltingly, however, we began to find common ground. It was not the political line I had heard at the commune's "brief introduction," but rather shared interests in family, home, and above all, food. While we chatted, the Yu family consumed their meal with exceptional gusto. In my notebook I wrote afterwards, "This food was the best, the simplest, and the healthiest I have eaten in China. And the attitude of the family was so friendly and positive that it wiped away the negative taste of all the confrontations with guides."

I peered out of a bus at the poster in Stalin Square, a vast expanse named in honor of the Soviet dictator at a time when Moscow and Beijing were allies in the 1950s. Now they were enemies, and the billboard read, Be Prepared for Surprise Attacks by Social

IMPERIALISTS! We were in Dalian, northeast China's most important port, a city of imposing commercial buildings, wide streets, vast dockyards, and charming green electric trams, a legacy of the first half of the century when the city was a Japanese colony. It all seemed tranquil enough, but Dalian was just six hundred miles from the Soviet border, and the Russian threat was taken very seriously.

From the ideological disagreements and bitter personal hostility between Mao Zedong and Nikita Khrushchev in the late 1950s, to the open breach of the early sixties, to the bloody border clashes of 1969, conflict with the Soviet Union had long been a decisive factor shaping China's domestic politics and its interaction with the rest of the world. Preventing China from becoming the "revisionist" bureaucratized state he saw emerging in Khrushchev's Soviet Union was a driving force behind Mao's Cultural Revolution. Countering the Russian threat was the chief rationale for Beijing's thaw with the United States and the reason why the Chairman ordered the construction of a nationwide series of underground tunnel systems whose scale defied the imagination.

In the basement of a hotel just off Stalin Street, Comrade Wu, the "responsible cadre" from the Dalian civil-defense organization, pushed a small button and the floor opened up. We tramped down a long flight of stairs and entered an empty underground city built in 1970 in response to Chairman Mao's call to "dig tunnels deep, store grain everywhere, and never seek hegemony." The tunnel appeared fully equipped to carry on with daily existence: it held barbershops with revolving chairs, dining rooms with sets of chopsticks laid out on the tables, hospital wards, and classrooms. There was even a bookstore and a "club" for cultural performances, with twenty-five rows of stone seats, nine Mao quotes, and a stage lit in red neon.

"If there is a Soviet attack," Comrade Wu told us, "conventional, chemical, or nuclear, each of the five tunnel networks in Dalian is designed for eighty thousand people to take refuge, carry on with normal life, and, if necessary, fight."

Having grown up during the Cold War, I had memories of classroom civil-defense drills and of my parents stockpiling food and water in our basement at the height of the Cuban Missile Crisis in 1962. It all seemed faintly unreal at the time, but what the Chinese had created was mind-boggling. Our hosts, in permitting us to visit such a closely guarded facility, seemed confident we would both understand the tunnel's significance and put the right political spin on these defensive preparations when we spoke or wrote about our visit after returning home.

"We will not attack unless we are attacked," Comrade Wu declared, quoting Chairman Mao as we emerged, blinking, back into the sunlight. "But we will certainly counterattack if we are attacked. Down with Soviet social imperialism!"

The following day, I cradled a rifle in my hands and tried to imagine vicious Soviet social imperialists at the foot of the reddish brown hill in front of me.

"All right," said the eight-year-old boy in white shirt, green pants, and red kerchief standing next to me, "now hold steady, carefully take aim, and fire."

The explosion broke the afternoon silence. It was the first time I had ever fired a weapon, and, not surprisingly, my target was still standing. The boy walked over and took the rifle from me.

"It's like this," he said.

Within seconds, all eleven targets were full of holes. The other boys and girls put their rifles down and laughed and clapped. As far as they were concerned, the Russians wouldn't stand a chance.

Even in a city where anti-Soviet vigilance was the watchword, Dalian's Xigangchun Red Guard Elementary School stood out, and not only because its students took target practice every afternoon. Located in a hilly neighborhood well away from the harbor, the school was staffed by teachers who worked with their students to dig their own remarkable tunnel system into the hillside next to the playground. At the entrance was a large slogan: MAINTAIN OUR VIGILANCE, PROTECT THE MOTHERLAND. Stumbling along the packed mud floors while mounted loudspeakers played scratchy music, I entered a room where a seventh-grader with long pigtails stood up and provided a "brief introduction" in a tone that made her sound more like a drill sergeant than a schoolgirl. "Digging this tunnel was a heroic experience, in which we were guided by the teachings of Chairman Mao," she declared. "All the teachers and pupils of the school can fit inside. We can do homework and even cook in here."

From the tunnel, we were taken to visit several classrooms. We watched one group of students loudly recite tales from the life of Lei

Feng, a Maoist model soldier-hero whose self-proclaimed goal in life was to be "a rustless cog in the giant machine of socialism." In a music class, a girl sporting a Mao button led the youngsters in a rousing rendition of "Let the Red Flower of Daqing Spread All Over the Country," a tribute to the model Maoist oil field of Daqing. Then the students lined up and marched back to the field behind the school. Rifles were distributed and, one after another, the make-believe social imperialists bit the dust. The scene was astonishing. To watch these youngsters literally act out the Maoist slogans my friends and I had chanted at antiwar demonstrations in the U.S. left me speechless.

Finally back in Beijing after our adventures in the Northeast, we were taken to visit Qinghua University, China's foremost institution of scientific and technical learning. As students who had spent more time organizing protest demonstrations than doing our homework, we were very eager to hear about the revolutionary activities of Chinese college students and professors. The stories we heard were nothing like our own.

Ren Yansheng, a tall, round-faced young man with brush-cut hair, told us that he was one of the earliest activists in the Cultural Revolution, having put up a highly inflammatory wall poster, or *dazibao*, denouncing the wife of the country's then-president, Liu Shaoqi, in 1966. His attack on China's first lady was an opening salvo in a Maoist offensive that eventually led to her public humiliation at a mock Red Guards "trial" on the Qinghua campus. Ren participated in the first and most dramatic of eight rallies in which millions of young Chinese gathered in Tiananmen Square to demonstrate their loyalty to the Great Helmsman.

Within the campus, one of his targets was Tong Shibai, the dean of the electronics department. Educated in the United States before the revolution, Tong had returned to China in 1955 in order to contribute to the rebuilding of his country. With his Western background, he was quickly singled out for criticism when the Cultural Revolution erupted. He spent several years "reforming his reactionary thinking" by doing compulsory work in a factory, but insisted his punishment had been a liberating, uplifting experience, rescuing him from a wayward path and confirming his faith in the wisdom of Chairman Mao. "The key question," he said, "is what

48

class should education serve? We're not educating successors to the capitalist class here. We're educating successors to the proletarian revolutionary cause."

Ren Yansheng too was sent to "remold his thinking" by "learning from the peasants" in the countryside, an experience he too described in glowing terms. Were Tong and Ren representative of the new Maoist man forged in the crucible of the Cultural Revolution? I wondered. Making professors and students share in the life of workers and peasants appealed to my egalitarian convictions. I *wanted* to believe them. But their uncritical enthusiasm for what seemed to amount to forced labor troubled me. Not for the first time on this trip, I doubted I was getting the full story.

"Important news has just been announced on the radio," our guides Zhu and Yin told us breathlessly the following evening. "The Tenth Congress of the Chinese Communist Party has just been successfully concluded!"

My initial hunch was right. There had been a reason why we had been whisked out of Beijing so quickly at the start of our trip.

Within minutes of the announcement, somnolent, orderly Beijing erupted into total pandemonium. Roused from sleepy sidewalk conversations, from their homes, or from late-night factory shifts, many of the capital's citizens clogged the usually empty streets and moved toward Tiananmen Square. Some carried giant red flags and portraits of Chairman Mao. Others banged gongs and cymbals or beat large, colorful drums mounted on the backs of pedicabs. Everywhere, people chanted: "Long live the revolutionary line of Chairman Mao!" "Long live the great, glorious, and correct Chinese Communist Party!" "Ten thousand years life to Chairman Mao!"

My friends and I left our hotel and ran with the surging throng past the floodlit red gates of Zhongnanhai, the compound where senior party leaders lived and worked, guarded by two soldiers and two carved lions, and into the square, whose main buildings were suddenly brilliantly illuminated, their outlines shining in the misty evening. In the square, loudspeakers had been turned on to broadcast the official Tenth Congress communiqué and the names of the party's revamped leadership. The disembodied voice of the announcer echoed through the immense space, mingling with the din of the crowd and the pop of firecrackers.

I strained to listen for details of what had transpired. My Chinese wasn't good enough to get it all, but what I did understand was significant. The last Party Congress, held at the height of the Cultural Revolution in 1969, had proclaimed Marshal Lin Biao as Chairman Mao's designated heir. But Lin had died in a mysterious plane crash in 1971, amid rumors he had tried to assassinate Mao. The just-finished Tenth Congress would spell out a new leadership lineup and proclaim the country's future political direction.

"The Congress indignantly denounces the Lin Biao anti-party clique for its crimes," the broadcast intoned. "The Central Committee of the Communist Party of China expels Lin Biao, the bourgeois careerist, conspirator, counterrevolutionary double-dealer, renegade, and traitor, once and for all!" The announcement also disclosed the promotion of thirty-six-year-old former Shanghai textile worker Wang Hongwen, who was named to the party's top ruling body, the Standing Committee of the Politburo. Three years later, Wang would become the youngest member of Madam Mao's notorious Gang of Four.

My mind still spinning, I joined a group of banner-waving marchers leaving Tiananmen. Two men carried a huge portrait of Chairman Mao mounted on two bamboo poles. On a bicycle with a platform attached to it, a large drum had been mounted. Sweating profusely, a plump middle-aged man banged furiously away.

But I somehow felt slightly uneasy, struck, almost against my will, by what appeared to be a lackadaisical quality to the whole event. The people waved flags, paraded around, and seemed to be sincere. But their manner appeared perfunctory, without the electricity I had expected for such a momentous occasion. Near the hotel, I saw a Chinese TV crew train its cameras on the march. As the bright lights were turned on, two men acting like cheerleaders led the crowd in chants and clenched fist salutes. The moment the lights went off, the chanting stopped.

And I wondered, how could Lin Biao—second only to Mao, and whose personal introduction graced every single copy of the Chairman's famous *Little Red Book*—now be reviled as a traitor? In retrospect, I should have paid more attention to whether this political somersault would be credible to the Chinese people. I must confess that, at the time, I didn't give it much thought. The experience of marching with tens of thousands of Chinese through the heart of Beijing remained uppermost in my mind. My last journal entry for that night was, "In the U.S., with a demonstration like this, there would be tear gas, and we would all be throwing rocks. But here, everyone is a good guy, except for Lin Biao!"

My last morning in Beijing, two days after the end of the Tenth Congress, I took a long walk by myself, wandering down Changan Street and through Tiananmen. The square was curiously quiet, the red flags on the rostrum and the Great Hall of the People hanging limply in the late-summer heat. I passed the Beijing Hotel, where the most important of the steadily growing trickle of foreign visitors to China were put up, and turned onto Wangfujing, the capital's main shopping street. Here, at least, people were blasé about seeing foreigners. Peering into book and department stores, reading newspapers posted on the walls with their banner headlines about Chairman Mao and the Congress, I attracted almost no attention. Turning off Wangfujing, I strolled along some of the old *hutongs*, or alleys, with their elegant gray walls and dark red wooden doors. I peered into courtyards, watched children play while old folks gossiped on the corners, and soaked up the rhythm of daily life. In a way I had not felt before, I had a sense of commitment—to China, to understanding its incredibly complex yet oddly appealing revolution, to making my way as a journalist. Whatever else I might do, China would remain part of my life. I would be back.

CHAPTER THREE

Year of the Dragon

The clouds were low and gray. A slight drizzle was falling, and the smell of coal smoke floated through the damp chilly air. Suddenly several gunshots rang out. Hunching my shoulders, I scuttled away from the center of the street and, heart pounding, huddled for protection beneath an old billboard. Looking up, I found myself peering at an enormous slogan: POLITICAL POWER GROWS OUT OF THE BARREL OF A GUN.

The quotation from Chairman Mao was spray-painted on an old ad for Guinness stout. Barely six months after my first China trip, I was dodging bullets in an IRA-dominated neighborhood of Belfast, Northern Ireland. On my return from the People's Republic to the States, I had written a few articles about China for my home-town paper in Massachusetts, mostly (in my youthful enthusiasm) of the I-have-seen-the-future-and-it-works variety, and I started applying once again to papers and news agencies for an overseas reporting or stringing job. My trip to the still generally inaccessible People's Republic, where visas even for big-name foreign corres-pondents were few and far between, might, I thought, make me more employable.

The rejection letters were nicer, more thoughtful, and more encouraging this time around, but, given my youth and inexperi-ence, it became clear the chances of a full-time international reporting job, especially dealing with China, were slim. I was now twenty-two, the same age at which my hero, Edgar Snow, began his remarkable journalistic career. Like Snow, I saw in China both the mystery and romance of a distant land and culture as well as the very contemporary revolutionary struggle to find a new way of dealing with age-old injustices. I, too, felt an instinctive sympathy for the underdog and a basic distrust of established power. But the revolutionaries Snow admired, and whose struggle to overthrow their oppressors he had chronicled by sneaking past corrupt border guards, holding clandestine meetings with guerrilla fighters, and witnessing foreign invasion and internal upheaval, had now been in power in China for almost three decades, and they continued to keep their country largely closed to outsiders. Yet China embodied so much of what I was interested in that getting there remained my ultimate goal. The route, however, would be long and indirect. For now I would have to satisfy my political and intellectual interests, as well as my wanderlust and taste for adventure, elsewhere. Sitting in Massachusetts, the nearest available revolution appeared to be in Northern Ireland, where the IRA was locked in a "national liberation struggle " against British imperialism. A cheap excursion fare from Boston made the trip affordable.

It was not my first jaunt to Ireland. In 1971, for a course at Yale, I decided to write a term paper about British imperialism in Ireland because I could combine a stop in Dublin with a Christmas visit to my parents, then on sabbatical in London. One windswept afternoon, I turned up at the Dublin office of Sinn Féin, the IRA's political wing, to collect some pamphlets—and ran smack into the most wanted man in Northern Ireland. I was invited into a back room for a "wee yarn," only to find Joe Cahill, until recently head of the IRA's Belfast Brigade, sitting under a poster reading IRELAND UNFREE SHALL NEVER BE AT PEACE. He gave me a passionate introduction to the cause of Irish Republicanism. Spellbound, I studied his face. Cahill was unshaven, with gray stubble on his chin, a receding hairline, bushy eyebrows, and a large, bulbous nose on which thick, black-rimmed glasses perched precariously. But it was his eyes that struck me. They had a slightly hooded quality, almost like those of a cobra, and they were absolutely cold.

It was heady stuff. Here was a real revolutionary, in disguise and on the run. The Cahill interview became my first "scoop," detailed in a long article for the *Yale Daily News*. I took it terribly seriously.

And I was not altogether pleased, I must confess, when the editors relegated my triumph to a spot next to a cartoon written by fellow Yalie Gary Trudeau, featuring a then-unknown character called Doonesbury.

I saw Northern Ireland itself for the first time five months later. Again my parents' sabbatical created the opportunity. In 1972, my sociologist father was invited to give a lecture at Queens University in Belfast, and I asked to come along. We flew over for what turned out to be one of the most tumultuous weekends in a very violent year. My pulse raced as we passed burning barricades and Catholic "no-go" areas, where teenaged gangs stockpiled Molotov cocktails to keep British troops at bay. But after two days of nonstop riots, frequent explosions, and the almost constant clatter of gunfire, my excitement dissolved into raw fear. My head spun with terrifying thoughts. Any parked vehicle could be a car bomb. A sniper could open up from any corner. Would there be another explosion while we waited to get on the train to Dublin?

What was I doing here? I was too young to die!

Nearing the train station, I started to walk faster, then involuntarily broke into a trot. My father, more than a little anxious himself, tried to calm me down, but only after the Belfast-Dublin Express crossed the border into the Irish Republic, and I had chewed several antacid tablets, did I finally began to relax. If I was going to be a foreign correspondent, I had a lot to learn.

Despite my fears, Northern Ireland captured my imagination. It was not just the politics. The lilting, lyrical accents, the richness of the language, the drama of the history, even the brooding, temperamental weather made it overpoweringly romantic. To the amusement of my friends at Yale, I began to recite quotations from Chairman Mao and the poets of Dublin's 1916 Easter Rising with equal aplomb. In my mind there was some kind of connection between the two. With no other job possibilities after my China trip, it made quixotic sense to me to return to Belfast and try my hand at freelancing.

The first thing I did in Belfast was to resume the walk that had ended in panic on my 1972 visit with my father. Along a road known locally as "death row," a half-mile wasteland of burned-out buildings and rubble separating a small, militantly Protestant neighborhood from a stronghold of the IRA, I was stopped at a British army checkpoint.

"All right, lad," a British officer said gruffly, cradling a rifle against his camouflage flak jacket. "We've had a bit of aggro down the road. Are you a Protestant or a Catholic? Before I let you pass, I need to know your religion."

"I'm Jewish," I replied. "And I'm from the United States."

He looked at me as if I was crazy, then he shrugged and grinned. "Right then, no problem."

He pointed with his right arm. "There's people on that side of the road with machine guns. And on the other side there's people with rifles. Cheerio. Off you go now. Keep your head down!"

A moment later, a burst of gunfire sent me diving for cover.

I discovered to my surprise that my nerves were steadier than I had anticipated. I soon fell into a pattern. I sought out key personalities on all sides, tramped through the dark and often dangerous city streets, and spent endless hours in political discussion over pints of frothy Guinness stout, collecting material for articles I hoped to offer to my hometown newspaper, to a radical Boston weekly called the *Phoenix*, and to the *Guardian*, which had sponsored my China trip. I befriended some local reporters and spent many afternoons in their downtown office playing darts, drinking tea, talking politics, and waiting for something to happen. A loud bang, the wail of sirens, or a column of smoke curling up in the distance was usually sufficient to prompt them, with me in tow, to race to their cars, or sometimes just to run down the block, looking for trouble. For a novice, it was a wonderful learning experience, and it gave me my first taste of the camaraderie of reporters under fire.

"Would you like to visit Long Kesh?" a fellow I met in a pub on the Falls Road asked me one evening. I jumped at the opportunity. Journalists were not allowed into the infamous prison camp where the British had interned hundreds of suspected IRA members without trial (and where in the mid-1990s many convicted "terrorists" were still incarcerated). A visit would be a real scoop. I was to be passed off as the visiting American cousin of an IRA internee, complete with false papers and a carefully rehearsed story. With my heart pounding and sweat pouring down my back despite the chill, I made it past a series of searches and interrogations to the visitors' room deep inside the heavily guarded compound. There I spent half an hour with a young man detained for possessing explosives. If he was startled to see me, he didn't let on. Tall, gentle, and surprisingly serene, he launched into a lengthy explanation of how IRA inmates coped with the pressures of prison life. Gulping antacids on the way back to Belfast, I couldn't wait to get to my typewriter.

A few days later I landed an even better story. After a month of feelers, the Provisional IRA allowed me to spend a weekend with two of its "volunteers." My hosts, two brawny young men named Mickey and Seamus, showed me around the New Lodge, a Catholic working-class neighborhood of tiny terraced houses, dominated by one large high-rise apartment complex with a British army observation post on the roof.

At night, the two beckoned me to follow them through a maze of side streets and alleys to a small residence. As we walked, they explained why they had become guerrillas. Beaten, humiliated, and interned by the army in 1971, they had concluded that only violence would drive the British away. Inside the house, Mickey pulled a chest from underneath a couch to show me dozens of gleaming new Armalite assault rifles. Wrapping kerchiefs over their faces, both men picked up a weapon and posed for photographs.

I snapped the shutter with a wave of excitement. I was sharing, if only briefly, the clandestine existence of guerrilla fighters in a cause for which I had some sympathy. I felt I had come a long way from collecting signatures on petitions to bring the troops home from Vietnam. To my surprise, I wasn't frightened. In front of the house, Seamus finished a cigarette and looked at his watch. "We must be off. My wife will see you safely out of the area tomorrow. We've got an operation on tonight. Take a few digs at the Brits."

I did not see Seamus or Mickey again. Watching them walk off into the gloom, I felt something of a bond with these two young men. We were the same age, and I understood the choice they both felt they had been forced to make. I wondered how I would have behaved if I too were a Northern Irish Catholic living under such circumstances. The next morning, the radio reported that the IRA had shot and killed two British soldiers near the New Lodge Road. With decidedly mixed feelings, I wondered if my friends had pulled the trigger.

The long, dark Northern Irish winter slowly turned into a spring of more bombing and shooting. My three months in Belfast had given me a crash course in the complexities of Irish politics, a taste of the foreign correspondent's life, an appetite for further adventure, and above all a growing confidence that I could cope with intense pressure. It was clear, however, that there was no long-term career for me in Belfast. As I immersed myself in Ireland's ancient hatreds, I realized that I had accomplished what I could, and that my deeper interests continued to lie in Asia. Pounding away on my final Ulster dispatches, I made two decisions: I would acquire some formal training by attending the Columbia University Graduate School of Journalism, to which I had applied some months earlier; and I would take the time before the new academic year began to return to the Far East.

I had long ago promised myself that I would not visit Taiwan until I had spent a significant stretch in mainland China. A bastion of anti-communism, the Republic of China, ruled by the aging despot Generalissimo Chiang Kai-shek, was the epitome of American-backed right-wing Asian dictatorships that I had spent much of my college career demonstrating against. Unfortunately, with the People's Republic still largely off-limits to Americans, Taiwan remained the best available place for an aspiring student of Mandarin Chinese. Having fulfilled my vow by reaching Beijing the previous year, and seeking to further both my linguistic and political education, I took the money I earned from selling my articles on Northern Ireland, swallowed my ideological scruples, and purchased a ticket for Taipei.

Almost from the moment I arrived on an unbearably hot and muggy day in June 1974, I felt like a spy. Since 1949, when the Chinese Nationalist Kuomintang, or KMT, fled to the island to escape Mao's victorious Communist armies, Taiwan had been under martial law. Critics of the government, especially those advocating independence for the island, were routinely harassed or jailed. Enormous effort went into denigrating the validity of the "communist bandit" government in Beijing. Foreign publications like *Time* and *Newsweek* were strictly censored. Photographs of Chairman Mao and other Chinese leaders were completely blacked out. Each newspaper reference to the title of a mainland official, such as "Premier" Zhou Enlai, was printed with quotation marks to underscore its illegitimacy, and the KMT insisted on calling the Chinese capital not Beijing ("Northern Capital") but its prerevolutionary name, "Beiping" ("Northern Peace"). The local media acted in many ways like their counterparts on the mainland, only in reverse, extolling the global struggle against communism and highlighting visiting delegations from obscure groups like the "World Anti-Communist League," whereas the mainland Chinese press promoted anti-imperialism and gave prominence to visitors from such unknown Maoist splinter groups as the "Communist Party of New Zealand—Marxist-Leninist."

I arrived in this environment with a guilty secret. Not only had I been to the enemy capital, but I harbored more than a little sympathy for the enemy's political goals. This was one secret I would have to be exceptionally careful about sharing. I rented a tiny room in a building near the campus of Taiwan University, with a window that looked out on a swamp. On my first night as I prepared for bed, I was terrified to see a lizard crawling up the wall. Seizing my umbrella, I skewered the reptile and threw it out the window. Only later did I learn it was a gecko, renowned throughout the Orient as a symbol of good luck. Running it through with my umbrella tip was not an auspicious start to my trip.

My introduction to the fear-laced politics of Taiwan came from two American missionaries who had worked on the island since the 1950s. At the urging of mutual friends in New York, I looked them up at their residence in the hills of Yangmingshan, the mist-covered mountain that marks the northern edge of Taipei. They were strong supporters of Taiwan independence, a sentiment shared by many of the island's native Taiwanese majority, who resented the high-handed authoritarianism of the mainland Chinese-dominated KMT. Sitting on rattan chairs in their lush tropical garden, and keeping an eye out for the deadly bamboo snakes that slithered freely through the Yangmingshan undergrowth, I listened as the missionaries told me of Taiwanese friends imprisoned in a notorious penal camp on a tiny island just off the coast. They talked of their own difficulties with the Garrison Command, Taiwan's secret police, of being followed and monitored, and of the ever-present possibility of being expelled.

Against this backdrop, I pursued my study of Chinese. Having insufficient funds to enroll in a formal language school, I found a private tutor. Her name was Christina. She was a nineteen-year-old art student with an exquisite oval face and long, glossy black hair. She soon became more than my language teacher. With Christina at my side, I discovered another part of Taiwan—the face of traditional China, virtually wiped out on the mainland but still alive and vibrant here. She took me to Buddhist temples hidden in narrow lanes, where devotees made offerings of fruits and cakes before altars dotted with incense sticks that sent wisps of fragrant smoke into the air. We went to outdoor puppet shows, performed before raucous crowds in neighborhoods so distant from the traffic, smog, and construction of the city center as to be almost rural. And she introduced me to real Beijing opera—not the one-dimensional "revolutionary" performances I had seen on the mainland, but a spectacular display of nimble acrobats in garish costumes and painted faces twirling across the stage, their shrill tones mingling with drums and gongs in a fantastic cacophony. Even with Christina's constant instruction, my Chinese was wholly inadequate to understand the complex lyrics and allusions to classical legends of romance, intrigue, and heroics, but I was entranced as she patiently explained and translated again and again, seeking to draw me into the private world of her imagination and aesthetics.

Christina's favorite place was the Palace Museum near Yangmingshan, home to the priceless Chinese art treasures the Nationalists had taken with them when they fled the victorious Communists in 1949. Indeed it was here that I had first met Christina soon after arriving in Taipei, when I stopped to admire a sketch she was making of a traditional Chinese landscape and we struck up a conversation. We had wandered the long corridors together and I marveled at the richness and subtlety of Chinese culture, a side of China far removed from the revolutionary politics that had first sparked my interest in the country. Despite occasional courses and lectures in college, I had been so preoccupied with the changes in new China, I had neglected, or simply dismissed, the old. Now my eyes were opened to the vitality and complexity of China's traditional way of life and thought. My enriched appreciation was to grow in the years ahead, sustaining my attraction to things Chinese, even as my initial political enthusiasm waned. Still, I felt uncomfortable, not with Christina but with the fact that, for all its glories, this culture also represented the corrupt old system that the

Communists had overthrown. I felt there were good reasons for the Chinese revolution, and I found the KMT's attempt to use the glories of classical China to justify its own hold on power more than a little irritating. Yet I also loved the performances and art that Christina showed me. My conflicting emotions were hard to reconcile, but my romance with Christina provided a human dimension to what until then had been largely an abstract political and intellectual fascination. I never looked at Chinese issues quite the same way afterward.

Yet as I sat at my favorite eatery, Earl's Hot Noodles, where the waiter cleaned the chopsticks by wiping them under his arm, I looked around and saw a society that was, more than anything else, excruciatingly dull. Both in terms of its political conservatism and its rigid social conformity, Taiwan seemed to be a throwback to the 1950s, a place that had completely missed the convulsions that had provided the defining moments for my generation. At the time of my visit, the frenzy of economic development and consequent political liberalization I would cover for CNN two decades later had not yet begun. Taipei was a drab, gray, ramshackle place, with weather so bad I felt as if I were living in a giant sauna. Despite my affection for Christina, we were both too young for this to become a serious relationship, and midway through the summer I decided to leave. My next destination promised a good deal more excitement. Having grown up in the shadow of the Indochina war, I decided to see Vietnam for myself.

Vietnam had been such a formative force in my life that setting foot in Saigon was something of a letdown. En route, though, I had spent two weeks in Laos, and I found the charm of this decadent colonial outpost exciting and wonderfully exotic. I could sit in a French-style cafe in the capital, Vientiane, enjoying excellent coffee and freshly baked baguettes while watching delicate Lao women in swirling peasant dresses glide through streets filled with Indian shopkeepers, Chinese money-changers, Buddhist monks, government soldiers in red berets, and AK-47–toting troops of the Communist Pathet Lao. The golden spires of Vientiane's many Buddhist temples were visible in the distance, and a short walk brought me to the morning market. It offered vegetables, spices, handicrafts, household products, and, to my surprise, large quantities of marijuana, which, along with opium, was openly sold in the city.

In Saigon, I found simply despair. After driving from Ton Son Nhut Airport through a midafternoon monsoon downpour to the city center, I took a room in the Continental Hotel, immortalized by Graham Greene in his classic novel of Vietnam, *The Quiet American*. Its open-air terrace, known locally as the "Continental shelf," had in the old days been the gathering place for a generation of reporters, diplomats, spies, and adventurers. But when I arrived, the lizards that crawled on the ceiling outnumbered the drinkers in their rattan chairs.

By the summer of 1974, the war in Indochina had faded from the headlines. With American combat troops withdrawn and the South and North Vietnamese armies locked in a dreary stalemate, interest among editors, news executives, and the general public had waned. Vietnam was just no longer considered much of a story. After a decade of constant infusions of American money, personnel, and aid, Saigon itself appeared to have run out of energy. Under a leaden sky and almost continual rain, its yellow French-style villas, with their peeling orange-tiled roofs, seemed decrepit rather than romantic. The streets were full of hustlers offering girls, dope, and money-changing services. But there were no takers. Every time I left the hotel, deformed beggars clustered around me, their twisted hands clutching at my shirt and shoulder bag. A one-eyed pedicab driver—his other eye socket, a round hole surrounded by scar tissue—grinned hideously at me, trying to catch my attention. Next to him, a five-year-old boy, balancing a younger child in his arms, stuck out his hand for money. Walking along the banks of the Saigon River, past sandbagged cement guardhouses and faded advertisements for Buicks and Coca-Cola, I could see thousands of shacks made of corrugated tin and cardboard, packed with refugees who'd fled to the city to escape the fighting. Outside one such shack, a man washed himself with water from a puddle on the street.

Repulsed and depressed, I abandoned plans to travel outside Saigon or to look up other diplomats and journalists. Lost in my thoughts, I walked the streets alone for hours, talking to no one, ending each day nursing a coffee on the "Continental shelf" while watching the human debris of years of war pass by on the streets outside.

Oppressed into inertia, I decided to leave early and stop in Hong Kong before returning home. On my last afternoon, I walked across the street for a snack in a small restaurant. As I sat staring out the window, I was startled by a tap on my shoulder. A young woman with shoulder-length hair, wearing black bell-bottoms and a purple shirt, was standing beside me.

"Excuse me," she said. "Would you mind taking a walk with me?"

Puzzled, I invited her to sit down. Her name was Nguyen Thi Tam, and after I bought her a Coke, she poured out her story. She was twenty years old, from Can Tho in the Mekong River delta. Her father was dead, and her three brothers were all in the South Vietnamese army. Previously employed as a secretary for the U.S. military in Saigon, she was now without work and desperately short of money.

"When the Americans were here," she said, "I was happy. Life was good. I had a job. I had money. Can you help me? Now I have nothing. What I want is for an American to love me, to take me to the U.S. I would do anything for him. Before, when I walked down the street with an American by my side, I felt so happy. The Americans were here for so long, I thought they would never leave."

At the back of the restaurant, someone put a coin in the jukebox. The air was filled with the strains of Roberta Flack's "Killing Me Softly with His Song." Suddenly a youngster with a missing hand pushed his deformed stump into my face and demanded money. Overwhelmed with guilt, I dug a few coins from my pocket.

Nguyen Thi Tam was on the verge of tears.

"Today, no one has any money. Everyone is hungry. Sometimes I stay with a friend. Otherwise I have to sleep in the street. Sometimes I think I will just lay down and die. Please, will you walk with me?"

We left the restaurant and walked together in silence down Tu Do Street. We passed the hideous bronze statue of two heroic soldiers that dominated the square in front of the opera house, and the numerous girlie bars and shabby souvenir shops. The sky was darkening. Finally I said I had to leave for the airport.

"Please, can I come with you to Hong Kong," she pleaded. "I don't know how I am going to live here. I have no hope."

I made a feeble excuse and, embarrassed and ashamed, turned away. On the drive to the airport, I realized that, to Nguyen Thi Tam, I was no different from any other American who had come to her country in previous years. She had been seduced by the false hopes and dreams of the America that I represented in her eyes. I thought of the GI graffiti in a Saigon bar I had once read of in the newspaper: "Vietnam—fuck it and leave it." Nguyen Thi Tam had certainly been screwed. As an American, I wondered whether my opposition to the war made me any less guilty. Visiting the country gave me no satisfaction, no vindication for my years of antiwar activism. I was immensely relieved when my Air Vietnam jet lifted off a few hours later.

A year after I left Vietnam, I was again preparing to hit the road, this time armed with a master's degree and a serious commitment to be a full-time journalist in Asia. My two semesters at the Columbia University Graduate School of Journalism had given me the rigorous training in the craft of journalism to complement both my desire for adventure and my intellectual interest in politics and the Far East. Under the tutelage of the huge, boisterous, dominating Fred Friendly, the broadcast pioneer and the partner of another one of my heroes, Edward R. Murrow, I learned how to write fast and clearly, to be unafraid of deadlines and intimidating editors, and always to keep Friendly's favorite maxim in mind. "Mike," he would bellow in his gravelly voice, "you've got the makings of a good journalist. But never forget: You've got to have fire in the belly." In fulfilling my journalism school assignments—from covering the press conference of the winner of the Miss All-Bare America contest, in which the main speaker wore only red shoes, to an extended television project on the sex life of the giant panda, shot on location at the National Zoo in Washington—I tried to remember those words.

At Columbia, I learned how to edit film (in the days before video became the standard medium of broadcast journalism) from Tom Bettag, later producer of the CBS Evening News with Dan Rather, and I received constant support from the school's acting dean, Frederick T. C. Yu, a refugee from China who noted my interest in that part of the world and did everything in his power to encourage it. His most important gesture came midway through the academic year, when he arranged for me to receive the Columbia East Asia Journalism Fellowship, which enabled me to take courses on the Far East and provided me with a small stipend and a one-way air ticket to Hong Kong to use upon graduation.

Personal tragedy made it impossible to take advantage of Dean Yu's offer immediately. In April 1975, just before I was due to receive my master's degree, my father was killed in an automobile accident. He and my mother had put the usual parental anxieties aside to encourage and support me in what must have seemed a hopelessly romantic, if not downright foolish and dangerous, endeavor. There was no way I could express my gratitude for my father's confidence at this crucial turning point in my life, except to continue to search for my own way forward. But for several months, I put my life on hold, trying to help my mother and younger sister cope with our devastating loss. By the fall of 1975, I was finally ready to leave.

After graduation, I had contacted CBS News about job possibilities, and Tony Brunton, the head of CBS Radio, indicated there might be a slot available as a radio stringer in Hong Kong. But there was one problem. Columbia had taught me important skills, but the Journalism School felt it was beneath its dignity to teach such showbiz concepts as a zippy delivery, let alone what to do about makeup and hair styling. In the real world, I soon discovered these things mattered. Brunton told me that while my credentials were impressive, my broadcast voice was not. At his urging, and with the promise of at least a vague commitment from CBS as the reward, I started taking speech lessons. For several weeks that fall, I stood in front of a mirror for an hour a day doing neck exercises and reciting tongue twisters, while using my spare time to firm up other stringing arrangements with a self-styled alternative news agency in San Francisco called Pacific News Service, and with the *Chicago Daily News*.

In late autumn of 1975, I left the United States for Hong Kong. I would give myself about twelve months, I thought, to see if I had any chance of achieving my dream of becoming a foreign correspondent. I could not know that the British colony would turn out to be my base for the next eight years, and that it would be two decades before I would again live in the United States.

I made an appointment with the Hong Kong bureau chief of CBS News in the first week of January 1976. Brian Ellis greeted me at the door. Formerly CBS boss in Saigon during the chaotic final days of the Vietnam war (where he had become something of a hero for helping many Vietnamese who worked for Western news agencies to escape), Brian was now in charge of the network's operations throughout the Far East. To my delight, he told me that CBS executives in New York had left a message requesting a sample radio spot from me as soon as I arrived. If my speech lessons had produced any improvement in my delivery, the CBS Radio string was mine.

A large, cheery man, Brian wore a custom-made, perfectly pressed tan safari suit—typical, slick, big-time TV executive, I thought, standing there in my wrinkled sports jacket (the only one I owned) and shaggy hair. But Brian's thoughtful and engaging manner changed my mind. He quickly impressed me as a serious newsman who cared less about my tailor than whether I knew what I was talking about. Sitting in his plush office with its panoramic view of Hong Kong's spectacular harbor, he told me that, with the end of the Vietnam war, most of CBS's old Asia hands had moved on to other assignments, leaving something of a staffing vacuum in the region. It was my good fortune to appear on the scene at just the right time. In their Hong Kong bureau, a new TV correspondent named Barry Kalb had just been hired. Barry was no relation to the two famous Kalbs at CBS, the brothers Marvin and Bernard, and Brian implied he was no China expert either. My background in Chinese affairs outweighed my lack of experience. I might just be useful.

More than a little intimidated by the bureau's aura of money and power and by the sleek self-assurance of the CBS staffers, I nervously sat down at a desk in the newsroom, scribbled a few lines based on an article in a local Chinese newspaper, and recorded my test story. I felt rather foolish as I tried to remember my voice coach's admonitions to overarticulate my D's and T's and not to pop my P's. Brian promised to feed the spot to New York and said he'd be back in touch.

I set out to find a place to live. For two months before reaching Hong Kong, I had traveled rough in South Asia while doing a little freelancing, slipping into Bangladesh just days after a failed bid by left-wing soldiers to seize power, and riding a third-class train across India, then in the grip of Prime Minister Indira Gandhi's dictatorial emergency. It was a stimulating, sobering introduction to the complexities of the Indian subcontinent, but I was eager to turn my energy toward China. However, my journey had left me almost penniless. I got off the plane in Hong Kong in late December with exactly four dollars in my pocket. As payments for my India and Bangladesh stories trickled in, my finances were replenished, but it was a pittance. After much searching, the only place I could afford was a shabby apartment in a back alley of Tsimshatsui, the gaudy tourist strip at the tip of the Kowloon Peninsula just across the harbor from Hong Kong Island. For the privilege of living a ten-minute walk from the Star Ferry, and just a few steps from a row of Chinese herbal medicine shops, fruit stands, all-night eateries, and a tawdry girlie bar called the Four Sisters, my landlord, an Indian merchant from Calcutta, charged me $220 a month. I thought it was a fortune.

Hong Kong was teeming with tycoons, skyscrapers, neon signs, shops bursting with expensive electronic goods, and restaurants serving everything from Beijing duck to steak-and-kidney pie. With its devotion to the naked pursuit of wealth, it seemed to me to be as different from mainland China as it was possible to imagine. I wandered through streets that were a riot of noise and color and energy, jammed with double-decker buses, Rolls Royces, creaky green trams, and ubiquitous red Japanese-made taxis. Lining the distant hillsides of the Kowloon Peninsula were squatter huts and tenements. Looking in the other direction, I could see the mansions of the super-rich stretching up 1,800-foot-high Victoria Peak. An even more striking contrast was to be found in the heart of the central business district. Just yards from the garish Hilton Hotel, the Hong Kong Club, and what used to be the premises of the Cricket Club, sat the Bank of China. Mounted on its roof and casting a shadow on the square below were giant Chinese characters declaring LONG LIVE CHAIRMAN MAO. The massive and forbidding bank was a symbol of the British colony's ambiguous role as both a booming capitalist entrepôt and the gateway to the world's most austere socialist state.

Nineteen seventy-six, my first year in Hong Kong, was the Year of the Dragon according to the Chinese lunar calendar. The Chinese believe the dragon is the most powerful of creatures, and tradition holds that dragon years portend momentous, and often disastrous, events. As I awaited a reply from CBS, China's first disaster struck. On January 9, I turned on the radio in my tiny apartment to hear the stunning news that Zhou Enlai was dead. The Chinese premier had been ill for some time, but to many in China and abroad, myself included, he remained a towering figure, a pragmatic statesman who had kept China intact during the Cultural Revolution and orchestrated its return to the international community afterward. News of his death plunged the People's Republic into grief and anxiety. Press reports from Beijing described tens of thousands of sobbing mourners filing past Zhou's open coffin. Over a million people lined the streets on the day of his cremation. There was mounting speculation about a final showdown between Zhou's reformist protégé, Deng Xiaoping, and Chairman Mao's wife, Jiang Qing, leader of the Cultural Revolution radicals.

In Hong Kong, too, there was real sadness. Motivated by journalistic curiosity as well as by a genuine sense of admiration, I joined more than 20,000 local residents to pay my respect to Zhou at the Bank of China, where a memorial had been set up. Hours before the doors opened, long lines of mourners, many wearing black armbands, stretched completely around the bank building. Waiting in the sunshine, I struck up a conversation with a tall, friendly man who identified himself as Tsang Tak-sing, a reporter for a Hong Kong newspaper called *New Evening Post*, one of three so-called patriotic publications considered to be Chinese mouthpieces in the colony. Despite his impeccable, British-accented English, Tsang was a committed leftist who, I later learned, had been imprisoned for two years following anti-British rioting that erupted in Hong Kong at the height of the Cultural Revolution. We found we had many interests in common and agreed to stay in touch. Tsang was to become a close friend, and, in subsequent years, as he rose to become a leading pro-China spokesman in Hong Kong as well as a member of the Chinese Parliament in Beijing, he remained one of my most insightful guides to the twists and turns of Chinese politics.

Inside the Bank, a huge auditorium had been transformed into a memorial hall dominated by a black-bordered photograph of Zhou. Countless wreaths, bouquets, and messages of condolence were piled up beneath it. As we filed through, stopping briefly to bow our heads in front of the portrait, a funeral dirge echoed from a loudspeaker in a corner. Many of the mourners were in tears.

The following night, I stayed up late to watch the televised news reports of the state funeral for Zhou in Beijing. Chairman Mao did not attend the rites for his longtime comrade, fueling speculation about his own health. Instead the eulogy was delivered by Deng Xiaoping. It was the last time Deng would be seen in public until after the death of Mao. The political crisis in China had begun to boil.

A week after Zhou's funeral, the telephone rang. It was Brian Ellis. "We finally heard back from New York. Your tape is fine," he said.

"Welcome to CBS News."

I would be paid thirty-five dollars for each radio spot the network chose to air. I was too excited to quibble about the meager compensation.

CBS was located in New Mercury House, an ugly fourteen-story building fronting the harbor in Wanchai, an area known more for its topless bars, nightclubs, and restaurants than its news bureaus. Across the street was the Luk Kwok Hotel, the setting for *The World of Suzie Wong*, the famous novel about a Hong Kong prostitute with a heart of gold. In the nearby streets, hundreds of real-life Suzie Wongs aggressively plied their trade, dragging gullible tourists, adventurous locals, American sailors on R and R, and assorted Hong Kong gangsters into dimly lit bars with names like Pussycat, Starlight, and, of course, The Suzie Wong Club.

The bureau itself was ultramodern, with giant picture windows facing the harbor on one side, rooms packed with cases of expensive camera equipment and editing machines, a separate radio studio, telex and wire machines, and clocks displaying New York, Hong Kong, and Greenwich mean time. Apart from Barry Kalb, the rest of the staff consisted of producer Keith Kay, once a legendary cameraman in Vietnam whose rugged features made him look as if he'd just stepped out of a Marlboro ad; Udo Nesch, the current cameraman, a stocky, hard-drinking, chain-smoking German whose habits and manner suggested he had seen far too much in Indochina; Udo's soundman/editor, a soft-spoken New Zealander named Dave Thomas; and a tall, thin Chinese man, Joe Yue. "Uncle Joe" bore the scars of several wounds sustained while filming battles in Vietnam and Cambodia. At the height of the war, one of his jobs was to take newly arrived CBS reporters on their first combat, or "bang-bang," assignments. Having survived enough close calls to know when to stop pushing his luck, Joe was now doing freelance shooting on a part-time basis, preferring to spend most of his days fishing.

I was somewhat puzzled to discover that, apart from Brian, none of CBS staff seemed terribly interested in the latest political developments in China. This was not as surprising as it seemed to me at the time. For even the most enthusiastic American reporter, covering China was an exercise in frustration. The Chinese refused to allow any U.S. news organization to open a bureau in Beijing. Even occasional, limited visits were extremely rare. Moreover, ideo-

logical treatises in the *People's Daily* did not make for very interesting television, especially when compared to the excitement of
Vietnam. The upshot was that while my new colleagues played
cards in the office or went for long lunches at the Foreign Correspondents' Club as they waited for CBS to send them on a sexy
assignment somewhere else in the region, the unfolding but still
obscure political drama in Beijing was largely left to me.

Every day I looked for clues, poring over clippings in the official
Chinese news agency, Xinhua; combing the local Hong Kong press,
which was often full of interesting (if frequently incorrect) speculation; and examining the reports of the handful of European and
Japanese journalists based in Beijing. In China's secretive system,
obscure historical references or subtle changes in the order in which
leaders were listed at a mundane official event were codes that often
signaled momentous political developments. At the enormous U.S.
Consulate in Hong Kong, which monitored, translated, and made
available a daily digest of Chinese provincial radio broadcasts, I
befriended young political officers like Mark Mohr, Scott Hallford,
and Chris Szymanski, who in later years would hold important jobs
at the U.S. Foreign Service, particularly at the American Embassy in
Beijing. I attended academic lectures at the Universities Service
Center in Kowloon, a gathering point for China scholars conducting
research in Hong Kong. I interviewed refugees, businessmen, even
missionaries, and I sought to cultivate local Hong Kong Chinese
journalists with close ties to Beijing. I began to meet regularly with
Tsang Tak-sing, the cub reporter for the *New Evening Post*, who,
though loyal to the Chinese cause, was a sophisticated analyst able
to discuss serious issues without lapsing into party rhetoric. I
became friendly as well with a senior official at the Xinhua News
Agency, which functioned as China's unofficial "embassy" in Hong
Kong. His card described him as a reporter, but he was in fact a high-
ranking diplomat and Communist Party member. Although initially
suspicious of all Western reporters, once he discovered I had visited
China with a "friendly" delegation and was not as cynical as many
other foreign journalists, he became a good friend and an invaluable
source. I also met Dr. H. C. Ling, a South African–born Chinese
who worked for the most influential pro-Beijing newspaper, the *Ta
Kung Pao*. Elegant and silver-haired, with a taste for expensive
Western food and, apparently, an expense account to pay for it, Dr.

Ling frequently took me to lunch at the Pheasant and Peacock, a dark, wood-paneled restaurant in the central business district. Sitting among impeccably attired Western business executives, Dr. Ling, with the patience and faith of a true believer, tried to answer my questions and quell the mounting skepticism I began to express about the confusing course of events in China.

In the wake of Zhou Enlai's death, the signs were indeed perplexing. Seeking to gain the upper hand in the battle to succeed the eighty-two-year-old Mao, Jiang Qing and the leftists had mounted a new campaign to topple Deng Xiaoping. In a steadily rising crescendo, the official media denounced Deng as a "capitalist-roader." Staying at the bureau long after everyone else had gone home, pulling together the information and insights I had collected, I churned out spot after spot for CBS Radio. The story topics, which I listed in my journal, capture something of the flavor of those swiftly moving events: "Deng Called Chinese Khrushchev," "Anti-Deng Posters in Beijing," "Attacks on Deng in Shanghai," "Where Is Deng?" "Mrs. Mao Blasts Deng for Criticizing Revolutionary Opera." In late winter, one of my spots aired for the first time on the CBS World News Roundup, the broadcast program pioneered on the eve of World War II by Edward R. Murrow and William Shirer. Now anchored by Dallas Townsend, it still set the standard for radio news, showcasing such well-known correspondents as Connie Chung, Bob Scheiffer, and Leslie Stahl. "Look what company I'm keeping!" I wrote to my mother with some amazement. China in the Year of the Dragon was shaping up to be a very interesting story. I began to feel it just might launch my career.

In mid-March, however, things suddenly got very quiet in Beijing. From the outside, it was impossible to judge if this meant an end to the political crisis or simply the calm before a new storm. But for the moment, the steady stream of China stories for CBS Radio began to dry up, and with it my steady, if modest, source of income. I decided to take advantage of the lull to do a little traveling for my major print outlet, Pacific News Service. I booked a ticket to Bangkok, a place that turned out to be anything but quiet.

Nearly a year after the fall of Saigon, the U.S. defeat in Indochina was still sending shock waves throughout Southeast Asia. Nowhere were the reverberations more sharply felt than in Thailand. During the height of the war, thousands of American servicemen had been stationed on Thai soil. Now, seeking to accommodate Thailand's newly triumphant Communist neighbors in Vietnam, the government of Prime Minister Kukrit Pramoj, in the face of bitter opposition from the conservative Thai military, had reluctantly ordered the four thousand remaining U.S. troops to leave Thailand by March 20.

Flying in a few days before the deadline, I found Bangkok to be in a state of high tension. The city's nerves, normally stretched almost to the breaking point at this time of year by the relentless pre-monsoon heat and humidity, were further frayed by clashes between anti-American leftists and right-wingers opposed to a U.S. withdrawal. With the nation on military alert amid rumors of a possible military coup d'état, traffic on Bangkok's normally impassable streets had thinned out, some shops had closed down, and many anxious citizens, fearing trouble, were staying at home.

Taking a room for two dollars a night at a hippie hotel called the Maya Guest House, I made contact with Thanam, a radical Thai journalist whose name I had been given by mutual friends in the antiwar movement. We hit it off immediately. Educated in the United States, Thanam took me under his wing, introducing me to other Thai reporters and to leading student activists involved in the campaign for a U.S. pullout. With him, I joined thousands of anti-American students at a rally in a park next to Thailand's gilded and ornate Royal Palace. For eight hours under a baking sun, I watched the protestors listen to speeches, sing songs, and sip soft drinks out of red, white, and blue paper cups emblazoned with leftist political slogans. As night fell, the sun's fading rays glimmered on the golden spires in the distance. Sweaty and tired, I worked my way toward the front of the gathering to listen to what I hoped would be the final speech of the day. Suddenly I heard a bang. There was a flash and a scream. Someone had thrown two hand grenades into the seething mass of humanity around the rostrum. One exploded, wounding two students. The crowd dissolved into chaos as people stumbled over each other to get away. Struggling to keep my balance, I tripped over a hard object. I looked down at the ground. It was the second grenade, which had rolled to a stop at my feet without exploding. For a moment, I was frozen in terror. Then I, too, threw myself into the stampede. The device was a dud.

The next afternoon I was even luckier. The students had organized a march to the U.S. Embassy. Carrying posters proclaiming U.S.-THAI AS EQUALS NOT PUPPETS and NO TO KISSINGER'S MILITARISM, ten thousand students moved through Bangkok's clogged and fume-ridden streets. For several sweaty but uneventful miles, I tagged along, chatting with the smiling, laughing demonstrators and taking notes, all the while feeling as if I were at a college antiwar rally transplanted to the tropics. Moving up to the front of the march, I noticed just ahead a restaurant I had discovered on an earlier trip. Smitty's Pancake House served the best pancakes in Asia. Hot, tired, and hungry, I couldn't resist. I decided to pop in for a brief snack and a reinvigorating blast of air-conditioning.

Moments later, as I dug into a large stack of strawberry pancakes, I heard a muffled boom and raced outside. Up the street, the march was in chaos. Youthful bodies were sprawled on the bloody pavement, some writhing in pain, others terrifyingly still. From the top of a nearby building, a right-wing fanatic had lobbed explosives at the students passing below. Four young demonstrators were dead and eighty more were seriously injured. Scribbling furiously in my notebook as I struggled to take in the scene, I suddenly stopped short. Among the bloody youngsters being comforted at the side of the road were several I'd been chatting with just a few minutes before.

Shaken by my two narrow escapes, I was grateful for Thanam's invitation to dinner. After stopping for ice cream at an American-style coffee shop, he suggested a stress-relieving visit to a massage parlor. Curiosity and lust overcame my qualms, and, bemused by the paradox of a Thai leftist offering to introduce me to the sensual delights of Bangkok, I agreed.

Thanam took me to Darling's, a huge palace with an illuminated fountain outside and elaborate carvings of naked nymphs in the lobby. Inside, sitting behind a one-way window, were some of the most beautiful women I had ever seen. Each of them was scantily dressed, with a number pinned to her satin gown. For a price, each was available. I discovered that Darling's was a particular favorite of the Bangkok press corps. The women there counted among their regular clients many of the foreign correspondents I had met in the city. Indeed, one young lady, while ministering to me in ways I had never imagined, regaled me with more journalistic gossip—rumors of staff changes, travel plans, career moves—than I had heard from anyone else since I'd moved to Asia. She even told me of one reporter who regularly filed his dispatches from Darling's, phoning his foreign desk while she massaged him in the bathtub. Not exactly my image of the intrepid foreign correspondent, yet, to my surprise, the Bangkok sex scene was far less sordid than I had expected. The women were mostly from the countryside, and they were ambitious and shrewd enough to come to the city, learn some English, and earn far more than would ever have been possible had they stayed at home to work with their parents in the rice paddies. Many formed lasting relationships with their clients. For most of these young women, however, I knew a fate of disease and despair lay ahead. As someone whose sexual values had been shaped by the emergence of the women's movement in the U.S. in the late 1960s, my whoring in a Third World capital was as politically incorrect behavior as it was possible to imagine. But my leftist friend Thanam appeared to have no qualms, and I was troubled far less by such thoughts than I perhaps should have been. In Bangkok's torrid atmosphere, my moral and political certainties dissolved into ambiguity.

I returned to Hong Kong on Sunday, April 4, the day of the Qing Ming Festival, when the Chinese traditionally sweep the graves of their ancestors and pay homage to the honored dead. On this warm, sunny afternoon, thousands of local residents jammed buses and trains to the New Territories, loaded down with food, fruit, incense sticks, and other offerings to place at ancestral burial sites. Unpacking in my tiny, stuffy apartment, the heady experiences of the past three weeks in Thailand still fresh in my mind, I was ready again to turn my energies toward China. Monday was a public holiday in Hong Kong. I didn't expect to have anything to file, but I planned to drop by the CBS office anyway and start to catch up. It didn't look like I'd missed much Chinese news during my absence.

I was wrong.

Beneath the quiet surface in Beijing, popular resentment of Mao's wife, Jiang Qing, and her Gang of Four Cultural Revolution radicals had been steadily growing, fueled by their ideological campaign against Deng Xiaoping. The Qing Ming holiday provided the spark for an explosion. On Sunday, thousands of Beijing citizens had laid wreaths in memory of Zhou Enlai at the Monument to the Heroes of the Revolution in Tiananmen Square, the same monument where the student demonstrators were to make their stand in 1989. The veneration of Zhou, a moderate who had sought to blunt the worst excesses of the Cultural Revolution, was a thinly disguised protest against the extremist policies of Jiang Qing. Overnight the wreaths and posters were carted away by police. As I arrived at CBS on Monday, unaware of any of these events, fresh crowds gathered at Tiananmen Square to discover that their Qing Ming tributes of the previous day had been removed.

The first reports of trouble came at midday with a flash on our Reuters wire machine. A disturbance had broken out in the square after thousands of people defied government orders and placed new wreaths and photographs of Zhou Enlai at the monument. Except for an office assistant, I was alone in the bureau. I immediately booked telephone calls to a half dozen Western embassies in Beijing. There was no such thing as direct dial to China, so I sat impatiently, often for more than an hour, waiting for my calls to come through. Eventually the diplomats I did reach were able to provide independent confirmation—as well as eyewitness details—of one of the most extraordinary events in the history of the People's Republic. In a gigantic, spontaneous act of protest, over 100,000 people had massed in Tiananmen, shouting slogans, waving placards containing oblique criticisms of Chairman Mao and the radicals, scuffling with police, overturning vehicles, and ransacking and burning a building used by the security services on the eastern side of the square. The scale and boldness of this public outburst were breathtaking. As I phoned in first one, then two, then eventually a half dozen spots to CBS Radio, I could hardly believe what I was reporting. By midevening, after the crowds ignored the mayor of Beijing's broadcast appeal for calm, the militia moved in. In a brutal confrontation, large numbers of people were beaten and arrested. It was well past midnight when, exhausted, elated, and more than a little worried about the future of China, I left the bureau for home.

The fallout came almost immediately. As I kept track of reports that soldiers and security agents had been mobilized to maintain order in the heart of Beijing, the Communist Party's Politburo met in an emergency session to condemn the Tiananmen demonstrations as a "counterrevolutionary act." At the urging of the Cultural Revolution radicals, a feeble Chairman Mao agreed to blame the disturbances on Deng Xiaoping, an ironic twist in light of what was to happen in 1989. As the dimensions of the story became clear, I joined the rest of the CBS staff on the sixth floor of New Mercury House to monitor the evening news bulletin on Chinese television. Broadcast every night at seven o'clock from Canton, ninety miles away, the signal was picked up by a receiver installed on one of Hong Kong's tallest peaks and beamed to our building. CBS and the other foreign networks in Hong Kong shared the cost of recording it. Invariably grainy and of low quality, Canton TV nonetheless provided the only television pictures regularly available from China. In the dimly lit control room, we watched the image flicker as an announcer in a Mao suit read a historic proclamation: "On the proposal of our great leader Chairman Mao," he intoned, "the Political Bureau of the Chinese Communist Party unanimously agrees to dismiss Deng Xiaoping from all posts inside and outside the party."

Having been rehabilitated only three years earlier, Deng, for the second time in his political career, was out, the victim of another campaign by the radical leftists. Hua Guofeng, a colorless and previously unknown apparatchik, was appointed prime minister and Mao's designated successor. It seemed that yet again I was an eyewitness, albeit from a distance, to historic events in China.

There was also fallout at CBS from the Tiananmen crisis. My fortuitous presence at the bureau on that Qing Ming holiday had kept CBS Radio abreast of a major breaking story. The radio editors were extremely complimentary. CBS foreign editor Sid Feders, however, was angry that Barry Kalb, the staff correspondent, had not come in on that crucial first day. Kalb, in turn, blamed me for stealing his story. Although bureau chief Brian Ellis backed me up, the episode provided my first lesson in the harshly competitive world of network news.

Undeterred, I continue to log twelve- or sixteen-hour days at the bureau, reading the Chinese press, making phone calls to diplomats in the Chinese capital, and monitoring Radio Beijing on CBS's new and powerful shortwave. In May, as spring arrived with gray skies, constant rain, and humidity that peeled the paint in my apartment, there was renewed concern about Mao's failing health. Early in the month, New Zealand Prime Minister Robert Muldoon passed through Hong Kong after a state visit to China. Granted a fifteen-minute interview at a luxury hotel, I asked about his painful meeting with the Chairman. Muldoon told me Mao seemed very frail and had difficulty speaking. I wondered whether the Chinese leader was coherent enough for his comments to be translated accurately. Muldoon was noncommittal. When late one night the Xinhua News Agency announced that Mao would no longer see foreign visitors, I raced to catch the last Star Ferry to file the story. Gazing out at the now-quiet harbor as the lights of Hong Kong's high-rise buildings twinkled on the jet-black water, I felt that an era in China was about to end, with consequences no one could predict.

As the Mao deathwatch continued, I had my first brush with television. With Barry Kalb on vacation for three weeks, Brian Ellis assigned me to go with veteran cameraman Joe Yue to shoot a demonstration organized by a group of radical Hong Kong students to denounce the post-Tiananmen crackdown in Beijing—another presage of events in 1989. The handful of youthful protestors was vastly outnumbered by reporters, photographers, and TV crews. It was clearly not going to be a story CBS would broadcast. But for me, carrying Joe Yue's batteries and tripod, watching him change the canisters of film, and listening to the stories of his various adventures was an introduction to the way a TV crew worked in the field. I was fascinated. I hoped I would have a chance to do it for real someday.

Soon after, Brian Ellis sought and received authorization from CBS New York for me to do an on-camera audition.

"Panda," said Joe Yue, using the nickname he had given me, "it's about time you went out and got some TV clothes."

With no little embarrassment, I purchased a tan safari shirt with epaulets—the uniform favored by most TV correspondents in the tropics. I spent hours drafting a short commentary on China to read into the camera. The night before my tryout, I was so anxious that I went out and got drunk at the Four Sisters Bar near my apartment and took one of the women back home with me. Not normally a heavy drinker or womanizer, I was tired and more than a little hung over the next morning, but I donned my safari shirt and joined my camera crew on the roof of New Mercury House. Standing with Hong Kong harbor in the background, my hair slicked down to disguise its length, holding the microphone in my left hand and looking and feeling very nervous, I did three takes of my commentary. To my surprise, despite the buzz in my head, I was able to recite it from memory. The crew said I'd done a good job, but I realized I was not yet going to take Walter Cronkite's show by storm.

I was now feeling very comfortable living in Hong Kong. I enjoyed its fast pace, its exotic mix of races and cultures, its proximity to China. But the forces shaping my life were pulling me in contrary directions. I was put off by the colonial snobbishness of many of the wealthy foreigners I encountered, as well as by the territory's obsession with money. Most of the other foreign reporters seemed so cynical that I found talking about China with them to be an exercise in frustration. My closest friends were turning out to be the local pro-Beijing Chinese journalists. They may have been apologists for the Chinese government, but we enjoyed each other's company, discovering over dim sum and dumplings that we shared many similar views, as well as a keen interest in developments on the mainland. Yet as I followed events in China, I found my own doubts increasing, almost against my will. "News from China is pretty grim these days," I noted in my journal early in the summer. "Everyone is waiting for Mao to die. Infighting between rival factions continues. My enthusiasm for covering China has waned. It's a troubling issue for me. I had hoped my ideals would find an outlet by reporting the Chinese revolution. But it ain't so simple."

The prospect of a career in network radio or television also left me ambivalent. I had bought the required safari suit and joined the Foreign Correspondents' Club, whose men's room offered one of the best views of Hong Kong harbor. But the drunken hacks at the bar reminiscing about the good old days in Vietnam depressed me. One slow dreary Sunday, I sat in my apartment as rains from a typhoon pounded the windows, and reread Graham Greene's *The Quiet American*, in which the main character is a cynical, opium-smoking war correspondent in Saigon. "I identify with that figure enough to get disturbed at myself sometimes," I wrote in my journal. "I wonder how one can reconcile the desire to change the world with the necessity of reporting what is invariably an unjust and depressing present."

But I was too busy to spend much time soul-searching. Partly because of the tensions with Barry Kalb, I looked for some additional outlets beyond CBS. I began to freelance for the Long Island, New York, newspaper *Newsday* and to do an occasional story for the *Guardian* of London. Martin Woolacott, the *Guardian*'s thoughtful and vastly experienced Far East correspondent, had been extremely friendly and helpful during my initial months in Hong Kong. My first article for the *Guardian* examined how the Chinese, by monitoring the aberrant behavior of animals and charting changes in well water and soil composition, had achieved considerable success in predicting earthquakes. I thought I had written a bright, clever feature. A week after the story came out, China was devastated by the worst earthquake in its history, which no one had predicted.

When I arrived at the bureau on Wednesday, July 28, I heard the Radio Hong Kong announcer report in his clipped, BBC-style voice that the colony's Royal Observatory had recorded a massive earthquake in northeastern China. Measuring 7.8 on the Richter scale, the tremor's epicenter was in the industrial city of Tangshan, home to a million people. So far, there had been no official confirmation from the Chinese. Barry Kalb and the crew had left Hong Kong early in the morning for a previously scheduled assignment in Thailand. Once again, by sheer coincidence, it looked as if I might have a big story to myself. As in April, I began to work the phones to Beijing with the help of Chinese-speaking CBS office assistants Mike Lam and Tommy Cheng. I felt a bond with these overworked and underpaid low-ranking members of the bureau, which they reciprocated by going out of their way to be helpful. Unfortunately my initial inquiries elicited only sketchy details. Western diplomats confirmed that the tremor had been felt in the capital, and that many citizens had rushed into the streets despite pouring rain. But the authorities were saying little, and nobody seemed to have any clear idea of how serious the damage had been elsewhere.

The next morning, I was finally able to report China's first official statement. The Xinhua News Agency acknowledged that the quake had caused "great losses to people's lives and property." In particular, Xinhua said, Tangshan, one hundred miles southeast of Beijing, had suffered "extremely serious damages and losses." By now diplomats in Beijing were telling me the talk there was of potentially huge casualties. I was uncertain how to report this important development. Neither diplomats nor the few Beijing-based foreign journalists were being allowed anywhere near the worst-hit areas. In fact, I had little more than speculation and common sense to go on. But the somber tone of the Chinese media reports suggested this was a major disaster, and so, with careful qualifications, I stuck my neck out. In my stories I began to raise the possibility that thousands, and perhaps even tens of thousands, might have died.

I made regular pilgrimages across the harbor to the Hong Kong train station, trying to meet and interview travelers returning from China, hoping, above all, to find someone with a home-movie camera who had filmed the remarkable scenes I had been hearing about. On that score, I did not succeed. I did hear of one businessman who'd filmed the countryside while his train passed through Tangshan just days after the quake. But fearful of losing his access to China, he refused to give the material to CBS or any other news organization. Tangshan remained a radio story.

It wasn't until much later that the full scale of the horror became clear. My initial estimates, bold as they seemed at the time, vastly understated the extent of the tragedy. A quarter of a million people died in the quake, and another quarter million were injured. It was the worst such disaster the world had seen this century. For the superstitious Chinese, it seemed that the Dragon had roared.

Barely a month later, the Dragon roared again. On September 9, Chairman Mao died. But my string of remarkable journalistic luck had run out. In early September, I had returned to the States to see my family for the first time since I'd set out the previous autumn. I was at my mother's home in Massachusetts when I tuned in the CBS *World News Roundup* and heard Barry Kalb reporting Mao's death. I was crestfallen, but having just arrived on a cheap ticket I had paid for myself, I reluctantly decided not to rush back. Instead I tried to relax while staying glued to the radio and television and wondering how the Chinese would cope with the loss of their "Great Leader," the driving force of their revolution for nearly thirty years. I consoled myself that there would be plenty of news awaiting me when I did return.

I got back to Hong Kong just hours after the Chinese announced that Jiang Qing and her radical Gang of Four had been ousted from power. I'd been delayed briefly in Bangkok, where plans for a few final days of R and R had been ruined by a bloody right-wing military coup that took place just before I arrived. Scores of left-wing students had been massacred near the site of the anti-American rallies I'd attended in March. The Thai capital had been transformed into a frightening city of curfews, roadblocks, and mass arrests. Thanam and my other radical friends were either in jail or had fled to the jungle. I was tempted to stay, but it was clear that momentous events were taking place in China. I did not want to miss anything more.

Returning to CBS, I was no longer greeted as an inexperienced newcomer. Brian Ellis and most of the others in the bureau were eager for me to put my China expertise to use right away. It was hard to imagine a news story that could top Zhou Enlai's passing, the riots in Tiananmen Square, the purging of Deng Xiaoping, the Tangshan earthquake, and the death of Mao. But the drama that now unfolded in Beijing was absolutely sensational. In utter astonishment, I reported the arrest of Chairman Mao's widow, the collapse of her scheme to succeed her late husband, and the explosion of joy which the news of her disgrace set off throughout China.

Not all the pieces of this puzzle fell into place at once. On Friday, October 22, 1976, United Press International in Hong Kong mistranslated a Chinese news agency dispatch saying the ouster of the Gang of Four had "liquidated a bane in our party" to mean that Mrs. Mao and her cohorts had been executed. Without checking with the Hong Kong bureau, CBS Radio interrupted the World Series to report Jiang Qing's death. More than a little dubious, I made some calls to Beijing. One was to a Canadian friend studying at Beijing University who had been extremely helpful during the past several months, giving me consistently reliable insights and information on the scene in the Chinese capital. Now she told me her Chinese classmates were saying they'd attended briefings closed to foreigners where officials declared that the Gang of Four were alive, in detention, and would be put on trial. After considerable discussion, CBS Radio agreed to broadcast my report. Two weeks later, senior Chinese officials publicly confirmed to visiting foreigners the accuracy of the information I had obtained, although it would take four years of complex internal political battles in Beijing before Jiang Qing appeared in court.

The fall of the Gang of Four was by no means a sure thing. In the days just after Mao's death, Jiang Qing had sought to claim the Chairman's legacy as her own. It was widely believed she was on the brink of moving against her rivals when she herself was detained. For a brief period, the country faced the prospect of yet another prolonged and destabilizing rift at the top. When it became clear the danger had receded and Mao's widow had been neutralized once and for all, the country erupted in celebration. The popular elation was accompanied by one of the most vicious campaigns of character assassination China had ever seen, with articles, poems, wall posters, and cartoons vilifying, insulting, and mocking Jiang Qing. Press accounts depicted her as a latter-day empress who carried her own food and luxurious toilet when she traveled, who ordered the navy to cordon off beaches when she swam, and who systematically undermined Chairman Mao's key policies. Jiang Qing was undoubtedly a scapegoat. The savagery of the attacks on her was as close as the Chinese public could get to denouncing the man who was really to blame for China's recent suffering, but whose image remained untouchable, the Chairman himself. But the national sense of relief and liberation was unquestionably real.

It was a historic turning point for China, and, for those of us covering the country, one of the most remarkable stories ever to emerge from the People's Republic. Yet Beijing still refused to permit American journalists to visit. Stuck in Hong Kong, my colleagues and I had no way to witness the exuberant celebrations in the streets, to sample the heady atmosphere, or talk to the people. However vitriolic the denunciations of Madam Mao, recounting the editorials in the *People's Daily*, or rebroadcasting the grainy images from China Central Television (CCTV), did little to convey the flavor of a moment when it was not an exaggeration to say that an entire country was changing course almost overnight. For TV, with its need for compelling pictures, it was especially frustrating, although as a radio reporter, I left that headache to my colleagues.

One November afternoon, as the reports of nationwide rejoicing flowed into Hong Kong, I ran into Judith Lubman, a veteran China trader who had been among the first Americans to do business with the Chinese, and whom I had met at the home of mutual friends. Judith had just returned from the semiannual Canton Trade Fair, which had taken place amidst a mood of frenzied celebration, and where she'd photographed a series of remarkable wall posters. As she described them, I realized they might well make a highly unusual television story. She generously agreed to give her photos to me. With the approval of Brian Ellis, I had the pictures enlarged for cameraman Udo Nesch to film. They were indeed astonishing. Jiang Qing was depicted as a witch and a four-armed insect. One poster showed her with a snake's body, waiting to be crowned empress and about to change into a Superman suit. Another portrayed the other three members of the "Gang" kissing Mrs. Mao's feet as she lay in a bed ringed with dollar signs. I had never done a real TV story before, but Brian decided this would be my first chance. On a Saturday afternoon, I recorded a narration after several nerve-racking tries, and the material was air-freighted to New York. For the first time since I returned to Hong Kong, I decided to take Sunday off.

On Monday morning, when I walked into the bureau, Brian Ellis was beaming. He handed me a telex from the staff of *CBS Evening News*. "Ellis for Chinoy: Congratulations from all here on a splendid network television debut." I had a long way to go in mastering the medium of television, I knew, but this was certainly a promising start. For my own reasons, I breathed a silent thanks for the fall of the Gang of Four.

CHAPTER FOUR

Good Guys and Bad Guys

The crowd was a sea of blue—padded jackets, padded trousers, peaked caps—pressed so tightly together I wasn't sure I could move. With a mounting sense of anticipation, I pushed my way forward, trying to keep my feet on the ground as the assembled mass lurched first one way and then the other. "*Duibuqi*," I repeated. "Excuse me." Slowly, as people noticed the Westerner in their midst, a path was cleared. In a moment, I was standing in front of Democracy Wall.

Made of gray brick, stretching about two hundred yards along Beijing's Changan Street at Xidan Street, west of Tiananmen Square, the wall seemed surprisingly modest in scale. But for one exhilarating year, from late 1978 to late 1979, it was the center of the most remarkable outpouring of free expression since the founding of the People's Republic. In the *dazibao*, or big character posters, plastered on the wall, Chairman Mao was publicly denounced for the first time in China, sending shock waves across the country. Emboldened by a new, more tolerant political climate in the wake of Mao's death, thousands of ordinary people gave vent to grievances they had long been forced to suppress. Soon came calls for the ouster of all remaining Maoists in the leadership, including the Chairman's designated heir, Hua Guofeng, and the rehabilitation of those persecuted during the Cultural Revolution. There were shocking revelations of official lies, hypocrisy, and brutality, and demands for human rights, the rule of law, and, above all, political freedom.

In my office in Hong Kong, I had watched the development of Democracy Wall with amazement and intense frustration because I couldn't be on the scene. I had spent hours on the phone with friends in Beijing and eagerly awaited the transcripts of important posters as they became available. The most powerful was "The Fifth Modernization," written by Wei Jingsheng, an outspoken young electrician at the Beijing Zoo, who became the most prominent figure of this period. I was moved by his passionate argument that China would not achieve what a reformist government headed by Deng Xiaoping called the "Four Modernizations"—agriculture, industry, science, and defense—without a "Fifth Modernization," democracy. Clear-sighted, courageous, and charismatic, Wei seemed a most impressive figure. I hoped one day to meet him.

Now, at last, I had managed to secure a visa to China, giving me an opportunity to see Democracy Wall for myself. With dozens of Chinese peering over my shoulder, I studied the handwritten posters. There were essays, poems, complaints, and diatribes. One demanded justice for a man who'd been exiled from Beijing and forced to work as a peasant in the countryside at the time of the Cultural Revolution. Another called for the release of political prisoners. Scribbling in my notebook, I could feel the sense of excitement in the air. I turned to a young man standing next to me. "What do you think of all this?" I asked. Unlike many previous encounters in China, where people either parroted a line or averted their eyes and turned away, he looked directly at me and smiled. "The Chinese people need freedom," he replied. "This is good, very good!"

Democracy Wall stood just a short distance from the Minzu Hotel, where I had stayed on my first visit to China. In 1973, I had walked right by it, following the large crowds marching into Tiananmen Square to hail Chairman Mao and his radical policies at the end of the Communist Party's historic Tenth Congress. Now, six years later, the message from the posters and from the crowd in which I found myself was very different. In the poignant accounts of despair and suffering and the angry demands for justice, the wall projected the undeniable aura of truth. In my early political enthusiasm, I had been willing to gloss over China's flaws, convinced that morality lay on the side of the revolution. Now, with Democracy Wall providing a glimpse of the reality missing in all those *jieshao*, "brief introductions," I recognized that I had been attracted to an illusion. It was a sobering moment. As I stood there, I felt the last of my youthful idealism about China disappearing in the chilly Beijing wind.

In its place, though, came not simply disillusionment. On the day of my visit, Democracy Wall was already under attack by the authorities. Within months, the crowds would be gone, the posters hosed down and replaced with advertisements for batteries and toothpaste. But the people around me had survived unspeakable trials and tribulations. Their earnest, intense faces represented a triumph of the human spirit. Although my hopes for Mao's revolution were shattered, I retained a sense of hope for the Chinese people and their future.

My presence at Democracy Wall in 1979 was itself one sign of change in the People's Republic. Although the Chinese remained unwilling following Mao's death to permit the U.S. broadcast networks to open bureaus in Beijing, the government had begun to relax its once-stringent visa requirements for American journalists. Slowly, access to the People's Republic became easier. In May of 1977, barely half a year after the fall of the Gang of Four, I got my first glimpse of China's emerging post-Mao reality. Relieved and excited by the turn of events in their homeland, my Chinese Communist friends in Hong Kong opened the door, lobbying on behalf of my application for a visa to cover the semiannual Canton Trade Fair, the event at which, six months previously, my friend Judith Lubman had photographed those remarkable cartoon caricatures of Jiang Qing. When permission came through, it was considered a major breakthrough, producing many envious comments from frustrated colleagues who held far more lofty positions in Hong Kong's competitive journalistic community. Of more importance to me was the chance to see for myself what was happening. In my journal I wrote, "I hope it will rekindle some of my enthusiasm for China that has been bashed around so much by the political changes of the last eighteen months."

It didn't turn out that way.

At my request, the Chinese agreed to take me back to the Hongmian Textile Mill in nearby Foshan, which I'd visited in 1973. The factory was the same noisy, gloomy place I remembered. Now, though, a pigtailed young woman named Lin Ping gave me a "brief introduction" with a message that was exactly the opposite of what I'd heard four years earlier.

"The Gang of Four claimed that if you paid attention to the welfare of the workers, you were behaving like a bourgeois capitalist," she explained. "Anyone who criticized this line was suppressed. So leading members at the factory were confused and didn't dare do anything to motivate the workers."

Lin Ping pointed out that outstanding workers had begun receiving rewards and bonuses. I thought about Comrade Zhuang, the ebullient Maoist official who'd lectured us on the evils of using material rather than ideological incentives to motivate the workers when I visited in 1973. My request to see him was met with a blank stare. When I asked what had happened to him, Lin Ping replied, "I'm not too clear about that."

At my other stops—a commune, three factories, two cultural performances, and the trade fair itself—I could see the first tentative signs of a return to more rational, pragmatic policies. The presence of hundreds of Western businessmen, including many Americans, was the clearest evidence that China's door was opening. In the once-empty Dong Fang Hotel, where I had stayed in 1973, traders packed a newly opened rooftop bar dubbed the "Top of the Fang," a faint glimmer of nightlife in a city where everyone seemed to go to sleep by nine P.M. Most of the time, though, I was bombarded with lectures on the evils of the Gang of Four, and the heroic deeds of Mao's successor, the new Party leader Chairman Hua Guofeng. A cult deliberately imitating that of Mao was being created right before my eyes. The posters of Hua in downtown Canton showed him with a haircut and facial expression uncannily like those on the still ubiquitous Mao portraits. At one particularly awful song-and-dance performance, the featured numbers were "Presenting Rugs to Chairman Hua," "Chairman Hua Came to Our Commune," and "Whom Chairman Mao Trusted So Do We." I couldn't help but laugh. If the Communist Party's political line was different, the clumsy way it was being communicated seemed very much the same. "I am so sick of the line about Jiang Qing and the Gang of Four being the cause of all problems," I wrote in my journal, "without a word about Chairman Mao. The Chinese know that's a lie, but they won't admit it."

Two months later, in July 1977, came the clearest sign so far of the new path China was taking. Deng Xiaoping, purged during the Cultural Revolution, rehabilitated in 1973, and purged again following the Tiananmen Square riots of April 1976, was restored to power for an unprecedented second time. He made his first public appearance at a televised soccer match in Beijing. It was a major story. As it happened, I was manning the CBS Hong Kong bureau that evening while the rest of the staff were traveling, but I wasn't completely on my own. A few months earlier, at a raucous party in Stanley, a village favored by British expatriates on the far side of Victoria Peak, I had met a woman named Alison. Attractive and reckless, she had fled the grimness of her native Scotland to find adventure in the tropical excitement of Hong Kong. Earning her living by teaching English to Japanese businessmen, she was something of a lost soul, trying to find her way while bringing up a two-year-old son, the product of a relationship that had ended unhappily before the boy was even born. For all my professional progress, I, too, was rather lost emotionally—still recovering from the death of my father, struggling to cope with the unraveling of the political beliefs that had originally drawn me to China, and not certain of myself in Hong Kong's competitive and status-conscious society. At my office, I was still the low man on the totem pole, and I felt very much on my own. Alison and I each seemed to meet a need in the other, and we soon began spending time together. She had no interest in politics. Instead our relationship focused on domestic matters. We cooked elaborate meals together, took young Sean to the park or the beach, and lazed around reading or watching TV. It did not exactly fit my romantic image of the life of a foreign correspondent, but it was a welcome antidote to my solitary, workaholic existence, and the little boy and I soon became devoted to each other.

I did not anticipate any major news on this sticky midsummer night. So, while Alison went out with her girlfriends, I volunteered to look after Sean for a few hours and brought him with me to the office. Shortly after we arrived, the news about Deng broke. Within minutes, the phones were ringing and the telex was clattering. CBS New York wanted pictures for the *Evening News*. I had never coordinated a satellite transmission before, let alone produced a TV story on my own. Now I had just a couple of hours to arrange for the Canton TV film to be processed, find an editor, write and narrate a script, and set up a feed. Meanwhile, Sean, excessively stimulated by his late-night excursion, was having a ball. Soon he had crumpled the tape from the telex machine and the wire copy from our UPI and Reuters machines into large piles on the floor. Adding the coffee and Coke I was drinking, plus bits of discarded film and audiotape, he rolled about in the disgusting mess until both he and the floor were coated in paper-encrusted slime. As I tried to sound knowledgeable, cool, and professional on the phone with CBS New York while dealing with one of the biggest China stories of the year, I knew the editors could hear whoops of childish delight in the background. Luckily no one asked me what was going on, and, to my amazement, the feed went off without a hitch. At four in the morning, totally exhausted, I brought the still-excited child home to his considerably annoyed mother. When the local CBS staff came to work a few hours later, they thought the bureau had been hit by a bomb.

Soon after, I took Alison and Sean for a brief holiday to Taiwan. I had already been to Taipei earlier in the spring, when I had written an article for *Newsday* about human rights abuses on the island. I concluded that conditions had not improved significantly since my first trip in 1974. On the visit with Alison, however, reporting was the last thing on my mind. I had promised her a break from politics, and we intended simply to enjoy ourselves. As I presented my passport at Taipei's Sung Shan Airport, I was detained and ordered to leave on the next plane back to Hong Kong. It seemed clear that someone high in the government had taken offense at my *Newsday* article. I asked how deporting an American journalist would improve Taiwan's image on human rights, but airport officials remained silent. Tired and sullen, Alison, Sean, and I boarded a flight back to Hong Kong. I found it ironic that I had been put on Taiwan's blacklist at precisely the moment when my attitude about Communist China was growing increasingly skeptical. Oh well, I thought, there may be a silver lining. Being on Taipei's blacklist wouldn't hurt my chances of better access to the mainland. Despite protests from *Newsday*, CBS, and the State Department, it would be twelve years before I made it back to Taiwan, by then a thriving democracy where, in the aftermath of my reporting on the Tiananmen Square crackdown for CNN, I was greeted as a heroic fighter for freedom.

In the spring of 1978, NBC's Hong Kong bureau chief, Bud Pratt, offered me a job. Although reluctant to end my professional association with my mentor Brian Ellis, I was getting fed up with the unpleasant CBS office politics and the network's unwillingness to upgrade my status from lowly paid stringer. As Brian raged at the refusal of CBS bosses to make me a counteroffer, I gathered my files and moved from the eleventh to the twelfth floor of New Mercury House, where the NBC bureau was located just next door to ABC News and the Associated Press. I was much happier in my new surroundings. Officially the network's "Asia Radio Correspondent," I was no longer a stringer. I now had a contract, a regular salary, a private office of my own, full responsibility for all radio coverage, and the prospect, I hoped, of eventually becoming the backup TV reporter to NBC's senior regional correspondent, veteran Asia hand Jack Reynolds.

The move to NBC coincided with another important personal change. My romance with Alison, passionate but ultimately unworkable, ended. Our largely amicable parting had been hastened by my attraction to Alison's roommate, Lynne Curry, who seven years later was to become my wife. A tall, sandy-haired American whose soft voice held just a trace of a southern accent, Lynne had also arrived in Hong Kong in 1975. She was studying Mandarin at the Chinese University's language center in Kowloon while trying to sort out what to do with her life. Courses at Duke University had left her entranced with the Orient and determined to experience it for herself. Taking a huge gamble, she convinced her parents, who expected her to settle down to a conventional middle-class suburban existence, to let her go to Hong Kong, where she arrived with no job, no plans, no place to live, and no prospects, lured only by a sense of adventure and discovery. She threw herself into life there with limitless energy and enthusiasm. Several days a week she would rise at dawn and cross the harbor for *taiji* lessons. In the evenings, she took Tae Kwan Do lessons with a martial arts master in Kowloon. She was attracted by Chinese mysticism and began studying *feng shui*, the ancient Chinese art of geomancy and fortune telling. She was also running out of money and took a job at UPI's commodities news wire to make ends meet, a move that would eventually lead to a career in business journalism.

For a long time while I was involved with Alison, Lynne and I had been friends. But I began to realize that our frequent, intense conversations, often conducted while Alison was in the next room with Sean, represented something more. Late at night, Alison would often grow impatient as Lynne and I continued to talk. But I didn't want the discussions to end.

Alison handled the somewhat awkward situation with surprising grace. Moving on to other things in her own life, she seemed genuinely pleased for Lynne and me and remained friends with both of us.

Hong Kong was certainly a romantic place for a fling. Lynne and I spent evenings lingering over dinner on the Peak, watching the lights of the harbor twinkle below. We went dancing at the Scene, the disco in the basement of the Peninsula Hotel that was Hong Kong's "in" spot. (I was a terrible dancer.) We wandered through boisterous back streets full of markets and food stalls, ate memorable Chinese meals, and took ferries to the outlying islands for hiking and swimming, all the while talking endlessly about each other, the future, and things Chinese. Two years later, after many ups and downs, we decided our relationship was serious enough to take an apartment together, a small place on Hing Fat Street, overlooking the waterfront.

Lynne and I were part of a group of young people who were drawn to Hong Kong by a shared fascination with China and Asia, and who were struggling to find professional outlets for our interest. One of our best friends was Donna Liu, a widely traveled Chinese-American who worked as a subeditor at the French news agency AFP. Like NBC and UPI, AFP was located in New Mercury House. After work, the three of us often met across the street in Wanchai at a tiny Shanghai restaurant called 369. Despite the rats in the corners, a clientele consisting largely of Hong Kong gangsters, and a menu offering such memorable typos as "bean crud" and "stewed crap," the food was first rate. Our late-night gatherings to exchange office gossip and guesses about what was happening in China became something of a regular ritual, even after Donna left AFP and, at my instigation, took over the CBS Radio string I had recently given up. Many years later, Donna and I became colleagues at CNN and experienced the drama of Tiananmen Square together.

Lynne and I began to spend time as well with Nayan Chanda, the brilliant, vastly knowledgeable Indochina correspondent for the *Far Eastern Economic Review*, and his wife Geeta, a warm, sophisticated, French-educated woman from a distinguished Sikh family in Delhi. A Bengali from Calcutta with the air of a college professor more than a journalist, Nayan had an unparalleled understanding of the region. I admired his remarkable ability to unearth priceless nuggets of information couched in the Marxist-Leninist rhetoric of the official Vietnamese, Cambodian, and Chinese media. I envied the fact that, as an Indian, he had been able to maintain contact with key officials in Hanoi and Vientiane, traveling there regularly since the fall of Saigon, when Americans could not do so. Over Geeta's memorable Indian meals and on outings with their two young sons, Nayan and I regularly shared ideas, insights, and sources, developing a close personal relationship and a professional partnership that was to prove exceptionally valuable to both of us in the coming years.

Lynne introduced me to her Chinese language teacher and *feng shui* master, Lin Yun. A colorful, rotund man from Taiwan whose twinkling eyes missed nothing, Lin Yun did not fit my image of a Chinese fortune-teller or a sage of the Black Hat Tantric Buddhist sect. Apart from his Mandarin classes at Hong Kong's Chinese University, Lin Yun's life appeared to consist of an endless round of elaborate Chinese dinners at the fanciest restaurants in town. He frequently invited Lynne and me to these gatherings, where we were often the only foreigners present. We watched with amusement and fascination as local film producers, tycoons, and a seemingly endless supply of gorgeous movie starlets beseeched Lin Yun for advice on *feng shui*. The mystical Chinese belief that the alignment of wind, water, and the *qi*, or breath of life, affected the course of events, was taken very seriously in Hong Kong. Most major companies, I discovered, would not open an office or begin a new business venture without first checking with a *feng shui* expert. Knowing references were made to a building along the waterfront reputed to have bad *feng shui*. It was plagued by broken elevators, discolored windows, and crashing tiles that endangered the pedestrians below. Lin Yun's services were very much in demand. At first, despite Lynne's deep-seated fascination, I thought *feng shui* was little more than Chinese mumbo jumbo. However, one evening, Lin Yun abruptly warned a friend of Lynne's to be very careful because her *qi* was in dangerously short supply. We were all taken aback. This time there was no twinkle in Lin Yun's eyes. At the end of the evening he repeated the warning with the utmost seriousness, implying that her life might be in danger. A week later, while Lin Yun and I were having lunch,

Lynne rushed in with shocking news. Her friend was dead, asphyxiated by a malfunctioning gas heater. I stopped making fun of *feng shui,* and when Lin Yun gave me a small Chinese coin with the trigrams of the *I Ching* carved on it for good luck, I never let it out of my sight.

With the door to China gradually opening, Beijing's de facto embassy in Hong Kong, the Xinhua News Agency, began to organize month-long visits to the People's Republic for local diplomats and academics. Very occasionally, one or two Hong Kong–based reporters would be invited as well. There was intense competition and lobbying within the press corps for a coveted slot on one of these delegations. Because I had developed close friendships with people at Xinhua and other pro-Beijing organizations in Hong Kong, I managed to secure invitations for several such trips. In keeping with a long-standing pattern, the Chinese preferred to take occasional visitors like us to places from which the resident correspondents in Beijing were usually barred. The assumption seemed to be that as outsiders, we would know less, ask fewer difficult questions, and make fewer awkward requests. Altogether, under Xinhua's auspices, I visited ten provinces, ranging from the frozen wasteland of Heilongjiang near the Sino-Soviet border to the semitropical forests of Yunnan in the southwest, close to China's frontier with Vietnam.

For all the "brief introductions" and often obnoxious government guides (including a short, owl-faced, foul-tempered man we dubbed "Martinet Ming," whose main interest was preventing us from deviating from the official schedule, and "Playboy Zhao," with his stylishly cut Mao suit and insistence on taking us to kitschy souvenir shops), these trips were a revelation to me. China was in transition, and I could sense the profound nature of the changes under way.

"Excuse me. Are you Americans?" asked a thin, elderly man in halting English who came up to me and a colleague on a street in the southwestern city of Kunming.

"Yes," we replied.

"I knew an American once," the man said with a faraway look in his eyes. "He was a missionary here over thirty years ago who built a Bible school where I studied. Perhaps you know him. I am a Christian. Would you like to come to my home?"

Looking around nervously to make sure our Chinese guides were not in sight, we accepted his invitation. We followed him to a small building, walked upstairs, and entered a tiny one-room apartment furnished only with two beds, covered by mosquito nets, and a small, plain wooden desk. A map of China was plastered on the wall. Carefully he reached under a bed and pulled out a ragged copy of the Bible in Chinese and a companion book in English called *Favorite Bible Verses*.

A middle-school teacher educated by American missionaries, Xia Bing, or Philip, as he insisted we call him, had suffered greatly because of his religion.

"There used to be between ten and twenty thousand Christians here in Kunming, and ten Protestant churches," he told us. "But the Communists closed them all and turned many into factories. We're not free to worship." He paused for a sip of tea. "During the Cultural Revolution, I was denounced and sent to a labor camp. It was like Siberia, with two thousand prisoners, including six Christians whom I knew, all of us accused of being counterrevolutionaries. I was there for more than a decade and was only freed after Chairman Mao died. But there are still a thousand inmates there today. Every night in prison I prayed secretly."

We all were aware that labor camps existed in the People's Republic. At the time of my first visit, I consciously played down this and other distasteful aspects of Chinese society, unwilling to join the chorus of U.S. China bashers opposed to better Sino-American relations, in favor of the Vietnam War, and supportive of U.S.-backed right wing dictatorships elsewhere in Asia. Working as a journalist in Hong Kong, especially after the death of Chairman Mao, I had to confront the increasingly disturbing reports coming from China. Hearing Philip Xia Bing's story made the harsh reality of Chinese life come alive in a way that was not possible watching the country from a distance. I thought of my earlier political enthusiasm for Mao. How could I have been so naive?

As we parted, Philip gripped my hand. Lowering his voice, he said, "If anyone asks you about your visit to my home, tell them we only discussed ways of teaching English. And don't forget to read your Bible daily!"

I traveled from Chongqing, China's World War II capital, through the Yangzi River gorges, whose fabled beauty had long inspired Chinese poets and painters. In a dense fog on a raw autumn morning, I boarded a rusty passenger ship called the *East Is Red 47*, which slowly made its way past sampans, ferries, tugs, and other vessels to the center of the swirling, muddy Yangzi. China's greatest river was as treacherous as it was spectacular. Not so many years before, the only way for boats to navigate its dangerous waters was to be pulled by half-naked coolies who struggled along narrow tracks carved into the cliffs on either side of the river. Now the *East Is Red 47* shook and shuddered as its sturdy, crew-cut captain, forty-nine-year-old Lu Rorong, guided it through whirlpools and rapids so violent they made the waters boil with whitecaps.

The gorges came into view at dawn. With a blanket draped over my shoulders, I stood at the prow of the ship, a powerful wind blowing in my face, watching the night sky turn pink as the craggy peaks rising from the river gradually took on shape and color, some lined with forests, others with orange groves or strange rock formations stretching into the mist. Steeped in legend, they evoked the richness of China's past: Horse-Lung and Ox-Liver Gorge, Witches Gorge, Flying Phoenix Peak. I felt as if I had been dropped into an ancient Chinese painting, and the country's political struggles seemed very far away.

The cold interrupted my reverie. In the ship's lounge, whose velvet curtains had been drawn back to allow passengers to enjoy the view, I ordered a cup of hot tea to warm myself and struck up a conversation with a soft-spoken, middle-aged man named Li Le. China's present reality once again pushed aside images of its classical past. Li Le told me he was one of thousands of investigators sent out by the central government to reexamine all reported cases of unjust persecution during the Cultural Revolution. His mission was part of a broader initiative spearheaded by the recently rehabilitated Deng Xiaoping and his reformist allies. The intention was to "reverse the verdicts" not only on the Cultural Revolution but on Mao's vicious "anti-Rightist campaign" of 1957, in which tens of thousands of intellectuals were imprisoned, and on the 1976 Tiananmen riot, which was now being praised as a courageous act of defiance against the Gang of Four.

Over endless cups of tea, the chain-smoking Li Le described some of the cases he was looking into. One involved a nineteen-year-old farmer who, at the height of the Cultural Revolution, cut himself while clearing a field. In his pain, he tore off the Mao button pinned to his jacket and stomped on it. The local police heard about the episode and immediately sentenced him to five years in prison. The young man served his sentence, but the previous month, after Li Le's intervention, the farmer's conviction was ordered removed from the record books, and he was given more than a year's salary in compensation. At the moment, Li was working on the case of a man sentenced to fifteen years for allegedly failing to admit that he had once been a soldier in the Chinese Nationalist army before 1949. The victim insisted he had long before acknowledged the "error" of his prerevolutionary ways, but he was imprisoned anyway. Li was now en route to the man's village to learn more. I found it hard even to imagine the scale of the suffering Li Le was describing.

"There are so many cases connected with the Cultural Revolution," he sighed. "The Ministry of Public Security has asked me to travel to thirteen provinces. My estimate is that in up to 70 percent of the cases I am investigating, the victims were unjustly condemned."

"Reversing the verdict" represented more than just another flip-flop in the Party line. At a stroke, China's new rulers were repudiating virtually everything done in Chairman Mao's name for the preceding two decades. In a society where Mao's Communist Party had for so long claimed a monopoly not only on power but on wisdom, I realized the implications would be profound. In seeking to rectify twenty years of injustice, Deng Xiaoping was also sowing the seeds of heightened public disillusionment and growing doubts about the legitimacy of the party's mandate to rule.

Even as people like Investigator Li started to help China come to terms with its tortured past, the tensions stirred up by this process became painfully clear when a new crackdown began in Beijing. Angered by the increasingly bold criticisms pasted on Democracy Wall, Deng Xiaoping sanctioned the detention of key activists like Wei Jingsheng. It was an abrupt reversal for the man, who by the end of 1978, had made himself China's supreme leader and had initially tolerated the wall-poster campaign as part of his effort to discredit the excesses of radical Maoism. Dependent as I was on the carefully structured Xinhua trips for much of my access to China, I missed the opportunity to meet Wei before his arrest. In October 1979, he was put on trial. Pictures from the proceedings were broadcast on Chinese TV. They showed a youthful-looking Wei, dressed in prison garb, his head shaved and bowed, listening to the verdict before a panel of stony-faced judges and a carefully selected audience of five hundred people. I had read his essays and seen for myself the hope generated by Democracy Wall. Now, working late at the NBC bureau in Hong Kong on the day Wei was sentenced to fifteen years in jail for "counterrevolutionary incitement," I was angry and upset.

Although intellectually I recognized that profound changes were still under way in China—holding out, over the long term, the possibility of a more humane society—it was hard to be neutral and dispassionate watching such a travesty of justice. My feelings became even stronger when I acquired a copy of the transcript of Wei's trial, which had been surreptitiously tape-recorded and distributed by other activists not yet under detention. Standing before his accusers, Wei refused to admit to any crime. Instead he forcefully defended his ideas of democracy. His courage in the face of a certain guilty verdict and long prison term was astonishing. I wished I could do something to help. The only consolation was that NBC News had enormous clout. At least, I told myself, I could publicize Wei's unhappy fate.

The crackdown on outspoken political activity did not, however, mean an end to social liberalization. Several weeks after Wei Jingsheng's conviction, I was back in Beijing on yet another Xinhua trip, where I went to the Peace Café. The dismal, smoke-filled room with its ugly fluorescent lighting and plain plastic tables and chairs in a ramshackle building on Goldfish Lane didn't amount to much by Western standards. But in a city where almost everything shut down by 7:30, the café had become Beijing's hottest new night spot, where college students and especially the children of senior Communist Party officials could drink, smoke, hang out, meet members of the opposite sex, and, most controversial of all, mingle with foreigners. In a system where the mere expression of interest in such recreation could still easily result in political trouble, the Peace Café unquestionably had the aura of forbidden pleasure.

I joined a young couple drinking beer at a corner table. The woman was wearing tight pants and, in a daring gesture of independence, her hair was done in a permanent wave. Her pimple-faced boyfriend spoke with a slight lisp. As they offered me a drink and small plates of cakes and peanuts, we were joined by another young man eager to practice his English. "Hello. How do you do? Do you like Chinese beer? In America, many young people smoke marijuana. Is that right? I'd like to try. Do you have any?" He and his companions roared with laughter.

Three African students sat down at a nearby table. My Chinese friends made faces. "The Africans come here only looking for girls," the pimply youth said. "But we Chinese don't like them. But you Americans, that's different." With a leer, he turned and asked, "Would you like to meet a nice Chinese girl? I can introduce you."

I was tempted. Rumor had it that a prostitution ring was being run out of the Peace Café. It might make an interesting story. But as the beer continued to flow, I found myself put off by my increasingly tipsy companions. Making a polite excuse, I paid for a final round of drinks and left. Police raided the café not long after my visit, closing it down and arresting more than a dozen young people, who were sent to labor camps. Change in China was clearly going to be uneven and frequently painful.

Yet there were astonishing new developments. I did stories on the official repudiation of Mao's *Little Red Book*, the rehabilitation of those he purged, the steady flow of horrifying details about the Cultural Revolution, and the adoption of ambitious plans to rebuild the economy through market mechanisms and foreign investment. I took a day trip across the border to watch firecrackers and dragon dances at the opening of the first joint-venture hotel in the newly established Shenzhen Special Economic Zone. Deng Xiaoping had decreed that Shenzhen and three other locations on China's southeast coast should become laboratories for experimentation with capitalist-style mechanisms. Shenzhen was still the quiet, nondescript village bordering Hong Kong through which I had passed on my first China trip, but now foreign firms were starting to arrive. One day I took a ferry up the Pearl River delta from Hong Kong to Canton to cover the first U.S. cargo ship allowed to make regular calls in China. I watched smug American executives exchange toasts with expressionless Mao-suited Chinese officials on the dock. Looking out across the water, I tried to imagine the scene nearly a century and a half before, when British gunboats had blasted their way up this same river to guarantee Her Majesty's clipper ships the right to sell opium to China. I did stories about China's decision to allow foreign oil companies to search for crude in the South China Sea; Beijing's first conciliatory overtures to Taiwan; the first commercial broadcast on Chinese television; the first fashion show in Beijing; and the departure of the first batch of Chinese students permitted to study in the United States. The pace of change was dizzying. In one of my NBC broadcasts, I wondered, "How will studying in the freewheeling U.S.A. affect students who have never been out of China before? What impact will American-trained Chinese students have on the country when they return? The last generation of Chinese who studied abroad, in the early part of this century, came back and staged a revolution."

As I made my way along the side of the Olympic-size swimming pool, my attention was repeatedly distracted by the breathtakingly beautiful bikini-clad Thai women lounging in the sun. In a corner, at a table underneath a colorful umbrella, sat a young Chinese-speaking Thai diplomat I had met in Beijing some months earlier. We had stayed in touch, and I came to respect his knowledge and insights. Now, on a hot, humid Saturday morning in November 1978, he invited me for coffee at the luxurious Bangkok Sports Club, where the capital's rich and powerful gathered to play.

There was nothing playful about the reason for our meeting, however. The topic of our discussion was war. For the past year, I had watched with surprise, dismay, and puzzlement as a bloody border conflict turned Cambodia and Vietnam, once allies against the United States, into enemies. The decades-old alliance between the veteran Communists in Hanoi and Beijing was unraveling too. With the Vietnamese siding with Moscow, and the extremist Khmer Rouge in Cambodia siding with the Chinese, Indochina had become the latest and most dangerous battleground in the Sino-Soviet rivalry.

I was in Bangkok to cover the historic visit of Deng Xiaoping. His goal was to enlist Southeast Asian support to counter what Beijing saw as the growing threat from the Vietnamese and their Soviet patrons. It was the first time I had seen Deng in action, and I was impressed. The chain-smoking, crew-cut Deng was dynamic and forceful, radiating energy and confidence. True to his reputation as a pragmatist, he put ideological scruples aside in his determined effort to court the Thais. One afternoon, I watched as he visited the fabled Temple of the Emerald Buddha in the heart of Bangkok. It was a scene of pomp and pageantry, with chanting monks, banging gongs, and clouds of incense filling the air. In the center of the ornate, gilded temple stood the crown prince of Thailand, his head shaved, clad in a saffron robe, taking the vows of a Buddhist monk. To one side stood the new monk's father, Thailand's immensely popular King Bhumibol, resplendent in a white jacket with a gold sash and gold epaulets, accompanied by the rest of the Thai royal family and the country's prime minister, Kriangsak Chomanan. Next to Kriangsak, dressed in a stark black Mao suit, stood Deng, holding a bundle of joss sticks to present to the crown prince as a congratulatory gift.

Soon after, I squeezed into a packed room at Bangkok's luxurious Erawan Hotel for Deng's only meeting with reporters. Speaking in Mandarin so thickly overlaid with the accent of his native Sichuan province that I had trouble understanding him, he warned his hosts, and the world, about the dangers on the horizon. "You should all know that the Soviet Union and Vietnam desire to dominate not only the region, but the world." Gesturing emphatically, he continued, "Vietnam is the hooligan of Southeast Asia. It is a small hegemonist, but it is cooperating with the big hegemonist, and, together, they pose a threat to Southeast Asia, the Pacific, and the world."

Months of clashes along the Vietnam-Cambodia border had raised fears that Hanoi might soon launch an all-out attack to dislodge the brutal Khmer Rouge regime of Pol Pot and install a pro-Vietnamese government in Phnom Penh. As Deng left Thailand for stops in Malaysia and Singapore, I wondered what the Chinese would do under such circumstances. As I sipped my drink by the side of the Bangkok Sports Club pool, my Thai diplomat friend gave me the answer. He confided that he was one of only four Thai officials, including the prime minister, who participated in the meetings with Deng. I asked if there was more to the talks than what had been officially announced. He smiled. "If I tell you," he joked, "I probably ought to seek asylum in another country." Nonetheless, as we talked back and forth, I repeated my question. Eventually, my friend turned and said, "Deng told us there is a real possibility Phnom Penh might fall to the Vietnamese. This would not be the end of the war, but the beginning. For strategic reasons, Deng said China must save Cambodia at all costs, despite the brutal domestic policies of the

Khmer Rouge. Deng made it clear to us China would take appropriate measures, including, if necessary, the use of force."

This was a bombshell. Deng had in effect bluntly told the Thais that if the Vietnamese toppled the Khmer Rouge, China would likely take military action against Vietnam. Since Hanoi had just signed a twenty-five-year treaty of cooperation with Moscow, the possibility of a major war among those who stood on the same side against the United States in Indochina was ominously real. Back at my hotel, mulling over what I'd learned while rebuffing incessant offers from the bellboy to provide female companionship at discount prices, I realized the episode was yet another hard lesson that served to strip away one more layer of naïveté from the way I looked at the world. In my journal I wrote, "It's awfully hard to judge what's right and what's wrong now. It all seems to come down to big power politics and national interest. It is indeed ironic how many people I saw as the 'good guys' in the old days have turned out not to be very nice. This holds true for the Chinese, the Vietnamese and the Cambodians."

That was putting it mildly. For months, I had been devoting much of my time and energy to covering the appalling human tragedies caused by the communist governments of Vietnam and Cambodia. I could see the results just by looking out the window of the NBC Hong Kong bureau at the colony's bustling harbor below. Tens of thousands of Vietnamese boat people, the majority of them of ethnic Chinese origin, were pouring into Hong Kong, fleeing a systematic campaign of harassment organized by the government in Hanoi.

One day, four hundred of them were rescued at sea by a U.S. navy ship, the *Whipple*. I rented a small motorboat and set off for the outer reaches of the harbor with an NBC camera crew to film the vessel. It was midafternoon before we reached the *Whipple*, worryingly close to the satellite deadline for the *Today* show. The ship was packed to the bursting point with tired, frightened, disheveled refugees. Its normally immaculate decks were covered with blankets, laundry, and cooking utensils. The Vietnamese called and gestured to us, but the ship's skipper did not allow us to get close enough to talk with them. Conditions in Vietnam must be pretty bad, I thought, that entire families would risk setting to sea in flimsy wooden boats, often no more than rafts, at the height of the typhoon season. Knowing we would need as much time as possible to develop the film and edit the story, cameraman Lim Youn-chol, an enormously experienced Korean, shot very sparingly. Bobbing back toward the city center, we passed my former colleagues from CBS. They had chartered a large luxury yacht packed with cases of beer, and as they looked condescendingly down at us in our small sampan, they seemed to be having a very good time. But we would have the last laugh. The CBS crew shot so much film they didn't have enough time to get it all processed before the satellite feed, and their story never got on the air. A minor competitive triumph, it was a gratifying moment for me, as I had left CBS only a few months earlier.

I bounced out of the NBC bureau to treat myself to a big dinner. As I savored a steak at the Peak Café overlooking the harbor, my mood suddenly darkened. The day's professional success stemmed from the suffering of hundreds of people who were still stuck on a smelly, hot, overcrowded ship somewhere amid the twinkling harbor lights below me. I was swept by a wave of guilt. Was I just a voyeur, trading off other people's misery? Was this what journalism was supposed to be? Did the fact that I could treat what I'd seen as just another day at the office mean I was losing my own sense of values?

I had no easy answers. I left the steak on my plate half-eaten.

The heartrending exodus from Vietnam became a staple of my reporting. It climaxed with the dramatic arrival in Hong Kong of the *Huey Fong*, a 4,000-ton Taiwanese freighter carrying 3,400 refugees, including 1,000 children. For nearly a month, the ship sat off Hong Kong while the territory's government tried to compel the captain to sail on to Taiwan. As I fought to control my queasiness, we sailed repeatedly through the choppy seas to get a closer look at the battered, rusty ship. Marine police prevented us from boarding, but it was clear that conditions on the *Huey Fong* were appalling. I could see many people huddled on the deck, their thin blankets affording little protection against the wind and rain. Some of the refugees shouted down to us that supplies of food and water were running dangerously low. Although the captain insisted he had picked up the Vietnamese at sea, it became clear that the refugees had been forced to pay millions of dollars to leave their homeland in an exodus deliberately promoted by the government in Hanoi. The people I had once admired for their heroic resistance to the military might of the most powerful nation on earth were now engaged in cynical trafficking of human beings for political and financial gain. Making my regular journeys to check up on the *Huey Fong* and its pathetic human cargo, I was sickened, and the cause was not the swells of the South China Sea.

But the plight of the Vietnamese boat people paled in comparison to the horror stories coming from Khmer Rouge–controlled Cambodia. On a trip to Thailand, I went to a refugee camp near Surin on the Thai-Cambodian border to see for myself. The accounts of mass executions, starvation, and disease were consistent and appalling. "The Khmer Rouge are executing all former policemen, soldiers, government officials, teachers, students, and Buddhist monks," one refugee told me. "If anyone is identified as an enemy agent, he must be killed."

The preferred method of execution was beating to death with clubs or shovels, because it saved bullets. Another refugee reported seeing five hundred people, their hands tied, taken away in trucks for execution. A third described to me how he managed to untie the ropes with which he had been bound and slipped into the jungle just before seventy of his companions were put to death. Later I was to see much more misery among displaced peoples—Palestinians, Chadians, Kashmiris, Afghans—but I was haunted for years by the horror of what I heard on that visit: the Khmer Rouge, for whom I had once had a sneaking sympathy during the days of the American war in Indochina, were responsible for the death of one out of every eight Cambodians—over a million people.

What Deng Xiaoping had predicted two months earlier came true at the end of 1978. In a two-week blitzkrieg that began on Christmas Day, Vietnamese forces invaded Cambodia, toppled their one-time Khmer Rouge allies, and occupied Phnom Penh. For me and other reporters, it was a uniquely frustrating war, because Western journalists were not able to witness the conflict. Sitting in Bangkok or Hong Kong, all we could do was monitor the drama from a distance. Luckily I had a secret weapon.

I'd gotten to know a U.S. intelligence analyst through mutual friends at the American Consulate in Hong Kong. Colorful, eccentric, and outspoken, with long hair flowing over his ears and collar, he didn't fit my preconceptions of a spook. Instead he looked like an aging hippie. An old Vietnam hand now based in Washington, his job involved analyzing photographs from spy satellites and reconnaissance planes, intercepted communications, and other raw intelligence data on Indochina and China. He was a walking gold mine of classified information. To my surprise, he appeared eager to share what he knew, especially after he realized that, with my frequent visits and excellent contacts, I might have some interesting insights on China to offer him. As tension mounted in Southeast Asia during the following months, we talked frequently on the phone. In return for details of the intelligence crossing his desk, I told him what I had gleaned of Chinese thinking and policy. And now that war was under way, we spoke two or even three times a day. For a one-time sixties radical, I felt more than a little strange trading information with an American intelligence operative, but I recognized that this was part of a time-honored journalistic tradition: I was using him and he was using me. We both knew exactly what we were doing. And I felt I was getting the better half of the deal.

Day after day my "Western intelligence source," as I identified him in my stories, provided updates on the fighting that few other reporters seemed to be getting. He gave me precise details of Vietnamese troop movements; a running tally of which key Cambodian roads and towns were being overrun well before such developments were announced in Hanoi; what kinds of aircraft and artillery were being used; and insights into Vietnam's military and political strategy and the nature of the Khmer Rouge resistance. His information was consistently correct. One evening, after almost two weeks of battle, he told me, "I can confirm that the Vietnamese have captured Phnom Penh. Large columns of Vietnamese armor, infantry, and artillery are moving toward the western part of Cambodia. There is no more Khmer Rouge regime."

As the fighting intensified, I began meeting almost on a daily basis with Nayan Chanda of the *Far Eastern Economic Review*, along with a senior Chinese diplomat based in Hong Kong with whom Nayan and I had both become friendly. We pooled the information we were receiving from totally different sources, and shared our insights and ideas. Together we were able to assemble a surprisingly accurate picture, both of what was happening on the ground hundreds of miles away and of the behind-the-scenes diplomatic intention of the key players on all sides. I was able to use what I had learned to produce a series of exclusive reports charting the course of the conflict. In the absence of television images from the battlefront, NBC New York devised computer-generated graphics and maps to illustrate my stories. They ran regularly on the *Today* show and the NBC *Nightly News*. Bud Pratt told me my star was rising at the network.

It was a wildly exhilarating time for a young reporter. As the fighting in Cambodia eased, another huge story broke to replace it. Deng Xiaoping traveled to the United States to mark the normalization of Sino-American relations, which the two countries had agreed on in December 1978. I had been deeply moved by the decision to establish diplomatic ties. On the day of the announcement, I celebrated by inviting my friends from the Xinhua News Agency to a big Chinese meal, which we punctuated with frequent toasts to "friendship." I had been waiting and hoping for normalization for a long time. In a very modest way, I believed I had helped to promote closer contact between Americans and Chinese, and I was thrilled to see the process reach its logical climax.

And I had another reason to be excited. With the opening of formal ties, the Chinese would almost certainly allow American news organizations to open bureaus in Beijing. When permission came for NBC, I was confident I had a reasonable chance of being offered the assignment.

Throughout Deng's trip to the States, where he won numerous admirers by wearing a cowboy hat and generally confirming his image as the "cuddly Communist," I made regular phone calls to my friend in Washington. What he told me was alarming.

"We have unmistakable evidence," he said, "of a huge Chinese military buildup on the border with Vietnam. According to spy photos and electronic intercepts, a 150,000-strong Chinese strike force, backed by hundreds of planes, armor, and artillery, is being deployed on the Sino-Vietnamese border." We both agreed Beijing was preparing for war, and my Chinese friends in Hong Kong did little to dissuade me from that impression. At the same time, my intelligence source said there was evidence of a Russian naval buildup in the South China Sea. Events seemed to be spiraling out of control.

Early on Saturday, February 17, 1979, Bud Pratt called me to come to the office immediately. The Xinhua News Agency had just announced a Chinese attack on Vietnam. I called my friend in Washington before leaving home. Xinhua was right, he told me. A massive Chinese force, backed by armor and aircraft, was pouring across the border into Vietnam. For the second time in as many months, I had a huge story to cover but, again, not as an eyewitness. Swallowing my frustration, I immediately began analyzing the usually contradictory Chinese and Vietnamese press announcements, comparing notes with diplomats and experts, and meeting regularly with my Chinese contacts.

On the second day of the war, my Chinese diplomat friend spelled out China's goals over lunch at the Tung Hsing Lou, an excellent Beijing-style restaurant that was our favorite meeting place. "Our objective is to inflict so much damage that Vietnam cannot cause any further trouble on its border with China, and to curb its expansionist tendencies in Cambodia. To do this, we have to humiliate the Vietnamese. We don't think the Russians will intervene. But if they do, it is better to have a war now and be done with it. China is not afraid." I hardly felt like a war correspondent, hundreds of miles from the fighting, but at least I was getting on the air as Beijing's troops drove forward, encountered fierce Vietnamese resistance, inflicted and took horrendous casualties, stopped, declared victory, and finally withdrew back to China. In the process, I was learning for myself the disturbing lesson that many other correspondents had discovered over the years. War, even covered from a distance, is good for your career.

Covered close up, it is even better. Nine months after the Chinese invasion of Vietnam, the Soviet Union invaded Afghanistan. Two days later, I was on the first flight from Delhi into Kabul. On landing, I was stunned by what I saw: menacing green Soviet tanks and row after row of MI-24 helicopter gunships lined the runway. Armored personnel carriers resembling large, mechanized centipedes sped back and forth. Giant AN-12 transport planes rumbled into the air every few minutes, ferrying Russian soldiers to other parts of the country. Soviet troops in thick winter uniforms drilled alongside unused airstrips, the thud of their boots audible during quiet moments between aircraft departures.

Unfortunately I didn't get beyond Kabul Airport. The communist authorities ordered all reporters who had flown in that morning to leave on the next plane out. But I realized even the little I had seen represented a historic moment. Back in Delhi, I filed nine radio spots and one television narration on a crackly voice circuit in the chilly, dimly lit Overseas Communications Center—NBC's first eyewitness reports on what would become one of the biggest news stories of the 1980s.

NBC ordered me to Pakistan to work with the network's stringer cameraman there. At first glance, the stout, graying, elderly man who introduced himself as Kamal Hyder hardly looked like an intrepid network cameraman. Now retired after forty years as the news editor of the *Pakistan Times*, Kamal had purchased an ancient film camera and taught himself how to take pictures both as a hobby and as a way to pick up a little extra cash. He complained constantly about NBC's lack of generosity and unwillingness to provide him with better gear, but he was full of energy and good humor, and he was delighted to have a real assignment. As we shook hands, he said "Chinoy—very interesting. Are you a Muslim? Chinoy is a Muslim name!" Delicately, I said no, explaining that, in fact, my grandparents were Russian Jews. I wasn't sure how this would go over in a country where President Zia ul-Haq seemed determined to impose Islamic law. But Kamal just laughed heartily and said, "Never mind. Welcome to Pakistan!"

Later I discovered that Chinoy was a very common name in Pakistan. There were lots of Chinoys, especially in Karachi, and I was forever receiving telexes at my hotel addressed to "Abdullah Chinoy," "Ahmed Chinoy," and so on. Unfortunately I could never figure out if there was any connection between the Muslim Chinoys and my immediate ancestors, the Russian Jews who fled the pogroms in the Ukraine for America at the turn of the century.

Kamal and I left immediately for Peshawar, the colorful northwest frontier city straddling the Pakistan-Afghan border, which, since the days of Kipling, had been the scene of intrigue, mystery, and violence. Zahoor, the young, mustachioed Pakistani driver we'd hired in Islamabad, inched his battered Toyota through streets packed with motor scooters, oxcarts, rickshaws, and horse-drawn vehicles, where turbaned, rifle-toting Pathan tribesmen mingled with women covered from head to toe in black burkas. It was overpoweringly exotic and romantic. I was entranced.

The next morning, we set out for the fabled Khyber Pass in search of refugees. Winding through the barren, rock-strewn mountains, past the ruins of fortifications from years gone by, the road was largely deserted. I was overwhelmed by a sense of history. It was through the Khyber that Alexander the Great led his marauding armies over two thousand years before, and the Mogul emperor Babur and countless other conquerors had followed in his wake. Implausible as it sounded, the question on more than a few minds now was whether Russian troops would be next. Such anxieties were being openly expressed in capitals from Islamabad to Washington.

My musings were abruptly interrupted by the loud disco beat of Donna Summer. In my rush to leave Hong Kong, I had grabbed only one audiotape. Stimulated as much by the sexy photo of the scantily clad disco queen on the cover as by her music, Zahoor insisted on playing it over and over again. We descended toward the Afghan border with the steamy moans of "Love to Love You, Baby" resounding through our tiny car.

I saw the refugees out the right-hand window, a small group of men with bristly mustaches and white turbans and women in black veils, sitting on the stony ground beside their camels. They told us they had been on the road since soon after the Soviet invasion, sleeping outdoors in some of the world's most rugged terrain in a desperate effort to escape advancing Russian troops. The long columns of refugees had been repeatedly strafed by Soviet planes and helicopters, and friends who had set out with them had died along the way. I pressed for more details. "We can't say anything else," one refugee replied. "We're too sad."

They were the first trickle of what would become a massive torrent of refugees. Eventually nearly four million Afghans, a quarter of the country's population, would flee their homeland, jamming into makeshift camps in Pakistan and creating at the time what was the worst refugee crisis in the world. We had stumbled onto a major story. Racing back to Islamabad, I talked a dubious British Airways flight attendant preparing to work that night's nonstop flight to London into carrying our film to the NBC London bureau. The next day my piece became the first report on the Afghan refugee crisis to be aired on American television.

Western journalists soon began to descend on Pakistan, where NBC asked me to stay on for the next three months. With Kamal Hyder tied up assisting additional NBC crews with logistical matters, at my suggestion the network hired Joe Yue, my old mentor from CBS, as a freelance shooter to work with me. With visas obtained from the Afghan Embassy in Islamabad, which for a few days defied orders from Kabul and granted entry to reporters. Joe, an experienced combat cameraman, and I headed for Kandahar, the main town in southern Afghanistan.

Kandahar had just been swept by a citywide anti-Soviet strike: mobs had attacked the police station, public buildings, and government troops. The receptionist at the hotel the next morning urged us to be careful.

"The other day," he warned, "three Russians went to the bazaar from the local airport, which the Soviets have occupied. They were dragged from their jeep and stoned to death. So watch out."

Lighting a cigarette, Joe said to me, "Shit, Panda, this place gives me the creeps. What the hell have we gotten ourselves into?"

The tension was palpable on Kandahar's muddy streets, with Afghan Communist soldiers guarding all major buildings and manning checkpoints every few blocks. But there were no Russians visible. It appeared the Soviets were prudently keeping a low profile at the airport.

By now, Joe and I were famished, but as we made our way through the city, there didn't seem to be a single place to eat. Suddenly we rounded a corner.

"Joe, look!" I exclaimed. The large sign in English read BROWNIES, COFFEE, APPLE PIE. I was ecstatic. The restaurant owner, a burly man with a stubbly beard who introduced himself as Ghulam, was thrilled to see us.

"Before all this trouble, I did such good business," he said bitterly. "Young people from America, Europe, they all come for my brownies. Now it is finished."

Devouring my brownies and pie, I had a sudden flash of realization. In the sixties and seventies, Afghanistan was at the heart of the "hippie trail" from Europe to Asia, a magnet for travelers lured as much by the cheap drugs as the spectacular scenery. Ghulam's business had flourished because of the "munchies," the acute desire for sweets often felt when coming down from a marijuana or hashish high. Now, though, there were no hungry hippies. With soldiers patrolling outside, I was as sober-headed as I could be, but I appreciated Ghulam's hospitality and his insights about the savage mood of the local citizens toward the Soviets and their Afghan allies.

During the next few days, Joe and I got close enough to the airport to see the Soviet planes landing and taking off. But the holy war was as elusive as it seemed omnipresent. Only at night did the fighting come close to us, when we heard the ubiquitous gunshots and, one evening, the huge explosion that destroyed Kandahar's power station, plunging the entire city in darkness. Both Joe and I were immensely relieved to return to Pakistan. Our powerful story made the *Today* show.

For television reporters trying to cover the ever-widening Afghan conflict, the biggest frustration was the lack of combat footage. Guerrilla resistance to the Soviets consisted of sporadic, isolated hit-and-run attacks. Even journalistic forays with the mujahideen did not guarantee that one would witness or bring back pictures of fighting. In Peshawar one day, I mentioned my frustration during a conversation with one of the mujahideen spokesmen. To my surprise, he offered to sell me several rolls of undeveloped super-8 film, which he claimed the guerrillas had shot themselves. His conditions were unusual. Apart from a cash payment of $1,000, he insisted that I personally carry the film for developing at NBC's European production center in London, and, while there, buy him a pair of high-quality British shoes.

"I am a spokesman for jihad," he said. "Here is a hundred dollar bill. When you come back, you will not only return the film but, Inshallah, bring me a new pair of good shoes."

Although a bit shaky, the pictures proved as good as advertised— rifle-toting mujahideen celebrating in front of three burning Soviet tanks, bodies of Russian soldiers laid out on the ground. Real "bang-bang." En route to Heathrow Airport for my plane back to Pakistan, I stopped in the shoe department at Selfridges department store on Oxford Street. Picking out a shiny new pair, I went to exchange the hundred dollar bill he had given me. After some delay, the man behind the counter returned the money. "I'm sorry, sir," he said, "but I can't accept this bill. It's counterfeit."

I used NBC cash to pay for the shoes.

Midway through my stay in Pakistan, Lynne finally agreed to join me for a few weeks. Absence had only intensified our feelings for each other. Our reunion was a joyous moment, as well as an excuse for me to take a desperately needed break. In the lobby of the

Islamabad Holiday Inn, Lynne noticed a tourist poster showing a yak caravan moving through snow-capped mountains of Skardu. Neither of us had any idea where Skardu was, but we both instantly agreed we had to see it. It took a frightening ride on an ancient, shuddery Pakistan Airlines F-27 propeller plane, which threaded its way without radar between the giant peaks of the Karakorum mountain range while following the path of the Indus River, to reach the remote town. Nestled in the foothills of K-2, the world's second-highest mountain, and surrounded by towering, snow-capped peaks, dotted with crystal-clear lakes and valleys full of apricot and apple trees, Skardu seemed like Shangri-la to us. We took long walks, climbed spectacular rock formations, rented row-boats, and hired a hashish-smoking driver to show us a nearby glacier. It was a passionate, magical few days.

But the fantasy ended all too quickly as I moved ahead with plans for a final project before winding up my three-month assignment—crossing into Afghanistan with the mujahideen. I had been developing contacts for this purpose for months, and NBC sent an experienced cameraman from the Tokyo bureau to accompany me. But the cameraman changed his mind, claiming the trip was not worth the risk. It was an extremely awkward situation. Weeks of careful planning and discussions with my Afghan contacts were now at risk, and yet I did not want to embarrass the cameraman or appear to NBC as an irresponsible thrill seeker. When the shooter flatly refused to go, I had no choice. The trip was canceled.

A year later, I finally got my chance, convincing NBC Radio to let me go with the mujahideen on my own, without a crew. Disguising myself as an Afghan tribesman, in gold and gray turban, baggy pants, and a green blanket draped over my shoulders, I slipped across the border with a mujahideen guide and a dozen guerrilla fighters. Our destination was a mountain range near the town of Khost, where a garrison of Soviet-backed forces had been under siege by the rebels for two years. My hosts were not certain if we would see any fighting, but they promised me a taste of mujahideen life.

After a full day's march over steep hills and plunging valleys, we stopped for the night at the hut of an old goat herder. Soaking my tortured feet in a cold stream under the starlit sky, I was joined by my guide Asef, a one-time Kabul rug merchant who had left everything behind to join the guerrillas.

"Our country is like our mother," he explained. "The Russians have come. It is right for me to fight, to spill my blood on my soil. I am not afraid of being martyred."

The next morning I came face to face with the war I'd been looking for. We set off at dawn through a narrow valley, with the rays of the rising sun casting a spectacular orange-purple glow on the surrounding mountains. Suddenly one of the guerrillas leaned down and pulled up a piece of jagged green plastic—the remnants of a Soviet antipersonnel mine. A few minutes later, I spotted another piece. I was nervous. I walked carefully, trying to follow exactly in the steps of the man in front of me, trying not to think about what could happen if I stepped on a mine. I knew the Russians had dropped thousands of such explosive devices, colored green to blend in with the terrain, in order to interdict movement between Pakistan and Afghanistan. A moment later I heard a loud rumble like a thunderstorm moving ever closer. "It's a Russian air raid," my guide said anxiously, directing me down a steep hill where we could continue to walk with less risk. I could hear the thud of exploding bombs but could see nothing. Soon the rumble faded away and I breathed a sigh of relief.

Nervous and exhausted, I felt easier when, the next afternoon, we turned around and headed back to Pakistan. Near the border, however, we were waylaid by Afghan bandits who threatened to hold me hostage if I didn't pay them a large sum of cash. Terrified, I readily agreed to their demand for a thousand rupees—about a hundred dollars. As soon as I paid, the bandits started laughing and smiling. My confidence returning, I turned to Asef. "Do you think you could ask them if they would mind signing a receipt for the money?" I asked. With their cash safely tucked away, the gunmen seemed happy to oblige. I ripped a page from my notebook, wrote a few words and asked the leader of the group to put a mark underneath. Moments later, we set out for Pakistan. In my pocket, I had a piece of paper reading "Received 1,000 rupees from Mike Chinoy as ransom for Afghan bandits." Later I submitted the receipt with my expense report to the NBC accountants. They approved it without question.

Getting a ransom receipt from my kidnappers was typical of the topsy-turvy world in which I found myself. In the Afghan war, the "bad guys" were the leftists advocating land reform, women's rights, and secular modernization—all worthy goals that I normally supported. Yet the intolerant and factionalized Afghan communists had sought to impose a Marxist revolution on their impoverished and deeply Islamic society, and now relied on Moscow to keep them in power in the face of massive popular opposition. The "good guys," fighting what communists would call a "war of national liberation," represented the most reactionary, inward-looking, fundamentalist forces in Afghanistan. Yet I found myself openly rooting for them. It made me realize there was no such thing as objectivity. The most a journalist could do was to report honestly and accurately what he had seen and heard, explaining both the local values and the larger context. I was convinced that simply doing my job—telling what was happening as I understood it—was helping the Afghans. Yet I found myself uncomfortably at the same end of the political spectrum as the knee-jerk anticommunists in the West I had so often disparaged. And that was not only true in Afghanistan. The revelations pouring out of post-Mao China, the horrors of the Vietnamese boat people and the "killing fields" of Cambodia, the war between China and Vietnam—two socialist countries with which so much of my youthful energy and idealism had been bound up—presented a challenge as painful personally as it was significant journalistically.

I had once believed that Asian socialism represented hope for the future, and initially I had viewed journalism as an instrument for my ideals. Only later did it become a calling in itself: the thrill of travel, the deadlines, the chance to witness history overshadowed and eventually marginalized my original, simplistic political thinking. I still retained my gut sympathy for the underdog and my ideals of social justice, but I was being forced to reevaluate where and how these values applied in the complex, untidy real world I was covering. There were no easy answers. Luckily the pressure of deadlines, and the need to keep track of so many rapidly changing crises and conflicts, helped me to avoid being consumed, and possibly even paralyzed, by soul-searching. And for this I was grateful.

CHAPTER FIVE

Fireman

It was a small gesture, but it repre-
sented a big breakthrough. In mid-1981, the Chinese granted CBS,
NBC, and ABC permission to station one radio correspondent in
Beijing, two years after the major U.S. print media had been allowed
to open offices there. The assumption was that full-fledged network
bureaus with camera crews were only a matter of time. In our Hong
Kong bureau, I thought NBC had three strong candidates for the job:
Jack Reynolds, the network's most experienced Asia hand; my imme
diate boss, the Chinese-speaking Bud Pratt; and myself. Apparently
for family reasons, neither Reynolds nor Pratt was particularly eager
to move to Beijing, where an acute shortage of housing for foreigners
meant newly arrived reporters would have to live indefinitely in
scruffy Chinese hotels. I, of course, desperately wanted to go, and I
lobbied strongly for the assignment.

When NBC finally made its decision, I was stunned. News division president Bill Small announced that he was sending Sandy
Gilmour, the network's Houston correspondent, to Beijing. I could
not imagine how a news organization with NBC's reputation could
assign a reporter with no China background, no Asia travel experience, and no Mandarin language training to cover one of the
world's most secretive and complex societies at a crucial moment of
transition. It boggled the mind. At that moment, after over three
years at the network, where I had learned a lot but had become

increasingly frustrated by the superficiality and the cavalier treatment of foreign news, I decided I wanted out.

While I actively pursued other job opportunities, NBC made my decision for me late in 1982. In a wave of budget cuts of the kind sweeping all the networks, NBC decided to close its Hong Kong bureau, transferring or firing all the personnel. After eight years there, I was without a job. I was dazed initially, and more than a little bitter. But the more I thought about it, the less upset I became. After all, NBC's management had only forced a decision I had already been contemplating. In retrospect, getting fired was the best thing that ever happened to me. In early 1983, I accepted a job with an unknown, struggling, all-news TV network called CNN.

"Mike," drawled Ted Turner, "this is a diagram showing all the Russian communication satellites. I'm gonna use 'em to beam CNN all over the world. I know I can do it. I'm friends with all those guys. See," he added, reaching again into his pocket, "here's a picture of me and Fidel Castro when we went duck hunting in Havana. He's my buddy."

Ted stuffed the paper and photograph back into his jacket.

"Well," he said, "nice to see y'all. I gotta go." And he raced toward the departure gate to catch his plane.

It was April 1984, and I had just met the founder and owner of CNN for the first time. Our encounter took place at Tokyo's Narita Airport, where, a year after joining CNN, I was en route to China to do a documentary for my new employers prior to a state visit by President Ronald Reagan. Turner was en route to Hong Kong for a sailing competition in the South China Sea. With the network's Tokyo bureau chief, John Lewis, in tow, Turner greeted me in the transit lounge. Bursting with energy, he insisted on carrying my suitcase, buying me a cup of coffee, and spelling out his vision for global television news.

As he left, I turned in amazement to John Lewis, a veteran Asia hand who'd been with CNN since its earliest days.

"Is he always like this?" I asked.

"Yep," John replied. "A lot of Ted's ideas sound crazy, but when you're in a room with him for ten minutes you think, yeah, that's doable."

Despite Ted Turner's big ambitions, when I started at the

network in February of 1983, I could understand why cynics had dubbed the fledgling CNN "Chicken Noodle News." Its headquarters was a former Jewish country club in midtown Atlanta, which resembled a decayed mansion from the set of *Gone With the Wind*. White columns framed the main door of a long, dilapidated building with a circular driveway in the front and spacious lawns sloping down the hill in the back. CNN was in the basement. Ted Turner's first cable TV venture, the "superstation" WTBS, occupied the rest of the building. In a cramped, chaotic newsroom, editors and newswriters hunched over shabby desks jumbled at odd angles. Other staffers scurried past rows of flickering monitors and control panels while an anchor desk stood prominently in the middle of the bedlam. The place had a manic energy: too many people jammed into an airless underground chamber, faced with the seemingly impossible task of putting out a newscast that would never end.

After years of being the junior reporter in Hong Kong, I was astonished at how young everyone was. I later learned CNN management was trying to save money by hiring staffers just out of college, with no experience, and paying them half the normal wage while they learned on the job. Hired as a London-based "fireman"—a guy who chases crises all over the world—for the first time in my life I felt, at age thirty, like a grizzled veteran. And in comparison to the youngsters racing through the basement of 1050 Techwood Drive, I suppose I was.

It was hardly surprising that such a breathtakingly ambitious venture didn't always go smoothly. In one memorable episode, the bank of TV monitors behind the anchor desk was accidentally switched in midbroadcast to a cable channel showing pornographic movies. In another, the moveable panels that made up the CNN weatherman's map went out of control, trapping the unfortunate forecaster's arm between high and low fronts as he desperately tried to maintain his unflappable on-camera demeanor.

But for all the glitches and amateurishness, I found the new network to be a bracing change after the stodginess and nasty internal politics of NBC. Reporters at CNN had virtually unlimited airtime. An average spot was allowed to run four or five minutes, and a sound bite—an on-camera quote—could easily run almost as long as the ninety-second spots that were the norm at the other networks. With twenty-four hours of airtime to fill, CNN's editors were eager, indeed desperate, for stories. Their appetite was inexhaustible, creating an atmosphere in which all ideas, no matter how different or even downright zany, were given serious consideration. The battles with power-hungry field producers, arrogant New York–show producers, or rival correspondents over airtime and story content that had so soured my experiences at CBS and NBC soon became unpleasant but fading memories. CNN offered a sense of freedom, experimentation, and energy that I found exhilarating.

If my previous bosses had been fairly conventional network executives, I quickly discovered the people running CNN were nothing of the kind. The man responsible for ensuring that this ragged collection of unknown, underpaid, and overworked people turned Ted Turner's fantasy into reality was Executive Vice President Burt Reinhardt. Around the network, Reinhardt had something of an intimidating reputation, so much so that when sighted, warnings of a "Burt alert" swept through the newsroom. A tough, no-nonsense penny-pincher, his passion for saving money went to extremes. Beneath the gruff exterior, however, was a warm, witty man of immense integrity. After the network became a success, Burt was universally acknowledged as the individual who kept CNN from going under during its early years.

The other half of top management was Ed Turner (no relation to Ted), a wry Oklahoman and former CBS veteran who ran the day-to-day news coverage. Something of an eccentric, he liked to sign his memos "ET," but no one doubted his commitment to hard news. My immediate boss, the person who really hired me, was foreign editor Jeanee Von Essen. A stout, boisterous redhead with a quirky style—when on the phone, she had a habit of waiting silently, often for several minutes, before saying a word—she was nonetheless a shrewd judge of people, who, between flattery and threats, seemed able to coax enormous amounts of work from her tiny crew of far-flung reporters. With the help of a tall, intense overnight deskman named Eason Jordan, the foreign desk and the miniscule CNN bureaus in London, Rome, Beirut, Jerusalem, and Tokyo set out to do battle with the larger, better-staffed, and incomparably richer competition. When I joined, CNN had exactly five foreign correspondents. Jeanee wasn't kidding when she promised I would be covering fires all across the globe.

I spent most of the next five years on the road for CNN. From my base in London, I logged hundreds of thousands of miles, dropping in and out of crises in Europe, the Middle East, Africa, and Asia with such regularity that I sometimes had trouble keeping track of who was fighting whom. Somewhat to my surprise, fighting turned out to be much of what I would cover. I had never expected that my interest in politics, revolution, and international affairs would lead me to become a "road warrior," chasing TV pictures of "bang-bang" from one hot spot to another. But my experiences would provide living proof of Clausewitz's famous maxim that "war is just an extension of politics." And I was to learn that the words and images I beamed around the world via satellite were themselves an increasingly significant factor in both politics and war.

Being a fireman also turned out to be a personal trial by fire. My travels not only kept me away from home for months at a time, but made me a regular eyewitness to mass murder, kidnapping, looting, famine, rape, tyranny, and pillage. When I wasn't worried about being killed, I struggled to cope with the turbulent emotions stirred up by the demands of my job. I was concerned that exposure to so much evil would scar me in a way I'd seen among many old Vietnam hands in Hong Kong. I did not want to become a hardened, unfeeling bystander, merely peering in on the terrible moments in people's lives. Yet I also found myself attracted by the danger, the excitement, the competition, and the camaraderie of being on the scene at historic turning points, however violent. It was a difficult balancing act, made bearable in part because in my reporting I was also able to chronicle the uncommon generosity and heroism among the many ordinary people I encountered who were caught up in extraordinary times.

In early March 1983, after I completed a three-week orientation in Atlanta, spending eighteen hours in the newsroom each day before returning to a local inn across the street dubbed, with good reason, the "Roach Motel," Jeanee took me aside. "I know you're supposed to be going to London to get settled in," she said, "but our man in Lebanon, Derwin Johnson, is due for a break. Would you mind going over and filling in? It'll just be for a couple of weeks." I spent six of the remaining nine months of 1983 in Beirut.

It was Lebanon's springtime of illusion. From everything I'd read—the vicious civil war that began in 1975 and left Beirut divided between a Christian East and a predominantly Muslim West; the subsequent Syrian Army intervention that imposed an uneasy and not very peaceful stalemate on the warring factions; the brutal Israeli invasion of 1982, which drove the Palestine Liberation Organization out of the city; and the intervention of U.S. Marines and a multinational peacekeeping force vainly seeking to pick up the pieces—I half expected having to dive for cover the moment I got off the plane. Looking out the window of the creaky, half-empty Middle East Airlines Boeing 707 as it descended toward Beirut, I saw row after row of blasted, pockmarked buildings rising from the red Lebanese soil along the shores of the Mediterranean. Armed soldiers patrolled the airport. But the atmosphere on this chilly, gray day in early March 1983 seemed surprisingly relaxed, and as I explored Beirut from my base at the legendary Commodore Hotel, home to the foreign press corps, I found a city awash in optimism.

It was perfectly safe to walk around, even at night. Shops and offices were open for business. Talk of reconstruction and of recapturing Beirut's former glory as the financial center of the Middle East was in the air. The main highway between East and West Beirut had been reopened, along with the city's long-closed port. On Rue Hamra, the commercial center of West Beirut, boutiques offered the latest French fashions. The cafés and restaurants were packed. Every night, I faced a difficult decision: where to dine? The only sound of war I heard came from the hotel's parrot, which had an unnerving habit of whistling imitations of incoming artillery shells from its cage by the swimming pool.

The calm didn't last long. First, five U.S. Marines were injured when a grenade was thrown at them in a Shiite Muslim slum. It was a warning shot from a previously unknown group called Islamic Jihad, whose campaign of bombing and kidnapping was to shake the Middle East for the rest of the decade. Soon after, my crew, John Towriss and Doug Habersin, two extremely talented young men from CNN headquarters in Atlanta, joined me to cover a Passover seder with Israeli soldiers at a heavily sandbagged farmhouse in the Chouf Mountains above Beirut. The mood was jolly, with much laughter and singing, and a bearded Army rabbi reciting the Passover story. The scene brought back childhood memories of holidays with my own family. Suddenly Islamic guerrillas opened fire with rocket-propelled grenades, killing two Israelis on guard duty.

Doug, John, and I spent a frightening night watching our angry, distraught dinner companions spray the nearby mountains with retaliatory fire.

The following morning I arrived back at the Commodore Hotel with that curious combination of elation, fatigue, and vague uneasiness that I had experienced on other big but troubling stories. I had survived a frightening encounter, and scooped the competition too. Once my report was written, edited, and filed, however, I felt a pang of sorrow for the two Israelis who had died. It was sharper and more personal than usual. As a Jew, I had an emotional bond with these soldiers. I understood why the Israelis called their faceless attackers terrorists. In my story, I sought to portray sympathetically the young men caught in the crossfire, but I worried that this sense of familiarity would affect my news judgment. Yet whatever my feelings for the young men with whom I had spent Passover, in Lebanon's larger political context, Israel, whose army was camped out in someone else's country, had a lot to answer for. There was good reason why so many in Lebanon wanted to drive them out. Yet again I was in the middle of a story where my emotions and my intellect collided.

There are moments that freeze time, and you are suspended within a stunned realization that history is changing course before your eyes. Such a moment occurred on Monday, April 18, 1983, when an Islamic Jihad suicide bomber destroyed the U.S. Embassy in the heart of Beirut. Hearing the explosion, my crew and I raced toward the embassy, weaving in and out of traffic, following the ambulances and fire engines. Stopped at an army checkpoint, we got out of the car and, with the camera already rolling, sprinted the last several hundred yards along the Corniche, as the seafront road is called.

We came upon a scene of utter devastation. The bomb had ripped apart the seven-story embassy building. Flames and smoke poured out of the shattered structure. The ground was covered with blood, shards of glass, masonry, and water from the fire hoses. Pushing our way forward, John and Doug aimed the camera at the American marines, French soldiers, and Lebanese Red Cross teams who were frantically searching the rubble. As sirens wailed, bodies, or pieces of bodies, were placed on stretchers or in plastic bags and carried away. Gaping at the wreckage, I saw suspended in the debris of an upper floor the body of a dead U.S. diplomat. Many of the searchers were weeping. More than sixty people, including seventeen Americans, were dead.

I had never before been this close to violent death on such a massive scale. Over the years, as I reported conflicts in other countries, I often wondered how I would react. As in my early trips to Northern Ireland, this horrifying carnage tested my professional and emotional discipline, as well as my intestinal fortitude. I was sickened by what I saw, but I discovered that the demands of covering the news not only took precedence over my emotions, but in fact helped keep my feelings in check. From sorrow, pity, fear, and disgust, my mind turned of necessity to more immediate problems. The top priority was getting reliable information, pounding out a script, composing a stand-up to do in front of the camera, plotting out possible times for satellite transmissions, and figuring out how to get in touch with the CNN foreign desk.

The three of us made our way back to the edge of the Corniche for a wide shot prior to leaving to arrange a feed. As the camera rolled, several Lebanese army soldiers in a state of extreme agitation suddenly charged at us for no apparent reason, flailing away with the butts of their rifles. Retreating and ducking and backpedaling, we were all hit. I barely missed having my jaw broken. I limped back to the bureau with a huge bruise on my leg and a sinking feeling that the bombing marked the end of the illusion that the United States and its Western allies could solve the problems of Lebanon.

CNN's coverage of this event provided an early sign of how radically different the network was from its competitors. Portable satellite dishes, miniaturized satellite telephones, and live broadcasts from distant locations were still in the future, but CNN repeatedly ran our bombing video raw and unedited, as I narrated and analyzed the story over the phone from the bureau. There was nothing slick or polished about our presentation. CNN's audience saw the same chaotic, jerky, and horrifying images John and Doug had seen through the lens of their camera. It was unsanitized reality—a foretaste of what CNN could do.

The next morning, a spectacularly sunny Mediterranean spring day, I went down for breakfast in the Commodore coffee shop with Lynne, who had joined me from Hong Kong some weeks earlier on the basis of my romantic descriptions of elegant restaurants, fascinating people, and a return to peace. Now we discovered an international press invasion. Overnight ABC had chartered a plane to fly in Peter Jennings from London. CBS had flown in its senior foreign correspondent, Tom Fenton. Dozens of other "firemen" were also arriving. The Commodore lobby was littered with TV equipment and buzzing with activity. It was a classic media "gang bang," with reporters swooping in like vultures, squabbling and competing to pick the carcass of disaster clean. I felt sorry for the resident Beirut correspondents "bigfooted" by the network superstars and their gaggle of producers who took over the story. Meanwhile, CNN's cost-conscious management dithered for a day about sending any reinforcements at all. Eventually Beirut bureau chief Derwin Johnson was called off his vacation and another crew added from London. The network's attitude was a mixed blessing. No one was "bigfooted," and there were no clashes over airtime. Instead I had the opposite problem. Even after Derwin returned, we were overwhelmed by the almost insatiable demands of a twenty-four-hour-a-day network. "Feeding the monster," we called it. Outmanned and outspent, we were pushed unmercifully by our bosses, who insisted we not only match but outdo our competitors shot for shot. When we didn't, there was trouble.

As I watched the network stars come and go in their chartered planes, we received another message from Jeanee. Concerned over the expense of keeping five people in the Commodore Hotel, CNN boss Burt Reinhardt wanted all six CNN staffers to sleep on the floor of Derwin Johnson's apartment. It would save the network $500 a day in hotel bills. Didn't I think it was a great idea? Six jaws dropped in unison in the ragged CNN bureau. Amidst curses and muttering, Derwin and I carefully composed a telex reply, which said—in so many words—get lost. Jeanee never raised the issue again.

After three long months, Jeanee finally agreed to let me fly to London just long enough to find an apartment and settle in. In those first hundred days in Beirut, I had done more television stories than in my entire career at NBC News, and every single one had been aired. My colleagues and I had shared a kind of camaraderie and élan I did not see among the self-important network crews and correspondents. Despite my exhaustion and CNN's stinginess, this was a reporter's network. I was convinced it represented the future. Once I got some sleep, I was ready to plunge back in.

CNN was happy to oblige. I spent a week in the central African nation of Chad, trying to report a war between the pro-American government and Libyan-backed rebels. We covered heroic young men dying from horrible war wounds—but only in the hospitals in the capital because the government barred all reporters from visiting the front. Instead my crew and I found ourselves stuck in a dingy hotel with broken toilets, a whorehouse in the lobby, and a garden restaurant where bats swooped low to pluck meals off the plates of astonished diners. Our efforts to report Chad's grim civil war turned into a comedy of errors worthy of *Scoop*, Evelyn Waugh's classic satire on foreign correspondents.

Soon after, I was back in Lebanon as Shiite militiamen battled the Lebanese Army for control of downtown Beirut. Shells blasted a hole in the Commodore Hotel, narrowly missing cameraman Jeff Martino and me as we tried to do a stand-up. I stayed on to watch Israeli troops withdraw from the Chouf Mountains, a move which set off a savage conflict between Druse Muslim and Maronite Christian militias. And I covered another Islamic Jihad suicide bombing that destroyed the U.S. Marine base at Beirut Airport, killing 241 U.S. servicemen. It was an exact repeat of the embassy bombing six months earlier. It was as if someone had just hit the replay button on a bad horror movie.

I had come to know the six-story marine-base headquarters well in the preceding months. At the height of the Chouf Mountain war between the Druse and the Christians, the marines allowed our camera crews to shoot the fighting from the roof of their building, which offered a ringside seat for the battles in the nearby hills. Huddling together behind rooftop sandbags, I had become friendly with these young American soldiers, who were stuck in the middle of a conflict that made no sense to them. Now, where the headquarters once stood, there was a mound of smoking, twisted rubble. I again watched marines and Red Cross workers, grim-faced, some weeping, searching through the rubble for bodies. I heard the same anguished questions about security, about who did it, and why. There was the same invasion of reporters and TV crews, the same demand from Atlanta for information and stories. With U.S. policy in Lebanon in tatters, I sensed it would not be long before the rest of the marines would be on their way out, leaving the Lebanese to sort out their feuds on their own.

I finally left Beirut at the end of November 1983, but not before one last nerve-racking episode covering bloody fighting between supporters and Syrian-sponsored opponents of Yasser Arafat in Palestinian refugee camps in the northern Lebanese port of Tripoli. It was a big story, I supposed, but I no longer cared. I was tired, depressed, and stressed out. I told Jeanee I would be willing to go back someday, but, for a while, I wanted to put my energies elsewhere. Four months later, CNN's new Beirut bureau chief, Jerry Levin, became the first Western journalist kidnapped by Islamic Jihad. Over the next two years, the wave of hostage-taking drove almost all foreign reporters out of the Lebanese capital. I never returned to Beirut.

It was April 1984, and Ronald Reagan was going to China, following in the footsteps of Richard Nixon in 1972 and Gerald Ford in 1975. Despite the rapid development of U.S.-China relations since President Jimmy Carter and Deng Xiaoping agreed to establish full diplomatic ties in 1979, Mr. Reagan's first visit to a Communist country was a major event, made even more significant by China's pathbreaking effort to reform its rigid socialist economic system by adopting some of the techniques of capitalism. CNN was planning to send a gaggle of White House reporters and crews, and foreign editor Jeanee Von Essen asked me to spend ten days there doing a series of "advancers" to air just prior to the president's arrival. Accompanied by a crew from the CNN Tokyo bureau, I returned to the People's Republic for the first time since 1981.

In a beat that had become a jumble of sudden plane flights to unanticipated and often dangerous places, going to China for CNN was not just another assignment. Unlike my other working trips, where I had to become an instant expert, reading clip files in airport transit lounges on everything from oil prices and the peculiarities of Libya's Muammar Qaddafi to Anglo-Irish diplomacy, Hindu cremation rites, and Philippine elections, China was my story. Although I would leave before the president and his Washington entourage arrived in Beijing, I was grateful to Ronald Reagan for creating an opportunity for CNN's cost-conscious bosses to send me.

The organization of a visit to China had not changed very much. "Minders" from the Foreign Ministry took us to carefully selected "units" to receive *jieshao*, "brief introductions." But I was amazed by the dramatic difference in substance. In a tour that included many of the same places President Reagan would visit, I heard barely a word of ideology. Deng Xiaoping's drive to achieve the Four Modernizations of agriculture, industry, science, and defense by the year 2000 was the hot topic. Madame Xie Xide, president of Shanghai's prestigious Fudan University and a graduate of Smith College, where my parents had taught, laid out the guiding principle of Deng's pragmatic new policies. "Not everyone can get rich at the same time," she told me in an interview. "Some people must get rich first in order for the others to follow suit." The changes I had begun to chart during my visits in the 1970s had now turned into a wholesale reversal of Maoist egalitarianism.

In dusty fields outside Xian, site of the famed Terra Cotta Warriors, gnarled peasants explained the "contract responsibility system," under which farmers, following the abolition of the people's communes, sold a portion of their crops to the state but were allowed to sell the rest on the free market, giving them, for the first time in years, an incentive to grow more. I wondered what Yu Kexin, the model Maoist peasant I met in 1973, thought of all this. In Shanghai we were taken to the city's first Sino-American joint venture, a precision instruments factory set up by the Massachusetts-based Foxboro Company. Shenzhen, the muddy village through which I had entered China for the first time in 1973, was now a construction site, full of Hong Kong–funded factories and new hotel and office blocks. In Beijing, I saw the first Coca-Cola bottling plant in China. I wondered if THE REVOLUTION GOES BETTER WITH COKE would be the next slogan to appear on China's walls.

Already signs of the insidiously subversive power of what Communist Party conservatives had called "bourgeois liberalization" were beginning to appear. On the Bund in Shanghai, along with the crowds doing *taiji*, I encountered pimply teenagers in blue jeans and leather jackets who wanted to talk not about "serving the people" but about disco music. In Shenzhen, I saw young people whiling away the time playing video games. A more striking change was apparent in the countryside, where Maoist restrictions on age-old social customs had disappeared. On one muddy road we saw a funeral procession made up of peasants wearing traditional white mourning costumes, burning incense, and paying homage to the spirits of the dead, a scene that would have been unthinkable just a few years before. I wondered about the long-term political implications of such loosening of Party control. If the social and economic liberalization continued, would it produce pressure for change? If so, how would the Chinese people, and the government, react?

Yet much of China remained poor and isolated from the rest of the world. We were taken to a village through which the presidential entourage would pass on its way to see the famous two-thousand-year-old Terra Cotta Warriors outside Xian. As we arrived, a huge, cheering crowd lined the main streets, clapping and waving. It quickly became apparent that these villagers, unused to foreigners, thought I was the president!

I returned to London with dozens of videotapes, plans to edit a one-hour special program, and a renewed desire to be based in China. I liked the texture and rhythm of Chinese life, as well as its language, history, food, and social behavior. It was an endlessly fascinating place, now moving in remarkable new directions. It would be exciting to live there and report on it for CNN. I had raised this hope with Jeanee in my earliest discussions, even before joining the network. Sending me on the Reagan advance trip was a clear signal that I would likely get the nod if that day ever came. CNN's still-precarious finances, however, left it very uncertain when the network might be able to open a bureau in Beijing.

Just off the plane from Hong Kong, where I had locked myself in a hotel for two days and had written the entire script, I settled into a crammed edit suite in the London bureau with cameraman/editor Mick Deane, to cut a program I had entitled *China in Search of Itself*. Unlike reporting spot news, editing a complicated, one-hour documentary would be a long, painstaking process. Predictably, however, CNN headquarters wanted to air the program in less than a week. Mick and I were going to have to hustle, but I didn't really mind. That was the CNN way.

A few hours after we started came a news flash. A British policewoman had been shot and killed a few blocks from our bureau by a diplomat firing from inside the Libyan Embassy. He had been aiming at Libyan exiles demonstrating across the street against strongman Muammar Qaddafi. Police had surrounded the embassy.

Apart from myself, there was only one other correspondent, Richard Blystone, based in the CNN London bureau. A gruff, hard-driving veteran of years at the Associated Press, for whom he'd covered the war in Indochina, Dick had been with CNN since its earliest days. A good friend, he was also, in my view, the best writer at the network, as well as the wittiest. I admired him greatly. But there was simply no way Dick and the second London bureau crew could meet Atlanta's demand that the Libyan Embassy siege be staffed twenty-four hours a day. With no change in the deadline for the China special, Mick Deane and I were hauled off our editing and sent to the stakeout at St. James's Park near Piccadilly Circus. Dick and I and the two bureau crews traded twelve-hour shifts, basing ourselves in a hotel room with a commanding view of the Libyan Embassy. Apart from watching and waiting, there was little we could do, except to run up a sizable room-service bill. Every day after I completed my embassy stint, however, instead of going home to get some rest, I returned to the bureau and stayed up all night with Mick working on the China program. As dawn broke, we went back to the siege. After a couple of days of this, we were on the brink of collapse. Following repeated and increasingly desperate pleas, Jeanee finally agreed to spend the money and fly in some help from the CNN Rome bureau. My colleagues arrived just as we finished the documentary. The whole episode, comic and macabre, left me with less than charitable feelings about Libya.

But it was nothing compared to the strangeness I encountered when I visited the country itself. In early 1986, Libya and the United States were on a collision course following a series of terrorist attacks on U.S. targets in Europe, which the Reagan administration blamed on Colonel Qaddafi. After much prodding from CNN, the Libyans agreed to issue us visas. On a chilly, wet Middle Eastern winter day, cameraman Phil Turner, soundman Mark Iredale, and I found ourselves in Tripoli, where we and other Western journalists were soon herded onto a bus and driven into the desert. Two hours later, we encountered Muammar Qaddafi madly driving a tractor across the sand.

Dressed in a traditional Arab gown, Qaddafi brought his vehicle to a grinding halt. His eyes were glazed, and as I moved closer it appeared that he was wearing makeup and perfume. His sinister-looking, tractor-driving security guards stopped a few feet away from him. Speaking first in heavily accented English and then in Arabic, Qaddafi launched into a sharp denunciation of the United States, and then drove back off into the desert.

A rare visitor to the Great Wall of China: me, August 1973

Under the gaze of a statue of Chairman Mao and an admiring crowd, our tour group (off-camera) plays Frisbee. Shenyang, China, August 1973

*With model Maoist peasants Yu Kexin and family, August 1973 (above),
and with Yu Kexin (and granddaughter), May 1993 (below)*

IRA gunman "Mickey" prepares to "take a few digs at the Brits." Belfast, Northern Ireland, 1974

Mike Chinoy, fledgling China watcher. CBS Hong Kong, 1977

China opens, albeit tentatively, 1978

"Democracy Wall," Beijing, October 1979

With the Afghan mujahideen, December 1981 (right) and February 1979 (below)

Reporting from the bombed-out U.S. embassy in Beirut, Lebanon, April 1983

Shooting a "standup" with NBC cameraman Kamal Hyder in the Khyber Pass, March 1980

"Chicken Noodle News" broadcasts the funeral of slain Indian Prime Minister Indira Gandhi. The microphone is taped to a lampshade in my hotel room. New Delhi, India, November 1984

On assignment in Hong Kong with CNN sound man Mitch Farkas and "shooter" Cynde Strand, March 1989

With Sherlock, Daniel, and Lynne in Beijing's Tiananmen Square,
January 1988

Such bizarre scenes were normal in Libya. Much of our time was spent at carefully organized government rallies, where officials led the crowds in ritualized chanting (in English, for the benefit of the cameras) of the slogan, "Down, Down U.S.A.!" The waiters in the hotel later joked that they were all suffering from "Qaddafi arm," a malady brought on by having to wave their fists in the air at such rallies for hours on end. Often surrounded by female bodyguards, it soon became apparent Qaddafi also had a taste for female Western reporters. As the visiting press corps jockeyed for greater access to the Libyan leader, late one night his aides came to the hotel and invited first a female reporter from the *New York Times* and then one from the Associated Press for exclusive encounters in the colonel's desert tent. Our colleagues returned with hair-raising stories of trying simultaneously to conduct an interview and resist Qaddafi's amorous advances. With our all-male crew, CNN got no further access to the colonel. As word of his preferences leaked out, one of the other networks immediately added a very attractive female producer to their team in Tripoli.

I was in Geneva covering a meeting of ministers from the Organization of Petroleum Exporting Countries (OPEC) when the phone rang on October 31, 1984. I heard the precise, BBC-like tones of my English producer, Peter Humi.

"Mike," he said, "Indira Gandhi's been shot. It just crossed on the wires. Atlanta wants us to leave immediately for India."

Eighteen hours later, Peter, cameraman Jeff Martino, soundman Mark Iredale, and I arrived in Delhi. The situation at the airport appeared normal enough, but as we hired a rickety old truck to take us and our fifteen cases of equipment to the Hyatt Hotel, I wondered about the long, thin black lines of smoke I saw curling upward in the distance. Bouncing along toward the city center, I realized what was happening. The assassination of Prime Minister Gandhi had plunged the capital into complete, terrifying chaos. We didn't know it yet, but we were driving into the worst communal riots India had experienced since its establishment in 1947.

Mrs. Gandhi had been walking in her garden when she was shot dead by two of her own bodyguards. The killers were members of the Sikh religious sect, exacting vengeance for the prime minister's crackdown earlier in the year on armed separatists fighting for an independent Sikh state. On our way to the hotel, we stopped to take some shots of a crowd of Hindus about to torch a Sikh school. As we approached, the mob seemed friendly enough to us. Teenaged boys laughed and clowned in front of the camera. Suddenly several men who appeared to be the ringleaders began gesturing angrily in our direction, apparently upset that we were going to record their attack on the school. Without warning, the atmosphere changed. Screaming and shouting, the crowd charged at us. We leapt into the cab of our truck and yelled at the driver to go. As the truck lurched away, some of the rioters tried to pull Mark off the back of the vehicle. I was certain he would be killed if they succeeded. A tug of war ensued, with me, Jeff, and Peter holding on to one of Mark's arms while the crowd yanked at the other. Finally the momentum of our truck won out and the rioters let go. Frightened but relieved, Mark slumped back into the truck.

At the gates of our hotel we saw a burned-out car in which, we were told as we checked in, two people had been killed a few hours earlier. As darkness fell, we could hear the sound of guns nearby. The whole city seemed to have gone mad. In the next three days, the death toll would reach three thousand. Late that night, Peter Humi braved more gunfire and marauding bands of vigilantes to make a wild ride to the TV station with our story. Soon after he returned, John Lewis and a correspondent and crew from Tokyo arrived. They had come under fire at three police roadblocks before the one-eyed driver to whom they'd been forced to pay $100 dumped them and their gear on the highway near the hotel and vanished into the dark. They were more than a little shaken. I was happy to see them.

Amid the carnage, Jeanee announced that CNN wanted to broadcast Mrs. Gandhi's funeral live by picking up Indian TV's transmission, with me providing the commentary. In the absence of studio facilities, the only way we could pull this off was for me to watch Indian television in my hotel room and provide live commentary and narration over the phone as the Indian TV pictures went out over our own network. Given the appalling unreliability of Indian telephone lines, the general chaos in Delhi, and the uncertainty over whether Atlanta could arrange a satellite feed to pick up the coverage, we weren't very optimistic.

In my room, we attached a microphone to the telephone and taped it to the lamp shade next to my bed, on which I had spread out the notes I hoped would sustain me through three or four hours of continual live commentary. Turning on the local TV, we booked a long-distance call to CNN headquarters. As we feared, the line was crackly and frequently cut off. Then John Lewis came up with an inspired idea. He and Peter went downstairs and found the hotel operator. A few minutes later, the two producers came back beaming. "Well, dude," John said, "you should be okay now. We just paid the operator fifty dollars. And we'll keep bribing him every hour until this thing is over." Hunched over the bed, speaking into the microphone hanging from the lamp, I tried to share my insights as Indian TV showed hundreds of thousands of frenzied mourners following Mrs. Gandhi's funeral procession through the heart of Delhi to the cremation site on the banks of the sacred Jumna River. In the often antiseptic world of Western television, this was certainly the first cremation ever seen live on TV in the United States, and to my amazement, the program went almost flawlessly, except for one brief interruption. As I was about to make what I thought was an important point about the future of Indian politics, I, and millions of viewers, heard a disembodied voice replace mine over our live phone hookup. "Excuse me, please, excuse me, please. I am calling from Mexico. Is this the Hyatt Hotel? I would like to reserve a room for January." I feared our producers in Atlanta would have heart failure. John and I cracked up.

During my frantic early years at CNN, I took time off for a special trip back to my hometown of Northampton, Massachusetts, where, on a warm, slightly overcast day in June 1985, Lynne and I were married at the Smith College Chapel. We had made the decision on a cold, rainy night in London the previous December, soon after I came back from India. We had now been living together for four years. To my relief, Lynne had shown herself able to handle the tensions created by my constant and abrupt departures. She was lonely and didn't like it, but she didn't run off with someone else. Instead she made a life for herself, developing her own set of friends and freelancing about the business scene in London for the *Christian Science Monitor* and the *International Herald Tribune*. She understood the emotional, temperamental, and intellectual forces that were driving me, and she respected my choice. For my part, I discovered that the inevitable sexual temptations of life on the road, to which many colleagues regularly succumbed, held little appeal for me. Being away from Lynne was the hardest part of my work, but I was determined not to let the frequent separations totally over-shadow the rest of my life. I did not want our relationship to join the long list of casualties of the foreign correspondent's lifestyle. We shared too many interests and values, and were too committed to each other.

We designed the ceremony ourselves, incorporating elements from Lynne's Presbyterian and my Jewish tradition in a civil cere-mony. Over a hundred people came, including friends from Hong Kong and even Beirut. My cousin John Krich, now a successful writer, was best man. I had not been in the serene, white, classical New England building since my father's funeral there a decade ear-lier. But it was a fitting place to be married, a reaffirmation of the continuity of life in the face of all its inevitable tragedies. Though I was suffering a case of nerves far worse than in any war I'd ever cov-ered, everything went smoothly until I tried to put the ring on Lynne's finger. My hands were shaking so much it took several tries before I succeeded, to the great amusement of our relatives and friends. Afterward we held a reception in the elegant lobby and out-door courtyard of the Smith College Theatre building, overlooking Paradise Pond. As we began a round of toasts, the sun finally came out.

After the wedding, we headed to my family's summer house on Martha's Vineyard for a week-long honeymoon. We swam in the Atlantic Ocean, cooked lobster dinners, and relished each other's company with no other pressures to worry about. One night, out of curiosity and habit, I turned on the TV news. It was not a smart move. A TWA jet had just been hijacked to Beirut, its passengers held hostage by Islamic extremists. The screen was full of reports from the Lebanese capital, mostly done by friends of mine. I worried that CNN might try to call me off my honeymoon, forcing me to choose between my new wife and my demanding bosses. In fact, I learned later that Jeanee Von Essen did try to contact me. She called London bureau chief Françoise Husson and demanded to know where I was honeymooning. I had given Françoise our phone num-ber for emergencies, but to her everlasting credit, she insisted to Jeanee that she didn't have it. CNN would have to wait.

Twenty-four hours after returning from my honeymoon, CNN

ordered me to Damascus, where the TWA hostages would go if they were freed. Still feeling like a starry-eyed newlywed, I had to leave my bride of just one week to plunge into the political and journalistic vortex of the Middle East. The hostage crisis had become a huge story. In the Syrian capital, I found the other networks pouring in money, personnel, and equipment in anticipation of the hostages' release. Anchor Tom Brokaw flew in for NBC. Predictably enough, CNN chose to staff Damascus with only cameraman Jeff Martino, a freelance sound technician, and me. Lynne, alone in London, was depressed and upset by my absence. I desperately wanted to be with her, but until the crisis was resolved, it was clear that CNN wouldn't let me leave. I might be stuck in Syria for a long time.

After several anxious days, the Islamic militants in Beirut finally released their captives. Syrian television agreed to provide camera facilities to broadcast the ex-hostages' news conference in Damascus, and to allow all four networks to use its camera for reporters to do a live debrief with their anchors back in the U.S. We drew lots to see who would go first. Amazingly, CNN won. Still, Jeff and I had a huge problem. Unlike the other networks, CNN was too penurious to pay to install international phone lines in the hotel ballroom. We thus had no way of communicating with CNN headquarters. I wouldn't be able to hear instructions from a producer or questions from an anchor in Atlanta. Yet in my last conversation from my hotel room, Jeanee had made it clear that CNN expected me to do a live shot, and expected it to work.

The news conference ended, and the Syrian TV engineer motioned to me. If I was to do a live shot, I had to get ready. In a last-minute huddle with Jeff, we suddenly had an idea. Standing in front of the camera, I asked the Syrians if the feed was up yet. They nodded. I clipped on a microphone.

"Hello, Atlanta," I said into the camera. "This is Damascus. I don't know if you can see or hear me, but if you can, this is how we're going to do our live shot. When I give the signal, we will synchronize our watches. I will wait exactly two minutes and then start to talk. Please have an anchor make a very general introduction, like, 'Here's Mike Chinoy in Damascus.' I will say my piece and sign off. No questions. That's the only way to make this thing work. I'll begin two minutes from ... now!"

I looked at my stopwatch. Every fifteen seconds, I called out the remaining time to Atlanta. As the seconds ticked away, I grew more and more nervous. After two minutes, I plunged in. "Hello, this is Mike Chinoy in Damascus. The ex-hostages are on their way to a plane for Germany now, after a news conference here in which they talked about their experiences in captivity."

I signed off several minutes later. I had no way of knowing whether CNN headquarters had seen or heard anything I said, let alone put me on the air. Jeff and I made our way back to my room to call Atlanta and find out. Jeanee picked up the phone. She was whooping with delight. "It was fant*aaastic!*" she shouted. "It looked great!" Back in the lobby, our network colleagues appeared glum. I asked what was going on. "Nothing," said one reporter. "Since CNN got its live shot out first, the other nets canceled theirs."

Amid all my travels, I had not lost the soft spot in my heart for Northern Ireland. My colleagues in the CNN London bureau joked about my enthusiasm for the awful weather, undistinguished food, and ancient quarrels. But I chose to make Northern Ireland, less than an hour's flight from London, part of my beat. The other U.S. networks had long ago lost interest in the province's endless conflict. Most of the time, my crew and I had the place to ourselves, choosing story topics based on our own judgment and interest, with no worries about competition. Although shootings and explosions remained a feature of daily life, there was something comfortingly familiar about the Irish "troubles" that made it a welcome change from the even uglier passions I had covered in other hot spots. And the pleasures of sitting down in a cozy pub for an evening of Guinness, Irish music, and political gossip made the daily discomforts and dangers bearable.

But it didn't make them go away.

One sunny afternoon in August 1984, Northern Irish police killed a man just a few feet from where I was standing. Cameraman Jeff Martino and I had flown to Belfast to cover a rally at which Martin Galvin, the head of the IRA's American support group Noraid, was scheduled to speak. The British government had banned Galvin from entering Northern Ireland, a move virtually guaranteed to inflame the situation. We were certain that Galvin would try to circumvent the ban, and the Royal Ulster Constabulary, truncheons and rubber-bullet guns at the ready, were out in force to catch him if he did.

Jeff and I worked our way through a boisterous but peaceful crowd of several thousand in Belfast's staunchly Catholic Andersonstown district. Bullhorn in hand, Gerry Adams, the bearded leader of Sinn Féin, the IRA's political wing, stood on the steps of an old white building making a speech. I had met and interviewed Adams several times. He struck me as smart, sophisticated, charismatic, and utterly ruthless. As he finished speaking, Galvin burst out of the building's front door. The police charged through the crowd, blasting rubber bullets at point-blank range. Jeff and I were nearly swept off our feet by a sea of panicked people. "Are you rolling?" I shouted, struggling to keep my balance amid the chaos and din.

Suddenly a few steps ahead, I saw a thin young man with a mustache grab his chest, lurch backward, and collapse. "Someone's been hit, someone's been hit!" people cried. The police poured past us, their faces contorted with rage and anger, hitting and shooting wildly as they swarmed over the wall and into the house into which Galvin had fled. Amid the chaos, Galvin got away.

The young man now lay on the ground, and a small crowd gathered around him. Someone tore open his shirt. Horrified, I saw a large red mark the diameter of a coffee mug across his chest. Frantically, people tried to revive him but it was no use. Twenty-two year-old Sean Downes was dead, hit in the heart by a rubber bullet. I turned to Jeff.

"I think we have almost the whole thing on camera," he said quietly.

This was one place where I felt no conflict between my emotions and my professional obligations. I was almost as angry as the people around me. I knew that the world should see what had just taken place before my eyes. A straight account of the facts was damning enough. Rushing to the Belfast office of the BBC, we booked a late-afternoon feed to London. Jeff was right. His graphic videotape showed Adams's speech, Galvin's appearance, the police charge, the puffs of smoke, the fusillade of rubber bullets. Amid the pandemonium, there was a brief and shaky shot of Downes moments after he was hit, followed by hysterical scenes as the young man lay dying on the pavement. CNN put the story on the air moments after it was received in London.

Throughout my years in London, the Irish "troubles" were never far from the headlines, from the IRA's nearly successful attempt to assassinate British prime minister Margaret Thatcher in October 1984, to the signing of an Anglo-Irish agreement to promote a political solution, which I covered the following year. I could travel throughout a dramatically changing world, only to return and find the mean streets of Belfast still frozen in time. It was still business—and bloodshed—as usual.

The crowd was the biggest I had ever seen, almost a million people packed into Luneta Park next to the Manila Hotel. Standing on the hotel roof next to dozens of reporters and cameramen, I watched a sea of banner-waving demonstrators singing, cheering, and chanting. The object of their adoration was a tiny, middle-aged widow in a yellow dress who sat quietly on the stage. Rising slowly, she walked toward the podium. The vast throng erupted. "Cory, Cory, Cory," they cried, their shouts echoing across the vast expanse before fading away over the waters of nearby Manila Bay. It was Sunday, February 16, 1986. Under a fierce tropical sun, Corazón Aquino was launching a nationwide campaign of nonviolent protest to topple Philippine president Ferdinand Marcos. The movement she led would be known as People Power.

Along with London cameraman Jeff Martino and soundman Phil Turner, I had arrived in Manila a week earlier in response to desperate pleas for help from Tokyo bureau chief John Lewis. For a month John, along with one reporter and two crews from Tokyo, had struggled to keep on top of a rapidly developing, increasingly complex story. It had begun in November 1985, when President Marcos called a "snap presidential election" to be held the following February. Marcos had ruled the Philippines, often with an iron fist, since 1965. He had run the country as if it were his personal property, looting the national wealth and allowing his wife Imelda and a clique of cronies to monopolize all important sectors of the economy.

I had visited the Philippines often during my years in Hong Kong. I found it a strange, occasionally charming, but often pathetic and usually depressing place with a serious identity crisis. A U.S. colony until 1946, the streets of its capital resembled a dingy American suburban strip, lined with McDonald's, Dunkin' Donuts, Shakey's Pizza, and other fast-food joints. Many of its people talked in Americanized English and adopted American-style nicknames. The defense minister, Juan Ponce Enrile, was known as "Johnny," and the head of the Philippine Constabulary, Lt. Gen. Fidel Ramos, was "Eddie." There was a surprisingly popular political party whose sole platform was to make the Philippines the fifty-first American state. It was also Asia's only Catholic nation, the result of centuries of Spanish rule, but it was Catholicism with a peculiarly Philippine twist: here, believers had themselves "crucified" for an hour every Easter; Cardinal Jaime Sin, the archbishop of Manila, laughingly greeted visiting reporters by saying, "Welcome to the house of Sin;" and, during a visit by the Pope in 1981, enthusiastic bar girls in Manila's ubiquitous red-light districts offered customers "papal discounts."

If ever a country was ripe for revolution, it was the Philippines, with its exploited peasants, urban slums, ranks of beggars, and desperate people foraging through garbage dumps. Yet the people, cowed by their colonial heritage and intimidated by Marcos's iron-fisted rule, had seemed unable to rise up. When Marcos blatantly rigged the elections, he assumed the traditional pattern would hold true. This time he miscalculated. Aquino and her supporters refused to accept the result, and the Philippines was plunged into crisis.

From the outset, the American media, especially television, played a central role in the unfolding drama. Indeed Marcos had announced his decision to hold an election during an appearance on ABC's *This Week with David Brinkley*. Given the immense clout of the United States, which maintained two strategic military bases in the country and was the Philippines' closest ally, both political camps deliberately sought to use the cameras to influence U.S. public opinion. American TV programs, including CNN, could be seen by ordinary citizens inside the Philippines via the U.S. Armed Forces Television Network. With most of the local media muzzled by the Marcos regime, our reports on the political struggle assumed a special significance, both as a pipeline to the Philippine people and a source of immediate, firsthand information for decision makers in Washington and Manila.

As usual, CNN was vastly outgunned by the competition. The other three networks had set up offices and a joint satellite transmission pool at the luxurious Manila Hotel, where General Douglas MacArthur had once made his headquarters nearly half a century before. CBS rented the hotel's Presidential Suite on the eighteenth floor, with private wading pool, and had constructed a small set for live broadcasts. ABC hired a black Mercedes for each of its producers and for the steadily growing number of star correspondents flying in. Each network brought in scores of engineers, technicians, makeup artists, computer experts, and videotape librarians, and deployed close to a dozen camera crews, arming them with walkie-talkies, radios, and portable telephones.

When Jeff, Phil, and I arrived from London, we found John Lewis and our Tokyo colleagues holed up in the Hilton, a dingy, dimly lit monstrosity that clearly had seen better days. Under instructions from Jeanee to save money, John had secured rooms there for fifty dollars a day, less than half the cost of the Manila Hotel across the park. For an even smaller amount, he had hired two broken-down cars—without air-conditioning to protect us and our gear from the brutal heat and humidity—to ferry CNN staff from one breaking event to the next. With CNN headquarters demanding three, sometimes four, stories a day, it was no surprise John was pleading for reinforcements.

As the crisis intensified, every day sent us chasing across Manila and into the provinces in pursuit of dramatic new developments: official vote counters walking off the job to denounce ballot-rigging by the Marcos forces; the murder of a key Aquino supporter; the activities of special U.S. envoy Philip Habib and the numerous American politicians who had come to monitor the election; press conferences by Marcos; an interview with Aquino; popular boycotts of Marcos-controlled businesses; frequent protest demonstrations; speculation about violence from the extreme left or a possible military coup; and mounting fears that Marcos would soon order a crackdown on the growing resistance. Staggering back into the Hilton late at night, we crowded into our makeshift editing room, shooed the cockroaches from the edit decks, and put spot after spot together, rushing them to the Manila Hotel in the wee hours of the morning to send them from the network feed point, before resting briefly and heading out again. We were surprised ourselves at the volume of material we were producing. But it soon became apparent that the amount of airtime CNN was devoting to the story was having an impact, generating support at home and abroad for Aquino and undermining Marcos's credibility.

It was a feverish atmosphere, accentuated by the corruption and decadence in the capital. Among the many contacts in both camps who kept John Lewis and me abreast of the swiftly moving events was an executive at a Marcos-controlled television station. His hatred for the president that his station was forced to glorify was matched only by his fondness for the capital's sleazy nightlife. He regularly took us to a notorious joint called Hot Lips. Sipping our beers, we watched giggling, naked go-go dancers do extraordinary things with unlikely parts of their anatomy, including waving small yellow flags to show their support for Mrs. Aquino, while our friend regaled us with the latest gossip from inside the Presidential Palace.

The Philippine TV executive was hardly the only person seduced by Manila's cheerful depravity. One CBS engineer, who had been in Asia for several years, actually became part-owner of a girlie bar in the Ermita red-light district, where a sign on the wall read OUR SPECIALTY: BLOW JOB ON THE ROCKS. Late one evening, he brought two attractive young women from the bar to the network transmission point at the Manila Hotel. With the nightly feed done, the women began to do a striptease on the CBS live-shot set, while the technician enthusiastically taped them. Somehow the signal was inadvertently punched out on the satellite. From control rooms at CBS, NBC, ABC, and CNN headquarters in the U.S. came the same startled query, "What the hell is that?" "Holy shit!" the CBS technician exclaimed to the others in the feed point, quickly flicking a switch. To his bosses, he replied with forced casualness, "I don't know. Somebody else's transmission must have crossed our line."

Meanwhile, the political situation was a standoff. From within the military came rumblings of ever greater discontent over the president's corrupt and high-handed ways. On Friday, February 21, I filed a long analytical piece on the Reform the Armed Forces Movement (RAM), a group of military dissidents who, I predicted, could play a decisive role. Flooded with spot news from Manila and elsewhere, CNN never got around to airing my story. Twenty-four hours later, under the leadership of Defense Minister Enrile and Constabulary Chief Ramos, RAM moved against President Marcos.

When the coup started, I was already worn-out and I'd developed a huge cyst on my cheek, forcing me to wear gobs of makeup that dripped unpleasantly in the tropical heat each time I did an on-camera stand-up. John Lewis, who had been awake for eighty consecutive hours, became so punchy and incoherent that CNN headquarters ordered him to go to bed. It was early, on what we all hoped would be a quiet Saturday evening, when the story broke. The message, from an old journalist friend of John's with close connections to RAM, was brief. With a small number of soldiers, Ramos and Enrile had occupied Camp Aguinaldo and Camp Crame, two military compounds facing each other across a large highway in suburban Manila. Here they declared their opposition to Marcos. Before leaving the hotel, I called the CNN Foreign Desk. Maybe, I suggested, it was time to run my still-unused report on restiveness in the military. Somewhat embarrassed, my colleagues in Atlanta promised to put the package on the air at once.

It was dark and eerily quiet when Jeff Martino and I arrived at Camp Aguinaldo thirty minutes later. Defense Minister Enrile, wearing a flak jacket, looked grim. So did the three hundred rebellious troops he'd brought with him. Outnumbered and outgunned, they all knew that if Marcos decided to strike they stood no chance. As I watched, it dawned on me that my own chances of survival wouldn't be so great either. Locating a phone in an unoccupied office, I called John Lewis back at the Hilton and filled him in on what was happening. He told me CNN headquarters was frantic to hear from me. After several attempts, I managed to get a call through to Atlanta. A few moments later, I was on the air, describing what I was seeing: the somber rebel soldiers chain-smoking and pacing the halls of the Philippine Defense Ministry on the Camp Aguinaldo grounds, their vulnerability to attack, concerns about Aquino's safety and whereabouts. Live telephone reports from the scene of the action were to become a central feature of our coverage for the rest of the crisis.

As soon as I hung up, I dialed the international operator again and put through a call to my old friend Nayan Chanda, who had moved to Washington for the *Far Eastern Economic Review* in 1984. We had stayed in close touch after my departure from Hong Kong, and I had spoken with him frequently since my arrival in the Philippines two weeks earlier. Now I woke him early on a Saturday morning, U.S. time, to tell him that a revolt was under way. He promised to call his contacts in the State Department, and we agreed to speak again shortly. Two hours later, I managed to reach him again. After giving him a quick update—Aquino's brother Butz had just arrived at Camp Aguinaldo—I asked what he had learned.

"I spoke to my source at the State Department situation room," Nayan replied. "He told me everyone was glued to the TV, getting all their information from CNN."

Walking out to the main gate with my crew, I noticed a small group of Aquino supporters gathered in the street outside. Some of the demonstrators told me that Cardinal Sin, who, along with most of the Catholic Church hierarchy, strongly supported Aquino, had gone on the church's radio station to urge people to take to the streets. Before long the crowd had swelled to twenty-five thousand, a sea of bodies protecting the rebel soldiers. I was astonished and excited. This was indeed something new. Only now I couldn't get an international call through from Camp Aguinaldo. Frantic, I called John Lewis at the Hilton. A few minutes later, he told me one of our technicians had jerry-rigged the hotel phones so local calls to the hotel could be patched directly through to CNN headquarters in Atlanta. My live description of the unfolding events continued without interruption.

By midday Sunday, at least a million people jammed the streets between Camp Aguinaldo and Camp Crame to support the anti-Marcos forces. Early in the afternoon, word came that Marcos had sent tanks, armored vehicles, and three thousand Philippine Marines to attack the rebel headquarters. A final showdown appeared imminent. With my crew, I threaded my way through a now fearful throng to witness the confrontation. I didn't believe what our camera was recording. Nuns and priests knelt before the oncoming tanks. Chanting civilians put flowers into rifle barrels and pleaded with the troops not to attack. Unprepared for such a reception, the hardened soldiers stopped in their tracks. People Power had overcome military power. I didn't realize it then, but this was the turning point. Marcos had lost his chance to crush the revolt by force. His downfall was now only a matter of time.

But the Marcos forces hadn't given up. At dawn the next morning, loyalist troops tear-gassed a thinned-out crowd in front of rebel headquarters and set up mortars nearby. After the elation of the previous day, I suddenly became extremely nervous. The rebels and their leaders spoke of a possible bloodbath. With an open phone line to CNN, I braced myself to broadcast a live account of events until the final assault made it impossible. Suddenly I heard helicopters. As a fiery red sun rose, I saw several choppers sweep in and land, but instead of shooting, I heard cheering. The pro-Marcos troops on board were defecting to the opposition. Soon after, cameraman Jeff Martino was standing at the front gate when two military aircraft flew overhead. The rebel soldiers cocked their weapons, expecting bombs to fall at any moment. But the planes returned, swooped low, tipped their wings in salute, and roared off.

A few hours later, Marcos himself appeared on television with his Army Chief of Staff General Fabian Ver, the man widely believed to have organized the 1983 murder of Mrs. Aquino's husband, Benigno, popularly called Ninoy. Sitting in a small, unused office, I watched on a little black-and-white TV set and described over the phone to our audience the astonishing scene unfolding. Trying to force a military solution, Ver announced plans to open fire on the rebels, whose command post was a few yards from where I was speaking. Not for the first time, I felt like a sitting duck. Marcos, evidently trying to appear statesmanlike, overruled him. With the cameras on, the two argued in English for several minutes. It was the strangest television performance I had ever seen. Moments later, with Marcos still speaking, the TV screen went blank. The rebels had captured Channel Four, the main government television station. They cut Marcos off in midsentence.

After forty-eight straight hours of exceptional tension and non-stop broadcasting, I was exhausted, but my crew and I headed off immediately to Channel Four. We were replaced by a reporter and crew from the CNN Cairo bureau, flown in on short notice to help out after our pleas to Atlanta for more people. The TV station was now guarded by anti-Marcos soldiers and a large crowd. Inside, pro-Aquino activists had swiftly gone on the air, adding this new weapon to their arsenal in what was becoming more a political, psychological, and propaganda battle than a straightforward military confrontation. Yet fear was in the air. Everyone expected a Marcos counterattack to regain control of the airwaves.

As darkness fell, we looked for a vantage point to set up our cameras for what promised to be a long and frightening night. About two blocks away from Channel Four, I noticed a large, gray building with castlelike turrets and a neon sign reading CAMELOT HOTEL. We were in luck. It was only when I turned the lights on in our room facing the station that I realized this was not your average hotel. All the room lights were red. We had just checked into a "love hotel," whose sleazy basement nightclub was apparently notorious through-out Manila. After mounting our camera on a tripod by the window, we turned on the TV. To my dismay, I realized most the broadcasts from Channel Four were in Tagalog. I had no way to figure out what was happening. Suddenly I had an inspiration. Walking downstairs, I approached the doorman.

"Can you get me a nice girl?" I asked in as lecherous a manner as I could fake. "Can you get me two of them?"

He grinned. "No problem, boss."

"Okay, then," I continued. "I want two girls. The only thing is they have to speak English, and they both have to be supporters of Cory Aquino." Raising his eyebrows, he gave me a look suggesting he'd catered to all kinds of kinky tastes, asked for fifty dollars, and promised two girls within an hour.

Wearing heavy makeup, skin-tight slacks, and see-through blouses, the two young women were taken aback to discover their clients consisted of a half dozen tired, sweaty young men who had strewn piles of cables, videocassettes, and other TV equipment around the room. I immediately put them to work. "I want you to watch Channel Four and tell me what's going on," I said to one. I asked the other to monitor the radio. Then the women asked, "Don't you want a massage? We give very nice massages." I promised to schedule another rendezvous when things had calmed down. The young pros-titutes took to their tasks with gusto. Throughout the night, they provided a running translation of the continuing drama as the rebels in control of the station exhorted the people to stand firm against Marcos. But every hour or so, they tried again to interest me in a mas-sage. As day broke, I paid them off, wondering how I would claim the cost of two prostitutes on my CNN expense report. Eventually I listed them as "translators."

Twelve hours later, after an eventful day highlighted by a brief but fierce gun battle between Marcos loyalists and rebel forces, the phone in the Camelot rang. It was one of our ladies of the previous night. "Is that Mr. Mike Chinoy?" she said. "I have been watching you all day on Armed Forces TV. I just wanted to tell you that I have heard rumors of crowds gathering to storm the Presidential Palace. I thought you would like to know." I gratefully promised her dinner one day and immediately called John Lewis. He quickly dispatched

Cairo correspondent Ben McNitt and a crew to the Palace, and told us to grab our gear, check out of the Camelot, and head back to the Hilton as quickly as we could.

By now word was spreading through the city that Marcos had fled into exile. As a noisy mob surged into Malacañang Palace, tens of thousands of jubilant people began to celebrate. Chanting, singing, waving banners, some riding in packed buses or open trucks, they lined the streets in a joyous display of liberation. Driving mile after mile through this nonstop fiesta, I looked back on what had become a real-life morality play. For once, the good guys had actually won. The villain had gotten what he deserved. In the process, the Filipinos had regained a sense of dignity and pride whose absence had for so long troubled me. I shared the exultation of the crowds we passed. I was cynical enough not to expect this happy ending to be the final word. But People Power was more than a great story. I felt proud that my reports had played a role in shaping local and international perceptions of such historic events. Over the next six years in office, Aquino hardly solved the country's problems. She was plagued by her own inexperience, several attempted coups, natural disasters, and continuing economic decline. But at the end of her term in 1992 she handed power over to Fidel Ramos, a key leader of the 1986 uprising, after what was, for the Philippines, a relatively fair election. The country is still one of the poorest in Southeast Asia. But it remains one of the most democratic, due in part to the heady days of People Power.

The events in Manila marked a milestone for CNN, too. This was the first long-running international crisis in which the network was able to provide round-the-clock live coverage, even if it was primarily by telephone. For all their resources, the other networks were limited to brief segments in the regularly scheduled news programs. Time after time, CNN was hours ahead with fresh information and pictures aired directly off the satellite, often raw and unedited. In his memoirs, then–Secretary of State George Shultz wrote, "Yet another novel development of the 'information age' came to the fore [during the uprising in Manila]. Via CNN, millions followed the Philippine drama as it was occurring."

And People Power was only the dress rehearsal for what would come next, when I moved to China as CNN Beijing bureau chief and told the world the story of Tiananmen Square.

CHAPTER SIX

Beijing Bureau Chief

Deng Xiaoping strode firmly to his seat on the platform in the huge auditorium of Beijing's Great Hall of the People. China's eighty-three-year-old paramount leader, wearing a carefully pressed Mao suit, had a satisfied, confident expression on his face. Despite his diminutive stature—he was less than five feet tall—he carried himself regally as the Chinese photographers and TV cameramen in front of him backpedaled furiously to get their shots. Standing just a few feet away, I could feel the force of Deng's personality. His toughness and determination came from surviving years of intra-party purges and turmoil, twice including his own ouster and subsequent political rehabilitation. Behind him, I saw Zhao Ziyang, Deng's handpicked successor, at age sixty-nine the new, reformist general-secretary of the Chinese Communist Party. Zhao was followed by a smirking Li Peng, a conservative soon to be named acting prime minister, and the rest of China's senior leaders. With floodlights illuminating a giant red hammer and sickle mounted above the stage, the men who ruled the People's Republic stood to attention, along with two thousand delegates, as a Chinese army band struck up the communist anthem, *The Internationale*. The Thirteenth Congress of the Chinese Communist Party, an event that would go down as a critical turning point in the country's political history, was under way. For the first time, Western journalists were being allowed to witness the proceedings.

I had arrived in Beijing a month earlier, in September 1987. After four and a half years of chasing wars, coups, and revolutions from my base in London, CNN had asked me to set up a bureau in the Chinese capital, fulfilling at last my dream of living and working in the People's Republic. Typically, however, I was offered the assignment at the most inopportune moment. Lynne was six months pregnant with our first child, and we were finally feeling settled in London. It took considerable argument for me to convince CNN management to delay my departure at least until the baby was born. But with a lively, healthy infant who had inherited his father's energy and, unfortunately, his ability to go without sleep, Lynne and I departed for Beijing. On my first night there, I sent foreign editor Jeanee Von Essen a telex: "I am pleased, no, make that absolutely thrilled, to report that the Beijing bureau is now open for business."

Cynde Strand, an adventurous CNN veteran who had worked with me as an editor in Beirut and stayed on in Lebanon for several years to become a resourceful and artistic camerawoman, joined me as bureau shooter. Since I had last seen her, she had traveled throughout the Middle East and Africa, had taken a year off to study Chinese in the Yangzi River city of Nanjing, and had spent the summer before the bureau opened wandering the mountains of Tibet. Our soundman/editor was Mitch Farkas. Born and raised in Hong Kong, he was the son of a Korean mother and an American father who was himself a well-known freelance cameraman with over thirty years' experience in Asia. In fact, I had worked with Mitch's father during my time at NBC in Hong Kong. Mitch was young, handsome, temperamental, and very talented. He and Cynde were colorful additions to the journalistic scene in Beijing.

As we settled in that fall, the mood in China was upbeat. To many people, the Thirteenth Party Congress became a symbol of the country's hopes for a brighter future. For months, political tension between reformers and conservatives in the leadership had been growing, heightened by an outbreak of student demonstrations the previous winter and the dismissal, at the instigation of hard-liners, of liberal Communist Party chief Hu Yaobang in January. Now Deng Xiaoping and his reformist allies, who favored accelerating the pace of change, appeared to have gained the upper hand. The decision to let journalists cover the Congress was one clear sign of the trend toward greater openness. As Cynde, Mitch, and I picked up our credentials at a newly established Chinese press center and lugged our equipment into the Great Hall of the People for the opening ceremony, I thought back to my first visit in 1973. Then the Party's Tenth Congress had been held in absolute secrecy, with news of its proceedings released only after it concluded. Now we buttonholed delegates for sound bites. "The people want reform," one official told me as he walked into the Hall. "We want a more liberated China."

Inside, Zhao Ziyang delivered a 34,000-word political report as our camera rolled. "Marching Down the Road of Socialism with Chinese Characteristics" was a blueprint for sweeping new reforms, including more private enterprise, family farming, and factories run by managers, not party bureaucrats. Even more important, Zhao devoted much of his speech to political reform, urging greater separation between the activities of the party and the government, the creation of a professional, nonpolitical civil service, and the recognition that differing groups in Chinese society might legitimately have divergent views. As Zhao spoke, I noticed Hu Yaobang, still technically a member of the Politburo despite his dismissal as Party chief earlier in the year, sitting at the back of the stage. He was watching with a satisfied look on his face.

The gathering concluded a week later after more open debate and diversity than any Congress before it. Having apparently achieved his goal of consolidating the reform process, Deng Xiaoping resigned from the Politburo, taking with him many of the elderly conservatives opposed to faster change. It was an important triumph for the moderates and a major setback for the remaining party hardliners. At an unprecedented post-Congress news conference, I watched as a confident, almost cocky Zhao Ziyang, dressed in a stylish, double-breasted pinstripe suit, met the press. Chinese leaders rarely spoke to foreign journalists, let alone spent a full hour in unrehearsed give-and-take with reporters. Yet Zhao laughed and joked as he answered dozens of questions while walking through a reception room packed with correspondents who had been covering the Congress. It was a virtuoso performance.

Late that night, we filed a story via satellite from the dimly lit and rudimentary feed facilities at the state-run China Central Television (CCTV), where all transmissions, or "birds," from Beijing originated. Our feeds during the week of the Congress were our first in China, full of confusion and shouting as the harassed CCTV engineers juggled the competing demands of CNN and a host of other foreign networks. Still, they worked. Heading back to the hotel late that night, I felt our bureau had begun to make its mark. Impressed with Zhao Ziyang and convinced that Deng's reformists were now in charge, we had a good story to cover.

We set up our bureau at number 20 Wangfujing Street, on Beijing's main commercial thoroughfare, not far from Tiananmen Square. Our presence there was a sharp departure from the usual practice, in which the Chinese Foreign Ministry required all foreign news organizations to be located in one of four diplomatic compounds. With guards at the gate to keep ordinary Chinese out, these ugly apartment complexes provided offices and housing for virtually all resident diplomats and journalists. At Ted Turner's behest, however, CNN had signed an agreement of cooperation with China Central Television—an example of his vision of television as a means of building bridges with countries long cut off from the United States. One result was that CCTV, not the Foreign Ministry, provided us with a translator and driver, as well as our bureau space. This arrangement was unique in a system where the operations of Western reporters were rigidly controlled.

So Cynde, Mitch, and I found ourselves on a street full of history—the very same street, I discovered, where, almost a century earlier, "Morrison of Peking," the legendary China correspondent of *The Times* of London, had made his home (at number 98 Wangfujing). Morrison was one of those colorful figures I had loved reading about during my early years as a student of China. When he wasn't traveling to the most remote corners of the country or shouldering a rifle to defend Beijing's foreign legation against Chinese mobs during the Boxer Rebellion of 1900, Morrison wrote dispatches that shaped the policies of the British Empire. In his honor, Wangfujing had actually been renamed Morrison Street in 1920, and returned to its original Chinese appellation only after the communist victory in 1949.

Wangfujing was a quiet, tree-lined street of small shops, antique stores, and restaurants when we moved in. Apart from the ancient green and yellow electric trolleys, the noise of cars was usually not loud enough to drown out the jingling of bells from thousands of bicycles and pedicabs. Along one stretch was a glass-enclosed display board where the latest issues of the *People's Daily* and other newspapers were tacked up for passersby to read. Unlike my experience in Shenyang in 1973, this time no one tried to prevent me from taking a look.

Wangfujing was also home to the Beijing Hotel, a monstrosity that occupied a full city block just a few minutes' walk from Tiananmen Square. Run by the Beijing city government, it had for many years been the hotel of choice for visiting VIPs because of its central location and spectacular views of Tiananmen and the Forbidden City. In the late seventies and early eighties, its lobby and coffee shop had also been the favored meeting place for members of Beijing's foreign community, although several new Western-style joint-venture hotels such as the Great Wall Sheraton and the Jianguo had begun to provide serious competition. We soon started to eat at the Beijing Hotel's Chinese restaurant regularly. Unlike the few small eateries elsewhere on Wangfujing, which kept typically Chinese operating hours of 11:30 to 1:00 for lunch and 5:30 to 7:00 for dinner, the one in the Beijing Hotel stayed open slightly longer. With our hectic and unpredictable schedules, we at least had a chance of getting a meal.

From the window of my office, I enjoyed looking down a narrow lane or *hutong*, one of many that ran off Wangfujing. With its long, gray walls topped by curved roofs and its faded red gates opening to inner courtyards, it was a reminder of an old Beijing, one rapidly disappearing to make way for the large apartment and office blocks that increasingly dominated the skyline. The building housing our bureau was one of those new constructions: a shabby, rectangular example of Soviet-style architecture. The elevators were routinely out of order, power outages were common, the guaranteed air-conditioning rarely worked, and the two rooms we had been given were located just across the hall from a foul-smelling bathroom, which also usually didn't work. A public water boiler downstairs provided hot water that was delivered in thermoses daily by the elderly men who were supposed to keep watch over the building, but spent most of their time sitting in the lobby, smoking and chatting. The water gave our instant coffee an unpleasant industrial odor. Seeking to save money, Jeanee Von Essen was reluctant to authorize purchases of what I thought were essential office furnishings. Initially we were forced to mount our editing machines on top of equipment cases, while I tried to manage the bureau from a rickety desk without direct-dial telephones, a computer, a fax, or a copying machine. As Atlanta was unwilling to pay for a new car, we bought a creaky 1981 Toyota from CBS for $3,000 after the network declared the vehicle hopelessly obsolete and ordered its Beijing staff to get rid of it.

Pleased as I was to be working outside the confined and isolated atmosphere of the diplomatic compounds, there were days when I cast an envious eye on my colleagues' relatively clean, spacious, well-equipped, and efficient premises. I was even more jealous of their apartments. I had applied for three flats in the compounds for Cynde, Mitch, and for me and my family as soon as we arrived. But the opening of China had produced something of a gold rush. More and more foreigners—diplomats, reporters, and business people— were flooding into Beijing, and demand for housing was acute. The Foreign Ministry's notorious Diplomatic Service Bureau (DSB), which controlled access to these apartments, kept putting me off, insisting there was a waiting list of five hundred families. The scuttlebutt among my colleagues was that only a series of lavish banquets or a well-placed bribe could put one at the head of the DSB's list. I had little leverage without the budget or authorization from CNN to pay for either.

Nor did the company feel able to pay for us to stay in one of the city's few modern, Western-style, joint-venture hotels. Instead Lynne, four-month-old Daniel, and I joined Cynde and Mitch in taking rooms at a decrepit local hostelry called the Ritan Hotel. Its lobby was in perpetual darkness, and the food in the restaurant was inedible, forcing us to go out for every single meal. A fleet of taxis stood outside, but with their wages guaranteed by the socialist "iron rice bowl"—the cradle-to-grave social-security system—the drivers appeared to have little interest in taking us, or any other passengers, anywhere. Our eighth-floor "suite" of three tiny adjoining rooms was dusty, dimly lit, and full of cockroaches. Occasionally the floor attendants would arrive with brooms and rags to make a show of cleaning, but usually, displaying the same enthusiasm as the cabbies, they stayed in their own room down the hall, chatting, smoking, reading the newspaper, and ignoring our requests for help. It took eight months, and repeated trips to the DSB office, where I would deposit a screaming Daniel on the desk of a surly official and say, "Are you going to force this infant to spend his whole childhood in a hotel?" before we were given an apartment. Our new home was poorly built and overlooked what was then a construction site, as the DSB frantically sought to meet the demand for accommodations by adding buildings to the compound as fast it possible. On our first night, all the bathroom tiles crashed down on Lynne while she was taking a shower. Yet it was large and airy, and for ordinary Chinese it would have been an almost unimaginable luxury. We were grateful—and lucky—to be there. Cynde and Mitch would remain on the DSB waiting list for two more years.

Even our four-year-old Labrador retriever, Sherlock, was caught up in the Chinese bureaucratic maze. We had briefly left him behind in London. Now we were having him shipped to Beijing. Late one afternoon, with a blazing red sun setting over the fabled Western Hills, Lynne and I eagerly drove to the airport to collect him. It took two hours before the staff in the air-cargo department would confirm he was even on the flight. But our problems were only beginning. With the relevant documents, I walked into the customs office. A sullen official sat behind a bare wooden desk in a dingy room and glared at me.

"What *danwei* is your dog?" he snapped. "To what 'work unit' does this dog belong?"

I stared back. "Excuse me?"

Sherlock, bewildered after his eighteen-hour flight from London, peered through his traveling cage.

"Everyone in China must have a work unit," the customs officer repeated in his monotone voice, referring to the Chinese Communist practice of assigning all individuals to a *danwei*, or unit. For most Chinese, the *danwei* not only controlled wages and bonuses but also access to housing, education, medical care, travel permits, even marriage and divorce. In China, without a *danwei*, you were virtually a nonperson.

"Unless it has a unit," he went on, "this dog is not allowed to enter the country."

"But you're not talking about a person," I protested, trying to control my annoyance. "This is just a dog. It doesn't have a work unit. Beside, I have all the necessary papers, rabies certificate, health declaration, the airline waybill."

The young man gave me a look of thinly disguised contempt.

He stood and puffed out his chest, the buttons on the epaulets of his black uniform reflecting the glow of the single light bulb hanging from the ceiling. With an attitude suggesting a determination to defend the socialist motherland from Sherlock and all other dubious foreign interlopers, he declared, "No unit, no entry," and walked away. If this unpleasant encounter was a reflection of the ossified bureaucracy Zhao Ziyang and the reformers were trying to change, I thought, they were going to have an uphill struggle.

Daniel, nestled in Lynne's arms, began to howl. It took four more hours of tortuous negotiations, and the intervention of a senior customs officer who seemed to take pity on Daniel, before we were allowed to take the dog with us for delivery to a friend at the Associated Press, Charlene Fu. She had generously agreed to look after him until we were assigned an apartment. Sherlock still didn't have a unit, but he was extremely relieved to be out of his cage. His first act after setting foot on Chinese soil was to pee for five minutes straight.

Despite the frustrations and difficulties, I was thrilled to be in China. Apart from the Thirteenth Congress, no big stories broke during the first few months of my assignment. I was grateful, for I needed the time to brush up on my rusty Chinese, to get the bureau running, and above all, to settle in and take the pulse of the capital and its people. Wheeling Daniel in his stroller, Lynne and I joined the huge crowds celebrating the autumn harvest at Moon Festival, marveling at the acrobats in red, green, and pink silk pants showing off their skills on stilts, the musicians playing traditional Chinese instruments, and the vendors selling bowls of steaming hot noodles. On October 1, National Day, we strolled through the cheerful throngs that packed Tiananmen Square in a mood of optimistic celebration. We wandered the streets and the parks, where old men carried birds in ornate bamboo cages while others did *taiji* exercises in the early morning; we poked through markets bursting with vegetables, rice, fish flopping in plastic buckets, and slabs of meat still dripping blood; we peered at the busy families in the *hutong* courtyards, and watched women cook as children played and old folks squatted by the side of the tiny, teeming lane, gossiping or playing cards. This was the China that entranced us, not the petty bureaucrats and the surly staff in the hotel. These public rituals were a welcome antidote both to our dismal accommodations and to the isolation in which most foreigners in Beijing tended to live. Lynne and I knew we were barely scratching the surface of a reality both less colorful and more complex, but we always returned from such excursions with renewed enthusiasm for being in China.

Daniel caused a sensation. A fair-haired, blue-eyed boy in a society where male children were still prized over little girls was a rare sight. He was inevitably surrounded by Chinese mothers with infants tucked inside rickety bamboo prams, who grilled us on every detail, wanting to know what we fed him, how we disciplined him, what kind of clothes he wore, and how we got him to sleep. It was clear that Doctor Spock's book had not been translated into Chinese. We received numerous friendly lectures from the many Chinese women we met who thought we were doing everything wrong. "It's too windy. You haven't bundled him up enough to bring him outside!" "Why is he still in diapers?" We had brought hundreds of Pampers with us, and every time a colleague or friend went to Hong Kong, I asked them to bring back a fresh supply. Paper diapers were virtually unknown in China, where infants wore clothes with a slit in the back of their pants and parents pushed their children to "go" at a very early age. Many people were appalled by what they saw as our lack of strictness and our encouraging Daniel to explore his environment on his own. The Chinese swaddle their babies for the first few weeks of life and, for months afterward, tend to carry them around while discouraging independent activity—the earliest steps (we discovered) toward inculcating the strict social conformity so valued in Chinese culture.

Consumed as I was by the demands of my new job, I tended to shrug off these admonitions, leaving Lynne to cope with a new and stressful environment. A first-time mother who was adjusting to caring for an infant far away from family and friends, Lynne found the incessant prying, however well-intentioned, to be unnerving and irritating. Still, it was apparent to us how much the Chinese loved children. They dressed them colorfully while they themselves wore drab attire. The adults seemed to put into tending their youngsters the emotions that they repressed in dealing with each other. Time and again, we discovered that having Daniel with us was an invaluable way to break through the awkwardness that inevitably surrounded our encounters on the streets.

In addition to meeting ordinary citizens in the rounds of daily life, I also sought out Chinese journalists and intellectuals, foreign businessmen and diplomats, and my fellow reporters. So much had changed in the three short years since my last visit. The reforms that Deng Xiaoping had introduced a decade earlier to drag a still-backward China into the modern world were producing a far-reaching transformation. Orthodox communism was being replaced by elements of a market economy, allowing the Chinese people a measure of personal freedom unthinkable during the Mao years. Refrigerators, electric rice cookers, televisions, and other consumer goods beckoned from new department stores. The loosening of controls produced an explosion of private businesses offering services that had been lacking for many years—from barbershops and shoe and bike repair, to restaurants and privately run bars. The streets of Beijing and other urban areas boasted a new class of Chinese entrepreneur, the *getihu*—which is literally translated as the "individual household."

Inspired by Deng's exhortation that "to get rich is glorious" and by admiring reports in the government-controlled media about individuals whose efforts had turned them into instant millionaires, a whole generation seemed to be making up for all the years that money and material goods were denounced as "bourgeois decadence." Walking around Beijing, I could see the stalls of these merchants on almost every street corner. In a lane near our bureau was one such *getihu*, a fast-talking young man named Dong Aizhi, who wore tight pants and had his hair swept back Elvis Presley–style. In a large rented room, Dong, previously a worker at a rubber-processing factory, had opened a beauty parlor. Above the door was a sign in crudely written English: MAKE YOU BEAUTY AND PLEASURE HAIR SALON. Despite his lack of experience or training as a hairdresser, Dong cut hair and gave permanents to young people seeking to change their appearance to keep up with the changing times. He reveled in his independence. "It's much better to be your own boss," he told us as we took pictures in the salon one morning while Hong Kong pop music blared from a tape recorder. "I can earn so much more money, and nobody bothers me." That was not entirely true. Dong still faced enormous bureaucratic headaches and needed multiple official authorizations to stay in business, since the Communist Party had only recently begun to acknowledge the existence of private business. But he often earned more in a day now than the seventy yuan he had earned each month in the factory.

Equally striking was the widespread public fascination with all things Western. I had noticed this attraction on my 1984 trip, but now the speed with which the austerity and cultural deprivation of the Mao era was giving way to popular fashions long condemned by Party ideologues was mind-boggling. In Beijing and other cities, everyone seemed to be scrambling to learn English and to adopt Western-style fashions, music, and ideas. One sunny autumn afternoon, Mitch, Cynde, and I drove to the gaudy Beijing Exhibition Center to cover China's first International Cosmetics Exhibition. This was a very big event. Under the numbing conformity of Maoism, all makeup had been banned. Even now, with the current gradual relaxation, foreign cosmetics were generally a forbidden pleasure, and questions remained about the propriety of women wearing lipstick or eye shadow. But it was clear the climate was changing. We arrived at the Exhibition Center to discover thousands of impatient young women pushing, shoving, and scuffling with police. They weren't dissidents but would-be consumers, frantic to get in the door. After a perfunctory attempt to maintain order, the overwhelmed cops fell back, allowing the excited patrons to pour inside. We joked about covering a "makeup riot" as we followed them. In the main exhibition hall, the throng crowded around displays set up by foreign cosmetics companies such as Max Factor, Clinique, and Elizabeth Arden. They marveled as heavily made-up, stylishly dressed women from Hong Kong demonstrated the fine points of mascara and manicures. "For a long time we had to dress so plainly," one young Beijing woman complained to me. "I have no idea how to dress up or wear makeup. But I certainly intend to learn." With Max Factor eye shadow costing more than the average Chinese earned in a month, it was clear to me that imported cosmetics would remain little more than a dream, but now, at least, a dream that was politically acceptable.

The young Chinese weren't the only dreamers I encountered. "It's an unbelievable market, the greatest in the world," one sales executive from Elizabeth Arden gushed to me. "Can you imagine— a billion Chinese wearing makeup!" I smiled to myself. The wide-eyed cosmetics company officials displayed the kind of naive enthusiasm I often encountered among Western—and especially

American—business people during that rosy period. Lured by heady visions of the potential profits of the immense Chinese market, companies were spending millions of dollars to get a foot in the door.

Charting these and other consequences of the reforms and of the new open-door policy became the central focus of my reporting. We covered the opening of China's first Kentucky Fried Chicken outlet, located just a few hundred yards from the Great Hall of the People. It offered a commanding view of Tiananmen Square, allowing Chinese customers eager to spend the exorbitant sum of ten yuan to munch their southern-style chicken, mashed potatoes, and gravy while admiring Chairman Mao's mausoleum across the street. We interviewed executives from Western advertising firms and covered signing ceremonies for one new Sino-American joint venture after another. We followed the tourists to the Beifang Shooting Range, where China's leading arms exporter, the NORINCO company, sought to capitalize on the invasion of visitors by offering them the chance to fire everything from handguns to heavy artillery—for a price. We trekked out to the laboratory of entrepreneur Zhao Zhangguang, who had gotten rich marketing his Formula 101, a reputed cure for baldness. We watched leggy Chinese models parade down the catwalk in tight miniskirts and provocative blouses at a fashion show staged by a Shanghai silk factory, while the factory's marketing manager spelled out ambitious plans to market Chinese-made clothes abroad. Another Shanghai factory produced a Chinese version of Monopoly, the ultimate capitalist board game. The factory had sold hundreds of thousands of copies and could not keep up with demand. "We never had this sort of thing here before," factory manager Li Zhihui told us. "Buying houses, real estate, bankruptcy. For people to learn how to make and handle money is good for the country."

It was exciting to watch the Chinese enjoy new freedoms, wealth, and opportunity, and it was moving to sense them coming alive again and beginning to interact with the outside world. On CNN's news broadcasts, our reports were a revelation. China was so distant and obscure that the regular exposure to how ordinary people lived, worked, played, and thought helped our viewers see the Chinese as less alien, more like themselves. The network aired virtually every spot we did. The demand from show producers for new material, especially lifestyle stories, never ceased. At a time when my friends at the CBS and ABC Beijing bureaus had trouble getting on the air, and my old employer NBC didn't even bother to maintain a resident correspondent in the Chinese capital, I felt we were filling a major gap in public understanding of the largest nation in the world.

Our reports were even filtering back to China too. One consequence of the open-door policy was that many of the new joint-venture hotels in Beijing were able to install satellite dishes to receive foreign satellite TV broadcasts, including CNN. Given the generally tight control over the media, I found this an amazing development. The explanation seemed to be that satellite television was an issue the authorities in Beijing had never had any reason to think about. In the absence of any regulations, hotels and other units simply made their own deals with local public security officials, who appeared willing to tolerate the new medium.

Yet as I charted the unfolding changes in China, I found myself confronting mixed emotions. I had long ago lost the last of my youthful illusions about the Mao era. But I wondered whether China's flirtation with consumerism would become a new faith as unquestioningly accepted as the abandoned Maoist dream. As a radical student, I had rejected the competitiveness and materialism in my own country, which the Chinese were now so enthusiastically embracing. Would the harsh principles of the market work in a country as undeveloped and overpopulated as the People's Republic? I could understand the appeal of an exotic foreign import like Kentucky Fried Chicken to a people who had suffered an endless diet of political propaganda and grim living conditions, but I was troubled by a sense that many Chinese, especially the young people, had lost their way, scornful of the values and ideas of earlier generations, but with no new substantial positive values of their own.

"I do what I want to do. I don't want anybody telling me what to do," an attractive young woman named Wang Shanshan told me one evening. A former nursery-school teacher, she had opened her own bar with the help of some friends, one of the first such privately run establishments in Beijing. It was cold, tiny, and full of cigarette smoke. But here Shanshan could wear the latest Western fashions, indulge her passion for imported rock videos, and escape China's still strong pressure for social and political conformity. She was hardly a dissident, though. "I don't care about politics," she insisted when I asked for her views on current developments in the country. "I care about my life. That's what's important. I have the right to control my life."

So strong was the sense of youthful alienation created by the collapse of faith in socialist ideals and the spread of a consumer culture that, in 1988, two Chinese intellectuals published a book on the phenomenon. *The Fourth Generation* described how, in contrast to the veteran communists who staged the revolution, the bureaucrats who administered it in the 1950s, and the Red Guards who turned everything upside down in the 1960s and 1970s, the current generation of Chinese youth was turning inward, motivated not by politics or ideology but by the country's new materialism. Chatting in our bureau one evening, one of the authors, twenty-five-year-old Zhang Yongjie, said, "In the past, the value system here put the group or the collective first. An individual had to adapt to that. But today, young people are increasingly looking out for themselves. Getting what the individual wants has now become the top priority."

Into this spiritual void came a growing public interest in religion. In contrast to my secretive encounter in Yunan nearly ten years before with Philip Xia Bing, the persecuted Christian who'd just been freed from a labor camp, I was now able, with official permission, to spend my first Christmas in China at the Chongwenmen Protestant Church in Beijing. Built at the turn of the century, it had been closed during the Cultural Revolution, when practicing Christians were denounced both for their religion and for the Western "contamination" such beliefs represented to the Red Guards. The church had reopened just a few years earlier and now attracted hundreds of worshipers. Many were elderly, and from their deeply lined faces and haunted eyes, I could imagine the terrible ordeals they had undergone.

I spoke with the church pianist, a white-haired man named Lu Jia. In a quiet, unemotional voice, he told me how his fingernails had been pulled out during the Cultural Revolution to prevent him from playing the piano. Merely to be in the church now represented for him an almost unimaginable triumph of faith. Officiating at the service was the Reverend Kan Xueqing, a portly, bespectacled man who had been through his own hell in the 1960s, although he made it clear that he didn't want to talk about his experiences. With a few colored light bulbs hung from the altar to create a Christmas spirit,

Kan read from the Bible and led the congregation in a series of traditional Western Christmas songs sung in Chinese. A surprising number of young people were in attendance, perhaps as many as half of the thousand-strong congregation. These men and women had grown up solely on a diet of communist thought and, unlike their elders, had almost no exposure to other ideas. When I asked some of them to explain the appeal of going to church, I heard a familiar refrain. They had lost their faith in the Communist Party, like many other young Chinese. The church offered spiritual fulfillment they could not find elsewhere.

In this relatively relaxed atmosphere Chinese journalists cautiously began to press for more openness. Soon after the Thirteenth Congress, in a clear signal of the reformists' political strength, Party chief Zhao Ziyang announced that the Communist Party's theoretical journal *Red Flag*, associated with hard-line ideologues, would cease publication. It was replaced by a new publication, *Qiu Shi*, or "Seeking Truth," a title drawn from one of Deng Xiaoping's favorite pro-reform admonitions: "Seek truth from facts." Increasingly I noticed the boldness with which normally timid Chinese reporters now asked questions at news conferences and the prevalence of exposés of corruption and official misconduct in Chinese newspapers. Because of CNN's formal cooperative relationship with China Central Television, I was in close touch with Chinese TV reporters and editors, who began to express cautious hope that CCTV might begin to resemble a more conventional, less ideological news organization. It became clear that part of CCTV's motivation for collaborating with CNN, and in assigning CCTV staff to my bureau, was to expose its own personnel to the inner workings of a Western TV news operation.

As Beijing's harsh, dusty winter turned into spring, we visited "English Corner," a wooded area of the Purple Bamboo Park in northwest Beijing where every Sunday hundreds of Chinese spontaneously gathered to practice their English, with a visiting foreigner if possible or with each other if necessary. Despite their often rudimentary language skills, the conversations were animated as the crowds of people struggled to articulate their thoughts, displaying an almost desperate desire to communicate with the outside world. "This is the time for China to open even wider," one young man told me. "English is a worldwide language, so we must learn it." As we discussed topics ranging from the Iran-Iraq war to the American women's movement, nobody seemed to mind the presence of our camera. There was a sense of freedom in the way people talked to us, as if the large crowds and the entirely uncontroversial purpose of improving language skills made "English Corner" a politically safe place for Chinese to mingle with foreigners and speak their mind. "People can say whatever they want here," said one man. "We don't have to worry about getting in trouble." I thought back to my encounter with a group of Chinese on the street in Shanghai in 1973. Although we had discussed little more than the weather, the police had swiftly shooed me away. Now Cynde, Mitch, and I lingered all morning and returned regularly, with no interference from the authorities.

We knew, however, that even in this time of relative relaxation, the government, firmly convinced that all foreign journalists were spies, kept close tabs on everything we were doing. There was no question that our phones were tapped at the bureau, as they were at the hotel, and, after we moved in, at our apartments. Our driver Lu Boqian, and office assistant Li Sanwei, although supplied by China Central Television and not the Foreign Ministry, were still required to report on our activities. So too was Li Xiu, the young Chinese woman the Diplomatic Service Bureau assigned to us when Lynne and I asked to hire a baby-sitter for Daniel. Her presence was an intrusion that created tremendous tension at home, as all of us learned to be discreet in discussing our plans, opinions, and, especially, our dealings with Chinese people. We assumed that we were watched, if not actually followed, everywhere we went. The surveillance was part of a system of controls aimed at preventing reporters from learning too much about how Chinese society actually worked.

In most instances, permission to visit or film a school, factory, government ministry, business, hospital, farm, theater, or any other Chinese work unit, required authorization from its Foreign Affairs Office, or *waiban*. Usually we were asked to put all the questions we intended to raise in writing ahead of time, and *waiban* officials invariably insisted on accompanying us everywhere we went, trying to prevent free and spontaneous exchanges with the people we were reporting on. Regulations for travel outside Beijing were equally rigid. All trip proposals, including a list of interview questions and details of exactly what pictures we wanted to take, had to be submitted ten days in advance to the *waiban* in the city or province we wished to visit. Requests to cover stories that might reflect unflatteringly on the system were usually rejected, and I quickly learned to disguise my intentions in drafting story ideas for submission to the authorities. I discovered as well that failure to spell out every single step carried a price. In the northeastern city of Shenyang, for example, we once requested permission to visit an automobile plant. Our local guides duly drove us to a plant one morning, where we discovered there were no workers in sight. The assembly line was shut down for the day, and all we had to shoot were silent machines. "You asked permission to visit an auto factory," our guide replied when I complained. "We have granted your request. You didn't inform us you wanted to film the workers, too!"

Most frustrating of all was the way in which this system was deliberately designed to prevent normal contact with the people. Individuals brave or foolhardy enough to become friends with foreigners, especially foreign journalists, at a minimum risked pressure and criticism from their work unit, if not harassment or worse from the security police. With every encounter I worried whether I was putting a Chinese friend or colleague at risk. Making real friends became a complicated, tension-filled, and uncertain process.

Yet I was determined not to be defeated by the challenges the system posed to living and working in Beijing. Over time, Lynne and I developed a number of good Chinese friends. Among them was Yang, a young reporter for the business section of the *China Daily*, the government's official English-language newspaper, set up in 1981. We met at a news conference that Lynne, who had started freelancing for London's *Financial Times*, also attended. Our initial discussion centered on the politically safe topic of iron and steel production. But Yang seemed eager to stay in touch, and soon we began to meet regularly. He introduced us to his wife Lili, an attractive young woman who had studied English in college. Yang was a sophisticated man who knew a great deal about the Chinese economy and retained a keen interest in economic and political affairs, both in his own country and abroad. But over frequent meals, he made clear that working at the *China Daily*, despite the gradual moves toward more openness, remained an exceedingly frustrating experience. He described a system, not only at the *China Daily*, but throughout the government-run media, in which even the blandest of stories were frequently spiked for fear of offending senior leaders; where positive stories were regularly manufactured, regardless of the truth; and where foreign news items were carefully sanitized in case China's "foreign relations" might be affected. "Eighty percent of what we know we aren't allowed to publish, even with the reforms," he complained to us, "while eighty percent of what you foreigners publish, you don't know what you're talking about!"

Yang and Lili lived with his mother in a decrepit house with communal toilets and no running water, fronting on a courtyard in an old *hutong* off Changan Street. One evening, ignoring the still-strong social pressure against being friends with foreigners, they invited us for dinner. Groping our way through the darkened, unlit alley, we found the two-room residence. There was barely enough space to move in the tiny living room, but Yang's mother had somehow cooked up an elaborate feast on two small burners, which we ate while squeezed around a plain circular table illuminated by a single light bulb. Most of the conversation centered on Yang and Lili's desire to travel to the United States. For them, and for many young people in China, the reform process and the more tolerant political climate had opened up previously unimaginable possibilities. Both seemed almost desperately eager to experience life outside the still-rigid confines of Chinese society, to soak up new ideas, acquire new skills, and seek new opportunities. Because we were journalists, Yang and Lili were convinced that we had some special clout at the United States Embassy that could help them secure visas. In China, where almost everything was done on the basis of *guanxi*, or connections, it was not an unreasonable assumption, but it was not true.

Lynne and I were to meet many Chinese who, based on their experience of how their own system worked, would ask us for a similar favor. Although we did try to offer whatever advice we could, I don't think Yang, Lili, or other Chinese friends ever fully accepted our insistence that we couldn't go through the back door and help them obtain the coveted permission to travel to the U.S. Some months later, without any assistance from us, Yang and Lili received their American visas and left to study in Philadelphia. They were there when the tanks rolled into Tiananmen Square in 1989. It would be several years before either of them would return to China, even for a visit.

At the end of the meal, inspired by the delicious food, Lynne asked Lili where she could take a Chinese cooking class. Pulling out a copy of the *Beijing Evening News*, Lili found an advertisement for a cooking school and gave Lynne the address. Surprisingly, we were still naive enough to think it would be that simple.

The school was for trainee chefs, and virtually every head in the room turned when Lynne walked in the door. But the young men seemed friendly enough, gathering round in a curious crowd, eager to chat with the attractive visitor. When Lynne explained in Mandarin her desire to study Chinese cuisine, the severe, middle-aged woman who appeared to be in charge raised no immediate objection, and agreed to let her remain for that day's session. As soon as the class started, the director made an announcement. "Please welcome the foreign reporter who has come to watch our class. Let us give her a round of applause." Once the clapping stopped, the students swiftly averted their eyes. When the session ended, no one lingered to chat. Lynne realized that by introducing her as a journalist, the director had, in a typically subtle Chinese way, sent a clear signal to everyone in the room to keep their distance from the dangerous foreigner.

"You are welcome to continue to study here," the director told Lynne. "But you must first get permission from the Chongwenmen district Foreign Affairs Office." Excited and still hopeful, Lynne came home and immediately called the Chongwenmen *waiban*. After repeated attempts, she finally reached a surly man who told her to call the *waiban* of the Beijing city government. There she spoke with an official who, although more polite, was no more helpful. "If you want to study cooking," he told her, "why don't you contact the Diplomatic Service Bureau? They are trained to help foreign guests. They will send an English-speaking chef right to your home. There is no need to worry about attending classes anywhere else in Beijing." Lynne was crushed. Sharing an experience with local Chinese was her chief reason for wanting to take cooking classes. For days she raged at the way the system kept her cooped up in the foreigners' ghetto. The one class she had attended provided a new recipe for stir-fried beef, but the experience left a bitter taste.

Having Chinese visit our new apartment, which the DSB had finally provided us in April 1988, was equally fraught. At an embassy reception at the Great Wall Sheraton Hotel, where Chinese officials authorized to meet with foreigners mingled awkwardly with frustrated diplomats seeking new insights on current political developments, I struck up a conversation with a burly, middle-aged man named Sheng who analyzed international politics at a government think tank. To my surprise, he accepted an invitation for dinner and we quickly agreed on a date. He explained, however, that he could not come directly to our compound. If his driver knew his final destination, he told us, it would be reported to his superiors and he would get into trouble. We agreed that Lynne would pick him up in front of the Sheraton Hotel. On the appointed evening, the rendezvous went off without a hitch. Although he was terrified of Sherlock, I could see that Sheng was pleased to be at our house. But he was also exceedingly nervous, repeatedly darting his head toward the window while limiting his conversation to vague pleasantries. We had barely finished dessert when he announced that he must go or else his driver meeting him at the Sheraton might become suspicious. Lynne drove him back to the hotel. When we tried to reach him again, he didn't return our phone calls. We presumed his fear of foreign contamination outweighed his genuine desire to be friends.

The remarkable place I now called home was vibrantly alive, frustratingly opaque, compellingly interesting, and maddeningly secretive. Tyrannized by its history even in the midst of liberalization, China was changing literally in front of our eyes. Figuring it out was an all-consuming passion. Apart from talking about our cheerful, growing baby, it dominated my discussions with Lynne, who shared my fascination, and it was virtually the only topic of conversation when I got together with my colleagues in the Beijing press corps. In the mid-1980s, China was still considered a remote and difficult assignment, primarily attracting those with a special interest or background in Chinese affairs. My closest friends among the resident correspondents were usually those who, like me, had long been drawn to China, studying its language, history, politics, and culture in the hope of one day having a chance to probe its mysteries firsthand. It was an obsession that produced as much anguish as exhilaration, but, once you were hooked, China seemed impossible to put aside.

Thrown together in the foreign ghetto, we developed a camaraderie based on our common desire to escape from our gilded cage and peer inside the Chinese system. With few movies, concerts, or other forms of nightlife, and most local restaurants, apart from those in the handful of joint-venture hotels, closed by 7:00 or 7:30 P.M., our favorite form of recreation became intense dinner-table discussion and debate, comparing notes on the day's events and how we had covered them, and swapping ideas on the latest political trends, rumors, and gossip.

My regular companions were a colorful lot. Dave Schweisberg, who arrived in Beijing a month after I did to become bureau chief for United Press International, was chain-smoking, bearded, and overweight, with a keen mind and an acerbic wit. A veteran with previous stints in Hong Kong and Tokyo, he had stayed on at UPI— even though the news agency had been in chronic decline for decades and now hovered near bankruptcy—because it gave him the freedom to do what he wanted. He and I quickly became friends and collaborators, working on stories, playing squash together, and sharing sources, tips, and insights. He and his Hong Kong–Chinese girlfriend also fell in love with our dog and cared for him for four months, after Schweisberg's competitor at the AP, our friend Charlene Fu, decided her own one-room flat was too small to accommodate Sherlock indefinitely while we waited for an apartment. Our professional partnership benefited both of us. Cynde, Mitch, and I could rely on UPI's monitoring of events on a minute-by-minute basis, the staple of wire service reporting, while we provided Dave and his understaffed, underfunded, and overworked, but exceptionally aggressive and well-informed, staff access to the resources and clout of a major TV network. In a city of limited entertainment, Dave was also part of an unusual Beijing creation, a rock group called the Back Door Band, in honor of the Chinese practice of using back-door connections to get things done. His fellow musicians were an unlikely combo: a guitar-playing political officer from the U.S. Embassy and two musically talented Western businessmen. Performing at parties and, occasionally, at local discos, the Back Door Band livened up many a dreary Beijing night, and gave me and my crew a colorful local feature to file for CNN.

Zorana Bakovic was the correspondent of the Yugoslavian newspaper *Delo*. A Serb from Belgrade married to a Croat from Zagreb, she had first lived in China as a student in the 1970s, becoming a government interpreter before moving on to journalism. She had spent so many years in Beijing that she confessed to feeling more Chinese than Yugoslav. I admired her astonishingly good Chinese and her remarkable range of Chinese contacts and sources, especially among intellectuals. I thought she was the most insightful foreign journalist in the capital, living confirmation of my long-standing view that the Yugoslavs, because of their socialist background and years of "comradely" relations with the Chinese, had a particularly good understanding of how things worked in the People's Republic. She had a son the same age as our Daniel, and we often spent weekend afternoons together talking politics while the children played.

My chief professional rival was Jack Sheahan of CBS. A veteran of two decades at the network, he had been in Beijing for several years. Although he had no China background, he was a tough and aggressive reporter. He was also a charming and courtly eccentric who wore only black and held elaborate dinner parties replete with caviar and champagne. His chief frustration was the difficulty of getting on the air at a time when China was no longer in the headlines and CBS headquarters seemed to have little interest in the story. Although we were officially competitors, Jack was privately delighted with our presence in Beijing, hoping that a steady diet of China stories on CNN would rekindle interest on the part of his own editors. To the extent that he could, he went out of his way to help us and I was happy to reciprocate. The notion of the CNN and CBS Beijing correspondents collaborating would have horrified both our bosses. But ten thousand miles from the head office, struggling to operate in a system that treated all reporters equally badly, conventional notions of competition frequently made no sense.

Lhasa, the capital of Tibet, had been shaken by a series of violent demonstrations against Chinese rule just days after I began my China assignment in September 1987. Thousands of angry Tibetans, demanding independence for their homeland, fought in the streets with Chinese police and soldiers. Nearly a dozen protestors were killed by gunfire. It was the worst outbreak of anti-Chinese violence since Beijing suppressed a pro-independence uprising in Tibet in 1959, forcing the country's spiritual leader, the Dalai Lama, to flee into exile in India.

Much as we wanted to, there was no way we could get to Lhasa. Our camera equipment was still stuck in customs at Beijing Airport, and it would take almost a month of difficult negotiations before we could bring the gear into the country. Cynde, Mitch, and I were overwhelmed with endless application forms for press cards, residency permits, reentry visas, health certificates, drivers' licenses, and bank accounts. Indeed it took so long to open an account at the Bank of China that we ran out of money. I was forced to borrow $5,000 from Jack Sheahan simply in order to cover our daily expenses. Some of our Beijing-based colleagues, however, did make it to the Tibetan capital by ignoring the ten-day advance notice rule, flying to Chengdu in Sichuan province, and getting on the first available flight from there to Lhasa. To my surprise, the Chinese authorities, either through confusion or indecision, briefly allowed them to file on the tense situation they found. A few days later, though, the government cut all phone and telex links, ordered the journalists to leave, and declared that from now on the ten-day rule would be rigidly enforced. The result was a virtual news blackout that lasted almost a year.

Undeterred, I submitted monthly travel applications to the Lhasa *waiban*. I was eager to visit not only because the conflict between the Chinese and the Tibetans was a complex and compelling story, but because Tibet appealed to my sense of adventure. It was remote and forbidding, its very name evoking images of mystery and romance. I used every connection I could find to push our case. In the spring of 1988, the United Nations' Beijing office agreed to let us accompany a World Food Program delegation, only to have the *waiban* say no. In the summer, Tibet historian Tom Grunfeld, a longtime friend and fellow CCAS activist from the 1970s with good access to senior Chinese officials responsible for the territory, was allowed to visit Lhasa, where he lobbied on our behalf. Two months later, we were thrilled to receive a telex from the Lhasa *waiban* inviting CNN to Tibet. On September 18, 1988, Cynde, Mitch, and I swallowed our altitude sickness pills and boarded a creaky Air China Boeing 707 for the Tibetan capital.

Surrounded by soaring, snowcapped mountains, an average of 15,000 feet above sea level, and dotted with huge, crystal-clear lakes, vast open spaces, and Buddhist monasteries, Tibet seemed to me to be another world. Driving in from the airport, where, to our surprise and relief, no one from the *waiban* had bothered to meet us, we passed horse-drawn carts piled high with hay and groups of men and women in traditional Tibetan dress working the fields. I saw a hundred-foot tall Buddha, painted in blue and gold, carved into the side of a mountain. Entering Lhasa, I could not take my eyes off the whitewashed walls, terraced stairs, and huge brown towers of the Potala, the Dalai Lama's former palace. It dominated the landscape, looming starkly against the deep blue sky and the distant mountains. In the late afternoon, the sun cast a golden shadow over the city. The effect was magical.

We checked into the Lhasa Holiday Inn, a symbol of China's cautious efforts to open Tibet to the outside world. It was less than half full. Although my crew and I had no problems with the city's 12,000-foot altitude, for visitors unable to cope, an oxygen mask lay on the bedside table in each room. The coffee shop served "yakburgers," which I found stringy and tough, with a slightly gamey flavor, yet surprisingly tasty.

The next morning, with no sign of our minders from the *waiban*, we decided to strike out on our own to explore the capital. After decades of Chinese control, and in spite of Beijing's insistence that there were no serious problems between Tibetans and ethnic Han Chinese, it quickly became apparent that Lhasa was a city divided along racial lines. The Holiday Inn was located in the Chinese part of town, whose broad, bicycle-filled streets, drab, rectangular gray buildings, and scaffold-covered construction sites looked no different from that of any other urban area in China. The roads were lined with Chinese-run shops and stalls selling Chinese-made shoes, clothing, food, and other goods. Almost all the people I saw in this area were ethnic Han Chinese, who comprise over 90 percent of the population of the People's Republic, with other ethnic groups, including the Tibetans, making up the difference. Many of them were recent arrivals, drawn to the region by the economic opportunities of an untamed frontier, and encouraged by a central government eager to secure its political control. There was no doubt the Chinese dominated commercial as well as political life in Lhasa. In brief conversations, they seemed arrogant and disdainful of traditional Tibetan ways, viewing the locals as backward, dirty, and superstitious. "Han Chinese tend to think the Tibetans are lazy and won't work hard," a young Chinese woman told me. "There is a total lack of understanding. We are so different from them in terms of lifestyles, dress, and food. So, of course, the gulf is very deep."

A few minutes away, in the heart of Lhasa's old city, we came upon an utterly different scene: Tibetan faithful by the thousands, worshiping at the Jokhang Temple, the holiest shrine of Tibetan Buddhism. Before images of the Buddha dating back 1,300 years, crowds of people wearing colorful robes and mud-caked, fur-lined boots prostrated themselves over and over again, clasping their hands together and reaching out to touch the ground, sliding along a stone surface worn smooth by years of such devotions. Along the Barkhor, a sacred path around the Jokhang, we encountered an unending stream of pilgrims moving in a clockwise direction. Some prostrated themselves along the way, others sat on the ground, chanting, rocking back and forth, and twirling prayer wheels. A few, oblivious of the swirling crowds, sat in silent meditation. As we shot the scene, a young boy came over to us, raised his hand in a thumbs-up gesture, and said in a squeaky voice, "Dalai Lama, Dalai Lama." Next to him was a teenager with five photos of the Dalai Lama hanging around his neck. Amazed and enthralled, I found the scene both formidably picturesque and deeply moving, the expression of devotion and defiance all the more remarkable after decades in which the Buddhist faith at the heart of Tibet's culture and identity was the target of harsh Chinese repression.

We walked to a terrace overlooking the main square to take some high shots of the Jokhang with its two gold towers. On the way we passed small stalls selling pictures of the Dalai Lama, many of them showing him as a young man meeting Chairman Mao in 1954. Clever, I thought to myself; there was no way the Chinese authorities could object to that. As we filmed, a large open truck packed with fifty uniformed Chinese soldiers barreled through the square, a jarring contrast to the intensely religious scene I was watching. A young English-speaking Tibetan approached us. "All the Tibetan people love the Dalai Lama," he said to us under his breath. "We hope he will come back to Tibet."

Returning to the hotel, we discovered that our minders had been frantically looking for us. After a sharp warning not to take the camera outside the hotel without permission, they offered a *jieshao* and spelled out our official itinerary. It quickly became apparent that the authorities hoped to use our presence to show that tensions were easing, order had been restored, and traditional Tibetan religion and culture were flourishing under China's benevolent, modernizing rule. Over the next few days, we were taken to a primary school, Tibet University, and the local TV station to see how the Tibetan language was still in use; to the Academy of Social Science, where a Mandarin-speaking Tibetan academic tried to explain how the government was helping a backward society to modernize; and to a meeting with Mao Rubai, the Chinese Communist Party's deputy secretary for Tibet, widely rumored to be the most powerful figure in the territory. We were told it was his first television interview.

By Chinese standards, Mao Rubai was a moderate, committed to economic development, opening Tibet to the outside world, and tolerating religious activity. Polished and smooth, he patiently answered my questions for nearly an hour, but when I pushed him, his face tightened and I felt an undercurrent of anger in his voice. "Our policy is to protect normal religious activities," he declared. "But at the same time, we do not allow people to destroy public property or endanger the people's health. We will not allow that. The struggle against the separatists will continue. To stop the separatists from splitting the motherland, we had to arrest them." Mao Rubai's concern stemmed from more than just anxiety over street disorders in Lhasa. Although the various ethnic minorities in China, including the Tibetans, made up fewer than 10 percent of the total population, they inhabited a huge chunk of China's territory, much of it, like Tibet, remote but strategically vital border regions. For Beijing, I could see the specter of unrest in Tibet was a nightmare with broad implications. I was convinced that China would never voluntarily relinquish control over Tibet even though virtually every encounter we had with ordinary Tibetans left the impression of their overwhelming desire for independence.

From a distance the Ganden Monastery, cloaked in mist, its gold spires straddling a mountain ridge 14,000 feet above sea level, looked like a scene from the fictional land of Shangri-la. As our minivan edged closer, our sense of wonder was replaced by one of horror. The monastery, for seven hundred years a center of Tibetan Buddhist learning and home to five hundred monks, was a wreck, reminding me of a ruin from Greek or Roman times. It had been totally devastated by the Chinese in 1969, at the height of the Cultural Revolution. It was hard to believe that just a few years earlier it had been a vibrant religious institution. Slowly Cynde, Mitch, and I picked our way through piles of rubble, broken, jagged walls, and buildings with no roofs. In one corner was a slogan written in English: CHINESE GO BACK TO CHINA. In a hushed voice, Mitch turned to me and said, "This is how war must look."

But the story in Ganden, I discovered to my surprise, was not entirely bleak. Amid the destruction, the monastery was slowly coming back to life. That explained why the Lhasa *waiban* had taken us there. We were shown how the few remaining monks at Ganden were using donations and government funds to rebuild, fixing up temples, reprinting copies of the ancient scriptures, and recreating priceless paintings and sculptures. And I found this process under way at other religious centers too, such as the Drepung Monastery, where I saw worshipers spooning yak butter into urns to keep the candles on the altar going, and the Sera Monastery, where a dozen trainee monks in purple robes debated holy texts on a grassy, tree-shaded lawn.

It was clear the Chinese were not only permitting religious activity, but consciously trying to encourage the revival of traditional Tibetan culture. Whatever the horrors of the Cultural Revolution, the claims of critics outside China that Beijing was conducting a deliberate policy of religious oppression struck me as an incomplete and unsatisfactory explanation for the Tibet problem. The issue for the Chinese was that the Tibetans, unintimidated by repression, were also unimpressed by the current attempts at tolerance. Their religious beliefs and sense of independent national identity remained inseparable, with the monasteries the base for nationalist agitation. What the Chinese saw as a crackdown on political activism appeared to the Tibetans, and many others, to be a crackdown on religion. It was no surprise that I could feel the Tibetan animosity toward the Chinese everywhere we went.

Strolling with my crew along a corridor at the Sera Monastery, we came across a young monk sitting cross-legged against a red column and chanting. On his lap was a rectangular box holding a religious text. Seeing us walk by, he flipped the text over. On the other side were the English words FREE TIBET. With an impish grin, he beckoned us to take a picture. From down the corridor, another monk looked up and, seeing the scene, broke into a wide smile. As the camera rolled, I held a whispered discussion. "In March of this year, we had a demonstration here," the young monk told me. "The government sent a twenty-person team to investigate and throw the ringleaders out of the monastery. All Tibetans in their heart want an independent Tibet," he declared. "There will definitely be more protests. We will certainly have an independent Tibet. We want the Dalai Lama." As he finished his speech, he noticed our government guide walking up. Quickly flipping his sign over, he began to pray again, his chants echoing down the corridor.

Late one day, after our official program was over and our government minders had gone home, we draped a jacket over our camera and slipped out of the hotel, doing our best to appear as if we were simply taking a walk to enjoy the scenery. Our destination was a wooded area near the Lhasa River where we had agreed to meet a young, Chinese-speaking Tibetan man we had encountered on the street some days before. He was eager to talk on camera, but, fearing arrest if the authorities found out, he suggested the safest place for an interview would be an isolated spot along the riverbank. Sitting with his back to the camera, facing the river and the mountains beyond, he launched into an impassioned half-hour monologue as I anxiously looked around for Chinese police who, I thought, must have followed us.

"The Chinese say Tibet is part of China," he began. "We are completely different—our customs, culture, language, civilization. It was the Chinese who invaded Tibet. They say the Chinese government is improving the living standards of the people. They're only talking about the ethnic Han Chinese here, not us Tibetans." Given China's size and all-too-evident willingness to use force, I asked whether he thought independence for Tibet was anything more than a pipe dream. He sighed. "I know the possibility of independence is small," he replied. "Maybe our hopes don't amount to anything. We may never be independent. But I believe in our leader, the Dalai Lama. We will never give up." I admired this young man's passion and bravery as much as I doubted he would ever achieve his dream. He featured prominently, along with Mao Rubai and the others we interviewed, in a half-hour special on Tibet we prepared after returning to Beijing.

Fifteen months later, I sat in a sunlit reception room in the tiny Himalayan town of Dharmsala, India. Across from me, wearing a purple robe, wire-rimmed glasses, and large leather shoes, was the Dalai Lama. With a faint smile crossing his lips, he began to speak in a deep, rumbling voice. "The desire for freedom is something basic in human nature. It's an instinctive desire. It's there. No force can stop it. That is one of the main reasons why communism has been a failure everywhere."

We had gone to Dharmsala to interview the Dalai Lama just days before his departure for Norway to receive the Nobel Peace Prize in 1989. Since our visit to Tibet the previous year, renewed anti-Chinese rioting had led Beijing to impose martial law in Lhasa, and Chinese army tanks had crushed the democracy movement in Tiananmen Square. Honoring the man who was both the spiritual leader of Tibetan Buddhism and the political leader of Tibetan nationalism seemed an appropriate gesture at this moment of repression, despite the predictable outrage from Beijing.

Dharmsala, once a British summer retreat during the heyday of the Empire, was now an almost completely Tibetan town, headquarters for many of the hundred thousand Tibetans who had fled into exile with the Dalai Lama. After the tensions we had experienced in Lhasa, it was refreshing to see an authentic Tibetan community free of Chinese interference. At its core was the Dalai Lama. I found him a most remarkable man, who radiated a genuine spiritual aura but was at the same time modest, witty, insightful, and self-deprecating. As we began our interview, one of the light stands started to topple over. With extraordinary agility, the Dalai Lama leapt out of his chair and caught the stand before it hit the ground, to the immense gratitude of my camera crew. As we thanked him profusely, he replied with a laugh, "I've had a lot of practice reacting quickly. After all, I had to get out of Lhasa in a hurry in 1959 when the Chinese invaded!"

The Dalai Lama was in a contemplative mood, more interested in talking about the value of Tibetan culture than the mechanics of trying to negotiate with Beijing. Despite the Chinese government's harsh actions, and pressure within the Tibetan diaspora for him to take an even more militant posture, he clung to his insistence on nonviolence. "Some say the Dalai Lama is too soft. But I think that underneath my softness is a base of firmness. Sometimes I think softness will remain longer than a hard thing. You see, through violence, even if you achieve something, it creates new problems. Violence is like a very strong pill. It can cure some ailments, but it has very dangerous side effects."

With his quiet intensity, I could understand why the Dalai Lama was so venerated by the Tibetans and many others, and so disliked and feared by the Chinese. His faith in the face of terrible odds was inspiring. Meeting him brought home to me the difficulties of remaining impartial about Tibet. It was a land so unlike any other, with its awesome mountains, resilient people, ancient religion, decades of oppression, and mysterious attraction to the outside world, that the temptation to choose sides was overwhelming. In my heart, it was impossible not to root for the long-suffering Tibetans. My head told me it was a lost cause.

By the time Cynde, Mitch, and I returned from Tibet in late September 1988, the mood of optimism that had marked our first year in China had dissipated. Since the reformists' triumph at the Thirteenth Party Congress the previous October, the Chinese economy, freed from many of its constraints, had begun to career out of control. Convinced that price reform was the key to progress, Communist Party chief Zhao Ziyang, under the prodding of Deng Xiaoping, moved to allow prices for most goods to be determined by the laws of supply and demand. The result, not surprisingly, was an inflation rate of more than 20 percent, the worst since the founding of the People's Republic in 1949. The rising prices quickly eroded many of the economic benefits produced by the reforms and generated a sense of acute anxiety in a society where thirty years of government controls had kept the cost of virtually everything unchanged. As people desperately sought a hedge against inflation, there were bank runs, waves of panic buying and hoarding, and revived memories of the hyperinflation that swept China in the late 1940s, undermining support for Chiang Kai-shek's Kuomintang and helping to propel Mao Zedong's communists to victory.

China's race toward development had also spawned rampant corruption, profiteering, and nepotism among Party and government officials. I had to look no further than the manager of the building where I worked to see *guandao*, as official profiteering was called, in action. Portly and jolly, Manager Sun was in charge of the Television Services Building, as the premises housing our bureau was known. He ran a company that claimed a vague relationship to China Central Television but which in fact operated wholly on its own, trying to cash in on the country's economic boom. Apart from CNN, Manager Sun rented out office space to a couple of other foreign companies. Much of the rest of the building was used for a series of unsuccessful restaurant and nightclub ventures. The most puzzling aspect, though, were the TV sets and other electronic goods I regularly saw piled up in boxes by the elevator. Initially I couldn't figure out to whom they belonged or how they got there. Later, from talking to other building employees, I learned that manager Sun had been running a scam. He had acquired these products at minimal cost by using his official connections, and was reselling them—I was never sure to whom—at vastly higher prices, reaping a tidy profit in the process. Manager Sun was hardly unique. Many officials exploited their special access to obtain highly coveted goods for resale on the booming black market. Repeatedly I heard people complain that *guanxi*, or back-door connections, were the only way to get ahead. Few people were caught or punished for their misdeeds, but Manager Sun was unlucky. One day I arrived at work to discover he had been relieved of his duties. I never learned his fate, and no one at the building ever spoke of him again.

By late 1988, the economic crisis sparked by the dislocations of moving from a planned to a market-oriented economy had generated a political crisis, splitting the senior leadership. At the end of the summer, Prime Minister Li Peng and other Party conservatives, deeply concerned about skyrocketing inflation, had gained the upper hand, instituting a series of measures to cool down the economy and reassert state control while putting Zhao Ziyang and the reformists on the defensive. Paralyzed by division at the top, the market reforms, as well as the prospect of movement toward political liberalization, began to grind to a halt, alarming the intellectuals, dissidents, and artists who had been inspired by the relatively relaxed climate during the past year. Worried that the entire reform process might be reversed, they began to pressure the Communist Party to accelerate the pace of change.

At the forefront of this push was Fang Lizhi, an astrophysicist who had become known as China's leading human-rights advocate. Fired from his university job and dismissed from the Communist Party in early 1987 following the student demonstrations that led to the ouster of liberal Party chief Hu Yaobang, he now began to speak out after a long period of silence. One afternoon, Cynde, Mitch, and I drove to Fang's apartment in Haidian, the university district of Beijing. When the door opened on the eleventh floor of one of the hundreds of ugly, undistinguished high-rises dotting the capital's skyline, I saw a plump, bespectacled man with twinkling eyes. He ushered us into his study, where a small Statue of Liberty stood on the table and a poster of Albert Einstein hung on the wall. In the next room, his wife, Li Shuxian, sat at a table reading a book.

I began our conversation by asking Fang about the lack of political freedom in China. "We should have more human rights," he said. "We need freedom of thought, speech, and press. If you say something about the leadership now, you'll get into trouble." Fang was emphatic that China had no choice but to move away from Marxism. Forty years of socialism had produced nothing in China, he asserted, and the story in the Soviet Union was the same. "It's very obvious," he said. "Look at the Soviet Union, Eastern Europe, and China. Everywhere, people want change."

Fang also accused the United States of a double standard on human rights, criticizing the Russians but ignoring violations in China.

"If I had a chance to talk to President Bush about human rights, I would say the situation here is in some respects worse than the Soviet Union. We still have political prisoners. Our legal system still has an offense called counterrevolutionary crimes."

I said that some people argued democracy was not suitable for a country like China.

"I've heard that, too," Fang answered, "but I disagree. It doesn't matter which people or race or culture you talk about. Human rights is the same the world over. Freedom of speech and the press is the same. All countries should be judged by the same standard."

Such daring criticism had long ago infuriated Deng Xiaoping, who reportedly personally ordered the scientist dismissed from his job the previous year. But Fang's assessment of China's paramount leader was a mixed one. "I would judge Deng's contribution to our country to be about fifty-fifty," he said, using the characteristic Chinese tendency to make assessments in percentages. After Deng assumed power, for instance, the government had assessed Mao's historical role as 70 percent good and 30 percent bad. "In the area of the economy," Fang continued, "Deng has played an important and positive role. But in the political field, well, I don't think he's so good."

"Do you think Deng and the government are afraid of you?" I asked.

Fang laughed.

"That is very difficult to say. At the least, I know they don't like me!"

I, however, liked Fang immensely. He was witty, thoughtful, direct, and unafraid. The contrast to the evasive bureaucrats and timid officials I regularly encountered in my work was striking. And Fang had put his finger on perhaps the central question facing China: could it have economic development without democracy?

It was a time of ferment. Reports circulated of informal *shalong* (salons), where university students and faculty in Beijing met to discuss democracy, protest movements, and how to change China. In December, on the tenth anniversary of the Democracy Wall movement, I interviewed Ren Wanding, a soft-spoken, sad-eyed man who had spent four years in jail for his activism at that time. Now he, too, lent his voice to the calls for political reform. Soon after, Fang Lizhi sent a controversial open letter to Deng Xiaoping, calling on the Chinese leader to release all political prisoners, including Wei Jingsheng, the most prominent figure from the Democracy Wall period. Fang made the letter available to reporters, and on a chilly winter morning I went to see him again.

"I feel that right now, we intellectuals shouldn't merely think," he told me. "We have to do something, such as making public our opinions on politics. That's why I sent this letter to Deng Xiaoping, proposing that Wei Jingsheng and other prisoners be pardoned."

Fang justified the appeal for Wei's release on the grounds that 1989 would mark the fortieth anniversary of the founding of the People's Republic. This was one of a series of politically significant anniversaries in 1989, including the seventieth anniversary of modern China's first great student protest, the May Fourth Movement of 1919, and the two hundredth anniversary of the French Revolution. Any of them could become a catalyst for renewed dissent.

Fang's letter was followed by two more protest petitions, signed by dozens of prominent intellectuals. The government-controlled media blamed these organized challenges to the Communist Party's authority not on the chief organizers, but on an obscure young intellectual named Chen Jun. I had met Chen Jun some months earlier when, after studying in New York, he moved to Beijing to set up a small, privately run bar called JJ's, which he jokingly described as "the *danwei* [work unit] with a difference." With some friends, he also set up a human-rights monitoring group in a dingy hotel room not far from my home. As a U.S. green-card holder, he was an easy target for official allegations that "subversive" foreign influences were fueling the discontent. It was not long before the authorities detained him and put him on a plane back to New York.

On New Year's Eve in 1988, Mitch Farkas and I, along with a talented new bureau assistant from CCTV named Tan Yadong, found ourselves in the city of Nanjing, covering a series of anti-African disturbances on the campus of Hehai University. I had discovered that racial prejudice against Africans was common among the Chinese, as were tensions between African and Chinese college students, especially where women were concerned. But as we made our way through angry crowds of shouting, chanting Chinese on Nanjing's raw and chilly streets, I thought the degree of anger among those I spoke with went beyond the immediate complaints about the African students' behavior. The protests seemed to me in large part an excuse to vent frustrations over larger dislocations in Chinese society, such as corruption, inflation, and poor job prospects. For the Chinese leadership, the confrontation created an extremely sensitive situation. In addition to the worrying domestic implications, there was also the likely impact on China's diplomatic ties with Africa, where Beijing had always presented itself as a defender of African and Third World interests. Returning to the capital, we learned that senior officials had ordered CCTV not to transmit any stories on the protest shot by foreign TV crews, forcing us to ship our story by air for transmission from Tokyo. It was a day late, but it got on the air.

In this fevered atmosphere, U.S. President George Bush announced plans for a state visit to China, where he had served as head of the U.S. diplomatic mission in the 1970s. Unfortunately the trip took place while I was on vacation, so I could only read about the Chinese government's clumsy and controversial decision to stop Fang Lizhi from attending an official White House–organized dinner to which he had been invited. Not surprisingly, the move backfired on the Chinese. With the top White House correspondents of all the networks, including CNN, in Beijing, Fang's image and words were beamed all across the U.S. and around the world. So great was the crush of crews chasing him that Cynde Strand was knocked down by another cameraman and had her nose broken.

I had been slightly surprised that the U.S. Embassy in Beijing had recommended inviting Fang. My own encounters with U.S. Ambassador Winston Lord had left me with the impression that human rights was low on the Sino-American agenda. For Lord, an energetic, fast-talking man who had traveled to China as an aide to Henry Kissinger in the earliest days of the U.S.-China rapprochement, preserving the "relationship" between Washington and Beijing was the top priority. Always eager to cultivate the press, he regularly invited reporters to his home—once at 5 A.M. to watch the Super Bowl on satellite TV. I became friendly with him and his glamorous Chinese-American wife, the well-known author Bette Bao Lord, who was deeply involved in promoting Sino-American cultural exchanges. She frequently hosted leading Chinese intellectuals and artists—many considered hostile by the government—at the ambassadorial residence, and often arranged for distinguished American cultural figures to visit China. For us, she was always a good story, often more so than her husband. For example, once she helped movie star Charlton Heston direct Chinese actors in a Mandarin production of *The Caine Mutiny*, which was performed for the general public at the Capital Theatre, next to our bureau on Wangfujing Street.

I liked Ambassador Lord personally, but I shared the view of many other correspondents that there was a large gap between our perceptions of China and his. Lord was inclined to be an optimist, downplaying the scale of the economic crisis and public discontent, and dismissing our assessment of the bitter power struggle between reformist Zhao Ziyang and conservative Li Peng as one more of nuance than substance. Moreover, like Fang Lizhi, we were frustrated by the embassy's reluctance to pursue the human-rights violations we were reporting on a regular basis, in sharp contrast to the tough American line toward the Soviet Union.

I found this aspect of U.S.-China relations particularly interesting because there were growing signs that a Sino-Soviet summit to heal a rift dating back to the 1950s was in the cards. In February, Soviet foreign minister Eduard Shevardnadze came to Beijing. I attended a press conference at which he announced that Soviet president Mikhail Gorbachev would visit the Chinese capital in mid-May to meet with Deng Xiaoping and other top Chinese leaders. It would be the biggest China story in years, rich in global implications. As soon as the summit was announced, my bosses at CNN decided it deserved the full treatment. We began drawing up plans to bring anchor Bernard Shaw, a portable satellite uplink, and a staff of forty to Beijing in May. Meanwhile, my crew and I set out for the Sino-Soviet border. We flew to Heihe, a desolate town on the Amur River, just half a mile across the water from the equally grim Russian town of Blagoveschensk. Even in early spring, the weather was frigid, with bitter Arctic winds whipping down from Siberia and sending whirling flurries of snow through the mud-caked streets. Despite their proximity, the two towns had been separated by a vast political gulf for more than thirty years, and searchlights mounted on guard towers still swept the river at night. Now, however, the freezing conditions were contributing to a thaw across the frontier. The Amur River was frozen solid. Every day, we stood shivering along its banks, watching trucks rumble back and forth as the Chinese took Russian raw materials in return for consumer goods that were in desperately short supply in the Soviet Union. The mayor of Heihe was ecstatic about the evolving Sino-Soviet rapprochement. After years of living on the front line of a very volatile border, he told us that he now saw the possibility of prosperity and growth for his citizens.

One freezing night in Heihe, as we sat around the dismal hotel bar drinking beer with a Polish student who was studying the almost-vanished Manchu language, I put through a call to the Atlanta office. From this remote spot, I learned some big CNN news. Jeanee Von Essen had abruptly lost her job as foreign editor, and had been replaced by longtime overnight desk man Eason Jordan. Jeanee had hired me and I felt a strong debt of gratitude to her, but I had dealt amicably and efficiently with Eason for years, and after Jeanee's irritating idiosyncrasies, I believed his straight-talking style would be a refreshing contrast.

We returned to Beijing in early April, ready to devote our energies to the ambitious arrangements necessary to cover the summit live. For the moment, charting the tensions in Chinese society took second place to drafting memos, participating in conference calls, making hotel reservations, and applying for all the permits required to import our equipment. We were all excited as the summit came closer. But the ferment in China didn't abate. Just before our trip to the border, anti-Chinese rioting erupted again in Tibet. This time the Chinese government made sure no reporters got to Lhasa. But I had made alternative arrangements with a young American who, anticipating trouble, had taken a home-video camera and traveled to Tibet as a tourist. He captured and smuggled out graphic images of Chinese police beating Buddhist monks in street battles that led the government to impose martial law in Lhasa. Sitting in my office as the announcement came over our Xinhua News Agency wire machine, I phoned the news to Atlanta and was put on the air immediately. I was surprised by the Chinese decision. For all its repressive tendencies, the communist authorities rarely took such openly draconian measures. It was a sign of just how seriously they viewed this challenge to their authority. In my report, I noted that this was the first such declaration anywhere in China since the height of the turmoil during the Cultural Revolution. I could not anticipate that, just two months later, the government would be forced to declare martial law and order the army onto the streets of Beijing.

◤

CHAPTER SEVEN

The Soul of China:
Tiananmen Square

April 15, 1989, dawned smoggy and overcast, the kind of day that most accentuated the socialist drabness of Beijing. I was lying on the couch in my living room, playing with my little boy and my dog when the phone rang.

"Mike," asked Parisa Khosravi, an editor on the CNN Foreign Desk in Atlanta, "the wires are reporting that some guy named Hu Yaobang just died. Do we need to do anything about this?"

"Nah," I replied. "Hu was purged as Communist Party boss by the hard-liners two years ago and has been out of the limelight ever since. His death is not a big deal. I don't think it'll make much of a TV story. All you need is a fifteen-second anchor read."

How wrong I was! I knew that Hu Yaobang's dismissal for failing to crack down on student demonstrations in the winter of 1986–87 had made him a hero among many Chinese, but as I resumed my game of tug of war with Daniel and Sherlock that gray afternoon, I could not anticipate that the death of this outspoken but widely respected reformer would be the catalyst for an explosion of the long-smoldering tensions I had been charting in Chinese society during the past few months.

Over the weekend, students at Beida, as Beijing University is called in Chinese, in an immediate, emotional reaction to Hu's passing, put up wall posters praising the late Party leader and criticizing his conservative opponents. Others laid wreaths in his memory in

Tiananmen Square. Still thinking nothing major was brewing, I sent Cynde and Mitch on Monday to check out the Beida posters while I busied myself with what I thought were more pressing matters. CNN Special Events producer Alec Miran and engineer Ron Hacker were arriving the next day to survey the logistical nightmare of making the network's ambitious plans for live coverage of the upcoming Gorbachev-Deng summit a reality. As Beijing bureau chief, I was the point man for the local arrangements. We had to win approval from China Central Television (CCTV), the Ministry of Posts and Telecommunications (PTT), and the Foreign Ministry to bring in and operate a satellite uplink, or flyaway. We needed permission from the police to operate walkie-talkies and install microwave transmitters for live broadcasts from Tiananmen Square and a half dozen other locations. We needed a hotel willing to let us set up the flyaway, build an anchor set, install cables, power supplies, and international phone lines, and provide office and living space for forty CNN staffers. They would require visas, cars, drivers, translators, and catering facilities. Putting together such a complex operation in barely a month would be a daunting challenge anywhere. To try to do so in China's secretive, bureaucratic, and inefficient society bordered on madness.

Shortly after I collapsed in bed that Monday night, the dreaded phone rang. Half asleep, I heard the gruff tones of my friend Dave Schweisberg, the UPI bureau chief. "I just got a call from someone out at Beida. Several thousand students have set out from the campus for the city center on some kind of march. I thought you'd like to know."

"Thanks, man," I replied. "I owe you one."

Stumbling out of bed, I quickly called Cynde and Mitch, rousing them from sleep. Still groggy, we each took up our appointed tasks. Cynde grabbed her camera and tripod. Mitch checked the cables and microphones on the recording deck. I found a pen and a notebook, and stuck a small case of makeup in my pocket. With a bad five o'clock shadow even first thing in the morning, I was under orders from CNN headquarters to apply pancake to my face before appearing on camera. A few minutes later, we arrived at Tiananmen Square. Apart from a handful of groggy journalists and a few dozen police, it was silent and empty.

Long before I could see the procession, I began to hear youthful cries—the initial stirrings of a long-silenced people regaining their voices—several hundred yards to the west, down Changan Street. Faint at first, the chants grew steadily louder, reverberating out of the darkness. *"Hu Yaobang wansui!"* ("Long Live Hu Yaobang!"); *"Minzhu wansui!"* ("Long live democracy!"); *"Ziyou wansui!"* ("Long Live Freedom!"). Suddenly a crowd several thousand strong emerged from the gloom. A dozen students carried a huge white banner with three black Chinese characters in a tribute to Hu Yaobang: THE SOUL OF CHINA. At the head of the crowd was a face that would soon become familiar to me, that of a slim, bespectacled Beida history major named Wang Dan. With the charismatic Wu'er Kaixi, and the emotional Chai Ling, he would emerge as one of the most important student leaders in the weeks ahead.

Clambering up to the first ledge of the Monument to the Heroes of the Revolution in the center of the square, several students secured the enormous banner while the crowd sang *The Internationale*. Just as they would turn the most powerful symbols of China's Communist revolution—from the Heroes Monument to Tiananmen Square—into weapons in their own struggle to change the system the revolution had created, the students would make *The Internationale* their own anthem. I remembered its words from my earlier years of radical political activism:

> Arise, ye prisoners of starvation.
> Arise, ye wretched of the earth
> For justice thunders condemnation.
> A better world is in birth.

As the crowd cheered and clapped, a young man climbed onto the monument and demanded that the Communist Party's entire Politburo resign.

"Hu Yaobang understood the way we young people think," one Beida student told me. "We are mourning the death of Hu Yaobang," declared another. "But our purpose is twofold. Right now, Chinese society is plagued by inflation, corruption, and *guandao* (profiteering). It is our responsibility to try to clean things up."

The atmosphere seemed remarkably relaxed, despite the passionate language. There was much laughter and joking, almost as if the students were on a recreational midnight frolic. Cynde and Mitch worked furiously to capture the astonishing scene on camera, the glow of her TV light casting eerie shadows on the sea of youthful faces. I hovered just behind them, wanting to view the demonstrators as Cynde was seeing them through her lens. There was no need to tell her what shots to get. We had been a team for long enough to understand each other's responses and styles instinctively. The size of the crowd around the monument seemed impressive, but when I stepped a few yards back, the protestors appeared to be swallowed up by the vastness of the darkened square. They seemed so vulnerable, should the state choose to exercise its power. Even now, I was astonished that the authorities had not interfered.

"Our Party is pretty enlightened," explained one student with tousled hair and a white paper flower of mourning in his lapel. "I don't think coming here to mourn the death of a former party leader should cause any trouble."

Watching the students press close to the carved frieze of muscle-bound, bayonet-wielding revolutionary heroes at the base of the monument, I wasn't so sure. Even under the pretext of mourning a fallen Party leader, this gathering in Tiananmen represented the most significant expression of student protest since the demonstrations two and a half years earlier that had caused Hu Yaobang's downfall. With growing popular discontent over China's crisis of faith and economic difficulties, with dissidents and intellectuals like Fang Lizhi already testing the limits, and with the Communist Party divided between conservatives and reformers, could these young people become a catalyst for wider unrest?

The seventieth anniversary of the historic May Fourth Movement was less than three weeks away. On May 4, 1919, Chinese students had marched to Tiananmen Square to protest government weakness and corruption that had led to China's humiliation at the Versailles Peace Conference after World War I. By inspiring a generation of intellectuals who saw themselves as the country's conscience with a responsibility to push for radical change, the May Fourth Movement helped give birth to the Chinese Communist Party in 1921, and contributed to the political ferment that led to Mao's eventual victory. After 1949, the Communists had enshrined the May Fourth protestors as shining examples of what patriotic intellectuals could do for their country. Now, watching the singing, chanting students around the Monument to the Heroes of the Revolution, I wondered whether a new generation was once again about to lead the way? And what would the Communist Party, usually so ready to crush any signs of dissent, do in response? With dawn breaking, I recorded a stand-up in the square. "How much longer," I asked, "will the government wait before moving to crush this challenge to its authority?"

Back at the bureau, tired but my adrenaline pumping, I called the CNN Foreign Desk. "We need to book a satellite feed," I told my colleagues in Atlanta, breathlessly describing the unprecedented gathering I had just seen. "This is worth it, even if we do so on our own." It was normal CNN practice to join and share the cost of feeds booked by the other networks. My budget-conscious editors almost never paid for unilateral transmissions, which could easily cost over $2,000 for ten minutes of satellite time. To my amazement, the evening news shows at ABC and CBS had no interest in spots from their Beijing correspondents. This simply wasn't a big enough story. It didn't take much, however, for CNN's new foreign editor, Eason Jordan, to be convinced that we had witnessed something with potentially momentous consequences for China. A feed was booked for 8 A.M., giving us barely two hours to write and edit. We raced off through the morning rush hour toward CCTV, weaving past bicycles, cars, and trucks, passing a now-empty, sun-filled Tiananmen Square. As the Chinese TV engineers watched our spot going out, I could see their eyes widen. Several of them looked at us and broke into smiles. Moments later, CNN put the story on the air. It was the first report on China's spring of protest to be broadcast on Western television.

Meanwhile, we were having problems with the Beijing Hotel. With a spectacular view of the Forbidden City and the northern half of Tiananmen Square, it provided an ideal vantage point for live coverage of Gorbachev's official welcoming ceremony, scheduled for May 15. I had been pleasantly surprised that the hotel had readily agreed to my request for CNN to install a flyaway and anchor set on its roof. I suspected that the $75,000 CNN was prepared to pay may have had something to do with it. Now, while Cynde and Mitch went home to rest after our night-long exertions, I came straight from the CCTV feed point to join my colleagues Alec Miran and Ron Hacker for a meeting at which Deputy Manager Mr. Li informed us that the hotel, run by the Beijing city government, was getting cold feet.

Despite earlier promises, Mr. Li now demanded letters from

both the Foreign Ministry and the Ministry of Posts and Telecommunications authorizing use of the uplink, and even if we got them, said that security concerns meant no CNN personnel would be allowed to remain on the roof when Gorbachev's motorcade drove by. This edict would effectively prevent us from broadcasting live pictures of his arrival at the Great Hall of the People. In a polite way, Mr. Li was telling us the deal was off. I was convinced this abrupt change in attitude was prompted by the overnight demonstration in Tiananmen Square. I suspected that the security forces wanted to use the roof themselves. As Alec, Ron, and I set off for the next in a daylong round of presummit planning meetings, I realized that I would now have to begin all over again the search for a hotel prepared to accommodate our needs. I hoped the students would stay quiet long enough for me to do so.

But by midday, the students were back in the square. I finally escaped, bored and exhausted, from the last of my meetings, and joined Cynde and Mitch late in the afternoon. "You are not going to believe what's happening," Cynde greeted me. Nearly a thousand students from virtually all of Beijing's leading universities were holding a sit-in directly across from the Great Hall of the People, surrounded by a much larger crowd of sympathizers and onlookers. With the setting sun slipping behind the Great Hall, casting golden rays across Tiananmen, I listened to a series of student leaders denounce the government and call on the Communist Party to accept a list of seven demands. These included allowing free speech and a free press, forcing officials to disclose their incomes and assets, allocating more money for education, stamping out corruption, and "reversing the verdict"—annulling the official decision dismissing Hu Yaobang. Their earnestness and idealism, and their hopes of reforming the system from within, brought back memories of the U.S. antiwar teach-ins I had attended in college. At that time, when I first became interested in China, I had never imagined I would see such protests in the heart of Beijing.

From what I could tell, the demands had been formulated by a loosely knit group of youthful activists. Although I'd been aware of the heightened interest in political action on Beijing's campuses earlier in the year, including the "democracy salons," where students gathered to discuss and debate new ideas, I knew little about the individuals involved. I was eager to learn exactly who they were and what they represented, but the effort and time required simply to make our way through the excited throng and get the video images and brief sound bites needed to meet yet another satellite deadline made this difficult to do in the heat of the moment. Our inability to undertake in-depth background investigations while capturing the ongoing drama proved to be one of my biggest frustrations through-out the "Beijing Spring." I covered almost all the important events of the next six weeks as they happened. But despite the dramatic images we broadcast, the demands of my job—coping with cameras, sound gear, cables, tripods, lights, batteries, shot angles, twice-daily satellite feeds, numerous other logistical and technical concerns, and the fact that successful coverage required the com-bined efforts of myself and my crew—imposed an enormous burden. As much as I wanted to, I found myself with little time or opportunity to dig for the stories beyond the immediate events I was witnessing. This constant problem for television news reporters was made even more acute by the complexity of the crisis in Beijing.

Keenly aware of what I could not do, I relied increasingly on my informal alliance with Dave Schweisberg and his capable col-leagues at UPI. We decided to collaborate, recognizing that none of us would be able to be on hand for every single important statement from student leaders, or to see all aspects of a demonstration, let alone have time to thoroughly scrutinize the official media. We provided UPI details, color, quotes, and information from all the events we attended, especially those that they missed. In return, Dave shared with us the insights he culled from UPI's coverage and his own sources, both on campus and in the government. By the time the crisis reached a climax, we were functioning as virtually one organization.

Despite my frustrations, nothing could compare with the thrill of being on the scene, in the middle of what we quickly realized were historic events. We all sensed what Cynde described as the "good vibrations" of these early gatherings. "What a party, what a pic-nic, perfect blue skies, banners, and speeches," she wrote one night in a diary she kept throughout the spring. "It is like a revival. The Chinese people are saved! Everybody is testifying. Some get carried away by the opportunity to speak their minds, but everyone gets a turn to express what is in their minds and in their hearts. The Chinese people are saved. Hallelujah!"

It was a sentiment I shared. Adjusting to life and work in the ossified, bureaucratic, and isolating atmosphere of Beijing during the previous two years had not been easy. I had begun to feel down about being in China, depressed by the growing sourness of the public mood as the country's economic and political crisis deepened, and the fact that the efforts of the dissidents I knew appeared fruitless. It was painful to watch the country and people that had meant so much to me flounder in a sea of discontent, however interesting I might find my work. These courageous young students were inspiring to the many ordinary citizens who came to the square to watch. They raised my spirits as well.

For the first time, I noticed that some of the protestors appeared to be consciously playing to the TV cameras, as when one unfurled a banner in English reading FREEDOM, DEMOCRACY, AND ENLIGHTENMENT. I saw the gesture as a sign of growing political sophistication, an indication that at least some students were aware of the power of international public opinion. More importantly, with the state-run Chinese media muzzled by the government, the students knew that foreign reports on the protest would be beamed back into China via the Voice of America and the BBC, giving them a powerful weapon with which to combat official silence or disapproval.

By now the other U.S. networks had become interested in the story, in part, I suspected, on the basis of the report CNN had aired the night before. A joint feed was booked for early Tuesday evening, in time for the Tuesday morning shows in the United States. Cynde, Mitch, and I again tested our nerves. I scribbled a script in the car as we raced from the square to the bureau, where Mitch took over for a crash editing job, slapping shots together while Cynde identified the best sequences, before the three of us dashed through the traffic to CCTV five miles away to file our second spot on the growing protest movement.

Later in the evening, while Mitch and I edited an updated spot for another feed coming up in the wee hours of Wednesday morning, I sent Cynde back to the square for a final look. It was a good call. She arrived to discover that thousands of chanting, banner-waving, singing students were surging down Changan Street toward Zhongnanhai, the headquarters and residential compound of the Chinese Communist Party leadership, a half mile west of

Tiananmen. Those at the head of the march tried to force their way inside, pushing and shoving the startled guards in one of the boldest gestures of political defiance in the history of the People's Republic. Moments before we were due to leave for CCTV, Cynde raced into the bureau and flung a tape on my desk. "This is great video!" she exclaimed breathlessly. "The cops and the students are mixing it up at Zhongnanhai!" With Cynde and me looking over his shoulder, Mitch edited frantically, managing to incorporate her dramatic pictures and the news of this latest development into our story.

At 4:30 A.M., on our way back from CCTV after a successful feed, Cynde and I stopped near Zhongnanhai. Several hundred police had arrived and were forcing the few remaining students, barely a thousand in all, to return to their campuses. Parking our car several blocks away, we walked swiftly through darkened alleyways to reach Changan Street. The police, who had formed a line across the street, ordered us to move out with the rest of the crowd. This was the first time the students had come face-to-face with the security forces, and even though there had been few arrests and virtually no violence, the confrontation seemed to me to mark a significant escalation in what I had just described in my story as "an open challenge to the Chinese leadership." It was too late to add the images of gesturing policemen and chanting students that Cynde now captured to our story, but I was certain this was only the beginning. There would be many more feeds.

Eighteen hours later, Zhongnanhai was the target of a second march, which followed a day of more demonstrations in Tiananmen Square. Cynde, Mitch, and I were at the head of the large, angry crowd as it reached Zhongnanhai's main gate and confronted a sizable contingent of police blocking the entrance. Shouts of *"Li Peng chulai!"* ("Li Peng, come out!") and *"Yaoqiu duihua!"* ("We demand dialogue!") echoed through the darkness. The three of us were sandwiched between the sweaty, agitated protestors and a phalanx of police who suddenly tried to push the students back from the entrance to the compound.

"The cops are coming!" Mitch called out. He and I both tried to shield Cynde with our bodies as the surging crowd threatened to rip the cable linking her camera to Mitch's record deck.

"Hold on, don't leave me!" she pleaded. Police officers attacked the crowd with clubs and brass belt buckles. Amid shouts of *"Buxu da ren!"* ("It is wrong to beat people!"), some students threw bottles and bricks. Cynde climbed up a small aluminum ladder and turned on her camera light to take a shot. A policeman immediately pointed his electric torch at us and a second cop rushed forward as Cynde quickly turned off the light. Unsure where we were in the darkness, the police lunged blindly ahead. They were about to reach us when a student picked up a bicycle and lofted it at them. The enraged and distracted cops turned and fell on the young man as the three of us escaped. It was a close call; a few of the police had kicked a similar ladder out from under the feet of NBC cameraman Gary Fairman, leaving him with an injured elbow. The crowds began to cheer when they saw Cynde with her camera, but she was disconcerted by the applause, convinced that the real hero was the young man.

If the authorities thought a show of force would discourage the students, however, they were wrong. The protests continued despite a driving rain on Thursday and again on Friday during the run-up to Hu Yaobang's official state funeral, scheduled to be held Saturday morning, April 22, at the Great Hall of the People. Still, there was no official response to the students' demands for dialogue. Instead the *People's Daily* published a commentary on April 21 warning against further antigovernment protests. And the Beijing city government announced that Tiananmen Square would be closed to the public on the day of Hu's funeral. Finally, I thought to myself, the Communist Party's patience is running out.

Fortified with a dinner of dumplings and soup at the nearby Beijing Hotel, my crew and I arrived at the already packed square around midevening Friday. The ranks of the protestors grew. Long columns of singing, chanting students marched from the university district to arrive just before midnight. It was apparent they intended to stake a claim to the square ahead of the official ban on their presence. The students ignored government threats and vowed to stay through Hu Yaobang's memorial service the next morning. I was convinced a confrontation was imminent. Expecting the police to arrive at any moment, the three of us joined other reporters to wait out the night at the monument. "We plan our strategy," Cynde wrote in her diary. "Will it be tear gas or water cannons or cattle prods? Do we shoot and run, and if so, in which direction? Or do we drop back and try to get behind the police, but which direction will they come from? One always has to think ahead. Nervous speculation and bad jokes get us through a chilly night." Just before dawn, we saw trucks move into the northeast corner of the square. "This is it," Cynde said, pointing her camera. "It looks like water cannons." We braced ourselves as the vehicles moved closer. Then we all broke into laughter; they were cleaning trucks, arriving to remove not students but garbage.

Beneath a rising sun that turned the morning sky a brilliant blue and cast a golden glow on the five-star emblem of the People's Republic hanging atop the entrance to the Great Hall of the People, the relieved protestors in Tiananmen held their own impromptu memorial service for Hu Yaobang. Bowing their heads in a moment of silence, the demonstrators laid a series of wreaths at the foot of the monument and sang China's national anthem. The words echoed across the vast expanse. "The Chinese nation is facing its most dangerous moment. Everybody must roar with defiance. Arise! Arise! Arise!" At eight o'clock, police began to cordon off the square. We readied ourselves for trouble, but it quickly became clear that those inside would be allowed to remain. The authorities, however, seemed determined to prevent any more people from joining the crowd. It was the same kind of ambiguous show of force we had seen all week— an indication, I thought, that the Party was either too divided or too fearful of the negative consequences to mount a harsh crackdown.

Suddenly we realized there was no one in our office to record the Chinese TV broadcast of the official Hu Yaobang funeral ceremony inside the Great Hall of the People, which Deng Xiaoping, Zhao Ziyang, and other leaders were scheduled to attend. We could not do a story without these pictures, and so, with great reluctance, I sent Mitch back to handle this important job. Arriving at the bureau, he discovered that our driver, Mr. Lu, was already there. Fired by the enthusiasm of the movement, Lu, who, like most Chinese workers, usually preferred to wait for instructions from me, had taken it upon himself to prepare a machine to record the CCTV broadcast. Mitch was grateful, but now, with the square surrounded by police, he could not rejoin us, and Cynde and I were on our own. We worried because we were running low on videotape and fresh batteries for the camera. We had also both been too busy to use the toilet since eight o'clock the previous evening, and the square itself had no public restrooms. If we left now for the toilets across the street, we wouldn't be allowed back.

"I don't know which is going to give out first," Cynde joked grimly, "my batteries or my bladder."

As the hour of Hu's funeral approached, Cynde and I witnessed an astonishing scene. A crowd of demonstrators, which I judged to be almost 100,000 strong, confronted columns of police within sight of a long line of elderly officials shuffling up the massive front steps of the Great Hall of the People for the official ceremony. Even at a distance, I could sense the bewilderment among these old revolutionaries, once at the forefront of the struggle to transform Chinese society, now facing a new generation of rebels. Hobbling on their canes, supported by aides and nurses, they peered down at the students in what seemed to be utter incomprehension. After some pushing and shoving, students and police alike abruptly sat down in the street to listen to the funeral service on giant loudspeakers. The police, holding their hats in their hands, bowed their heads. In an awkward, shared moment of silent respect, the students, just inches away from the police lines, bowed their heads too. As I listened to Communist Party chief Zhao Ziyang praise Hu as someone who "never tried to hold back his opinions," I tried to imagine the scene inside the Great Hall. The irony was overpowering. The old men who purged Hu Yaobang were going through the motions of paying respect to his corpse, while his young supporters were being kept at bay by police.

As soon as the ceremony ended, the demonstrators resumed their chants of "We demand dialogue," and "Li Peng come out!" Suddenly three young students knelt on the steps of the Great Hall, prostrating themselves for half an hour in a gesture evocative of supplicants begging the favor of an emperor in imperial China. Among the three was Wu'er Kaixi, already emerging as one of the more media-savvy student leaders. To no one's surprise, Premier Li Peng did not come out. Still, I was convinced that by defying the government and occupying the square, the students had scored an important political and moral triumph. Their action might push the leadership toward political reform in the hope of preventing further protests, or, more likely, I thought, trigger a crackdown like that which followed China's last major outbreak of student unrest, when Hu Yaobang lost his job. Whatever the result, we had witnessed a major change to the Chinese political landscape. Excited and exhausted, Cynde and I staggered back to the bureau to edit what we knew was a powerful story, after first making an emergency stop at the nearest public toilet.

I was ready to hug Vic Kimura. The sales director at the Great Wall Sheraton Hotel, located four miles from Tiananmen Square, had come through for me. When the Beijing Hotel backed out as political tension in the capital grew, Kimura readily agreed to provide a workspace, accommodations, and a Chinese-style pavilion in the Sheraton garden for an anchor set. The CNN portable uplink could be installed next to the miniature golf course, and microwave links to receive feeds from Tiananmen Square could go on the roof. Sheraton engineers and technicians happily sketched out plans to run cables and wiring from both locations to the ninth-floor suites we planned to transform into a newsroom and production center. Dealing with the Beijing Hotel had been a nightmare; our negotiations had been replete with all the political and bureaucratic problems I associated with the stagnant, inefficient state-run industries that China's reformists were trying to change. The Sheraton, in contrast, was precisely the sort of well-run, well-organized operation one would expect from a Sino-American joint venture. Our plans for live coverage of the Gorbachev visit were back on track.

Since Hu Yaobang's funeral, I had shuttled back and forth between meetings at the Sheraton Hotel and visits with my crew to the campuses of Beijing's main universities. Leading student activists, flushed with their success and encouraged by signs of broader support from intellectuals and workers who had swelled the ranks of the crowds the past weekend, had announced the creation of a new, independent student federation called the Provisional Beijing Students' Union. On Monday, April 24, they launched a boycott of classes to force the government to talk to them. What had initially been an amorphous collection of individuals and demands, fueled primarily by grief and mourning, was beginning to turn into an organized movement. It was, however, still so loosely structured that in order to get any idea of what was happening, my crew and I spent endless hours just hanging around, asking questions, waiting for protestors to come or go.

I understood why the students were disgruntled. On earlier visits to Beida and other campuses, I had seen students jammed six or even eight to a room in dormitories lacking heat and hot water, with laundry hanging from the rafters of dank corridors. With government spending on education slashed even as inflation spiraled out of control, university teaching, library, and research facilities declined, while students as well as professors found their meager stipends insufficient to get by. In a country where intellectuals had long considered themselves a privileged class, a good education no longer guaranteed a good job. Indeed, the average university graduate earned less than Dong Aizhi, the self-employed hairdresser I'd interviewed soon after arriving in Beijing. And growing numbers of students found that ability counted less than connections, or *guanxi*, in finding work. For many of the young protestors, the chant of "down with corruption" had a very personal ring, as their own grievances blended with the broader discontent simmering in Chinese society.

The dormitories were still cramped and dreary, but now I found the atmosphere at Beijing University to be electric. In the center of the campus, the walls were covered with posters supporting the student strike, demanding political freedom and an end to corruption. Written on red, pink, yellow, and white paper, they provided a colorful contrast to the bleak brown and gray walls of the campus buildings. I noticed savage caricatures of Deng Xiaoping, and a cartoon showing a grim-faced party cadre putting a gag on a crying student. On one pole hung a banner in English, obviously designed for the cameras, reading GIVE ME LIBERTY OR GIVE ME DEATH! Students crowded around the poster display, some dictating the contents into small tape recorders, others copying furiously into notebooks, reveling in the opportunity for the free and animated exchange of ideas rarely seen at Chinese universities.

I had seen the slogans, but I needed to know what the students *really* wanted, and what they *really* meant by terms like "democracy" and "freedom." In this feverish atmosphere of discussion and debate, establishing such definitions was not easy. I buttonholed students and put the question to them.

"A great many ordinary people don't understand what democracy is," asserted a bespectacled Beida student in a white T-shirt. "They haven't had any experience. But democracy must come from the people choosing their own government. I don't completely believe in the Chinese Communist Party. But I don't oppose it either. If we oppose the Party, China could slip into chaos. So I support the reformists in the Communist Party. I hope they will take China toward democracy. But ever since the dismissal of Hu Yaobang, I feel the reforms have slowed down. That's why I'm protesting."

"You shouldn't have a small group of so-called leaders deciding everything," a young woman, her hair in a pigtail, chimed in. "Democracy is when the people decide things for themselves."

"You can say that American democracy doesn't fit China," acknowledged a student from Qinghua University, one of the many activists from campuses all across Beijing who had flocked to Beida, now emerging as the nerve center of the movement. "But I still think we need to try some kind of democracy anyway, as well as studying what aspects of other social systems would be appropriate in our society, where the Chinese Communist Party is the biggest and most powerful institution."

For many students, influenced by exposure to Western ideas as China opened its doors in the preceding decade, democracy appeared simply to mean freedom of press and expression.

"Now China is in the grip of a dictatorial government," an intense young man with a slight stubble explained. "Right now, none of the media is publishing anything about our student movement. They can't print the truth. We need real news. We want our demands to be heard."

It was clear that the protestors were not talking about an American-style political system for China when they used such language. I wasn't completely comfortable with the way I and other reporters, faced with the limitations of daily journalism and its pressure to compress and simplify, tended to describe their protests as a "democracy movement." The more I listened, the more I became convinced that the students' top priority was not establishing a democracy, but simply securing formal recognition from the government for their movement. Theirs was not an attempt to overthrow the system but a clamor for a hearing, for legitimacy and respect from their elders—an acknowledgment that, as intellectuals, they, like the protestors of the May Fourth Movement, had a special mission to help improve Chinese society. The constant chants that called for "dialogue" and for Li Peng to "come out" and meet them— not unreasonable demands—appeared far less difficult to grant than, say, their cry for eliminating corruption. But in China's one-party state, I realized, it was the one demand the Communist authorities could not meet, because to do so risked setting a dangerous precedent. An officially sanctioned independent student federation could easily lead to demands for trade unions, churches, and other organizations free of Party control. It wasn't immediately clear to us, as Cynde, Mitch, and I roamed the campuses on those sunny April days after Hu Yaobang's funeral, but in the government's refusal to acknowledge the legitimacy of the students and their concerns lay the seeds of future tragedy.

Two documents occupied my attention on Wednesday, April 26. One was a letter from Vic Kimura, confirming all the arrangements Alec Miran and I had painstakingly negotiated for CNN to use the Great Wall Sheraton Hotel during Gorbachev's visit. The other was an editorial that dominated the front page of the *People's Daily*. Entitled "Take a Clear-cut Stand Against Turmoil" and inspired by Deng Xiaoping, it harshly condemned the student movement for seeking to "poison people's minds, create national turmoil, and sabotage the nation's stability and unity." It accused the students of conspiring to overthrow the government, and it warned the protestors to halt their activities. The editorial was a decisive moment in the crisis, locking the government into a hard-line position from which it would be difficult to deviate. It also showed that Deng Xiaoping, despite a decade of reform, was no more willing to tolerate direct political opposition now than when he ordered an end to Democracy Wall in 1979 and sent Wei Jingsheng to prison. In Deng's eyes, economic and political change remained two entirely separate issues. Open challenges to party rule would not be tolerated. Reaction from the campuses was angry and defiant. Ignoring the government's warning, the students announced plans for a march the next morning to Tiananmen Square.

Shortly after dawn on April 27, Cynde and I set out for Beijing University. We were on our own, as I had been forced to send Mitch and bureau assistant Tan Yadong back to the Sino-Soviet border for more material to be used during the upcoming Gorbachev summit. Lugging our equipment, we stood in the warm spring sunshine and watched thousands of students pour out of the university's main gate with a roaring cheer to link up with demonstrators from dozens of other campuses. As they headed toward the city center, the protestors sang *The Internationale* and chanted the now-familiar slogans. They were well organized, with marshals linking arms to protect the long columns of marchers. Equally impressive were the crowds of cheering workers standing on sidewalks or peering out of windows, some flashing victory signs, others offering food and drink. The students' complaints about corruption and inflation had obviously touched a responsive chord. Carrying the sound deck for Cynde while she composed her shots of the immense crowd, I lost any doubts about the extent of public support for the movement in Beijing.

In view of the government ban on such activities, I was less certain that the students would be allowed to complete their march, and was nervous, not only about the protestors, but about what might happen to Cynde and me if we were caught in the middle of a confrontation. Shortly after setting out, the protestors had punctured a thin cordon of police, but, further along, we saw a phalanx of cops with arms linked, blocking the road. Moving behind the police, Cynde picked a spot by a tree and mounted her stepladder to get a good view of the confrontation. Chanting "The People's Police Loves the People," the seething mass of humanity collided with the forces of law and order. The police line broke, pinning us and our equipment against the tree. "Don't hurt the cameraman," the students shouted as they swept by.

"I could not breathe. My ladder was gone, but my feet were not touching the ground," Cynde wrote in her diary. "I remember strong hot breaths of stale garlic on my neck as we all collapsed in a twisted heap on the ground. The same scenario played itself out again just down the street, another tangle of feet and cords and cables, but this time I lost my ladder for good."

By now, the police had been pushed to the side. An immense throng, perhaps as many as 150,000 people, surged toward downtown Beijing. As we caught our breath, a young man came running up. "Miss, Miss," he called to Cynde, handing her a piece of twisted metal, "You lost your ladder in the crowd, and I am returning it to you." A few moments later, another demonstrator arrived and offered to carry our bulky sound deck on the back of his bicycle. Shaken up and exhausted from lugging the heavy piece of equipment, I was enormously grateful.

Mile after mile, hour after hour, under a hot midday sun, we trotted along at the head of the exuberant procession. I felt a strong sense of identification with these young protestors. They reminded me of my own generation, only they were braver, challenging a system that in the past had not hesitated to imprison, purge, or kill its opponents. Tired and sweaty, Cynde and I eventually hitched a ride with a passing motorist who let us off outside Zhongnanhai near the entrance to the square. If the security forces were to make a final attempt to block the march, this was where I thought it would take place.

I was right: row after row of police, lining up four-deep, blocked the entire width of Changan Street. This time, Cynde climbed a lamppost, while, like a bodyguard, I braced myself below her. Colliding, pushing first one way and then the other, the oncoming marchers and the security forces seemed to be playing a giant game of tug-of-war. Finally, overwhelmed, the police cordon broke. As the excited youngsters rushed into Tiananmen, I saw that some of the police officers were smiling.

In the square, the students ran into a convoy of army trucks filled with soldiers. For a moment, I thought another, more serious clash was imminent. Then the protestors swarmed around the bewildered young troops, clambering onto the hoods and sides of the vehicles. In a day full of powerful images—students breaking through massed lines of police, factory workers offering the marchers water and popsicles, the broadest boulevards in Beijing jammed with banner-waving protestors—this was the most remarkable. In front of the Tiananmen Square rostrum, under the stern gaze of Chairman Mao's picture, soldiers of the People's Liberation Army found themselves helpless in the face of the largest antigovernment demonstration since the founding of Communist China.

It was, as Cynde put it, "a great shot."

Knowing her exceptional talent for turning news pictures into art, I was sure it would be a compelling picture. In Imperial China, when a dynasty no longer commanded the support of the public, people said it had lost the Mandate of Heaven. For the men who now ran the state Mao created, it was the Mandate of Heaven that now seemed to be slipping from their grasp.

My contemplation was interrupted by a quick reality check. Atlanta had booked a feed. Mitch, our usual editor, was at the Sino-Soviet border. Cynde and I had to scramble. She recalled the climax of this day in her diary:

> It is another crash edit. The energy and intensity of a good story takes on a life of its own. But none of it will matter if we don't make it to the television station in time. DEATH RIDE TO THE FEED POINT!!! Racing down crowded streets at bicycle rush hour, Mike guns it, swerving around riders. He takes out a stationary flatbed bicycle, which starts a chain reaction knocking down other parked bicycles. We have only minutes to get there. Stopping would tie us up for hours. Mike guns it again past the growing crowd. We run to the feed room but stop just short of the door. After all, you can't have the competition knowing how close you came to missing the feed. Mike and I and our twisted ladder and our heavy, out-of-date equipment feed the best story, beating out the networks with their army of shooters and producers. But, more important, we get the story out. The world begins to watch. The young technicians at CCTV put out extra effort to help us get the story on the air. You can feel their excitement is as great as ours.

A week later, the students did it again. For the second time, Cynde and I, now thankfully rejoined by Mitch, made the exhausting ten-mile trek from the university district to Tiananmen, along with an estimated 100,000 students and other demonstrators. It was May 4, one of the most politically loaded dates in the Chinese calendar, and the students had draped themselves in the mantle of their activist predecessors who, exactly seventy years before, had launched China's first student protest movement.

The march was the climax of a remarkable week of dramatic twists and turns. As the massive demonstration on April 27 drew to a close, the authorities, having failed to stop the protest, and taken aback by its size, announced their willingness to talk with the demonstrators, but only through officially sanctioned student organizations. Two sets of meetings with a limited number of students selected by the government were held, and both of them were shown on Chinese television. The official media portrayed the talks as proof that the Party was genuinely seeking a dialogue. On the campuses, the students I spoke to described the government's action as a "farce" and "trick." Frustrated with the lack of meaningful dis-

cussion, representatives of the independent student union met at
Beijing Normal University (Beishida) on Tuesday, May 2. Cynde,
Mitch, and I watched them emerge from a classroom building with
a list of twelve demands—official recognition chief among them.
Led by Wang Dan, who already had impressed me with his intellect
and quiet determination, they mounted their bicycles and set out to
deliver the petition to the Great Hall of the People. We drove alongside, stopping briefly to shoot, then racing on ahead to join the throng
of reporters who crowded around Wang Dan as he mounted the
steps of the Great Hall and handed the document to a low-ranking
official. Wang told us the students had given the government until
noon the following day to make a positive reply. Without a response,
they would take to the streets again.

Less than twenty-four hours later we and other reporters gathered at a news conference where government spokesman Yuan Mu
swiftly rejected the ultimatum, accusing student organizers of
"engaging in a political struggle against the leaders of the Chinese
Communist Party." Yuan had also been the official representative
in the failed attempts at "dialogue" the previous weekend. I was not surprised the talks had made no headway. I found Yuan so arrogant,
condescending, and patronizing that he was almost physically
repulsive. "Reptilian" was the description frequently used by my colleagues in the press corps. With his oily, slicked-back hair and leering
expression, he oozed insincerity. The contrast with the freshfaced, idealistic students could not have been greater. That afternoon, we
watched as the students met on the sunlit Beishida campus to decide
how to proceed. Halfway through the meeting, student leader Wu'er
Kaixi took the floor. Handsome and dashing, his shirt half unbuttoned,
playing as always to the cameras, he announced, "On Thursday, May
fourth, we will march to commemorate the May Fourth Movement!"
The crowd erupted into applause.

After Yuan Mu's threats, I was sure the students were on a collision course with the government, and I wondered how many more
humiliations the authorities would take. But to my surprise, there
were even fewer police at the May 4 march than at the demonstration the previous week. Ignoring the official warnings, the huge
crowd reached the square almost without incident, again occupying the Communist Party's hallowed ground at the base of the
Monument to the Heroes of the Revolution. The students found

important new allies on this day: in a striking gesture of defiance, three hundred journalists from the *People's Daily* and other state-run media joined the protest, lending new weight to the demands for freedom of the press. They carried banners reading DON'T BELIEVE WHAT WE WRITE. WE PRINT LIES. It was the start of agitation that, within days, led to the unprecedented drama of the official Chinese press for the first time openly and objectively reporting on antigovernment activity. There were demonstrations reported in Shanghai, Changsha, Xian, and other cities as well. The rebellious spirit of the May Fourth Movement was very much alive.

After the May 4 march, however, the students began to run out of energy and ideas. Within days, the independent student union voted to end its boycott and return to classes. But the decision was not unanimous. Signs of division had appeared within the students' ranks. The more radical leaders wanted to press on with action in the streets. The uncertainty was compounded by a conciliatory overture from Communist Party chief Zhao Ziyang. While the students rallied in the square on May 4, Zhao addressed two thousand delegates from the Asian Development Bank across the street in the Great Hall of the People. Ignoring the embarrassingly huge crowd protesting just outside, Zhao reversed weeks of government threats, declaring that "reasonable demands from the students should be met through democratic and legal means." With the momentum for street protests fading and the authorities apparently taking a milder line, it seemed that compromise might be possible. We learned later, however, that Zhao's speech infuriated Deng Xiaoping and other hard-liners, fueling a split in the leadership that made it increasingly difficult for Party moderates to explore the prospects for dialogue. The split in the Party was an important element of the story, but the leadership cleavage was not immediately apparent to those of us caught up in charting the daily drama on the streets and the campuses.

Like the students, Cynde, Mitch, and I were utterly exhausted, worn out by weeks of little sleep, constant action, unrelenting competitive pressure, and a lack of reinforcements. But our shared experiences over the past month had also solidified the strong bond we had already forged during the two difficult years we had just lived through while setting up the CNN Beijing bureau. We no longer operated as three individuals but as one seamless unit, fiercely loyal, protecting and guiding each other in the field. Just as soldiers in combat fight not for grand ideals but for the buddy who shares their foxhole, so we too became soul mates, sustained by a feeling that it was the three of us against the world. We responded to what we were witnessing in similar ways. We understood not only our own roles, but how the others would react. Although we remained understaffed, we felt we were giving our competitors a run for their money. While the other networks, with their greater resources, began flying in help, CNN was waiting until the Gorbachev visit before bringing in extra troops. Atlanta did agree to hire Donna Liu, my old friend from Hong Kong, on a freelance basis; she was visiting relatives in Beijing while on a sabbatical from CNN. I also gave more responsibility to the bureau's part-time researcher and newspaper clipper, a young Chinese-speaking English teacher at Beijing Normal University named Jessica Smith. But I watched the extra camera crews and reporters now assisting my colleagues at CBS, ABC, and NBC with considerable envy. When, in the wake of the massive May 4 demonstration, the pace of events slowed down, I was very relieved, not least because I had come down with an acute case of laryngitis.

As my voice gradually returned, I busied myself with writing and editing the background stories on Sino-Soviet relations that I had not found time to do amid the tumult of the previous weeks. By the time I was completely recovered, the army of CNN staffers assigned to the summit coverage at last began to descend on Beijing. Along with Alec Miran, who would run the operation, came anchor Bernard Shaw, Moscow bureau chief Steve Hurst, and New York–based correspondent Jeanne Moos. They were joined by a half dozen engineers, two additional camera crews, videotape editors, an assignment editor, a director, a newswriter, two studio lighting technicians, a computer expert, a shipping agent to handle importing all our equipment through Chinese customs, and a unit manager, Joyce Fraser. I was impressed by the scale of the CNN operation until I learned that CBS had more than twice as many reporters and crews, plus anchor Dan Rather. We weren't "Chicken Noodle News" anymore, but we were still outgunned by the big-three networks.

My old friend, Tokyo bureau chief John Lewis, flew in to work as a producer. He greeted me warmly in the lobby of the Great Wall Sheraton. "Yo, dude! What have you put these Chinese students up to? I get nervous every time you and I work together. The last two times we collaborated, we had an assassination and street riots in India, and then a revolution in the Philippines! What are you going to do for an encore here?" I laughed and expressed my hope that things might now be calming down.

The network's coverage plan called for Bernie Shaw to anchor segments of four different broadcasts for the week of the summit. Hurst, who regularly traveled with the Soviet leader on his overseas visits, would cover the Gorbachev events. I would be responsible for the Chinese angle, and Moos, one of CNN's wittiest writers, would do features and color stories. Apart from edited packages, all of us would be expected to do live shots and what were known as "donuts," in which the reporter provides a live, on-camera introduction and conclusion to a previously edited story. Largely through the heroic efforts of my Chinese colleague Tan Yadong, who used his negotiating talents and remarkable ability to get things done in the Chinese system, we had secured permission to broadcast live from the rostrum at Tiananmen. With its spectacular view of the entire square, it would provide a perfect vantage point for covering Gorbachev's planned arrival ceremony in front of the Great Hall of the People, set for Monday, May 15.

While our engineers assembled the portable satellite dish, ran cables, installed microwave links, and transformed the hotel's garden pavilion into an anchor set for Bernie Shaw, the more radical students, frustrated by the government's continued unwillingness to begin a meaningful dialogue and worried that their movement was running out of steam, decided to ratchet up the pressure. The imminent arrival of Mikhail Gorbachev suddenly gave them something they had so far lacked: bargaining power. Hundreds of journalists from all over the world, including scores of television crews, were now in Beijing to cover a summit that should have been one of Deng Xiaoping's most important diplomatic achievements. It was a historic event. The Soviet leader was coming to China's capital to heal a rift dating back three decades, one that had long shaped the face of global politics, and which had produced, among other things, the Sino-American rapprochement pioneered by Richard Nixon. Now these two giant socialist neighbors, both in the midst of profound internal change (the glasnost and perestroika pioneered by Gorbachev, and Deng's *gaige* and *kaifang* or "reform" and the "open door") were putting their long-strained ties on more equal and amicable footing. Moreover, Gorbachev's visit would mark the emergence of Deng's China as a major actor on the world stage, no longer simply a card to be played in superpower diplomacy, but a force in its own right. Much of the pomp and pageantry celebrating the occasion was scheduled to take place in Tiananmen Square.

Then, two days before Gorbachev's arrival, the students stole both the spotlight and the setting for Deng's diplomatic breakthrough. Following an emotional speech by Chai Ling, in which the attractive and eloquent Beijing Normal University student leader declared, "We, the children, are ready to sacrifice ourselves!" the students began a hunger strike in the square. They demanded genuine talks on an equal footing with Party leaders and official recognition that their movement was "patriotic and democratic," in effect a retraction of the hard-line April 26 *People's Daily* editorial authorized by Deng Xiaoping. Until their demands were met, they announced, they would not eat or leave Tiananmen, embarrassing the Chinese leadership before the world at its moment of triumph.

Cynde and Mitch were at the campus of Beijing Normal University, where several hundred hunger strikers had gathered before setting off for the square. Many of them had just finished a farewell banquet. Now, wearing headbands and carrying banners, they began the ten-mile walk, led by the colorful Wu'er Kaixi.

"Every movement needs a sexy star," Cynde wrote in her diary. "Wu'er is handsome and pouty, just the kind of person TV news producers love to gobble up for lunch and spit up on the evening news."

With his flair for the dramatic—he was first of the student leaders to play to the cameras, the first to be surrounded by what looked like Chinese "groupies" attracted by his media appeal, and he had managed to have himself carried on the shoulders of his fellow marchers during one of the earlier demonstrations—Wu'er Kaixi certainly made good copy.

Meanwhile, I was outside the Russian embassy, watching a student representative deliver a letter to the Soviet leader, inviting him to meet with the protestors during his stay in Beijing. To many young Chinese, Gorbachev was something of a hero because of the political liberalization he had overseen in Moscow. Echoing a theme that would surface repeatedly in the days ahead, the student told us, "Gorbachev's reforms have been extremely successful in the Soviet Union. China could learn a lot in this area, especially about political reform. We want to understand their methods for developing democracy."

Rejoining Cynde, I found the students had effectively taken control of Tiananmen. In front of the Monument to the Heroes of the Revolution, an enormous flag with the Chinese characters for "hunger strike" had been raised. Around it, the hunger strikers sat or lay on pieces of cardboard or newspaper, protected by a cordon of marshals. Behind them was a large and rapidly growing crowd of supporters. That night, student leaders held their first press conference in the square, spelling out their demands in front of a throng of reporters and cameramen. They were far more sophisticated in handling the media than they had been just a few weeks earlier, providing English translators for their remarks as well as signs and banners in English (GIVE ME DEMOCRACY OR GIVE ME DEATH) and in Russian (DEMOCRACY, OUR COMMON GOAL) for the crews and still photographers. They were aware that the media gave them leverage, and they clearly intended to use it.

The next day, nearly 3,000 students had joined the hunger strike, and the number of people in the square continued to grow. By midafternoon, the first students began to faint from hunger and heat exhaustion. Sirens blaring, ambulances began ferrying them to local hospitals as the government made a last-ditch attempt to convince the students to leave. Warning that a continued presence could jeopardize the position of Zhao Ziyang and the reformers, associates of the Party chief pleaded with student leaders to go. Skeptical of the government's sincerity and emboldened by the massive outpouring of public support, the students turned a deaf ear. This failure to bring the occupation of Tiananmen to an end before Gorbachev's arrival fatally undermined Zhao Ziyang's position in the leadership. Had the students departed, a compromise that would have protected their gains and preserved Zhao in power might have been possible. Instead, by disrupting the Soviet leader's visit and embarrassing Deng Xiaoping, the hard-liners in the Chinese government were immeasurably strengthened. Although it would not become clear until later, the final opportunity for compromise had disappeared.

As a red sun burned through the dawn mists on Monday, May 15, I stood on the roof of the Great Wall Sheraton Hotel and did my first live shot from Beijing.

"At this hour," I told our viewers, "there are growing fears of a serious confrontation between the Chinese students and their government."

Late Sunday, the police had announced that Tiananmen Square would be closed to the public. Everyone was ordered to leave by 8:30 on Monday morning. Walking through the square that night, past hunger strikers huddled in blankets, I could feel the fear. Yet, as the deadline approached, the police took no action. Either the government was being extraordinarily tolerant, or it was in such disarray that it was unable to respond to this latest in a long series of humiliations. Finishing up at the Sheraton, I raced to the square to join Steve Hurst and other colleagues for our initial live broadcast from the Tiananmen rostrum. It seemed clear that the story of the day was not going to be Mikhail Gorbachev's arrival in Beijing.

To go live from Tiananmen Square required CNN engineers to align a microwave link on the rostrum so that it had a direct line of sight with another microwave at CCTV, which then beamed the signal from our Tiananmen camera back across Beijing to the Sheraton, where our uplink sent it to a satellite, then down to CNN Atlanta headquarters, back up to another set of satellites and onto television sets around the world. Shortly before nine, our engineers tested the signal, as well as the audio link that would, by means of walkie-talkies patched through a phone line at the Sheraton, enable us to hear both the anchors and the instructions of producer Miran.

It all worked.

Moments later, Hurst and I were on the air, detailing the scene below us for Bernie Shaw and our global audience. The view from the rostrum was awe-inspiring, conveying far better than any ground-level perspective not only the square's immense size but its potency as a political symbol. With its vast open spaces, the huge obelisk of the Heroes Monument in the middle, the solid rectangular mausoleum housing the remains of Chairman Mao behind it, and the massive edifices of the Great Hall of the People on the west and the Revolutionary Museum on the east, it was indeed the center of China, a shrine to Mao's Communist revolution. As cameraman Mike Johnson panned down, I described a thin line of police stretched along both sides of Changan Street. But it was clear that the rest of Tiananmen belonged to the students. Gorbachev's plane was due in a couple of hours. It seemed impossible that his welcoming ceremony could be held while the students controlled the heart of Beijing.

With our first live shot finished, we took a short breather while waiting for the top of the next hour, when we would be on again. Suddenly I heard faint chants from the crowd. I turned to cameraman Johnson. "Whoa, to your right, Mike! They've broken through the line!"

Sure enough, in the square's northeast corner, a large crowd of students had surged forward, pushed the police back, and flooded onto Changan Street. I grabbed one of our portable radios.

"Tiananmen to base. We've got students breaking through police lines and running out to the barrier in the middle of the street."

For several minutes as the cameras rolled, the students pushed and shoved the police, who were far more skilled in controlling traffic than angry crowds. Eventually the police re-formed, leaving a small corridor in the middle of the street. It was a minor episode, but we could imagine how powerful such images must have looked to audiences tens of thousands of miles away, watching the event as it happened. And it was just a foretaste of the much greater drama to come in the days ahead. Shortly afterward, word came that the government had moved Gorbachev's welcoming ceremony from Tiananmen to the old Beijing Airport. There, he was greeted by Chinese President Yang Shangkun and given a twenty-one-gun salute. I could only imagine the anger and humiliation the veteran revolutionaries felt at seeing the students spoil a moment that had been years in the making.

Early in the afternoon, finally freed of my live-shot duties, I made my way from the rostrum across Changan Street and into the square to see up close the phenomenon I had been describing. It was like walking into a huge festival. There were perhaps as many as a hundred thousand people—students, workers, intellectuals, shop assistants, teachers, young couples strolling hand in hand, and parents with clinging infants. Many carried banners: WE WANT CLEAN GOVERNMENT, DENG XIAOPING RESIGN, DEMOCRACY IS OUR COMMON DREAM, HELLO MR. GORBACHEV. More compelling than the slogans or the numbers, however, were the expressions on people's faces. They were vibrant and animated, full of laughter and life, as if awakened after years of enforced silence. In this one corner of China, where the People's Republic was actually controlled by the people, the mask of emotional and political reserve I had often encountered among so many Chinese seemed to be disappearing before my eyes. The mere act of coming to Tiananmen Square was a liberating experience. Suddenly made citizens of their own free space, the students began to take responsibility for their lives in a way I had rarely seen in China. Instead of being routinely rude, people were polite and solicitous of others. Hostility or embarrassment toward foreigners was replaced by a sense of directness and pride. I could feel the air of freedom.

The square was now a vast camp with a student "command center," where activists cranked out leaflets from makeshift printing presses, blared announcements from a crude broadcasting system hooked up around the monument, operated a clinic, and tried to manage the huge, seemingly endless flow of people. At its heart were the hunger strikers, most now sitting or lying listlessly in the hot May sun, some smoking or reading, others singing or playing cards. Most of them were surrounded by a circle of supporters from their own university. In a country where food is an obsession, where many people were old enough to remember when millions starved to death in famines, and where a common greeting was "Have you eaten?" the students' decision to starve themselves stirred powerful emotions. More than the chanting of slogans, the speeches shouted through bullhorns, or the singing of *The Internationale*, the sound that dominated Tiananmen Square that week was the wail of sirens as ambulances carted away yet another student.

I spoke to some of the hunger strikers. "I feel now many more people are standing up," said one cigarette-smoking Beida student with a white headband and a green checked jacket. "They don't like what the government is broadcasting or saying. They know who is right and who is wrong, so I am very encouraged." Added a fellow striker, "Before the hunger strike, the government didn't take any notice when we demonstrated or boycotted classes. It wouldn't talk to us. So I think the hunger strike is the last resort. We must make the government recognize our student union and acknowledge that our action is patriotic. Please, tell the truth to the whole world."

I returned to the Sheraton for another live shot to "donut" my story, wrapping up the day's events, which I described as the latest in a series of humiliating retreats for the government. "This massive explosion of discontent has sent shock waves through the Chinese leadership," I reported, "fueling divisions between reformists like Communist Party chief Zhao Ziyang, who sympathizes with the students, and hard-liners opposed to political change. Ironically, the biggest loser today has been Deng Xiaoping. His power and prestige have been deeply eroded. This unprecedented challenge to his authority has overshadowed what should have been the crowning diplomatic triumph of his long career."

Late in the evening, I was back in Tiananmen, where things were getting out of hand. Someone with a bullhorn had urged the crowd to push their way into the Great Hall of the People. Suddenly police emerged from the doors, and a clash seemed inevitable. After much shouting, the protestors fell back. But the episode worried some thoughtful student activists. "These are Beijing citizens, not simply students," one of them said to me. "We students can't control them. The government must talk with the students as soon as possible. If they don't talk, there is going to be a problem." It was an early sign of trouble. The movement, which had held together precariously for a month, was beginning to fragment, even as its size and the stakes in its battle with the government continued to escalate.

At ten o'clock on Tuesday, May 16, Mikhail Gorbachev and Deng Xiaoping shook hands in the Great Hall of the People at the start of a two-and-a-half-hour meeting that officially brought the Sino-Soviet conflict to an end. Along with a camera crew and an engineer lugging the microwave equipment, Steve Hurst and I had arrived at the Tiananmen rostrum shortly after eight to discover that our permission to broadcast from that vantage point had been rescinded. A surly security officer told us the rostrum was now off-limits. With a live shot scheduled for the top of the next hour, we were stuck. Then the engineer suggested trying to set up the microwave in Tiananmen Square itself. We hauled the gear across the street, found an open spot just to the east of the flagpole at the north end of the square and set to work. After much testing and tweaking, the engineer let out a yell.

"I've got it!" he shouted. "I've got line of sight with CCTV. This is gonna work!"

At nine o'clock, Steve and I were on the air from inside Tiananmen, talking about the hunger strike and the historic meeting about to get under way.

211

The pictures from the square were riveting. We decided to make the camera and microwave position permanent, and to staff it twenty-four hours a day. After some scrounging, we rigged up a makeshift platform and strung some rope to keep the gawking crowds at bay. At the same time, CNN booked a room at the Beijing Hotel, just a few hundred yards away. Given my earlier, unhappy experiences with the hotel's management, we decided to take no chances. CNN producer Larry Register reserved the room in the name of "Register Surveying Company," explaining that the camera tripod he was carrying was actually surveying equipment. Whether they believed him or not, the hotel staff gave him the room he requested, with a balcony and a good view of the northern half of the square. With its phone line, power supply to recharge batteries, room service, shower, and bed, the room provided exhausted staffers a place to check in, take a break, and prepare to rejoin the masses outside. We dubbed it "Tokyo Base."

That afternoon, I drove to the Shangri-La Hotel in northwestern Beijing to interview Professor Steve Goldstein, a Smith College sinologist and old family friend who specialized on Sino-Soviet affairs. The Shangri-La was also the headquarters for CBS News. I stuck my head in the CBS office to say hello to Mike Lam, my one-time colleague from my days at CBS in Hong Kong, now working as a producer for Dan Rather. Greeting me, he took me to a corner and said admiringly, "How did you guys go live from Tiananmen this morning? Rather went ballistic when he saw it. He wants to know why we got beat by CNN."

I smiled and replied, "We just try harder."

At the end of the day, Rather and a CBS team arrived at the square with their own microwave equipment. Walking up to John Lewis at the CNN live-shot location, one of Rather's producers announced to him, "We're going to shoot here."

"No you're not," John shot back. "This is CNN's position. We've been here for hours. We've got it staked out."

Another, more senior, CBS producer walked over. Pointing to Rather, he lectured John, "Apparently, you don't know who he is."

"I certainly do. But you can find your own fucking live-shot location."

At that moment, Mike Lam raced up and pulled his pompous, angry colleagues away, and CBS set up in another part of the square.

The crowds on this second day were so big that Gorbachev was forced to abandon plans to lay a wreath at the Heroes Monument. Later visits to the Forbidden City and a Beijing Opera performance were also canceled, and the Soviet leader was compelled to switch his press conference from the Great Hall of the People to the government's state guest house, Diaoyutai. For a leader like Deng Xiaoping, who was accustomed to unquestioned obedience and total control, these indignities, broadcast around the world, must have been especially mortifying. How much more humiliation, I kept asking myself, could the government take?

Late in the day, Gorbachev met with Zhao Ziyang. The two men, both ardent reformers, appeared to hit it off. In full view of the TV cameras, Zhao mentioned that Deng Xiaoping was still the Communist Party's helmsman, who was consulted on all important decisions. On the surface, that didn't seem to be much of a surprise. But in the opaque world of high-level Chinese politics, it was Zhao's way of trying to shift the blame for the current political crisis directly onto Deng, an admission of his own powerlessness to resolve the situation. In the pressures of the moment, though, with CNN demanding instant analysis, I misunderstood its importance. I interpreted Zhao's statement as a sign that Deng was endorsing the surprisingly tolerant line the leadership had taken since Gorbachev's arrival.

I could not have been more wrong.

Nonetheless, the signs of moderation were remarkable. Despite rumors about the mobilization of troops, security forces were hardly in evidence. Moreover, an unprecedented wave of openness was sweeping through the Chinese media. CCTV began to broadcast regular, balanced reports on the protest, while the *People's Daily* and other official newspapers ran sympathetic articles about the students, as well as photographs of the huge crowds in Tiananmen. It was no wonder so many foreign reporters were convinced the students would win. I still remained skeptical. I had been studying China for too long to believe that the Party hard-liners would give in without a fight.

What happened the next day almost changed my mind. After our usual round of live shots in the first part of the morning, timed for the main Tuesday evening broadcasts in the U.S., I looked around and realized that something astonishing was under way. On this brilliantly sunny day, the huge crowds of the previous two days were dwarfed by an endless procession of marchers surging into the square. Beijing had never seen anything like it. Over the walkie-talkie, I pleaded with Alec for more airtime. We had to put this on live, I told him. It was just an incredible sight.

People from all walks of life were turning out to support the students. Among the protestors, I could see large numbers of workers carrying the banners of their factories, followed by hotel service staff, musicians, farmers, intellectuals, even a surprising number of old people. Most extraordinary were the representatives of the established order. One after another, organized groups from the *People's Daily*, the cadre training school of the Chinese Communist Party, China's national airline, CCTV, and the National Radio paraded past our live-shot location toward the center of the square. Then, to my astonishment, members of the Logistics Staff of the Chinese army arrived, not armed soldiers, but the military nonetheless.

The atmosphere was electric, a cacophony of banging drums, chanting, and singing against the backdrop of continuous wailing from the ambulances taking away hunger strikers, who were collapsing at a rapidly increasing rate. So much was happening that our shooter was forced to spin the camera from one scene to the next to keep up. The outpouring seemed to me to change the whole character of the movement. It was still peaceful, still good-humored. But with the general consensus among reporters that the crowds may well have exceeded one million, it had now taken on the character of a vast popular uprising, one laced with far more direct attacks on Deng Xiaoping than at the start. I was reminded of the People Power demonstrations I had seen in Manila in 1986, and I hoped this story would have as happy an ending. But a movement in which the students were joined by workers and other sectors of Chinese society was the government's worst nightmare. For all the government's restraint, I had a gnawing feeling the denouement was less likely to resemble People Power than the Prague Spring of 1968, which was crushed when Soviet tanks entered Czechoslovakia.

The bleakness of my mood was matched by an abrupt change in the weather and a sharp heightening of tension the following day. Overnight, Zhao Ziyang and Premier Li Peng visited a Beijing hospital and spoke with several hunger strikers. The meeting was broadcast on Chinese television, and the tape made available to

CNN and other foreign networks. It appeared to be a last-ditch attempt by the government to show its desire for a settlement and to convince the students to leave the square. My voice hoarse from overwork and lack of sleep, I began my live reports that morning by interviewing a hunger striker named Zhang Hongwei, who dismissed the gesture as meaningless. "It is far from enough," he told me, his eyes shining from his gaunt face. "Too many people have suffered from the hunger strike. The government must have a real dialogue with the students and recognize that we are patriotic. We are determined to fight to the very end."

Throughout the morning, as Mikhail Gorbachev wound up his official visit and left for a brief stop in Shanghai before flying home, I had the sense that Chinese society was unraveling. Workers walked off their jobs and headed for the square, among them the construction workers building a new office tower across from the CNN workspace at the Great Wall Sheraton Hotel. They joined the protest still wearing their green plastic hard hats. Lines of poster-draped buses jammed the streets, their horns honking as they followed the crowds in the streets. What seemed like the staff from every shop on Wangfujing Street had left work and were headed toward Tiananmen. One group carried a banner reading COMMERCIAL AND INDUSTRIAL WORKERS SUPPORT THE STUDENTS; others carried cartoon caricatures of Li Peng.

The protest movement had spread to other cities, including Shanghai. Cynde accompanied Steve Hurst to cover Gorbachev's stop there, and found herself in the midst of a 100,000-strong demonstration. She recounted the scene in her diary.

> When we arrived, we decided to film the protests, rather than Gorby. We headed to the center of town. The roads were clogged with protestors. Arriving at the main rally, we began filming. Our time was very tight and I had to work quickly. Disaster. I cannot find our van. All I could see was a sea of black heads where the van was once parked. Suddenly my heart leaped. I saw a van nosing through the crowd. Yes, it was our driver. he had gone to a store and filled the van with bread for the demonstrators to eat. The van is literally packed, door-to-door, floor to ceiling, with bread. We abandoned the van. Steve and company left for the air-

port and I attempted to get to the TV station. Walking in front
of a car, I held up the videotapes as people begin to help me
find a path. It was a ridiculous scene as the crowd yelled and
clapped "American TV, American TV, clear the way!"

In Beijing, I stood beneath Mao's portrait at the Tiananmen gate,
watching the square as dark rain clouds formed over the capital, turning the sky black in the middle of the day. Gusts of wind swept
through the streets, followed moments later by a torrential downpour. I didn't believe in heavenly omens or signs, but it would not
have been hard to interpret this as a warning of impending disaster.
The storm left the hunger strikers and their supporters miserable and
wet, and turned the students' encampment at Tiananmen into a
soggy, smelly mess, with shredded banners hanging limply in the
gloom and mist. By now, the few public toilets bordering the square
were filthy and clogged. The stench of garbage and human waste
floating up from the pavement was overpowering, and medics assisting the protestors began to worry openly about the deteriorating
sanitary conditions. I was relieved to return to the Sheraton at the
end of the day.

It was here that I witnessed the next incredible twist in a drama
where each day seemed to bring a development even more sensational than the day before. Finally, and in my view far too late, the
Party leadership agreed to meet with student leaders and broadcast a
videotape of the encounter on television. CNN was by now totally
consumed with the China story, and fed the CCTV broadcast back to
Atlanta for simultaneous rebroadcast around the world. Sitting in the
CNN workspace, I watched as Premier Li Peng confronted Wang
Dan, Wu'er Kaixi, and other prominent activists inside the Great Hall
of the People. It was a compelling drama. Unintimidated by the premier, Wu'er Kaixi, who had just arrived from a hospital after
collapsing from lack of food and was wearing striped hospital paja-
mas, brashly interrupted Li Peng, challenging him to meet the
students' demands. Wu'er's views were echoed by the other students.
This daring display of defiance left Li Peng visibly flustered and
angry as he issued a blunt warning to the students to bring the hunger
strike to an end:

"Disorder has already appeared in Beijing and is spreading across
the whole country. Beijing is in a state of anarchy. We cannot ignore
the current situation. We must protect the achievements of socialism."

The two sides were talking past each other and the meeting solved nothing. With Gorbachev now gone, the government hard-liners intensified their preparations for a crackdown.

Back in the square early Friday morning to resume our live transmissions, I found the mood to be one of frustration, disappointment, and anger over the students' fruitless discussion with Li Peng. Gone was the exultation on their faces so evident earlier in the week. Now they appeared grim and exhausted, talking quietly together in small groups or listening to broadcasts from their "Command Center." For the first time, I also detected some real anxiety, as word of troop movements and a possible crackdown swept the square. The rumors had been fueled by a dramatic appearance in Tiananmen by Zhao Ziyang. At 4:45 A.M., the beleaguered Party leader made his first and only visit to the fasting students. "I have come too late," he told them, his hands trembling and tears in his eyes. Defeated by the hard-liners in the Politburo, aware he could do no more to protect the demonstrators, Zhao appealed to the students to end the hunger strike. It was to be his last public appearance.

Throughout the day and into the evening, I watched Wu'er Kaixi, Wang Dan, Chai Ling, Li Lu, and other student leaders, having been tipped off about a likely crackdown, anxiously debating their next move. After Zhao's appeal, serious consideration was being given to ending the hunger strike and even vacating the square. "If Zhao's words represented the central government," said student leader Li Lu, "we also would make concessions. We would change from a hunger strike to a sit-in."

As darkness fell, Steve Hurst and I stood at the live-shot location and prepared to go on the air again. We continued to hear rumors that Zhao Ziyang had been sidelined, that the leadership had decided to crack down, and that the army was being called in to restore order. There was, of course, no way to confirm such information. In fact, throughout the crisis one of our biggest problems was dealing with unsubstantiated rumors. Secretive in the best of times, the Chinese government offered no mechanism with which to check such reports. Yet CNN was constantly on the air. The demand for fresh information was unrelenting, and the fact that our broadcasts were being seen inside China only intensified the pressure. There was little I could do but use extra care to sift through the rumors that were constantly sweeping the square.

Yet I was lucky because, in the feverish atmosphere of the past few days, I had befriended a young reporter from Radio Beijing named Liu. A thin, intense man whose father had fought with Mao in the revolution and was now a senior government bureaucrat, Liu had studied journalism in college and harbored ambitions of some-day becoming more than a vehicle for a propaganda organ of the state. During the past few nights, we had gotten to know each other, swapping information and insights, and sharing guesses about what might happen next. Sympathetic to the students, by virtue of his position and his family connections, he also had access to reliable information about the high-level power struggle now under way.

On this night, all the evidence pointed to decisive government action. Liu was saying he'd heard that the Politburo Standing Committee had voted four to one in favor of a tougher line, with Zhao Ziyang the only holdout. Dave Schweisberg told me his sources were reporting similar information. The main seven o'clock CCTV news bulletin, which CNN had been broadcasting with simul-taneous translation for the past several evenings, abruptly dropped its evenhanded coverage of the students in the square. Instead the announcers repeated Li Peng's call for the hunger strikers to give up. And at nine, while I was in the middle of a live report, the loud-speakers in the square suddenly began to blare out a strongly worded appeal for the students to leave.

Around the same time, students at Beijing University reported seeing military trucks moving toward the center of Beijing. As Bernie Shaw broadcast this news, CNN Moscow bureau producer Bruce Conover grabbed a handycam and headed out to the suburbs in search of the arriving troops. Back on the square, the tension was acute. The students seemed to recognize that the government had finally lost patience, and they braced themselves for the worst. Meanwhile, Atlanta wanted Hurst and me on the air more or less continuously. Luckily my sinologist friend Steve Goldstein joined us, giving me an articulate academic to interview about some of the broader issues raised by the crisis.

"I think part of this was a lack of appreciation by the leadership of the depth of social tensions in China, and how such tensions can explode in the way we've seen in the last few days," Steve noted.

Together we speculated that, with the departure of Mikhail

Gorbachev, a key reason for the government to show restraint had disappeared. Moments after we finished, the students announced that they were calling off the hunger strike. At this late hour, I did not think the government would be impressed.

Bruce Conover called in to report seeing fifty trucks full of soldiers in the outskirts of Beijing. The anxious students asked us not to use our camera light during our broadcasts for fear of making the live-shot location a target if the security forces moved in. Some minutes later, Conover's tape arrived back at the Sheraton and was immediately put on the air.

"As this convoy inched closer to the square," Bernie reported, "people were shouting to them 'Get off the trucks. Join the students in their cause.' And a group of people said, 'There's no reason to use force. Keep it peaceful. Step down and join us.' With six minutes to go before the midnight deadline for the students to leave the square," Bernie went on, "these are the live pictures from Tiananmen. In this capital city, everyone is watching to see what will happen here, and, of course, the world is watching."

By midnight, the crowd had thinned out somewhat, but the hard-core protestors showed no sign of leaving. In the darkness, I could hear the crashing of bottles from time to time. I told our viewers it was a political gesture: *xiaoping* also means "small bottle," and one of the acts of defiance we had seen was the smashing of small bottles to show their distaste for Deng Xiaoping. As I spoke, Bernie interrupted me. "We want to show our viewers something that's happening at CCTV. A slide is up, and we're hearing music now—an indication many times in nations around the world of something important about to happen on national television."

Moments later, our viewers around the world watched as Li Peng appeared on the screen and declared that the government's patience was at an end. The Communist Party, he announced, was taking "resolute and decisive measures to put an end to the turmoil." It appeared that a declaration of martial law and a military crackdown was imminent. In the square, the crowds became silent as Li's muffled voice echoed over the loudspeakers dotted throughout the vast, hundred-acre expanse. In the midst of the speech, we developed technical problems with our earpieces, making it extremely hard for us to hear the English translation being broadcast on CNN's air. Steve Hurst and I fumed in frustration, and the possibility that troops could be in Tiananmen in a matter of minutes left everyone nervous. We discussed with our crews what to do if the army arrived. Noticing a three-foot high concrete wall by the flagpole next to the live-shot location, we agreed that lying down next to it might offer a small amount of safety.

Alec Miran, who had managed to stay calm and keep the whole operation going all week, came up on the walkie-talkie to ask how many people were still in the square.

"A good number," I replied, "but it's thinning. I think it's only the most committed, because it's very clear what's coming. However, Alec, down to my left, a lot of the people have moved that way to confront the troops. Some of them have also moved down on the other side of the Great Hall of the People to be in a position to confront the troops there." Alec wanted to know what we were going to do. "Some of these buses are staying," I replied, "which is good, because we're going to stay. We're going to try to hide behind or in a bus. The cops around the flagpole have guns, and I am not sure they want us jumping in there."

I started to take my passport and checkbooks out of my bag in case we had to run, while in the background I could hear chants of "Down with Li Peng." As the premier's speech was rebroadcast on the loudspeakers, the square erupted in more boos, jeers, and catcalls. A convoy of motorcycles raced up and down Changan Street to demonstrate support. The students announced they were resuming the hunger strike.

From the outskirts of the city, where John Lewis had relieved Conover with the handycam, came more astonishing reports. The People's Liberation Army had been stopped—by the people. The videotapes being shuttled back to the Sheraton showed one remarkable scene after another, of huge crowds, people linking hands to surround the troop trucks and pleading with bewildered soldiers to halt their advance. This really was People Power—unarmed citizens putting their bodies on the line to block the military force of an oppressive ruler. The students announced over their loudspeakers that the soldiers had been stopped. With the approach of dawn, word of the crackdown was spreading across the city, prompting a huge new influx of outraged people to move toward the square.

It was just after nine A.M. on Saturday, May 20, when two officials of the Ministry of Posts and Telecommunications walked into the CNN workspace on the ninth floor of the Sheraton and ordered CNN to cease its live transmissions from Beijing in an hour.

"You are here to report on Gorbachev," they said. "Gorbachev is gone. Your task is over."

At the same time, loudspeakers in the square and the official Xinhua News Agency were issuing the same proclamation—martial law was being imposed, and would take effect at ten A.M.

Moments later, I received my summons from Alec Miran to return to the hotel at once. Driving away from the city center, I encountered enormous crowds of people streaming toward the square, angered by news of the government's decision, reinforcing my conviction that the masses in Beijing were on the side of the students. With correspondent Jeanne Moos on duty at the live-shot location, I joined Bernie and Steve Hurst at the anchor set in the Sheraton garden. Shortly afterward, John Lewis, who had been on the western side of Beijing watching "People Power" bring the advance of the PLA to a halt, joined us as we tried to put some last-minute thoughts together. Without enough chairs to go around, we stood in front of the anchor desk, sharing the one tiny microphone normally attached to Bernie's lapel. As we spoke, producer Larry Register passed along to Bernie details of the martial-law orders, which banned processions, demonstrations, boycotts, strikes and all news coverage by Chinese or foreign journalists.

"The thing that struck me when we just left the square," Steve noted, "is that you have the Chinese army on the outskirts of the capital and they can't get to town."

"The men who rule China are used to having their orders obeyed instantly," I added. "The notion that their armed forces would refuse to obey orders is mind-boggling, breathtaking. The implications are staggering. I think there is tremendous risk now in this situation and tremendous possibility of confrontation, if the government moves to carry out martial law. I think there is now a great danger of bloodshed. If they continue in power, it will only be through brute force."

At ten o'clock, Bernie started to count down the last ten seconds before the transmission ended. Nine floors upstairs, in the CNN control room, producer Larry Register said we were now operating on borrowed time. The camera panned away from us toward the CNN portable satellite dish.

"I've been told a representative of the Chinese government is now standing by at the flyaway," Bernie noted, "awaiting orders to pull the plug."

Two grim-faced Chinese officials in sports jackets walked back into the control room. Through our earpieces, we were told by producer Register that an ABC crew member had hooked up a video camera to our transmission cable and that the dramatic scene was being fed on the satellite and going out live on our air. One of the Chinese officials issued a warning. If we didn't obey and cease broadcasting, all our equipment would be confiscated by the Ministry of Posts and Telecommunications. Alec was unmoved. With assignment editor Vito Maggiolo standing next to him, he stalled for time, demanding a further explanation. Larry passed along word from CNN Atlanta to Bernie that President Bush was watching the scene at his summer home in Kennebunkport, Maine.

Suddenly the image on the screen froze. We appeared to have lost the satellite. We were told that CBS, which had been broadcasting from its own uplink at the Shangri-La Hotel, had also ceased transmission. Moments later, though, the link was reestablished. Miran was on the phone with an official from the Chinese Foreign Ministry, desperately improvising to keep us on the air.

"Are you telling us to stop as soon as possible or right now?" he asked. "Mr. Wang, our company's policy is that we would like a letter from you. What is the government afraid of?"

CNN vice president Jane Maxwell, who ran the Special Events unit, was now in the control room at CNN Center in Atlanta.

"Jane, I'm trying to make it clear that the policy of our company is to have a letter." In a hopeful tone, he asked, "Is that our policy?"

Jane answered, "Yes, Alec, we'd like it in writing because our lease to transmit on the uplink doesn't expire until tomorrow morning."

Alec picked up the other phone. "All we are requesting," he repeated to the Foreign Ministry, "is the same thing we requested in getting here, a letter."

Hanging up on Atlanta, Alec resumed sparring with the two ministry officials. Listening in, I became increasingly anxious. I thought Alec was doing a brilliant job of giving the Chinese bureaucrats a taste of their own medicine, leaving them utterly flummoxed over how to handle the kind of petty demands they invariably imposed on us, but, at the same time, I worried that we were pushing too far. If the situation wasn't resolved quickly, CNN could find itself in even bigger trouble, and as the resident correspondent, I worried that some of that would fall directly on me. I knew we had entered uncharted territory. Never before had a military crackdown against a popular uprising in a communist country, and against those who sought to report it, been televised live. Humiliated throughout the spring, an enraged and frustrated Chinese government was surely aware that its crude attempt to force us off the air was being seen around the globe. Once again, I asked myself how much more the authorities would put up with. Images of bayonet-wielding soldiers marching into our control room flashed through my mind. For my colleagues, at the worst it might mean a brief detention and then expulsion. But Beijing was my life. I had built a home here. This was not an obscure foreign crisis into which I had parachuted and could just as easily leave. Suddenly I was swept by a wave of anxiety for Lynne and Daniel, and even Sherlock. I'd hardly seen them for days. On my brief visits home for a shower or nap, I had noticed how Daniel, cranky and restless, had picked up on the tension and fear swirling around him. What would happen to our lives if the situation deteriorated further? I wondered. Would we even be able to remain in China? If we had to leave, could we get our belongings and our dog out with us? In an instant, I felt the whole fabric of our lives beginning to unravel.

The two Chinese officials were suddenly called to the telephone. One of their superiors was evidently watching and had phoned our workspace with new instructions. At 10:59, the younger of the two, Zhou Yanjun, took a pencil and began to write in Chinese on a yellow legal pad. When he finished, he looked up. I heard the voice of Vito Maggiolo saying "It needs a chop—an official chop, right?"

Good for you, Vito, I laughed to myself. Asking for an official seal, or chop, is just what they would demand.

On a split screen, our viewers watched as Alec asked Zhou to read his statement aloud in English. "As an observer of the Ministry of Telecommunications of China, and according to the directive from the superiors," he intoned, visibly uncomfortable, "Mr. Gorbachev's visit to China is over. Now I'm here announcing that CNN stop the moveable earth station and its transmission frequencies right away. Mr. Zhou Yanjun, 11:02, 20 May, 1989, Beijing summertime."

Alec turned to the microphone hooked to the audio circuit with Atlanta. "Jane?"

"Well," Maxwell replied, with CNN president Burt Reinhardt looking over her shoulder, "the government has ordered us to shut down our facility. I guess we'll have to shut it down."

"Okay," Miran answered. "Our policy is, the government has ordered us to shut down our facility. We are shutting down our facility. Okay, Bernie, sign off."

The camera switched to the four of us in the hotel garden. "Okay. We've heard the orders," Bernie said. "We've had our instructions from headquarters in Atlanta. For Steve Hurst."

"Goodbye," Hurst said. "It's been lots of fun. It's been very interesting. I've never seen anything like this."

"Interesting hardly describes what we've seen, Bernie," said John Lewis.

"The most extraordinary event I've ever witnessed in twenty years of following China," I added.

"In my twenty-six years in this business, I've never seen anything like this," Bernie said. "The situation in Tiananmen Square is that there is a standoff. The people are there. The troops are not there. They were ordered in, they came as far as they could get, five miles outside. They were talked to by the people—persuaded to leave. They turned around, promising never to come back. That's the story at the moment. For all the hardworking men and women of CNN, goodbye from Beijing."

The screen went to black. The plug had been pulled. Exactly two weeks later, troops and tanks of the People's Liberation Army rolled into Tiananmen Square.

CHAPTER EIGHT

Massacre

T he rumors swept the square like
the violent windstorms that descend on Beijing every spring, alternately intensifying and abating, only to return with even greater force: The People's Liberation Army, camped out in the suburbs of Beijing, was preparing to move. Army helicopters buzzing Tiananmen were carrying commandos for an airborne assault. A tear-gas attack was imminent. The students were preparing to leave. The students would stay until the bitter end. Zhao Ziyang and Communist Party moderates were under house arrest. Li Peng would be forced to resign. Zhao was winning the power struggle. The army was split between the crack 27th Division, loyal to the hard-liners, and the 38th, sympathetic to the students.

"Those of us who live in Beijing and have followed China for a long time," I noted in a live telephone report shortly after the Chinese pulled the plug on CNN's satellite feeds, "sit around Tiananmen Square watching this process unfold, looking at one another, scratching our heads, trying to figure out what could happen next. Where can this go? What are the implications? We simply don't know. We have entered absolutely uncharted territory."

The tide of resistance that swept through Beijing in the days immediately following the declaration of martial law on Saturday, May 20, ranged far beyond the historic, dramatic clashes of the previous weeks. I could hardly believe what was happening. Despite the government's edict and the harsh restrictions now technically in

225

effect, the city seemed to be slipping out of control as citizens abandoned their usual routines to join the protests. The machinery of government ceased to function. The traffic cops disappeared from the streets, offices and shops were left empty, and the supply of food from the farmers in the surrounding countryside began to dry up. Only the remarkable discipline and good humor of the demonstrators in the face of this collapse of central authority prevented a rapid slide into chaos.

Throughout the weekend of May 20–21, huge crowds, furious at the government's harsh measures, continued to hold convoys of soldiers at bay on the outskirts of Beijing, blocking roads and swarming over army trucks, sometimes slitting the tires, sometimes making emotional appeals to the soldiers not to move into the city center or use force against the students and their supporters. In Tiananmen, meanwhile, the number of demonstrators grew into the hundreds of thousands, perhaps even reaching a million. It became impossible, and almost pointless, to try to keep count. Crowds sealed off virtually every access road to the square in order to protect the students inside. Standing on the balcony of our "Tokyo Base," as we had dubbed our room at the Beijing Hotel, I described live over the phone for CNN the scenes I was witnessing. "The people are pulling cement barriers off the street, trying to move them and erect barricades across Changan Street in the city center. This presumably to block the movements of any military vehicles or tanks which might make a push toward the city center." Garbage bins, concrete bicycle-lane dividers, even some Beijing city buses were dragged into the roads. Earlier, walking through the square, as the wind swirled leaflets with government warnings in little circles through the air, I had watched demonstrators pass out gauze and cloth soaked in water to be used in the event of tear gas. Many had wrapped kerchiefs over their faces.

The protestors expected the worst. "Evil-doer" helped us gauge the increasingly grim mood. A young, round-faced painter we had met a few days earlier, he proudly wore a headband with this strange identification written in large, black English letters. "Evil-doer" told us he had once been a railway clerk. Disillusioned with the system, he opted out altogether, turning his energy to art. Every day, he came to the monument to sketch. When we first encountered him, his drawings of the landscape were full of bright red and yellow colors, reflecting the festive mood of the crowds. As tension mounted, his sketches turned to somber tones and dark shapes. His latest sketch of the monument was entirely in black.

Although expecting the worst, the students remained defiant. "This demonstration won't end until the government reverses its decision," insisted one young man who identified himself to us as a reporter for Radio Beijing. "Imposing martial law is against the will of the people. They may try to use force to stop the movement, but I think that's very stupid and would never work. Using force would mean suicide for the government."

Mitch Farkas managed to grab a few moments with student leader Wang Dan. Looking tired and subdued, Wang was in a pensive mood, but he insisted he wasn't afraid. "We don't think Premier Li Peng will get away with suppressing this movement," he told Mitch. "If I am arrested and jailed, I know my parents would understand that I was trying to do the right thing for my country." As to the students' plans, he revealed little.

By the night of Sunday, May 21, the tension had become almost unbearable. We were now maintaining a round-the-clock vigil at Tiananmen, with camera crews and John Lewis, Donna Liu, and other producers trading off twelve-hour shifts to ensure that the square was always covered in case the crackdown materialized. Following the satellite feed cutoff on the morning of May 20, we had kept our high vantage point at the Beijing Hotel and the Gorbachev summit workspace at the Sheraton. Sadly, with no more live transmissions, we had to abandon our live-shot location at the north end of Tiananmen, just across from the famous Mao portrait. Instead we staked out a small corner at the foot of the Monument to the Heroes of the Revolution. For the rest of the crisis, it was to become the CNN "bureau" at what we dubbed the "People's Republic of Tiananmen Square."

The square was in fact beginning to take on the characteristics of a small city. At the base of the monument, sympathizers on trucks or bicycle carts delivered food to be stockpiled along with water and medical supplies. The demonstrators erected new and better tents, purchased with money donated by supporters in Hong Kong and elsewhere outside China. They refined and improved the public address system so it could be readily heard across the vast distances of the square. Students were assigned jobs ranging from distributing meals to cleaning up garbage, while the leaders carved out a corner on one side of the monument for a more formal headquarters.

Meanwhile, we roughed out a scheme for keeping track of what was happening and of each other. In rotating shifts, the producers and crews who had joined my Beijing team for the Gorbachev summit coverage now cruised the square, taking pictures, doing interviews, and keeping a watchful eye on events. The student "runners" I'd hired to help out during the summit—a colorful collection of youthful China enthusiasts from Bulgaria, Yugoslavia, the U.S., and other countries—remained by the monument. They had the critical job of guarding the precious supplies of Snickers bars, M&M's, and the bottled water on which CNN staffers survived for the next two weeks.

Although the martial law restrictions barred reporting of the protests, we were determined to carry on. With no feed facilities, we began sending videotapes by plane for transmission from Hong Kong or Tokyo, using "pigeons"—either colleagues, friends, or, frequently, utter strangers we approached at the airport—to smuggle out our material. The level of sympathy for the students was so high that we rarely had a problem finding a traveling foreigner at the airport willing to carry the tapes. Our smuggling was technically a violation of the new martial-law regulations, but, for that matter, so was all reporting on the protests. So far, the government was making little effort to enforce the restrictions, and we, like most other news organizations, simply paid them no attention.

On this Sunday night, all the rumors of the past week suddenly crystallized into an overpowering, all-consuming fear. The army, which had amassed 150,000 troops, was coming. Li Peng had ordered Tiananmen cleared by daybreak. All through the night, our crews waited on the square, adrenaline pumping, nervously joking and pacing. Cynde watched the students tear up pieces of cloth for gas masks—little protection, she thought, if the army actually moved in. Equally jumpy in my balcony lookout at the Beijing Hotel, I saw the demonstrators grimly reinforce their roadblocks as I clutched a phone and, hour after hour, broadcast, in a hoarse voice threadbare with fatigue, what was happening below me: the crowds massed by the buses blocking Changan Street, surging back and forth from the square, clapping and chanting "Down with Li Peng!" It was an excruciating wait.

With the first rays of dawn, contrary to the fears and rumors, the army was nowhere in sight. Orders had been issued for the troops to withdraw. With many of the soldiers bewildered, disillusioned, some even weeping, the military convoys had turned around and headed out of the city. The overnight tension suddenly evaporated. The square was flooded by a wave of relief and euphoria. The exultation was fueled by indications that senior military officials were speaking out against the use of force to end the protest. Reports circulated that seven retired generals had drafted an open letter, signed by a hundred top military figures, urging the PLA not to attack fellow Chinese. To all outward appearances, it seemed the students had scored another victory.

The sense that the tide might be turning against Li Peng and the hard-liners intensified on Tuesday, May 23. Early in the morning, Donna Liu, staking out the monument with Tokyo bureau cameraman Jiro Mishina, noticed three uniformed soldiers arriving at the student headquarters. As Jiro grabbed his camera, one of the soldiers picked up a megaphone and announced to the crowd, "We support the students' democratic movement." Another, wearing glasses, raised his fists and led demonstrators in chanting "Long Live Democracy!" Later, several hundred thousand people again took to the streets in a show of support for the students, calling for Li Peng's resignation and demanding an end to martial law. In the midst of the crowd, three young men from Chairman Mao Zedong's home province of Hunan splattered the huge portrait of Chairman Mao on the wall of the rostrum with ink. It was an act of political sacrilege almost unimaginable in China, even during these turbulent times. The students, trying to keep their movement under control, were horrified. Struggling to keep his balance, Jiro fought his way through the crowd to videotape the three men as they were seized by the protestors, hustled through a corridor created when the students linked hands to break up the throng, and turned over to the police. It was not clear whether those responsible were activists or provocateurs. Whatever their motivations, all three were given long terms in prison after the movement was crushed.

Moments later, a huge dust storm blackened the sky. A howling wind raged through the city, slamming shutters, breaking windows, twisting trees, shredding flags, and sending soft drink cans and bits of debris whistling down the streets. Tiananmen Square suddenly seemed to disappear into the darkness. Out of the lowering clouds came sheets of rain, soaking the vast throngs. This must be what the wrath of God feels like, I said to myself. Or maybe it was the wrath of Mao. Whatever—it had to be an omen.

Yet at this very moment, the Chinese media, which up until that point had parroted the government line, began to report the views of those who disagreed with the emergency measures. The demonstration that afternoon, including the denunciations of Li Peng, was covered with surprising objectivity by the government-run Xinhua News Agency. China Central Television also changed its tone. Most surprising of all, early Tuesday evening we were advised by CCTV that the ban on satellite feeds had been lifted.

After an agonizingly slow drive from the square through rain-swept streets packed with protestors, I reached CCTV, five miles away, and raced to the transmission room, where I did the first CNN live shot since the plug was pulled four days before. "In an extraordinary reversal," I told our viewers, "Chinese television is now allowing Western broadcasters to transmit videotape of the events here in China from the headquarters of China national television. The decision is in direct violation of the martial-law regulations, which forbid foreign journalists from covering the unrest. It appears to be the result of a decision by the Ministry of Broadcasting and the management of China's Central Television to throw in their lot with the moderates in China's power struggle."

As I spoke, I saw the CCTV technicians grinning. Most of my friends and associates at Chinese TV had strongly supported the students and had reveled in their newfound, but all too brief, exposure to journalistic freedom. Outraged by martial law, they were clearly delighted to see the feeds resume. One of them gave me the victory sign. Another mouthed "Li Peng" and, with a scowl, drew the back of his hand across his throat. After analyzing the latest trends, I ended my report on a note of caution, pointing out that "the situation is extremely fluid, and at the highest levels of the leadership, we simply don't know what is happening."

My caution proved well-founded. Less than a day later, the Chinese reversed themselves again. With an advance warning of just a few hours, officials at CCTV abruptly announced that news transmissions were again to be cut off. The feedpoint was in chaos. Producers, technicians, and reporters—from CBS, ABC, NBC, and

CNN, from Britain's Independent Television News (ITN) and the BBC, from elsewhere in Europe, from Japan and Hong Kong—jammed the tiny facility, desperately seeking to send their video and arrange for live shots. Amid the shouting and din, the normal sense of competition was heightened to an absurd degree as each network scrambled and schemed to duplicate CNN's coup by being the one to be on the air as the Chinese cut off all feeds.

To me, all this scrambling seemed unnecessary theatrics. Enough drama could be found in the current crisis without reporters resorting to such artificial hype. Consumed as I was by the demands of keeping up with the fast-moving pace of events, I was at that point only dimly aware of what network executives, viewers, and governments around the world, especially in the United States, had realized during the past week. CNN's live broadcasts from Tiananmen, most notably the astonishing scenes as we covered ourselves being thrown off the air, had made broadcasting history. Never before had television played such an significant role in revealing and shaping the course of a near-revolution in a totalitarian state, especially one as large, important, and with as long a history of closing itself off to the outside world as China. When I had a minute to think, it became clear to me that by broadcasting live from the heart of the revolution, we had affected the dynamics and momentum of the very events we were covering. At a critical moment, CNN's broadcasts had deprived a Chinese government accustomed to absolute authority of a crucial political commodity: information. I had been forced to cover the anti-Chinese demonstrations in Tibet from my desk in Beijing two months earlier because the authorities prevented foreign journalists from entering Lhasa, but the present student movement was exploding in full view of the people of China and the rest of the world. In Beijing and other cities, Chinese citizens had been able to watch CNN's broadcasts of the uprising, viewing televisions at hotels and at the surprisingly large number of Chinese work units equipped with satellite dishes. Through CNN, millions more across the globe had witnessed a drama far more riveting than any novel. It was packed with action and suspense, peopled by idealistic heroes and scheming villains, and played out against a physical and political setting of epic proportions. I began to realize that an awareness of this huge international audience, and not simply internal divisions at the top, might well have dissuaded the authorities in Beijing from swiftly using force to end the protests. We might have helped to prevent—or at least delay—a crackdown. Beyond speculation was the fact that China had put CNN on the map. For better or worse, we were now part of the story.

For my colleagues and me, so used to being the understaffed, underpaid, overworked underdogs of TV news, often still dismissed by our condescending network competitors, it was a heartening reversal. Faxed newspaper clips began cascading into our Sheraton Hotel workspace from CNN's public-relations department. "These have been glory days for CNN," wrote the *New York Times*, also quoting my old Columbia Journalism School professor Fred Friendly: "I think CNN came of age with its China coverage." There were articles in publications from Paris to Taiwan. In *Newsweek*, the headline was "Karl Marx, Meet Marshall McLuhan." *TV Guide* asked "Can Global TV Topple China's Hard-Liners?" Added the *New York Post*, "Even *Dallas* Steps Aside for Beijing."

Although I had little time to read more than the headlines, I realized that CNN was becoming a worldwide phenomenon. After years of laboring in obscurity for the new and largely ignored network, I found myself abruptly thrust into the spotlight. Every television reporter wants to become well-known, and I was no exception. To some, my move to Beijing two years earlier had seemed to be a bad career choice. Before my departure, John Donvan, a good friend and fellow correspondent at CNN in London, urged me to reconsider: "You're far better off staying on as London fireman, where you'll be in on every big story. China is a backwater. You'll be out of the loop in Beijing. People won't remember who you are."

At the time, I thought he was probably right, but I didn't care. My dream was to go to China.

Now suddenly I was—at least for the moment—a "star." It was a bizarre sensation. I was certainly gratified by the recognition. China was "my" story. I felt I'd been preparing for it for years and was pleased that my moment in the spotlight had been earned for the work in Beijing, rather than in another distant capital. In addition, I had to admit to savoring a feeling of triumph over the Big Three networks. My unhappy experiences at CBS in Hong Kong during the mid-1970s and my firing by NBC early in my career still rankled. So did the snide remarks and frequently contemptuous attitudes of the network big shots I had encountered since then, including those I met on the streets of Beijing during the past few weeks. The enormous media praise for my upstart network must have been as galling for my competitors as it was rewarding for me. But however gratifying the recognition, I found myself so exhausted and preoccupied with the events swirling around me that I had little time and even less inclination to enjoy what I confidently expected would be nothing more than my own fifteen minutes of fame.

Even as my stature and that of CNN soared, our operation in Beijing was running into trouble. By the time the Chinese cut off satellite feeds again on May 24—this time for good—Bernie Shaw and Steve Hurst had been called back to their bases in Washington and Moscow. Alec Miran and his capable colleagues from the CNN Special Events unit had also moved on to their next assignment, a previous commitment to handle coverage of a NATO summit meeting in Brussels. They took with them not only the now-banned flyaway, but the computer system they had installed for the Gorbachev visit, as well as the walkie-talkies we had relied on for communications in the chaotic city, leaving the entire CNN Beijing team dependent on a couple of portable telephones. We did, however, acquire one piece of new equipment. Colleagues smuggled in a machine called a Pixelator, which transmitted videotape images as still pictures over the phone. It was slow, expensive, and complicated to use. But if the situation reached a crisis point, it would come in handy.

Of more significance, the departure of those brought in for the Gorbachev meeting deprived us of some of the network's most experienced and level-headed personnel, veterans of crises and big stories across the globe. While they were highly competent, Charlie Schumacher and Lindy Hall, the new producers sent out from CNN headquarters in Atlanta, had little experience overseas, still less in crisis situations, and almost none in Chinese affairs. Fresh reporters from other bureaus also arrived. Despite the ban on satellite transmissions, Atlanta's appetite for material had not waned. In addition to the twice-daily "pigeons," who took tape and edited stories to feed from Hong Kong or Tokyo, headquarters was now demanding live or recorded telephone updates almost every hour around the clock. Despite their lack of background, my new colleagues had been thrust on the air, sometimes within hours of arriving, and were asked by anchors in Atlanta to explain a series of events so complicated and fast-moving that even I, who'd spent years following China, was not certain what to make of them. This unfamiliarity with the complexities of China increased the danger of mistakes, exaggerations, susceptibility to rumors, and errors of judgment, analysis, or perception. As CNN was now being watched in China and in newsrooms, government offices, and foreign ministries around the world, I worried about the consequences. It wasn't just the reinforcements arriving in Beijing who concerned me during this volatile period. Although some of the anchors in Atlanta had a sophisticated grasp of the story, others seemed utterly uncomprehending. At one point, I was preparing to do a brief live phone report with an anchor who has long since left CNN. Before going on the air, I asked the show producer whether he wanted me to do a little question-and-answer session after my update. "Mike," he replied, "you know who's anchoring this show. Just say your piece, sign off, and hang up before you get asked a dumb question!"

As the network's most experienced China hand, my role now changed. Cynde, Mitch, John Lewis, Donna, and other colleagues were staking out Tiananmen Square around the clock, keeping track of the stalemate on the ground, where the students showed no sign of leaving, and the government gave no indication of backing down. Reluctantly I began to spend more of my time at our Sheraton Hotel work space than in the square. I briefed newly arrived staffers on the latest developments, acted as a sounding board and content editor for many of their packages, and helped plan each day's crew and story assignments. In Western-style comfort so sharply at variance with the endless days and nights I had spent camped out by the monument, I devoted the rest of my energy, fueled at this point almost entirely by adrenaline, to deciphering what was happening in the corridors of power.

During my years in Hong Kong, when access to a largely closed People's Republic was infrequent and tightly controlled, I'd honed my skills as a "China watcher," learning how to scour the official media for clues, trading theories and guesses with diplomats, academics, and fellow reporters. Suddenly, with martial law, the veil of secrecy that had always obscured the internal workings of the leadership was drawn even tighter. Even as the protests in the streets provided an extraordinarily revealing glimpse of the tensions flowing through Chinese society, I was forced to dust off my old China-watching skills to chart the behind-the-scenes power struggle that would, in the end, determine the outcome of the crisis.

The satellite feed cutoff on Wednesday, May 24, was not the only sign that reports of a comeback by Zhao Ziyang and the moderates were wrong. In the wake of the declaration of martial law four days earlier, much attention had been focused on Wan Li, the seventy-three-year-old head of the National People's Congress (NPC), China's rubber-stamp parliament. Wan Li was on an official visit to the United States when the crackdown was announced. Students in the square, as well as diplomats and other reporters, speculated hopefully: would he return to Beijing to rally the moderates by convening a special NPC session to repudiate martial law? But instead of traveling directly to the capital, Wan stopped first in Shanghai, where he was suddenly said to be urgently in need of "medical treatment." Rumors swept the square that Wan was detained in a government guest house as the hard-liners pressed him to join their camp. Whether he was held against his will or simply wanted to assess the situation before committing himself remains unclear, but the following weekend, he threw his support to Deng Xiaoping. The "Wan Li option," probably never more than wishful thinking anyway, disappeared.

My perusal of the official media offered other hints that Deng Xiaoping and the hard-liners were in charge. The *People's Daily* carried statements of support for martial law from six of the country's seven military regions and most of the provincial leadership. CCTV showed Li Peng meeting three newly accredited ambassadors from Burma, Mexico, and Liberia on Thursday, May 25. It was the first public appearance by any senior official since Li Peng's dramatic midnight speech six days earlier declaring a state of emergency. Defending his tough measures, the prime minister told the envoys the government was stable and that martial law was necessary to "restore order." Abruptly, the speculation about Li Peng's possible fall from power disappeared. The next evening, eighty-four-year-old economic planner Chen Yun appeared on CCTV. Speaking on behalf of a group of conservative party elders, Chen declared, "We, the veteran comrades, should step forward boldly. If we do not suppress this chaos started by a small number of people, China will never enjoy peaceful days. We must never make concessions."

My UPI pal Dave Schweisberg joined my efforts to decipher the opaque palace politics. Already good friends before the spring, collaborating on this story had created a special kind of partnership between us. I liked Dave's restless energy and admired his total cynicism and refusal to put up with official lies and deceit. Some months earlier, when the Chinese deputy foreign minister declared to reporters that criticism of China's human rights record in Tibet "hurt the feelings of the Chinese people," Schweisberg exploded. "Oh come off it, Minister," he almost shouted. "You know the Chinese people don't give a damn about Tibet. What hurts their feelings is when your government can't keep inflation under control." The minister's jaw dropped.

Now Dave was hollow-eyed with fatigue, and smoking far more than was healthy for a stocky man approaching middle age. Still, we met or spoke several times a day, trading insights gleaned from our separate sources. Sitting next to the ancient, noisy wire machines in UPI's cramped and scruffy one-room office in the Qijiayuan Diplomatic Compound fronting Changan Street, we agreed that the reappearance of the party elders was extremely significant. These were the same conservatives Deng Xiaoping had pushed out of senior positions at the thirteenth Party Congress, just weeks after Dave and I arrived to take up our Beijing assignments in 1987. One of the most memorable moments of that Congress occurred when a visibly ailing Chen Yun was helped out of his chair on the front row of the stage at the Great Hall of the People and, with the aid of a nurse, took several minutes to shuffle painfully to the exit. "This afternoon's photo opportunity," joked a cruelly cynical Associated Press photographer, "is Chen Yun water skiing!"

But the comeback of Chen Yun and other veteran revolutionaries was now no laughing matter. Dave and I both viewed it as an indication of Deng's determination to crush the students and hang on to power. I was not really surprised that China's paramount leader would enlist as his allies the conservatives who had long objected to his economic reforms. For Deng and the other men in charge of a ruthless Leninist party, resorting to force when challenged was a natural instinct. Deng himself had shown little hesitation in crushing earlier outbreaks of opposition. The more puzzling question was why Deng had allowed the protests to continue, and especially why the government had not stopped foreign reporters from operating. Apart from cutting off satellite feeds, we had encountered surprisingly little official interference, despite the newly announced restrictions.

We were still able to get around Beijing, to take pictures, to make international phone calls, to "pigeon" our stories out. I could only conclude that the leadership was too divided and preoccupied to act. I wondered how long this peculiar martial law, existing in name but not in reality, would be allowed to continue. In my gut, I felt time was running out.

Two additional bits of news deepened my pessimism. From separate diplomatic sources, Dave and I had both heard that Deng Xiaoping had made a trip to Wuhan in central China to mobilize support in the provinces and from regional military commands. Even more alarming, the diplomats, some with access to intelligence information such as U.S. spy satellite photos and electronic intercepts, confirmed the rumors sweeping the city that as many as 250,000 soldiers were now surrounding Beijing. The impression that the citizens had triumphed over the army, widely held among the crowds in the square and many reporters, was untrue. After the masses blocked their way the previous weekend, the soldiers had never left the outskirts of the capital. The official Chinese media was full of reminders of the PLA's presence. Most of the stories were bland enough, such as reports of local citizens offering gifts of food or assisting the troops to build temporary accommodations. But the message was unmistakable. The military had not gone away. Small PLA units had taken up positions inside ten key strategic installations, including the office of CCTV, Radio Beijing, and the *People's Daily* compound. Like me, Dave was convinced this was going to end badly. I left his smoke-filled office full of foreboding.

Soon after, in a state of agitation, I called Mark Mohr, an old friend from Hong Kong who was now a senior political officer at the U.S. Embassy. "Mark, I'm really nervous," I told him. "Can we talk?" When I arrived at his sparsely furnished apartment, Mark pointed to the ceilings and said, "This place is bugged. We can't talk here. Let's go to the Beijing Hotel." Sitting by the window of the hotel coffee shop, within earshot of the protestors in the streets just outside, I poured out my anxieties to him. "I am convinced there is going to be blood in the streets," I said. "I think it is going to happen soon."

I spelled out my worst-case scenario—the troops sweeping through Tiananmen, firing as they came. Mark had heard the reports of soldiers massing, but he tried to inject a note of balance. We went over the reasons why it would not be in the government's interest to shed blood. "Everything Deng Xiaoping has achieved since the reforms began in 1978 would be ripped apart," Mark said. "China would be condemned by the world. There have to be other ways to bring the protests to an end." Still, Mark, normally full of sardonic wisecracks and jokes, shared many of my anxieties. "I'll tell you what especially worries me," he confided. "What happens if there is a crackdown, and Chinese dissidents start clamoring for refuge in the U.S. embassy? What the hell are we going to do then?" It was an eerily accurate prediction. Less than two weeks later, China's most famous dissident, Fang Lizhi, along with his wife, would be given sanctuary in the embassy, creating a major stumbling block to rebuilding Sino-American relations that lasted over a year.

The atmosphere of popular defiance was increasingly mixed with fear. Driving toward the Beijing Hotel one afternoon, Lynne pulled over to join a small crowd reading a large red wall poster outside a construction site. She swapped rumors about troop movements with a student from Hunan province in central China who had recently arrived in Beijing to join the protests. Continuing their conversation in a nearby store, they were suddenly approached by two women who warned the young man in low voices that plainclothes police were entering the shop. He abruptly stopped in midsentence and turned away as the two plainclothes agents, wearing conservative gray Mao jackets, sauntered in. The two women, aided by the shop assistants, distracted the cops with sales talk, while another clerk discreetly pushed a sweater onto the counter for Lynne to examine. She pretended to study the garment while the young man moved to the other side of the shop. Soon the police departed. But the young man, now frightened, would not continue the conversation or give Lynne his name. He asked one of the shop assistants to accompany him for a few minutes as he said goodbye, just in case the cops were waiting outside. Lynne found the episode extremely unsettling.

The emotional roller-coaster of the past few weeks had left Lynne mentally exhausted. The crisis had forced her to put her free-lance business writing aside—there wasn't much business news to cover at this moment in any case—to concentrate on looking after two-year-old Daniel. Our son was becoming increasingly agitated by the tension he could sense around him and by my prolonged absences, as I worked twenty-four, forty-eight, even seventy-two hours at a stretch, returning only briefly for a shower and a nap. For

Daniel's sake, Lynne struggled to maintain a semblance of normal life. She took him to the German embassy doctor for his booster shots, to the free market in Sanlitun near our apartment to buy a new outfit, and to the sandbox in a nearby compound to play. Yet each trip required her to drive through streets filled with marchers and blockades. Our *aiyi*, or baby-sitter, still came every day, but when Lynne left Daniel to go out on her own, especially at the end of the day, she faced a nagging anxiety about getting back. "The nightly blockades mean one has to stay near home and not stray too far," she noted in her diary, "for fear of not being able to return until dawn."

There were other worries too. "Today there was a report that water and electricity might be cut off if order isn't restored," she noted a few days after martial law. "The Chinese press is already reporting shortages of gas, eggs, vegetables, milk, and other foods. Tomorrow I'm going to fill our car up with gas and go to the market again in search of eggs." Amid the constant rumors of a crackdown, Lynne found it hard to sleep, especially knowing I was out on the front lines almost every night. "Mike is unbelievably exhausted and anxious," she wrote late one night. "The stress on him is acute. As for me, when I finally get to bed, I fall asleep thinking of Armageddon and believing that I will wake up to learn there were tanks in the streets and bodies in Tiananmen Square."

For the first time, we began to worry that we might have to leave China in a hurry. Lynne collected all our valuable documents and papers in one place, and together we made a checklist of sentimental items to throw in a suitcase. Photographs, a treasured Chinese calligraphy, and some of Daniel's favorite toys were at the top of the list. I was also worried about Sherlock. Several months earlier, friends had pointed out that Chinese regulations required foreign dog owners to get an identification card, or *zheng*, for their pets, not only in order to own them legally in Beijing but in order to take them out of the country. It was one of those petty Chinese bureaucratic annoyances that we tried to ignore whenever possible. Now, though, it occurred to me that without a *zheng*, Sherlock might not be able to come with us if we did have to leave suddenly. Lynne decided to make acquiring a *zheng* for the dog her top priority.

The next morning, she drove to the police station that handled such matters. It was a stressful drive, past the barricades and crowds that had blocked most of the main roads leading to the center of

Beijing for days. The students, Lynne observed, and not the police, were directing traffic. The station was located in an old, gray-walled Chinese courtyard on Nanchizi, a small, tree-lined road off Changan Street, just a few hundred yards from Tiananmen. Walking through the gabled gate, Lynne went to the desk and announced in Chinese, "I'd like to get a *zheng* for my dog."

The policeman looked at her in astonishment. In the midst of a popular uprising in which he and his colleagues had literally been driven off the streets and found themselves virtually prisoners in their own station, a strange, fair-haired foreign woman was asking about a dog?

"You want a *zheng* for your dog?" he repeated slowly, not certain he had heard correctly. "All right, take these forms, fill them out, and come back with two pictures."

Returning home through the tumult, Lynne found a couple of old snapshots showing Sherlock's face and returned.

"*Buxing!*" ("No good!") the policeman barked when she walked in again. "These photos show only the dog's face. The pictures must show the entire animal. Now go and don't come back unless you have the right pictures!"

Wearily, Lynne threaded her way home again. The next morning, she was back, having found the full-body shots the cop demanded. He was clearly astonished, and not pleased to see her. Obviously she was not getting the message that he had more important things to worry about. Poring over the photos and forms, he said, "This is not sufficient documentation. Who legally imported this dog? To what unit does it belong?" Trying to control her frustration, Lynne explained that she was the wife of the CNN bureau chief, and the dog came with our personal belongings. "How do I know you are married to him?" the policeman barked. "I want proof, and a letter of introduction for the dog from your husband's work unit!"

Once again, Lynne slowly made her way back to our apartment, found a copy of our marriage certificate, and managed to arrange for my office assistant Tan Yadong to write a letter on CNN stationery "introducing" the dog and to accompany her back to Nanchizi.

"Oh, it's you again," the cop sighed in resignation when she walked in. With Tan by her side, the policeman realized he had been outmaneuvered. He filled in a small brown ID card very similar in appearance to the blue Foreign Ministry press accreditation I carried. On the line listing the "purpose" of owning the animal, Lynne told him to write "play." Finally, in exasperation, he stamped it with the police chop without which no document in China is considered official.

"Here's your *zheng*," he said. "Now get lost."

Clutching the valuable document, Lynne set off through the masses again. Two weeks after that, Sherlock became a Tiananmen evacuee.

It was the end of yet another long, uncomfortable night at the square, and Cynde Strand was in a bad mood. Hours and hours of announcements, songs, and chants over the students' loudspeaker system had left her head throbbing. After pushing the trash around her into a pile to stretch out on, her body ached. Now, at dawn, sitting uncomfortably on her metal ladder, she listened to her Walkman, watched an equally frustrated John Lewis obsessively playing with his Nintendo, and waited for student runners to make their way through the crowds with something to eat. Soon after, "breakfast" arrived—a plastic bag full of Snickers bars and Cokes. Again.

Cynde couldn't stand it. Grabbing the cellular phone, she called her favorite pizza parlor in New York. "I'd like a large pie with thick crust, extra cheese, anchovies, black olives, and peppers—to go, please." The woman on the other end asked, "And where should we deliver it?" When Cynde answered "Tiananmen Square," the woman hung up.

"Where the fuck is my replacement?" Cynde muttered. "This has gone on too long."

As May drew to an end, the euphoria of the days just after martial law were a distant memory. After weeks of occupation, Tiananmen Square more nearly resembled a squalid refugee camp than the center of a movement for freedom that had inspired the world. Baking in ninety-degree heat, the hundred-square-acre expanse was filthy, buried in garbage, and reeking of urine. With makeshift tents providing little shelter from the elements, more and more protestors were coming down with colds and intestinal ailments. Fears about a serious outbreak of disease mounted.

The movement was running out of steam. The crowds on the square began to dwindle. Puzzled and unnerved that huge numbers of soldiers were ringing Beijing, yet making no move to enter, and frustrated by the government's continuing refusal to respond to their demands, the student leadership started to fragment. Moderates urged a conclusion to the occupation, while radicals insisted on staying to the bitter end. The bickering students began to display the same bureaucratic and autocratic tendencies in their "People's Republic of Tiananmen Square" that they were trying to change in the government. The headquarters on the Heroes Monument, where Wang Dan, Wu'er Kaixi, Chai Ling, and other leaders spent most of their time, was now surrounded by rings of student guards to keep outsiders out and ensure that the insiders maintained their privileged status. Carried away by their own sense of self-importance, the student leaders became less and less available to the press, just like the elderly Party chieftains they so despised. Bodyguards refused access to journalists unless they could produce multiple ID cards and press passes. It was a farce, but a highly aggravating one. As Cynde noted in her diary, "The student security forces insist on seeing some kind of press pass before they will allow us on the monument. We present Sino-Soviet accreditation badges, credit cards, health-club membership cards, video-club rental cards." As long as we had enough cards, we could usually get past.

The self-styled "student security forces" became increasingly nasty to reporters and camera crews. One afternoon, a young man claiming to be an army cadet approached John Lewis near the monument and offered to do an interview. As John and Mitch Farkas finished shooting, disappointed that the cadet had very little of interest to say, other students walked over demanding the tape and insisting that we did not have permission from them to conduct such an interview. When John refused, the students began to push and shove. Swearing "fuck your mother" in his perfect Cantonese, Mitch created a minor distraction. John surreptitiously clicked open the tape deck, pulled out the interview tape, and switched it with a blank one, which he then gave to the angry students.

One evening, Wu'er Kaixi emerged to give a statement to the press, only to have his "security" detail demand that the camera crews keep their lights off. "If you want us to get Wu'er on tape," John argued, "we have to use lights." The students were adamant. Wu'er's remarks were recorded in darkness and never went on the air.

CNN's producers and crews now spent much of their time waiting around, chasing moments and moods without getting a handle on what was happening behind the scenes. "The crowd was like a huge, shapeless organism," Donna Liu recalled. "Every so often, it would be as if an amoeba would break off and we would rush to follow it. But it usually led nowhere." On my regular swings through the square, I huddled with John, Donna, and the crews who were staked out around the clock. It seemed clear that a large number of Beijing students who had been at the forefront of the earlier protests were now drifting away, sick of the stench and the boredom and anxious about a possible crackdown. The number of protestors eventually shrank from tens of thousands to just a few thousand, many of them from the provinces. These students were undisciplined and disorganized, drawn to the square primarily by reports of the excitement in the heart of the Chinese capital.

We were getting fed up. The world still saw the students as shining heroes. Their encampment was attracting politically sympathetic tourists and some oddballs as well. One day a group of Western environmentalists showed up and announced plans to bring a Greenpeace ship to Beijing. The next day, there were chanting Buddhist monks. But order and discipline were breaking down amid the power struggles and festering garbage. My own positive feelings about the movement began to change. They'd had a remarkable run, I felt, but now the hard-core protestors still occupying the square were in danger of overplaying their hand, discrediting themselves, sullying their achievements, and risking a potential bloodbath. Holding onto the square seemed meaningless. Why don't they just declare victory and go home? I kept asking myself. It seemed to be both the obvious—and the only—way out.

Some of the student leaders, notably Wang Dan and Wu'er Kaixi, appeared to reach the same conclusion. On Saturday, May 27, they held a press conference, which began with an unusually pensive Wu'er Kaixi, wearing his trademark blue T-shirt, trying to counter a growing sense of defeat. His comments struck me as designed as much for history as to keep the current movement alive. "I was an organizer of these protests," he said. "We wanted to get things going in two different directions. We wanted to adopt the thinking of the May Fourth Movement—democracy, science, freedom, law. That was the idea. The second goal was to promote a democratic revolution. In the first area, we have scored great victories. In the second, the struggle for a democratic system, we are convinced we will win."

Now, though, it was time to leave the square. Following Wu'er Kaixi, Wang Dan, speaking in his soft, melodious voice, announced that a decision had been made to end the occupation of Tiananmen the following Tuesday, May 30. There would be a final demonstration through the streets of Beijing to call for the end of martial law and democratic reforms. But Wang insisted that the movement was not over and that once they returned to the campuses the students would formulate a new plan of action. The relief in my voice when I broadcast this news that evening was palpable. So was my skepticism. An end might at last be in sight before the army intervened or I collapsed from exhaustion. First, however, the students had to follow through on their decision to depart.

It soon became apparent that the squabbles and ugly bickering that had eroded the movement's momentum in preceding days now prevented the protestors from leaving Tiananmen. The decision to retreat announced by Wang Dan was not unanimous. It was strongly opposed by radical students from outside the capital, many of them recent arrivals, almost all of them with no place else to go. Fixated on the symbolism of Tiananmen, they vowed to stay until at least June 20, when a special session of the National People's Congress was scheduled. And they acquired an important ally. Student leader Chai Ling had initially sided with Wu'er Kaixi and Wang Dan, but when the students from the provinces objected, she changed her mind, joining a hard core that was determined not to abandon Tiananmen. In an interview with another reporter, she said, "Only when the square is washed in our blood will the people of the whole country wake up."

My heart sank. There was no way out.

Rumors of the construction of a statue had swirled across the square all day. Students at the Central Academy of Fine Arts were building a symbol that protest leaders hoped would revitalize their flagging movement; dozens of them had been at work on the project for three days. Now, late in the evening of Monday, May 29, John Lewis waited by the monument with Mitch Farkas. Normally a soundman, Mitch had now begun shooting as well. The two were joined by Tom Mintier, an Atlanta-based CNN correspondent who'd just flown in from the U.S. Like all other CNN staffers sent to Beijing since the declaration of martial law, Tom had acquired a tourist visa in Hong Kong by pretending to be a holidaymaker. Beijing was no longer issuing press visas. An old Asia hand who'd been a U.S. Army combat cameraman in Vietnam, Tom had been with CNN for years, covering several crises around the world. Tom was not a China expert, but he was a good reporter, very thorough and careful. I was extremely glad to see him.

Suddenly these three heard the demonstrators break into cheers, some flashing the V-for-victory sign. In the distance, through the humid, heavy air, over the sea of black-haired heads, they saw a figure being carried on a flatbed bicycle cart. It had a raised pair of white arms, which bore a torch pointing toward the sky. Elbowing through the densely packed throng, past scores of other pushing and shoving photographers and crews, Mitch made his way forward, camera rolling all the time. Behind the first cart came a second, carrying the torso, and a third with the base. The Goddess of Democracy had arrived in Tiananmen Square.

At noon the next day, under a bright sun, the thirty-seven-foot-high statue, made of plaster, foam, and wood, was formally unveiled amid speeches and firecrackers. Positioned directly in front of Tiananmen Gate, looking like the Statue of Liberty, standing almost eye-to-eye with the portrait of Chairman Mao, it was a brilliant piece of political theater, a gesture of brazen defiance against the Chinese state. The Goddess served her purpose. Within hours, huge crowds were flocking to Tiananmen to stare at the remarkable white creation. The square was once again full of people. The movement appeared to have gained a new lease on life.

But as I talked things over with John Lewis, we agreed that erecting the statue was both an extremely brave and utterly foolish gesture. However riveting the image and however great the TV pictures, it was extraordinarily provocative. To many Chinese, even some sympathetic to the students, it appeared to be an American symbol in the heart of China. It was almost as if the students were taunting the authorities, daring them to act. If the army needed an excuse, John and I concluded, the Goddess of Democracy was it. To no one's surprise, the official media exploded in an orgy of condemnation. The *People's Daily* called it "totally against the law and against the will of the people." Whatever doubts the hard-liners may have harbored about a harsh crackdown simply dissolved.

As the statue was unveiled, word swept through the square of the arrest of three members of a new independent trade union. Organized worker activism had become a major factor only in recent days, although it had been clear much earlier in the spring that the students commanded widespread popular support. Inspired by the resistance to the military following the declaration of martial law, the Beijing Workers Autonomous Federation, led by a young railway electrician named Han Dongfang, claimed several thousand members. Less interested in abstract ideas of democracy than in bread-and-butter issues like inflation and corruption, the Federation had an uneasy relationship with the students, who were determined to keep control of the movement in their hands. By the last week of May, the Workers Federation was allowed to set up a continuing presence in the square, although it was relegated to the far-northwest corner, and its members were given little more to do than to act as security guards for the demonstrators in the event of a crackdown.

Among the hundreds of thousands who had participated in the occupation of the square, the three worker organizers were the first Tiananmen activists to be arrested. Their detention was a sign of how much the specter of a Polish Solidarity-style independent trade union emerging in China frightened the government. Several thousand protestors broke away from the main body of demonstrators and marched from the square to a nearby Public Security Bureau office to demand their release. Donna Liu followed the angry crowd with a camera crew as they sat in the street outside the police station, refusing to leave. Speaker after speaker harangued the crowd through megaphones with a stridency Donna had not heard on earlier occasions. Tokyo bureau cameraman Jiro Mishina stood by the gate shooting when a police cameraman walked up from inside and pointed his camera straight back at him. It was an unnerving moment. The three workers were eventually freed, but tensions on the street were rising. Donna began to worry that events were getting out of control.

After yet another twenty-four-hour day, Donna had just fallen asleep in her hotel room when she heard a pounding at the door. Her first reaction was panic. The game was up. The police had finally come. She was about to be arrested.

Cautiously turning the handle, she saw one of CNN's student runners standing in the corridor.

"Wake up," the young, redheaded Bulgarian exchange student shouted. His Chinese was excellent but his English was barely adequate. "I have message from Charlie. Shit is coming down."

Just before eleven P.M. on Friday, June 2, three civilians were killed when a speeding police jeep careened into the bicycle lane along Changan Street, several miles west of Tiananmen Square. Angry crowds gathered as news of the accident spread. Mitch Farkas and Atlanta-based cameraman Jonathan Schaer were in the bar of the Sheraton Hotel, drinking away the tension and fatigue of recent days. About to call it a night, they were walking, a little unsteadily, out to Mitch's car in the parking lot when Mr. Lu, the Beijing bureau driver, ran over and shouted, "The soldiers. They're coming toward the square! They're coming!"

"We were pretty drunk," Mitch recalled, "but suddenly, the adrenaline hit, and we said 'we gotta get down there.' We skidded off down the road, passing through mobs of people and roadblocks."

Reaching the Muxudi intersection on the western side of the city, they found the upturned jeep lying next to the shattered bicycles and bloodstains in the road. The mood of the people staring at the wreckage was ugly. A few blocks away, Mitch and John came across four busloads of soldiers surrounded by throngs of people. The angry crowd slit the tires, clambered aboard, and began passing large burlap sacks through the window. With a jolt, Mitch realized the sacks contained rifles, still in their wrapping. The crew grabbed their cameras and piled into the bus with the mob. Some people were slapping the soldiers around. One man mounted a helmet on top of a bayonet and held it up, to cheers and hoots. The video is great, Mitch said to himself, but with people tossing AK-47s around, this situation could get really ugly, and fast.

In front of the Beijing Hotel I could hear the shouts of "The army is coming! The army is coming!" I raced upstairs to "Tokyo Base" on the eleventh floor to get a better view and call Atlanta. It was just after 2 A.M., Saturday, June 3. Out of the gloom came several thousand soldiers, dressed not in military uniform but in white shirts and green trousers, many of them carrying satchels, jogging in formation from the east, down Changan Street toward the square. Activists who'd been camped out in Tiananmen and ordinary citizens roused from their homes marched from the opposite direction. A few yards below the balcony where I was standing, I watched the two crowds collide. Changan was turned into a seething, surging, punching, shouting mass of humanity. I strained to see if the soldiers were carrying weapons as I described the scene over the air. To my amazement, they appeared to be unarmed. Slowly the forward momentum of the troops was halted, then reversed. The columns broke up. Some soldiers hastily retreated. Others sat down on the pavement in bewilderment.

"Go! You're not wanted here!" The outraged citizens jeered and taunted the fleeing troops, displaying far more anger and violence than I'd seen in earlier confrontations. One soldier, his leg injured, hobbled away while two of his comrades propped him up. "We are all the sons of workers and peasants," a middle-aged man indignantly called out. "Our university students are also the children of workers and peasants. They are the future of China! The people don't need you to act like this!" By now Mitch and John Schaer had returned from the other side of the city and were moving through the crowds. "The soldiers were turned back by an unarmed group of people!" Mitch shouted in amazement to Schaer. "Did you see their faces? They were afraid, man. You see what's happened? That's a routed army!"

"The soldiers were not armed," I noted, speculating over the air about possible explanations for this strange episode. "They clearly were not in a position to sweep the square. There has been no sign of reinforcements. Whether this was intended as a show of strength or not is hard to say. Certainly it has had the opposite effect, galvanizing the protestors, bolstering their defiance, making the authorities look weak and indecisive."

This incident remains something of a mystery, even years later. Was it an attempt to slip soldiers into the area around the square under cover of darkness in preparation for the next night's assault? Or was it a deliberate provocation by the hard-liners to justify sending armed troops to the rescue? Whatever the motive, the events during the night brought tension to a fever pitch. As dawn broke, I saw the outraged citizens flocking toward the square to commandeer buses and turn them into new barricades.

Around the monument, students showed off army caps, gas masks, and other trophies from the night's confrontation, exulting in what seemed to be another triumph over the government.

"We've won this round," one protestor told Tom Mintier and

Cynde. "But only this round. We don't have much hope for the future. We will try to stay here, but we won't use force."

Nearby, the daily routine of occupation continued. Sleepy students brushed their teeth and rinsed off tired faces with pails of water. One young man, wearing jeans and a red T-shirt, picked at a guitar. Behind him, a sign on a tent read VICTORY BELONGS TO US FOREVER!

I finally returned home early Saturday afternoon, too tired to ponder the deeper meaning of what I had witnessed, hoping only for a nap long enough to recharge my fading batteries. Daniel, whom I'd barely seen for weeks, was thrilled. As I stumbled into bed, I felt terrible having virtually ignored him. Half an hour later, the phone roused me out of a deep sleep.

"Mike, soldiers are tear-gassing demonstrators outside Zhongnanhai," one of the producers shouted in my ear. "This may be it! You'd better get down there."

With an exhausted farewell to my family, I set off again for Tiananmen.

In the few hours since I was last there, the mood in the square and in the streets had changed. Something felt different, as if an invisible line had been crossed. I'd experienced tension and fear here before, had stood and listened to the fevered speculation about a military crackdown, but now, among both the protestors and the authorities, there was an anger and bitterness I had not previously sensed. Violence was in the air.

A thousand helmeted, rifle-wielding soldiers had burst out of the doors of the Great Hall of the People in midafternoon, only to be surrounded by a human barricade. Thwarted, the troops sat down and started to sing *The Internationale*. The protestors began to sing the song with them, even as some demonstrators at the back of the crowd began to tear up the pavement, throwing chunks of concrete toward the sitting soldiers. Cynde and Donna were recording the scene. Cynde felt as if the whole movement had broken down, gone out of control. "It feels like chaos," she noted in her diary. "Hoodlums are tossing huge rocks at the Great Hall, waving sticks at the soldiers. You can tell the soldiers are confused, a little afraid, and feeling trapped."

Turning to Donna, Cynde said, "Tonight is the night. The government cannot allow this to continue. They can no longer just debate what to do." As she spoke, more rocks crashed near her feet.

At dusk, the soldiers retreated inside the Great Hall. Donna and Cynde returned to the monument. Back in the Beijing Hotel, I pooled my own impressions with those of my colleagues, and then put in a call to Dave Schweisberg. Like me, he'd been frantically phoning sources and contacts around the city. From the window of his office a few miles to the east, Dave told me he could see truck-loads of armed troops surrounded by a crowd close to a nearby intersection. As citizens mobilized to block the entrance of the army to the city center, other press friends reported similar scenes throughout Beijing. I watched the CCTV evening news at seven P.M. in our by-now scruffy and crowded hotel room. Instead of a normal broadcast, the announcers read a series of sternly worded messages from the martial-law command, urging people to remain at home, stay calm, and not set up roadblocks or barricades. Anyone who ventured out, the announcer said, did so at his or her own risk.

Cynde's hunch was right: this was it. On the phone for an early-morning (U.S.-time) news broadcast, I struggled to summarize clearly the day's fast-moving events: "We appear to be shaping up for what could be a decisive confrontation between the security forces and protestors in the center of Beijing in the next several hours," I told anchor Patrick Greenlaw. "There's lots of activity on the streets, with everyone here in the capital expecting more to come as the light fades and we move into Saturday night and Sunday morning in Beijing."

The next day, June 4, was my thirty-seventh birthday. Despite the growing sense of crisis, after so much time apart in recent weeks, Lynne and I decided to have dinner together on Saturday night. Leaving Daniel with our Chinese baby-sitter, Miss Li, Lynne set off from our apartment, encountering angry, preoccupied crowds and newly erected barricades on her way downtown. The usual smiles for foreigners had vanished. Forced to park over a mile from Tiananmen, near the luxurious, recently opened Palace Hotel, she walked down Wangfujing Street to the Beijing Hotel. Inside the cavernous lobby, it was quiet, almost still. We sat down in a red-carpeted, virtually empty restaurant and ordered dumplings and soup. We had about an hour to eat. Atlanta wanted me back on the air at ten P.M., Beijing time. Our conversation was subdued and anxious. I didn't feel that there was much to celebrate. Every ten minutes I popped up and raced to the hotel door, just to make sure I wasn't missing anything outside. Still, Lynne was determined to do something nice for the occasion.

"I want to walk down to the square after dinner and buy you a T-shirt," she announced. "The students have made wonderful T-shirts with the word 'Democracy' printed on it. If I can find one, it would be a great present."

After paying the bill, I suggested we go upstairs and take a look from the balcony of "Tokyo Base" first.

As we walked into the room, a roar rose from the street below. Racing to the balcony, Lynne and I saw a thousand soldiers jogging toward the square. I grabbed the phone and called Atlanta.

"This is Mike in Beijing," I announced when someone on the Foreign Desk answered. "The army appears to be moving. I need to go on the air—*now!*"

A moment later, I described the scene for CNN viewers: "A thousand soldiers running in formation have burst through crowds on the eastern side of the approach roads to Tiananmen Square. About two hundred yards from the square, the column has run into a mass of humanity. Crowds of people have grabbed the soldiers, pulling them, pushing them, shoving them, kicking them. The soldiers appear to be no match for the outraged citizens. They're breaking ranks, retreating up a side street."

Lynne concluded it was not a good time to walk to Tiananmen and buy me a souvenir T-shirt. She was, however, torn. Every journalistic impulse told her to stay and witness the unfolding drama, but Daniel was home with a Chinese sitter. What would happen if the roads were cut off and she couldn't get back? Or if the sitter panicked and fled? She anguished while I finished my live report, and then announced that Daniel came first. She would try to get safely home. Leaving the hotel, Lynne turned up Wangfujing, where she ran into hundreds of shaken, bloodied soldiers, humiliated and upset, in full retreat from the angry crowds. Quickening her pace, she reached our car and headed away from the city center as fast as she could.

Around the Monument to the Heroes of the Revolution in the center of the square, the hard-core students awaited their fate with songs and chants of defiance, but also with growing anxiety visible in their eyes. Suddenly two young people ran up, waving a bloody shirt, shouting that demonstrators had been wounded and killed at the Muxudi intersection on western Changan Street. Mitch tried to coax more information from them, but the two were so hysterical they could only repeat, "*Muxudi, Muxudi.*" Finally, Donna suggested that Mitch take a camera and check the story out. He and soundman Eric Feigel piled into a car belonging to a French still-photographer and headed off toward the western side of Beijing.

There, a convoy of troop trucks had reached Muxudi, site of the fatal jeep accident the night before, at about 8:30 in the evening, only to encounter thousands of furious Beijing residents behind barricades of hijacked buses, vans, trolleys, and trucks. The crowd comprised a cross-section of the city—students, shop assistants, factory workers, bureaucrats, young and old. They were making their stand in a well-heeled neighborhood that was popular with senior officials and their families, within earshot of the State Guest House at Diaoyutai, where visiting VIPs were housed on state visits. For more than two hours the citizens threw rocks and bottles while the troops replied with stun grenades. Finally the soldiers were ordered to open fire in earnest.

Abandoning their car several blocks away, Mitch and his colleagues walked toward the distant din. "Suddenly frantic people started coming up and screaming," Mitch remembered. "I couldn't make out what they were saying. I shouted at them, 'Calm down! What are you trying to tell us?' Then a young man came up. He was holding his hair back, and he had a red gash on his head. He screamed in my face, 'Look at this! Look at this!' And then I heard a sort of 'bang, bang, bang' sound. I thought it was people banging trash-can lids. But the French photographer, who'd been in Beirut, said 'No! That's definitely gunfire! Something's happening! Turn that camera light off. That's gunfire, for sure!'"

An enormous, agitated crowd came into sight. Mitch filmed as the protestors set on fire trucks and piles of garbage across Changan Street. The gunfire picked up. Mitch thought it sounded like bees zipping over his head. Then he heard a *tang* and saw sparks as bullets ricocheted off the metal bicycle-lane dividers next to him. "Oh my God, they're firing all over the streets," he shouted to his soundman, Eric. "Let's get out of here. Let's go!" Escaping, Mitch noticed a group of people riding their bicycles into the gunfire. In a futile gesture of defiance, they threw bottles toward the advancing troops. What he could not see, or record, were the numerous men, women, and children on their balconies or in their apartments who were gunned down as the troops sprayed the neighborhood with bullets.

Like a steadily advancing thunderstorm, the first rumbles of the army's thrust began to echo through Tiananmen. With automatic weapons fire clattering in the distance and tracer bullets flying overhead, hysterical Chinese rushed up to Cynde and Donna. "One woman walked over holding up a guy with blood on his shirt," Donna recalled. "As she led him toward an ambulance, she cried, 'The troops have arrived. They're shooting down Changan Street right into the crowd. People are being killed.'"

Moments later, the first bodies were brought into makeshift medical tents in the square. Cynde collected her thoughts, sitting on her folded tripod, her hands clasped almost as if she were in prayer. Then she moved into action. The bulky camera on her shoulder, she stepped forward and recorded the cries of agony as hard-pressed medics sought to treat bloody, open wounds.

"Your mind begins to whirl," Cynde recalled later. "You shift into another gear. Where to get a shot and how not to get shot, how to stay alive and how to get tape out."

I, too, had shifted into high gear. I forced my emotions and fears into the background, and devoted all my energy to the task at hand. For now, the story came first. But I was desperately frustrated. I wanted to get out on the streets and, especially after all we had shared this spring, to be with Cynde and Mitch. But the only reliable phone to Atlanta within sight of the square was at Tokyo Base, and CNN headquarters understandably wanted continuous, live coverage. I was a prisoner, like a sports announcer forced to do play-by-play when what I really wanted was to be on the field with my teammates. Still, I was the link through whom everything we saw and experienced would be communicated to the rest of the world. I certainly had a good vantage point from which to watch the action. I put my frustrations aside.

"The assault on Tiananmen Square is now under way," I solemnly broadcast at 1 A.M. on Sunday, June 4. "There has been gunfire. There are people dead. There are people wounded in various places around Beijing."

Tom Mintier, after a brief rest, had joined me at the hotel, a second set of eyes to keep track of a chaotic situation. From the balcony, Jonathan Schaer trained a camera on the street below.

"I just saw a tracer round, straight in front of us," Tom said in an excited voice. "Something's coming this way. I can't tell what it is."

I resumed my live phone report. "From our vantage point, we have been seeing gunfire. Two, four, six, eight tracer bullets; eight, ten, twelve, firing through the air." Then the object Tom noticed emerged from the gloom. "An armored personnel carrier is now driving right in front of me, chased by about a thousand people," I reported from the balcony. "The APC just knocked over the flimsy barricades people had set up. We are still seeing tracer rounds, flashes of red, moving closer and closer to our vantage point."

With a roaring and grinding, the APC broke past the crowd and thundered toward the square, battered by rocks and bottles. The people running after it screamed abuse as it accelerated. I saw one man throw a pair of shoes at it. The gesture symbolized to me the astonishing courage and the utter futility of the resistance I was witnessing. Young men hauled more concrete bicycle railings into the middle of the street to make new barricades in front of the hotel. In the din, I heard Tom's low, level-headed voice. "Tanks coming from the western side of the square. You can hear the gunfire if you listen carefully."

Swamped by a sea of people in front of the giant Mao portrait hanging from the Tiananmen rostrum, the armored personnel carrier ground to a halt. Bombarded by Molotov cocktails, it finally burst into flames. Cynde moved closer to the fiery vehicle, into the frenzied crowd, toward the smell of sweat and gasoline. The three soldiers inside tried to escape, terrified of being burned alive, but they were assaulted by the club-wielding, brick-throwing mob. Within moments, two of the young conscripts had been beaten to death. The third, badly injured, was helped away by students aghast at the bloody turn of events.

"It looked like Dante's inferno," Cynde wrote afterward, "flames and cries of pain, faces plastered with shock and fear."

Now the gunfire was crackling overhead. It was time to step back, Cynde decided. But first, a final shot of the Goddess of Democracy, silhouetted against the backdrop of a burning APC.

Mitch had recorded the same scene from another vantage point at a corner of the square. Two sympathetic Chinese men supported his legs as he stood on a railing to get a better angle. "The APC was like a big dead roach," he remembered. "People were pelting it with sticks and rocks. Then it jumped forward again and tried, without success, to tear through the crowd. That's the shot I got. The people wanted this thing dead. They were really trying to kill it."

Walking back to the eastern corner of Tiananmen, Mitch encountered a group of teenagers carrying clubs in their hands. "We're going to fight," they proudly announced. Mitch was beside himself. "You're not going to fight," he shouted at them. "The army is shooting up there, and people are dying, and you're not going to fight!" The youngsters grabbed their sticks and ran off, yelling, "They're shooting! They're shooting! And we're going to fight!" Mitch began to cry. These children were walking into almost certain death, and there was nothing he could do about it. Suddenly drained, he decided to take his tapes back to the office. It was important that the world see images of the carnage. Making his way to Tokyo Base, Mitch handed the tapes off to a student runner, who took them back to the Sheraton. Here, Charlie Schumacher and Lindy Hall were working the Pixelator. It took almost an hour to transmit the images over the telephone, but soon the first eerie, grainy images, freeze-frames off the video, began to appear on the air.

The gunfire was consistent now, with volleys coming every few seconds. Dozens of red tracers whizzed through the air. "Jesus, they're getting close," I shouted to my colleagues, several of whom were peering over the edge of the balcony. "Anybody who doesn't have reporting responsibilities on the balcony, please get off!" By two A.M. Sunday, I could see the first line of troops on the north side of the square, establishing a cordon across Changan Street just under the Mao portrait. Two or three hundred yards to the east, right below my vantage point, a crowd of several thousand people stood defiantly, almost daring the soldiers to shoot. I described on the air what happened next.

"The troops are firing directly at the demonstrators! People are now running down the streets, bicycling down the streets as fast as they can. People are sprinting down the street. It's absolute panic, it's absolute panic! They're turning into side streets now, they're absolutely terrified. I can see someone carrying an injured person. There's an ambulance immediately in front of where I am."

The scene below me was the kind of thing you saw in movies, not on the main street of the city where you lived with your wife and child and dog. I kept talking, but my voice sounded to me disembodied.

"There are bodies, injured and dead all over the place."

A couple of hundred yards toward the square, just opposite Nanchizi—the street where the police station which had issued Sherlock's *zheng* was located—I counted at least a half-dozen bodies. It seemed a silly thought in the middle of a massacre, but I was glad that Sherlock had his ID. I had a strong feeling that we were going to need it to get him—and everyone else—out of the country. I watched in horror as a steady stream of flatbed bicycle carts carried casualties to waiting ambulances by the hotel entrance. I couldn't tell if the victims were dead or wounded. But I could see the pools of blood, and none of the bodies lying in the midst of the agitated, shouting crowds was moving. Early phone calls to hospitals confirmed that dozens had been killed so far. But in the smoke and gloom and bedlam, I could still see the white figure of the Goddess of Democracy, standing defiantly in the square.

Suddenly Atlanta told me that U.S. Secretary of State James Baker was about to appear for a previously scheduled interview on CNN's weekend talk show *Newsmaker Saturday*, hosted by my colleagues Ralph Begleiter and Charles Bierbauer. It was a unique chance to probe the secretary for his reaction to the unfolding drama. I was asked to provide a brief two-minute update in the middle of the interview. In his memoirs, Baker recalled the scene. "My most vivid recollection of that interview is that it was interrupted by a live telephone dispatch from CNN correspondent Mike Chinoy, who was watching the violence in Tiananmen Square. As Chinoy reported thousands of troops firing into crowds, my mind's eye carried me back to the Hungary of 1956, when, as a law-school student at the University of Texas, I'd watched the grim newsreel footage of Soviet tanks crushing the freedom fighters of Budapest." Despite his obvious distress, Baker, to my disappointment, used extremely cautious language in condemning the violence. "It is very important that excessive force not be used," he stated. "That would unfortunately appear to be the case, and this will disturb the United States government, and will disturb the American people considerably." This was the Bush administration's first high-level public reaction

The CNN live-shot
location during
the occupation of
Tiananmen Square,
May 1989

Covering the student
hunger strikers,
Tiananmen Square,
May 1989. Dan Rather
is in the background.

Reporting the would-be revolution in Beijing, Steve Hurst, John Lewis, Chinoy, and Bernard Shaw sign off as the Chinese prepare to pull the plug on CNN. May 20, 1989

Dave Schweisberg, UPI's Beijing bureau chief, my colleague and friend, at a Beijing news conference, 1989. He died of a heart attack in 1993, at age 39.

left to right: *Mitch Farkas, Cynde Strand, the Dalai Lama, and producer Phil Turner. I interviewed the Dalai Lama in Dharmsala, India, December 1989.*

Covering the Vietnamese withdrawal from Cambodia, November 1989

His reform policies dramatically changed the face of China during the years I covered the country. Rumors of his impending death fueled political uncertainty during my last years in China. I took this photo of Deng in Bangkok, Thailand, in 1978.

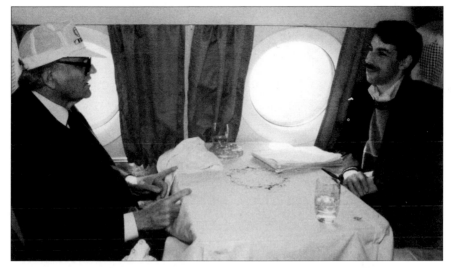

Chatting with the Reverend Billy Graham en route to North Korea at the invitation of Kim Il Sung, April 1992

Getting ready to go on the air in Pyongyang, North Korea, April 1994

The giant statue of Kim Il Sung at Mansudae Hill, Pyongyang, North Korea, 1994

Mitch Farkas and I with North Korea's "Great Leader," Kim Il Sung, April 1992

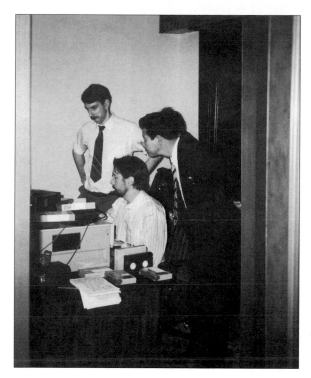

A North Korean "minder" (as we called our political chaperones) looks on as Tim Schwarz and I edit in a Pyongyang hotel room, April 1994

Broadcasting from Kim Il Sung Square, Pyongyang, North Korea, on the Great Leader's eighty-second birthday, April 1994

With Benjamin, Lynne, Daniel, and Sherlock in our "diplomatic compound,"
Beijing, Christmas, 1994

to China's decision to send in the troops. That it came on CNN in response to my live reporting while events were unfolding underscored the new and remarkable role the network was playing. Not only was CNN able to broadcast the action as it happened, it was able to elicit important reactions from some of the key players. It was only after the shooting stopped, though, that I realized how profoundly our work this night would shape American and international perceptions of China for years to come.

While Baker was speaking, Donna Liu slipped away from the square with two precious videotapes to deliver to the Beijing Hotel. Walking into the lobby, she was grabbed by a plainclothes policeman, who ripped her bag away from her. Donna struggled, but it was no good. The tapes were gone. Other returning reporters had similar experiences. Donna looked toward the bank of phones along the lobby wall. The wires of every single one had been cut. To go upstairs to Tokyo Base might prompt a police raid on the room. It was no secret we were there, and I was amazed the authorities had not detained us all already. There was no choice. In the tumult, she slipped outside. There was gunfire coming from the troops at the top of the square. Donna turned the corner up Wangfujing Street, heading back to the Sheraton.

At the monument, it was now decision time. Cynde huddled with soundman Kit Swartz and producer Bruce Kennedy, who insisted everyone should leave. Kennedy argued, not unreasonably, that the situation had become too dangerous, but Cynde refused to go.

"As a journalist and a shooter I cannot," she replied. "It's easy to take pretty pictures. But staying is my responsibility."

His pleas rebuffed, Kennedy departed, while Kit Swartz agreed to remain with Cynde. Into this atmosphere of fear and tension, a familiar, friendly face appeared. It was Dave Schweisberg, puffing on a cigarette. He'd been holding down the UPI bureau, writing lead after lead as his staff phoned in updates from around the city, often supplemented by my numerous phone calls, passing along what we had seen and heard. Now Dave had called his colleagues back to the office. As the boss, he felt it was his responsibility to take the risks at the moment of extreme danger. I felt a similar responsibility, but I was chained to the telephone at Tokyo Base. There was no way I could get away and still "feed the monster."

With flames pouring from the devastated APC, and bullets

flying in all directions, Cynde, Dave, and Kit discussed the best place to watch the final assault. They dropped back to the Great Hall on the western side of the square just in time for Cynde to shoot a tank rumbling by. Yelling "fascists," and "animals," the people threw rocks and even sticks. For the first time in years, Cynde smoked a cigarette. Moving back to the center of the square, the three found a hard-core group of several thousand students huddled around the monument.

At four A.M., the lights in Tiananmen suddenly went out. Still, the students argued about whether to leave or stay. Even faced with certain defeat and the prospect of death, most didn't want to abandon the symbol of their movement. Finally, in the hope of avoiding a bloodbath in the square, two intellectuals who had started a seventy-two-hour hunger strike in sympathy with the students the day before decided to contact military commanders to negotiate a withdrawal. After intense discussions, army officers reluctantly agreed. The students would file out of the square toward the southeast. At 4:40 A.M., the lights went back on, but the shooting continued. Over government loudspeakers mounted on the Great Hall came the order, "Students, clear the square immediately!"

Looking nervously over her shoulder, Cynde saw a wave of shapes moving across the street. Soldiers, carrying AK-47s began to pour out of the Great Hall of the People. "We were almost surrounded, trapped," she wrote in her diary. "As helmeted troops marched up the street six abreast, the crowd chanted abuse. People heckled them until gunfire scattered us. I remember thinking— I have to get a shot, at least some kind of shot. We sneaked into a group and moved up, shooting over the army lines. The tanks moved into the square. I was spotted. Shots cracked over my head. We ran for safety but stayed close to the square."

The terrifying roar in the distance came just before dawn. Moments later, I saw the first in a long line of tanks, armored vehicles, and troop trucks rumbling out of the gray light past the hotel from east Changan Street, in the direction of the square. Like some terrifying, prehistoric serpent, the line seemed to stretch for miles, an army of occupation arriving to reclaim Beijing from its own people. Some of the soldiers fired up at the hotel as they drove by, scattering the crowds in front of them, and sending us diving to the floor. To my utter astonishment, once the convoy passed, groups of angry citizens gathered again in the streets. It was either bravery or a suicide wish. Either way, I was profoundly moved. But there was no question about the outcome of the night's violence.

"The soldiers have now taken over Tiananmen Square," I reported. "The protest there is finished, squelched. There are still crowds in the streets, but the army is in command. The crackdown is going to take many more hours, if not days, before it is complete, before we will know how many people have died, how many are wounded, before we can judge what kind of damage it will cause to China's hope for political and economic reform and for taking its place as a respected member of the international community. For the moment, though, the iron fist of the People's Liberation Army has come down on Tiananmen Square. In the heart of Beijing, the student protest has been crushed."

While I spoke, the remaining students, surrounded except for a small opening in the southwest corner, reluctantly began to file off the square. As they did so, an armored vehicle knocked the Goddess of Democracy off her pedestal, crushing the symbol of the movement into pieces. Like athletes who have lost a championship match, the students moved slowly, their faces drawn and shocked, but still holding up the victory sign. One man without shoes shuffled along with rags around his bloody feet, weeping uncontrollably. A comrade admonished him, "Don't cry."

Dave Schweisberg walked behind a weeping student who had a cloth tied around his neck. The student lifted his arm in a clenched-fist salute. Cynde captured the entire mournful procession on camera. One blood-spattered man cried out to her, "When we left the square, the soldiers kicked and beat us with heavy sticks. They did this very roughly. Many students were pushed to the ground." A young woman came up shouting and declared: " Many students have been killed. I am very angry!" Added another, "The People's Liberation Army has been respected by the people for so long. But now they cannot do this violence to the students. This shows the government is totally mad."

It was over. Cynde, Dave, and Kit had been among the last reporters to leave the square. Now they had to figure out how to get away without having their equipment and precious videotapes confiscated by the omnipresent security forces. "A rickshaw driver stopped to take us," Cynde remembered. "With bodies bent over the camera, we rode past the main police station. It was eerie, the road mostly deserted. Changan Street looked like the aftermath of a battlefield. There was no sunrise this day. It just got gray." Reaching the entrance of the hotel, they ran into *Los Angeles Times* correspondent David Holley, who warned them that government goons were posted at the door to seize tapes and equipment. They hid the material in Schweisberg's car in a corner of the parking lot and, shattered, came up to the work space.

"It was Mike's birthday," Cynde wrote later in her diary. "So we put some cheese balls on a plate and sang 'Happy Birthday.' "

By now the tanks had been deployed facing east and west opposite the Mao portrait, protecting the entrances to the square. Crowds of demonstrators still lingered outside the Beijing Hotel, while in our room on the eleventh floor we debated our next move. We were convinced that it was only a matter of time before a roundup of reporters who'd witnessed the carnage began. Tom and I decided to pack the gear and tapes and slip away. Trying to look inconspicuous, we each carried duffel bags jammed with cameras, sound-recording equipment, and tapes, and strolled nonchalantly through the lobby. We found two rickshaws outside and asked them to head for the Palace Hotel up Wangfujing Street. Gunfire erupted just around the corner as we set off. A line of soldiers had leveled their AK-47s and shot directly into the crowds of demonstrators gathered at the front of the hotel. In the next few minutes, it became a pattern. A burst of fire, three or four bodies dropping to the ground, the people returning to claim the victims and taunt the troops, more fire, more bodies. A British businessman friend of mine, who had watched the night's events from his office on the hotel's sixteenth floor, recorded the scene: "We saw a platoon of soldiers rush forward and form into a line. The crowd broke as machine guns opened fire. Streams of people ran or pedaled for their lives, and the rhythmic shudder of the machine guns seemed infinite. We were ducking on our balcony—for good reason, with a whine a bullet passed close to our heads—but we had to continue looking. This was worse than random fire at hourly intervals. This was deliberate, cold-blooded slaughter."

Reaching the Palace Hotel, an oasis of luxury after the horrors of the past night, but, ironically, a joint-venture in which the army was a major shareholder, Tom and I called Tokyo Base for a fill-in from Jessica Smith, the bureau researcher who was keeping a look-out. Then, from the general manager's desk in the Palace Hotel lobby, we dialed Atlanta. Such was the noise in the lobby, however, that Tom, Cynde, and I had to crawl under the desk to file our report. Despite the bloodshed, I tried to be careful in assessing the number of dead and injured. As puzzled hotel guests stared at the three of us lying on the floor, I shouted into the phone, "There are all sorts of estimates, varying wildly. At this stage it is virtually impossible to come up with any final casualty figures, although if the violence continues, it is likely to mount in the hours ahead."

I hung up and we found a taxi. Twenty-four hours after I had staggered out of my apartment, I staggered back into the Sheraton Hotel. Lynne was there. I fell into her arms, weeping.

CHAPTER NINE

The Big Lie

"**M**ike? Is that you? Are you all right?" The sighs of relief, at both ends of the phone, were audible. I had not heard from Liu, my friend at Radio Beijing, since the shooting began. I was sure he'd been on the streets all night, given his sympathy for the students and his keen journalistic instincts, which had not been dulled while he worked for China's state-run radio station, and I was worried. Now, shortly after noon on Sunday, June 4, he called the CNN work space at the Great Wall Sheraton Hotel.

My hunch was right. In a state of extreme agitation, my friend poured out a harrowing tale of dodging bullets amid the crowds at the Muxudi intersection, site of the worst killing. "I saw men and women gunned down just a few feet from where I was standing," he said breathlessly. "The soldiers were firing randomly into the apartments nearby." Friends of his had died. Everyone at Radio Beijing was in shock, he told me, their anger compounded by the fact that the army was forcing the announcers there, and at CCTV, to broadcast little more than communiqués from the martial-law authorities. "I want you to know what happened," he said. "You, at least, can put the truth on the air."

But my friend was edgy not only because of the scenes of carnage he had witnessed. Shortly before calling me, Liu heard an alarming report from sources in the security forces. Having cleared the square, the army was gearing up to come after foreign journalists, especially those who'd photographed the crackdown. Because of

263

its almost continuous live coverage and the fact that it was still being seen in Beijing, CNN was at the top of the list.

"My sources said a detachment of security agents is already on its way to your office at the Sheraton," he said anxiously. "And you, because it was your voice on the air most of the night, you are a special target. There is chaos in Beijing now. Anything could happen. Be careful, Mike," he pleaded. "Your own safety could be in jeopardy. You are a marked man."

Deeply shaken, I put down the receiver and looked at my exhausted colleagues, who sat around the work space with dazed, frightened expressions. The room, normally humming with activity, seemed unnaturally quiet. Only the TV set in the corner tuned to CNN pierced the silence. The first videotapes of the massacre had finally begun to air, after being smuggled by a student runner to Hong Kong on an early morning flight and satellited from there to CNN headquarters in Atlanta. Watching Cynde and Mitch's powerful images of the citizens of Beijing facing the armed might of the People's Liberation Army, I slumped in my chair with relief. Whatever might come next, I said to myself, we had at least outwitted the authorities on this one. It was too late for the government to stop the world from seeing the military slaughtering the citizens of Beijing.

But if Liu's information was right, we could be just moments away from a raid by soldiers determined not only to shut down our operation but, in all likelihood, to confiscate the remarkable collection of videotapes we had compiled during the past few weeks.

"If they are going to rewrite history," I said to my colleagues, "they'd certainly want to start by getting rid of evidence that contradicted their version of events. It might be prudent," I suggested, "for me to take our raw tapes, our cameras, and myself, and find someplace safe for a while, out of reach of the army." No one disagreed.

I called Andy Koss, the soft-spoken, mustachioed press officer at the United States embassy. Andy was a good friend; he and his wife and children had often shared meals with Lynne, Daniel, and me in calmer days. "Andy," I said, trying to speak vaguely on what was undoubtedly a tapped phone, "I may have a bit of a problem here. Could I stop by your office with a bagful of goodies for you?" Andy understood what I was saying. "When do you want to come over?" he asked. "How about right now?" I replied.

Moments later, I piled several boxes filled with videotapes, plus two cameras and other pieces of equipment, into the trunk of the bureau's creaky 1983 Toyota and drove out of the Sheraton's parking lot. After dropping the cameras at the apartment of a sympathetic young Indian diplomat whose son was a playmate of Daniel's, I headed off through the eerily deserted streets, looking nervously over my shoulder, toward the American embassy.

The embassy's Press and Culture Section was located in a rectangular gray building at 17 Guanghua Road, just in front of the official residence of the U.S. ambassador. It was surrounded by high walls and a metal gate, but to my intense relief, the Chinese guards waved me through when I flashed my American passport. Andy Koss, Press Counselor McKinney Russell, and United States Information Agency officials Charles McLaughlin and Larry Daks were waiting at the door, and they quickly helped me carry the tapes and equipment. Once inside, I began to speak, but Andy put his finger to his lips and motioned me to keep silent. Walking past a framed portrait of President George Bush in the hallway, he sat down at his desk and began to write. A moment later, he held up a piece of paper.

"This building is not secure," I read. "Do not say anything you do not want the Chinese to know. We are going to put your tapes in diplomatic mailbags and keep them in our safe. We will put the gear in our storage room. The stuff will be safe with us. Okay?" Silently, I nodded. Andy ushered me into the office of McKinney Russell, a polished Cold War veteran who had spent many years based in West Germany. A TV set was tuned to CNN, playing Cynde and Mitch's pictures from the night before yet again. Turning up the volume, we were able to speak in hushed tones. I told the diplomats of the warning about a raid on the work space, and of my concerns for my own safety. McLaughlin, a burly chain-smoker with a handlebar mustache, indicated that the embassy had independently picked up the same rumors.

If these reports were true—and the fact that the embassy had received the same information I had suggested that this might be so—we agreed that it would be dangerous for me to leave. It crossed my mind that I might end up a hostage in my own embassy. "We thought that Chinese agents in black cars with no license plates were following you," he told me later. "We thought you were only minutes ahead of them."

With little to do but wait, I was able to get a sense of how the embassy relied on CNN for information during the crisis. All five TV sets in the Press and Culture Section were tuned to CNN, with staffers in rotating shifts monitoring the contents of our reporting and passing our information back to Washington. Later, James Lilley, the U.S. ambassador during the crackdown, told me that CNN was often well ahead of the embassy's political officers in reporting major developments, so much so that policy decisions in Washington tended to be driven more by what appeared on CNN than by the analyses of the U.S. diplomats on the scene. Hearing this confirmed my sense that CNN had suddenly become a player on the global stage, with potentially momentous consequences for those of us at the network as well as those about whom we were reporting.

However safe I felt, being stuck inside the embassy compound, watching CNN, was extremely frustrating. I needed to get back to reporting and didn't want to abandon Cynde, Mitch, Donna, Tom Mintier, and my other colleagues. We had pulled our cameras out of the Beijing Hotel, and most of our people were off the streets, holed up at the Sheraton trying to figure out what to do next in a chaotic, dangerous, and extremely fluid situation. Throughout the afternoon I spoke frequently with Lynne, who was waiting nervously at home with Daniel.

"The soldiers are not here yet," she would say to me. "They haven't showed up at the Sheraton. Are they down there?" As far as I could tell, there was no sign of the predicted raid. By early evening, after intense discussions with the embassy staffers, I decided to risk returning home. Charles McLaughlin and his wife, Judy, the embassy nurse, offered to accompany me. For extra security, I rode with Judy in her official embassy car with its diplomatic license plates, while Charles drove the CNN car. "That way," he remembered afterward, "if your car got stopped, I had a diplomatic passport and could say to the soldiers or police that I had just borrowed your car and didn't know anything about anyone they might be seeking." To avoid roadblocks, we took a back way past the North Korean embassy and down an alley near an adjacent vegetable market, before reaching the Ta Yuan compound where my apartment was located.

In the end, there was no swoop on the CNN office. Some days later, my Radio Beijing friend surfaced and told me that a group of plainclothes security agents had indeed been on their way to the Sheraton. However, in their civilian garb, they ran into trouble at an army roadblock. Perhaps, in a system as rigidly bureaucratic as China's, they didn't have the right passes for the jumpy soldiers on the streets to let them through. Possibly they were caught up in the tension between military units that was to fuel rumors of civil war in the days ahead. Whatever the case, they never completed their journey. I have never been able to confirm the truth of the reports that CNN was targeted for a raid. In the fear-laced climate of the time, it seemed frighteningly plausible.

"There's a guy! Do you see that guy?" Soundman Kit Swartz motioned to cameraman Jonathan Schaer. With mounting excitement, Swartz spoke again. "There's a guy in front of the tank!"

It was just past twelve noon on Monday, June 5. Following a meeting of CNN staffers in my apartment late the previous evening, we had decided that we had no choice but to ignore the rumors about a possible army sweep of our work space. With our tapes safe at the U.S. embassy, we retrieved the cameras stashed at the apartment of my friend from the Indian embassy and worked out a plan of action. Tom Mintier and I would trade off shifts doing live phone reports and edited packages, and we would immediately send a camera crew back to Tokyo Base, the eleventh-floor room at the Beijing Hotel with its sweeping view of Tiananmen Square. Since we had left with the gear midday Sunday in case the police swept in, Jessica Smith, the Beijing Normal University English teacher who worked part-time as the bureau researcher, had kept a lonely vigil at the hotel. Staring out the window with nothing to eat, she was petrified that Public Security goons would come and arrest her. "I kept thinking of all the alibis I could try if they grabbed me," she recalled. "I'm just a teacher, and I didn't want to stay on campus because it was too dangerous, or this was the first hotel I could think of in my panic to get out of the university, or I didn't realize it would be dangerous down here too." But she continued to carefully note down what she saw outside, phoning the information back to the Sheraton work space, where Tom incorporated it into his reports while I was holed up at the embassy. Now we decided to keep that vantage point staffed around the clock until we were forced to leave.

Twelve hours later, Swartz, the soft-spoken sound technician who had stayed with Cynde throughout the night of the massacre, and Schaer, an exuberant shooter I'd worked with during the People

Power revolt in Manila three years earlier, were perched on the Beijing Hotel balcony, keeping a watchful eye on Changan Street and the northern end of Tiananmen. Tom Mintier had joined them. Totally sealed off by the army since early Sunday, the square had been transformed into a military compound. In place of the students and their banners for democracy, hundreds of tanks, armored vehicles, jeeps, and squadrons of heavily armed soldiers stood guard. Suddenly a column of tanks in front of the Mao portrait on the Tiananmen rostrum began to rev up. I was in the Sheraton work space when Tom called to describe in amazement the scene unfolding below him. Quickly I called Atlanta and asked to be put on the air. For the next five minutes, with the call from Tom in one ear and the line to CNN headquarters in the other, I broadcast his account of the episode, which came to symbolize the continuing defiance of the Chinese people.

On Changan Street near the entrance to the Beijing Hotel, a single man in a white shirt, carrying a small satchel in one hand and a jacket in the other, stood in front of the oncoming column of tanks. Waving his arms, he motioned them to turn back. The lead tank, smoke puffing from its engine exhaust pipe, began to move toward the right. The man retreated and stopped in front of it, again bringing the column to a halt. A crowd of onlookers standing on the sidewalk began to cheer. I could tell from the tension in Tom's voice that he could hardly believe what he was seeing, expecting at any moment that the soldiers would either open fire or simply crush the lone dissident and move forward. At one point, the young man climbed onto the lead tank, squatted by the turret, and remonstrated with the troops. As he argued, there was a burst of gunfire, apparently warning shots. Undeterred, the man continued to call for the tanks to retreat. "Turn around!" he reportedly shouted. "Stop killing my people!" For five excruciating minutes, the drama continued as Schaer's camera rolled, and I blindly narrated the scene live over the phone. Finally three other men raced into the center of the road and dragged the young man away.

A moment later, the tanks rumbled off toward the eastern side of the city, and soon after, a student runner raced to the airport with the videotape. Six hours later, following a satellite feed from Hong Kong, the most dramatic image of the entire Beijing Spring, a symbol of individual resistance to the armed power of the state that captured the imagination of the world, was on the air—all five minutes of it, unedited, with no narration. Watching the extraordinary bravery of the young man, who was never identified and whose fate even now remains unknown, Tom Mintier and I had nothing left to say.

Beijing was a city consumed by rage and grief. The young man who stopped the tanks was not alone in his defiance. Stunned by the scale of the army's savagery, bands of angry citizens continued to hurl rocks, bottles, and curses at the armored vehicles and troop convoys racing through the streets of the capital. With a camera hidden in a duffel bag, Cynde Strand slipped into the Minzu Hotel on Changan Street to the west of Tiananmen Square. For two nights in a row, she watched and surreptitiously photographed from the balcony of her room as crowds erected barricades, torched buses, and skirmished with troops on the street below. I found the images she recorded especially painful. The Minzu was where I had stayed on my first visit to China in 1973. It was the place from which I had set out with such excitement to join the citizens of Beijing marching to celebrate the conclusion of the Communist Party's Tenth Congress. Now, in the very same place, they were fighting and being killed by the army that kept the party in power.

Mitch Farkas took a camera to the university district, where the protest movement had begun seven weeks before. He brought back pictures of grim-faced students, many of them weeping, gathered in small groups, trying to ascertain the whereabouts of missing classmates, and worrying that the campuses would be the army's next target.

But the popular resistance began to crumble under the weight of what amounted to a military occupation of China's capital, as trigger-happy soldiers drove through debris-strewn streets firing their automatic rifles at random. Yet the terror and uncertainty grew worse, fueled by what appeared at the time to be signs of conflict within the armed forces. Even before the crackdown, there had been widespread reports of opposition inside the army to using the military to crush a civilian protest movement. The commander of the 38th Group Army, the unit responsible for protecting Beijing in time of war, was rumored to have refused to lead his troops into the capital when martial law was declared, and a former minister of defense as well as other prominent retired military officials had also publicly opposed intervention by the PLA.

Now, late Monday afternoon, two dozen tanks took up positions on an overpass by the Jianguomenwai Diplomatic Compound, home to nearly a thousand foreign diplomats and journalists. Similar columns appeared at other strategic points guarding the approaches to the city. Western military attachés told us the tanks were in "battle formation." Their guns pointed not toward the heart of Beijing, where the protests had been most intense during the previous few days, but in the opposite direction, to the west, north, and south, as if ready to repel an attack by other soldiers. After the massacre, was it really possible that China now faced the specter of civil war?

Against a backdrop of sporadic gunfire throughout the night and the following day, we watched armored vehicles and troop trucks hurtle through the city's empty streets, without knowing who they were or where they were going. We also heard the muffled thud of explosions reverberating in the distance: two or three at a time, then silence, then two or three more. Standing on the roof of the twenty-one-story Sheraton, my colleagues and I strained to listen in the dark. We couldn't be certain, but it sounded very much like artillery or tank rounds.

Adding to the confusion was the continuing mystery as to who, if anyone, was actually running the country. Since the massacre, no senior Party leader had appeared in public or issued an authoritative statement taking responsibility for the crackdown. Government-run newspapers were appearing only sporadically, and CCTV was still broadcasting nothing more than communiqués from the martial-law command. And, of course, there was no official Chinese government or military spokesman to whom I and other reporters could turn for comment or guidance. In an information vacuum, rumors swept the city: Li Peng had been shot; Deng Xiaoping was dying of cancer; student leaders like Wang Dan and Wu'er Kaixi had been killed. Most widespread of all was the fevered speculation that the "good" 38th Group Army was preparing to fight the "evil" 27th Group Army, widely believed by the Chinese public to have perpetrated the June 4 massacre.

In retrospect, it is not hard to see how this rumor, which was at the heart of the "civil war" scare that swept China and agitated the world for several days, gained strength. Even after the demonstrators were crushed, many Beijing citizens could not believe that the PLA would sanction the brutality the city had experienced over the weekend. The army was one of the country's most revered institutions. From the days of Chairman Mao, who wrote that "the PLA men are like fish in the sea of the people," the Chinese Communists had gone to great lengths to make the PLA a "people's army." Unlike soldiers from earlier times, who were known for looting, raping, and pillaging, the PLA had a reputation for discipline, honesty, and integrity. Its troops not only defended the country and the revolution, they dug dams, built roads, and engaged in economic construction. Surely, people argued, the army that had liberated China in 1949 could not behave like this. It must have been a rogue unit that had crushed the protestors. The 27th Army fit the description. It was a force with a reputation for toughness and that had the responsibility in wartime of protecting Party and state leaders, in contrast to the 38th, whose commander's reluctance to support the crackdown was widely known. Hopes that the "good guys" would come to the rescue, a consuming desire to see those responsible for the violence punished, awareness of earlier reports of military dissent, and the apparent signs of internal conflict in the days immediately after the bloodletting, merged into fevered talk of Chinese soldiers turning their weapons on each other.

It wasn't merely speculation on the streets either. Those of us in the foreign press corps heard the rumors, often with numerous details, from Chinese journalists, intellectuals, and other usually well-informed local sources. Often I found that Dave Schweisberg and I had received almost exactly the same information from totally different people. Western military attachés from the American, Australian, Canadian, and other embassies also agreed that civil war might be a real possibility. Friends in Washington with access to photographs from U.S. spy satellites told me of indications of major troop movements elsewhere in the country. Something certainly seemed to be brewing. On the air, we speculated frequently about the possible implications of a showdown: all of them were frightening.

With our world crumbling around us, I urged Lynne to take Daniel and get out of China. I was determined to stay, but they would hardly be alone in leaving. Beijing's foreign community was fleeing in droves, some on their own initiative, others at the instruction of their embassies, all terrified by the disintegration of daily life and fears of civil war. Lynne didn't want to go, but many shops had closed, the postal service, garbage collection, and public transport had ground to a halt, food had disappeared from the markets, and water and gas supplies to our apartment had dwindled. When we realized that our discussions increasingly focused on questions about the ability of the compound's underground parking lot to withstand direct hits from artillery shells in the event of heightened conflict, Lynne reluctantly agreed that it might be time to leave. First, however, she wanted to be sure that Sherlock could go too. If there was going to be a civil war, or if I faced the possibility of being expelled, she didn't want to leave the dog behind.

On the morning of Wednesday, June 7, Lynne left Daniel with the *aiyi* and, accompanied by the wife of a Reuters photographer friend who also had a dog, drove through the deserted streets to the Jianguomenwai Diplomatic Compound. She was nervous, with tanks still positioned at the intersection outside, but she had no choice. Many international airline offices were located in the compound, and she was determined to find out how Sherlock could be shipped out of Beijing.

It turned out to be an exercise in frustration. Harassed airline staffers, deserted by their Chinese co-workers, who were too frightened to come to the office, struggled to cope with mobs of anxious foreigners desperate to leave. "I'm having trouble getting the *people* out of here," one ticket agent snapped at Lynne. "I can't bother with a *dog!*"

Discouraged, Lynne left Jianguomenwai and began to walk in the direction of the Jianguo and Jinglun, two joint-venture hotels a couple of blocks away. Suddenly she heard a horrible, crunching sound coming closer and closer. Turning around, she saw a convoy of tanks speeding toward her. Moments later, soldiers opened fire on the compound's fifteen-story apartment blocks, riddling the homes of foreign diplomats and journalists with bullets. In one flat, the Chinese *aiyi* of U.S. Embassy security officer Fred Krugh threw herself on top of Krugh's two children as the bullets passed just overhead. As windows shattered around them, Lynne and her friend ran for cover, quaking in fear as they huddled behind a wall. Later the martial-law command issued the preposterous claim that a sniper had fired at troops from inside Jianguomenwai. A more likely explanation was that the troops were trying to intimidate and discourage foreign TV crews and diplomats from photographing them or charting their movements from the windows of upper-floor apartments.

I had gone that morning to withdraw CNN's remaining money from the Bank of China on the western side of the city, driving past the burned-out remains of buses and army vehicles that lay in silent testament to the violence of the preceding days. To my surprise the bank was open, and I found it packed with people trying to retrieve their own or their company's cash. So great was the demand that the teller would only agree to let me take a third of the over $50,000 in the CNN account. On my way back, I spoke to several people who reported new troop convoys on the road to the Beijing Airport. The talk on the streets was that the army might soon seal it off, closing the only escape route out of the country. As I walked in our apartment, the phone was ringing. It was Lynne, calling from just outside Jianguomenwai.

"There's been a shoot-out here," she said, barely controlling her emotions. "And the tanks—they were horrible."

I was frantic. "Get back here as fast as you can," I urged her. "Take back roads, and be careful. I heard rumors they might cut off the airport. You and Daniel have got to get out of Beijing—now."

Half an hour later, she stumbled in, very shaken but in full agreement that it was time for her and Daniel to leave, even if we couldn't get the dog out.

Lynne's mind was racing as she suddenly faced the dilemma of what to take with her. It was not at all clear when or whether she and Daniel might be able to return, particularly if, as seemed entirely possible, I might soon be expelled or detained. I dumped a drawer full of Daniel's clothes into a suitcase while Lynne grabbed a few of his favorite stuffed toys and books. In another bag, we jammed our favorite photograph albums, along with documents like birth and marriage certificates. At the last minute, Lynne removed from its frame one of our most treasured possessions, a calligraphy by her old Chinese teacher and *feng shui* expert, Lin Yun. She rolled it up to take with her. It seemed an act of grim finality.

Walking out the door was heartbreaking. Miss Li, who had looked after Daniel from the time he was five months old, was sobbing. Even Sherlock, who had followed us from room to room with a quizzical expression on his face, looked upset.

But two-year-old Daniel somehow kept his composure. As we walked out, he turned to Miss Li and the dog, and said in Chinese,

"*Aiyi*, don't cry. Sherlock, don't cry." Now I burst into tears.

Downstairs, we were joined by Jessica Smith. The young English teacher from Beijing Normal University had kept her cool while maintaining a solitary lookout at Tokyo Base, almost until the moment we were forced to abandon it on Tuesday as the troops downtown tightened their grip. Initially she was determined to remain in Beijing, but earlier Wednesday morning, she had been at the airport helping a CNN crew shoot departing foreigners when she saw almost all her closest university friends swarm past and onto waiting planes. As she wrote later, "When the CNN van came to return to town, I hoisted myself in the seat and envisioned myself boarding the Titanic as everyone else was jumping off. A convoy of trucks drove past in the other direction, filled with armed troops heading toward the airport. More armed and helmeted figures lined the overpass—a final image that snapped my determination not to leave."

Now, with her wallet, passport, and sweater stuffed into a knapsack, Jessica squeezed into my old Toyota with Lynne and Daniel for the nerve-racking ride to the airport. We could see menacing-looking troops with rifles positioned along the way. But to our intense relief the road was open, and we were allowed to pass without interference. The airport itself was bedlam, as thousands of frightened foreigners, as well as many local Chinese, who held passports allowing them to travel, jostled for seats on the few outgoing flights. No one seemed to care about the destination; anywhere outside of China would do. I noticed the souvenir counters were empty. There would be no more tourists here for a while, I thought to myself. With no tickets or reservations, it was far from certain that Lynne, Daniel, and Jessica would be able to leave. I raced frantically from one airline counter to another seeking information. Finally word came that Cathay Pacific Airways was laying on two extra flights to Hong Kong. We waited nervously as the ticket agent called out the names of those on the waiting list. Suddenly I heard "Lynne Curry, Daniel Chinoy, Jessica Smith." Grabbing her tickets, Lynne took Daniel and set off for the immigration counter. There was no time for elaborate goodbyes. "I gave Mike a big hug and told him to take care," Lynne wrote in her diary. "Then I went through the gate, uncertain when we would be together again. Mike looked terribly sad, and I worried whether the Chinese would arrest him for his work. One of the last things he said to me was that he felt more strongly than ever that the real truth had to get out to the rest of the world, and he would continue to report it as long as he could. Finally the plane took off. Some of the passengers applauded. I didn't feel there was anything to clap about."

As she held Daniel on her lap, Lynne turned to Jessica in the seat next to her and said, "We spent two years building a life here. And now we don't know if we'll be able to go back."

I slowly drove home alone in the gathering dusk, suddenly drained. The combination of adrenaline and fear that had kept me going during the past few days had disappeared. Now I was just miserable and scared. Although I was rarely home, Lynne's emotional support, her presence with Daniel in our home, had sustained me throughout the tumultuous spring. They were my one anchor in a world turning upside down in front of my eyes. With their departure, I was on my own. Only poor old Sherlock, who greeted me with wagging tail and unrestrained excitement when I got back to our empty and disheveled apartment, remained as a reminder of the ordered family life I had suddenly lost. And I was worried about the dog. No airline would take him out of the country. It seemed silly and selfish even to try to send him away when so many people were still desperately seeking to leave. But if the situation should deteriorate further, or if I was suddenly detained or ordered out of the country, what would happen to him? The day before Lynne and Daniel left, I had arranged for the daughter of a diplomat at the U.S. embassy to look after him in an emergency. Two hours later, she called back to say that embassy dependents had been ordered out and that she was leaving for the airport. Now I called Charles McLaughlin, who'd been so helpful on the day after the massacre. To my great relief, he agreed to take the dog if anything happened to me.

The possibility of danger remained very real. Thirty-six hours earlier, dissident physicist Fang Lizhi and his wife had sought, and been granted, refuge at the U.S. embassy, where Ambassador Lilley hid them in the embassy clinic, just behind his official residence and the Press and Culture Section. Once President Bush's spokesman, Marlin Fitzwater, made the news public, the Chinese reacted with fury, accusing the U.S. of interfering in China's internal affairs. In the fear-laced atmosphere of Beijing, I speculated with my colleagues and friends whether the Chinese government might find a pretext to storm the embassy and seize Fang or perhaps detain an American in reprisal. Unpopular reporters certainly seemed an obvious target, and my Radio Beijing friend Liu continued to warn that my own high profile made me vulnerable, even urging me not to walk Sherlock by myself, because I might be set upon by government thugs. However far-fetched that sounded, with Lynne gone, I was too nervous to sleep at home. On the theory that there was safety in numbers, I decided to move into the Sheraton, returning twice a day to take the dog for a walk.

The hotel, which had been abandoned over the past few days by its usual clientele of Western business executives and tourists, was suddenly packed again. The new arrivals were mostly terrified diplomats and their families who had fled their apartments after the army opened fire at the Jianguomenwai Compound earlier in the day. Their faces pale and drawn, clutching suitcases and crying children, they thronged the lobby and coffee shop, speculating about how quickly they could get out of the country. After what was unquestionably a deliberate attack on the compound, in clear violation of the normal rules governing diplomatic behavior, fear that foreigners in Beijing could become the next targets on the PLA's campaign of violence had reached fever pitch. At the CNN work space, where the anxiety level over a possible army raid on the hotel was almost as great as among the diplomatic families, Tom Mintier and Tokyo correspondent Brian Jenkins, who had just flown in to help out, had willingly taken over all reporting chores for the past thirty-six hours so I could get my family out. I was extremely grateful for their help and understanding. As I was thanking them upon my return to the hotel, U.S. Embassy assistant army attaché Larry Wortzel walked in. A close friend of Cynde's, Wortzel was a short, stocky man bursting with energy. With his extensive knowledge of PLA operations and Chinese security matters, he had been a valuable source during the past few weeks. After briefly swapping rumors of rival PLA units engaged in shoot-outs and other soldiers refusing to follow orders—none of which proved to be true—Wortzel strode over to where I sat slumped in a chair and dropped a portable radio on the desk. "If you guys get into any trouble with the Chinese here tonight," he said to me, "I'm around the hotel. Call me!"

If Wortzel believed an army assault on the hotel was a real possibility, I thought to myself, then the situation was far worse than I had imagined. Soon after, Atlanta requested a telephone update from me. I was so unnerved by Wortzel's dramatic gesture that I decided it would be prudent not to broadcast from the work space. Deirdre Chetham, another embassy friend, offered me the use of her room on a different floor, where I described over the phone what I'd seen as I moved around the city during the day. I also talked about Lynne and Daniel's departure, dropping my mask of reportorial objectivity to share with our audience my personal anguish over what the tumultuous events in Beijing had done to my family life. "I spent the last day getting my wife and two-year-old son out of China—an experience so painful I hope I never have to repeat it," I told our viewers, my voice breaking. "It is as if one's whole life crumbles before one's eyes."

I was aware by now of the impact CNN's reports on the crisis were having around the world, but it wasn't until I mentioned my family that I got a sense of how personally involved with me many viewers had become. In the following days, letters, calls, and messages of concern about my family poured into Beijing and to CNN headquarters. I was amazed by the intensity of the reaction, which underscored the peculiar intimacy of television, and offered the sobering realization that for millions of people, I was the human vehicle through whom they were experiencing this momentous and tragic series of events.

Suddenly, at the height of the tension, the atmosphere abruptly changed. After a fitful sleep, I awoke the next morning, Thursday, June 8, to discover that the soldiers we had thought were on the brink of shooting each other were now devoting their energies to clearing up the debris of the past five days, hauling the burned-out shells of buses and military vehicles away, and tidying up the streets. For the first time since the army entered the city center, the troops moved their barricades back slightly, allowing the citizens to approach the edge of Tiananmen Square for a glimpse of the weekend's battleground. Tanks and armored vehicles still dominated the huge expanse, and there was no sign of the students' once-large encampment. The troops appeared to be under orders to go out of their way to be polite and friendly. Under a hot sun, buses, bicyclists, and shoppers reappeared. Some stores and restaurants reopened, and food again became available at local markets. After the trauma of the past week, it was as if the city were letting out a collective sigh of relief that at least a superficial calm had descended over the city.

The threat of civil war hovering over the capital quickly faded. In retrospect, it was evident that a combination of confusion, fear, and misinformation had fueled speculation well beyond what the reality on the ground warranted. This did not mean the tensions that my colleagues and I had sensed and reported were not real. That some troops did disobey orders and refuse to open fire on their fellow citizens seems certain. In fact, later in the year, internal party documents were leaked to newspapers in Hong Kong in which senior Chinese officials were quoted as confirming that over a thousand soldiers had faced unspecified disciplinary action for insubordination after the shooting. In addition, after reviewing the evidence, some Western military attachés told me that in the tumult of the assault on the square, different military units may have accidentally fired on each other. These unintended but violent encounters led to army casualties from "friendly fire." It was probably this heightened sense of distrust among various units that we interpreted as political divisions in the days after the massacre. There never was a real danger of civil war. The hope that somehow a faction of the military or the party elite would depose those responsible for the bloodletting was nothing more than wishful thinking.

How mistaken we were became clear the next day, Friday, June 9, when I turned on the TV set at the Sheraton work space to watch the seven o'clock evening news on CCTV. For the first time since the crackdown—indeed for the first time since his meeting with Mikhail Gorbachev on May 16—Deng Xiaoping appeared in public. His hands were shaking, his face was puffy, and his speech seemed slightly slurred. But, dressed in a blue-gray Mao suit, he was smiling broadly as he greeted members of the Politburo and the generals who were assembled in the Hall of Cherishing Benevolence at the Zhongnanhai leadership compound and congratulated them for crushing what he called a "counterrevolutionary disturbance whose goal was to topple the Chinese Communist Party." Walking beside Deng were Prime Minister Li Peng, as always with a smirk on his face, President Yang Shangkun, and several other conservative party elders who had played key roles both in the recent power struggle and in authorizing the decision to open fire on June 3. Conspicuously absent was Party General-Secretary Zhao Ziyang. He had not been seen since his tearful visit to the student hunger strikers in

Tiananmen Square the day before martial law was proclaimed in mid-May. It was widely believed that he had been purged.

As I watched the reappearance of China's paramount leader on the CCTV evening news that night, the message was clear: Deng was very much alive and in charge, heading a coalition of hard-liners and even some moderates who had joined forces to crush the threat to Party authority represented by the crowds in the streets. Just in case there were any doubts, the government swiftly launched the world's first televised purge, a nationwide witch hunt to track down students, workers, and intellectuals who had supported or taken part in the protests. In a macabre tribute to the power of TV, the mass arrests, interrogations, and trials became regular viewing fare on CCTV. So did repeated broadcasts of a list of the twenty-one most-wanted student activists, complete with mug shots, detailed descriptions, and exhortations to the masses to turn the criminals over to police. At the top of the list were Wang Dan, Wu'er Kaixi, and Chai Ling, all of whom were attempting to flee the country. "We can see clearly the true ugly faces of the student union," the CCTV commentator intoned. "Police in every province and region, on railways, airlines, highways, and border posts must immediately deploy units to arrest them and stop them leaving the country." The exhortation was only partly successful. Wang Dan was soon picked up, but Chai Ling, Wu'er Kaixi, Li Lu, and several other student leaders did escape to the West with the help of an underground network of supporters throughout China.

Night after night, my colleagues and I watched with disgust the grotesque images of frightened, manacled young people, some clearly badly beaten, being frog-marched into detention rooms or handcuffed to trees. On several occasions, young men convicted of arson or riotous behavior were shown being sentenced to death, the camera moving in for closeups of their terrified young faces just moments before they were led away to the execution grounds. In all, over thirty-five people were put to death in the weeks immediately after June 4. I found it significant that those singled out for execution— and for the most extensive TV coverage—were rebellious workers. The penalties for dissident students and intellectuals were much less harsh, and received much less publicity. It was a telling indication of the government's fear that the urban working class, in theory the bedrock of any Communist Party's support and legitimacy, might turn against the system. The authorities were determined to ensure that any politically restive workers got the message.

In one especially frightening episode, the Chinese intercepted an ABC News satellite feed from Hong Kong to its New York headquarters. The video showed a forty-two-year-old worker named Xiao Bin denouncing the massacre. It was almost immediately rebroadcast on CCTV with appeals for citizens to turn the man in. Xiao Bin was quickly arrested, and as punishment for his emotional remarks, he was sentenced to ten years in prison. This blunt signal on television warned Chinese citizens not to talk to the foreign media, and it was a grim reminder to us of the risks facing anyone who dared to defy the government's edicts. We anguished over how we would handle our coverage of dissenting opinions. Eventually, after discussions with foreign editor Eason Jordan, we decided that we would black out someone's face if we were asked, but that the decision would be left up to the individual being interviewed.

However, as the climate of fear enveloped Beijing like the oppressive summer humidity, the problem rarely cropped up. Hardly anyone was willing to talk to us at all anymore, let alone go on camera. I soon lost touch with most of my Chinese friends. I couldn't put them in danger by calling them, and they stopped contacting me, with the exception of the reckless and headstrong Liu at Radio Beijing. One day a mutual acquaintance did deliver a brief message from a theater set designer that Lynne and I had befriended earlier in the year. It said simply, " I cannot see you now. I am very sorry."

Cynde, Mitch, and I and a dwindling band of CNN staffers tried to continue to operate by playing a game of cat and mouse with the authorities. We shot enough surreptitious video of street scenes and helmeted, rifle-toting soldiers on guard duty to illustrate the mood in the city, edited those images together with CCTV's daily litany of arrests, confessions, and official pronouncements, and smuggled our spots to Hong Kong. It did not take long for us to run into trouble.

"Broke the golden rule today. I stayed too long in one spot," Cynde wrote in her diary in mid-June. Shooting the passing traffic on a leafy street one sunny afternoon, she, her soundman, and a visiting producer from CNN headquarters who had come to China on a tourist visa, were picked up by the cops. As they were escorted away, one Beijing resident yelled in protest. He, too, was quickly detained, as was the bureau driver, Mr. Lu. Sitting on a bench in the police station, the producer nervously dropped his cigarette on the floor and snuffed it out with his foot. "Clean up your mess, you filthy pigs," one officer exploded, his face reddening in anger. "We Chinese are not dirty animals!"

Each member of the CNN team was interrogated separately. Relieved because they hadn't been turned over to the army, Cynde decided to play the game the Chinese way, by admitting her "crimes" and begging for forgiveness. "In other words," she recalled, "I groveled. 'Yes, we broke martial law. I am so sorry. I didn't understand the rules. Yes, I'm just a stupid foreigner.'" All three were ordered to write self-criticisms. The police couldn't read that of the producer, a newcomer to Beijing. "What language is this?" they demanded. "He was so badly shaken," Cynde noted in her diary, "that his handwriting looked like Cyrillic."

Eventually the three were released, along with the driver, but only after their camera had been confiscated and they had been warned that the police would do whatever was necessary to stop foreigners from taking pictures.

"Funny thing," Cynde mused to herself as she left, "we were out to take pictures to show how life was returning to normal."

A few nights later it was Mitch's turn. Hiding behind a tree, he was shooting an army roadblock with a small and easily hidden handycam when he was spotted by the troops. Trying to walk away in as natural a manner as possible, Mitch casually dropped the camera in a bush. A moment later an army jeep roared up. Two soldiers with guns pointed threw Mitch against a wall as he heard a third soldier yell, "We've found the camera!" Two other cars full of men wearing civilian clothes and army helmets arrived. They had cameras and lights and began to videotape Mitch as they fired off questions.

"Who are you?"

"I'm an American journalist," Mitch replied.

"What were you doing?" they demanded.

"I was taking pictures."

"Why?"

"Because it's my job."

Sweating and scared, Mitch was bundled into an unmarked car and driven to a police station at a location he couldn't identify. There, an English-speaking army officer continued the interro-

gation, interspersed with remarks like "Why do you American journalists come here to make China look bad?" and "Why is your
President Bush insulting our country?" To this last one, Mitch
replied, "I didn't vote for him." His interrogators smiled, and suddenly the tension eased, although as Mitch completed writing his
self-criticism, the English-speaking officer announced that his passport was being seized. Deciding there was nothing to lose, Mitch
declared, "You can't take my passport."

"Yes, I can. I can take anything I want," the officer replied.

"Look," Mitch pleaded. " You can't take my passport. I'm about
to go on vacation to see my mother, and if I don't go, she'll be furious
at me."

"You are under arrest by the martial-law authorities," the officer
answered incredulously, "and you are more afraid of your mother
than of us?"

"To be absolutely frank," Mitch said, "yes."

The officer broke into laughter. "Come back in a week, and I'll
give you your passport," he said reassuringly. "Now get out of here."
A week later Mitch left on vacation.

Hoping to reduce the chances of decimating the Beijing bureau by
having more than one of us detained, or expelled, at the same time,
Cynde, Mitch, and I moved around Beijing separately. Mindful of
Liu's repeated warnings about my own safety, I deliberately kept a
low profile, and without a camera to attract unwelcome attention, I
was never picked up by the security forces. But I wasn't immune
from official denunciation. One morning I opened the *Beijing
Daily*, the official mouthpiece of the extremely hard-line Beijing
city government, to discover a blistering personal attack on me.
"Beijing-based CNN reporter Mike Chinoy hurled abuse and insults
at the People's Liberation Army troops until they were black and
blue," it thundered in a commentary entitled "How Was the Anti-
China Wave in the U.S. Stirred Up?" "His proud success," the paper
sneeringly continued, "was taking the gunshots he heard on the
streets of Beijing and broadcasting them back to America, to 'prove'
that the PLA massacred the peacefully demonstrating students.
What lies!"

My anxieties about being expelled, already high, now soared,
especially as the government had just announced that Voice of

America Beijing correspondent Al Pessin and AP reporter John Pomfret, both good friends of mine, had been given three days to leave the country. Still, I was actually rather pleased about the *Beijing Daily* article. In some ways I viewed it as a badge of honor, underscoring the fact that my straight reporting had enraged a government determined to suppress the truth.

And suppressing the truth now emerged as the central item on the government's agenda. With the situation on the streets under control and the dissidents being hunted down, the Communist Party launched a huge campaign to convince the people of China, and a skeptical world, that what my colleagues and I had lived through during the weekend of June 4 simply didn't happen.

Sixteen years before the Beijing massacre, I had followed crowds of marching Chinese into Tiananmen Square for the first time, at the conclusion of my initial trip to the People's Republic in August 1973. The occasion was a celebration of the Communist Party's Tenth Congress, at which Chairman Mao's designated heir, Marshal Lin Biao, was denounced as a "double-dealing traitor" who tried to overthrow the man he was tapped to succeed. In my youthful naïveté, I was astounded at the way the Party brazenly vilified a figure long praised as Mao's "closest comrade-in-arms." I remember wondering how the Chinese people would react to being told that a man who was a symbol of revolutionary correctness was now an example of counterrevolutionary evil. However, in a society numbed by years of mass campaigns, still largely cut off from the rest of the world, and dominated by a secretive leadership, there was little to prevent the Party from reshaping history as it saw fit. On the surface, it seemed, people had little choice but to accept the lie, and to draw from it clues about how a revamped ruling hierarchy expected them to behave in a changing political environment.

More than a decade and a half later, the Communist Party's instincts remained unchanged. Faced with a crisis, it reached for the old methods—repression, purges, and the "big lie." Now, however, there was a major difference. Through the experiences and memories of the citizens of Beijing and many other cities where protests had broken out, through the brief flowering of press freedom in Chinese newspapers and television in mid-May immediately before the imposition of martial law, through the Chinese-language broadcasts of the Voice of America and the BBC, and through the cameras of CNN and the rest of the international media, millions of people in China and across the world had seen and heard the events of the past few weeks for themselves. Erasing images so deeply engraved on the minds of so many would not be easy. It would take a disinformation campaign of breathtaking audacity and cynicism, which is precisely what the government engineered.

The message was blunt: there had been no massacre. The People's Liberation Army had used maximum restraint in quelling a "counterrevolutionary" rebellion against the state by "rioters and hooligans," led by a "tiny handful" of agitators out to sow chaos, in secret collusion with "hostile forces" at home and abroad. The first step in this rewriting of history was to control the discussion and debate by changing the terminology. Instead of a "democracy movement," the official media began to refer only to a *fangeming baoluan*, or "counterrevolutionary turmoil," that had been "suppressed" by the heroic soldiers of the PLA. The word "massacre" did not appear.

To buttress the Party's claim that the troops, not the citizens of Beijing, were the real victims of the violence, Chinese television began to show clips from the weekend of June 3–4, carefully edited to portray hoodlums running amok and attacking innocent soldiers. The images, taken from video monitors installed at key street intersections, as well as from footage shot by army cameramen, were often grisly, showing demonstrators setting fire to army vehicles, and the charred and mutilated corpses of soldiers killed by the protestors. But the clips, which were repeated night after night and soon made into a full-length documentary, were blatantly doctored. In many cases, the sequence of events was reversed. Even though the mood on the streets had indeed grown ugly in the hours before the army launched its final assault, with provocative acts on the part of some of the protestors, in the overwhelming majority of cases, the demonstrators had attacked the troops with rocks, bottles, bricks, or molotov cocktails, only *after* the troops had begun their advance or opened fire. The army vehicles set afire had been driving through the crowds, often at high speed, causing injuries and occasional fatalities. The sound was doctored, too: the audio of chanting mobs could be clearly heard, the sound of army gunfire not at all. Indeed some sequences showing the troops entering Tiananmen during the early hours of June 4 were silent, with no audio at all, even though I could recall hearing shots, cries, and screams at precisely that time from just a few hundred yards away.

Finally there was the question of casualties. Determined to show that the army was not responsible for the bloodshed, official spokesmen insisted that the troops did not kill anyone in Tiananmen Square, and that the total death toll that night did not exceed three hundred, a large number of them soldiers. Only a handful of students were acknowledged to have died.

The propaganda campaign was clearly a news story. Reporting its endless variations became a staple of my work in the weeks immediately after June 4. I had to concede that the government had managed its presentation skillfully. By relentlessly repeating the same lies and by showing the same doctored video over and over, the campaign began to have an effect. Afraid to talk about what they really saw, many people came under the Party's spell and started to doubt their own memories and perceptions. In a climate of intense fear and repression, the language one used to refer to the events of that weekend showed where one stood on the issue. To call it a "massacre" became a statement of political support for the students, while to use the word "turmoil" was to accept the government's version. Even among the foreign community, people began to back away from the reality of what had happened. Increasingly I heard diplomats, businessmen, and some reporters use the more neutral term "incident," or simply "the events of June 4." I found myself wondering too. Had I exaggerated the events of that weekend? Had I underplayed the intransigence or provocative acts of the students? However brutal its methods, was the government wholly unreasonable in wanting to clear the streets after so many weeks of disruption? Could it really have happened the way I remembered?

To preserve my own sanity, and for the public record, I decided to put together a long piece analyzing and countering the big lie. I reviewed my notes and tapes, not just from the night of June 3–4, but from the whole spring. With no Chinese willing to talk, I sought out numerous press colleagues who had watched events over the past few months, and who had had different vantage points on the night of the bloodshed.

As I pondered all the material, it was clear to me that the government's notion—that what it called a small group of "black hands" had carefully planned and orchestrated the whole uprising—was implausible, whatever minor violent episodes had preceded the weekend of June 3–4. The sheer size and diversity of the movement made this virtually impossible. My own experiences covering the protests—the mixed political signals from the students, the constantly changing announcements, the internal confusion, the sense that nobody had the authority to tell anybody what to do—underscored the lack of a central, organized leadership. The movement had exploded so rapidly that there was no individual or organization capable of fully controlling or directing the forces let loose on the streets of Beijing. This was one reason why efforts to find a face-saving compromise with Zhao Ziyang's supporters during the few moments prior to Mikhail Gorbachev's arrival, when that might have been possible, had ended in failure. It contributed to the reversal of the students' May 27 decision to declare victory and clear the square, which could have avoided the confrontation the following week. It was also one reason why various unruly elements began to get out of hand and add to the dangerous atmosphere in the days just before the army moved in. Moreover, the overwhelming support and involvement of the ordinary citizens and workers of Beijing, and the spontaneous acts of resistance to the military, both when martial law was declared and on the night of the crackdown, fatally undermined the argument for a carefully organized plot.

The claim that the students and their supporters were determined to create turmoil and overthrow the government also seemed a wild exaggeration. If anything, I had been struck by the mildness of the students' initial demands, which were for a freer press, an end to corruption, and more open government. The students' desire that the Party recognize the legitimacy and patriotic nature of the protest underscored their hopes of reforming—not toppling—the system that they were being trained to inherit. Only after it became clear that the Party had no interest in a meaningful compromise or dialogue did student leaders begin to harden their demands, the intransigence on both sides adding to the dangerous tensions created by the rapid escalation in the size and scale of the movement during the week of the Gorbachev visit.

But it was on the question of violence and casualties that I found myself most outraged. With my own eyes I had seen people killed, so the attempt to ignore or denigrate their deaths struck me as obscene. Yet when forced to confront the veracity of my own experience, I had to acknowledge that we in the media had made mistakes that played into the government's hands. Specifically, too many journalists and editors had focused excessively on Tiananmen Square itself, ignoring the much greater violence elsewhere in Beijing that night. Moreover, a lack of precision in reporting had allowed the term "Tiananmen Square Massacre" to slip into our vocabulary. The result was to create an opening for the Chinese authorities to distract attention from the scale of the killing throughout the rest of the city. The fact is that in a narrow, absolutely literal sense, Beijing's contention that no one was killed in the square itself might have contained a grain of truth. Within the actual confines of the square, the bloodletting appears to have been minimal, and the protestors gathered around the Monument to the Heroes of the Revolution were allowed to walk away as Cynde took pictures at daybreak. But as the Chinese government undoubtedly knew, focusing on the narrowly defined borders of the square was a false distinction, because while Tiananmen became synonymous with the democracy movement, the terror that night was not confined to this symbolic heart of Beijing.

From the balcony of the Beijing Hotel, I had watched as victims of army gunfire were wheeled away on the backs of pedicabs, and the colleagues I interviewed for my report saw similar scenes. Lewis Simons, a longtime Asia correspondent for the *Washington Post* who was then working for the Knight-Ridder newspaper chain, was observing events in the northeastern corner of the square early on the morning of Sunday June 4. "I watched troops with machine guns fire at waist level into a crowd of 400 people three separate times," he told me. "The first time I counted five bodies. The second time I counted six bodies. The third time I counted more than twenty bodies, possibly thirty. Now that's murder. And that, as far as I am concerned, was in Tiananmen Square."

Jan Wong, a reporter for the *Toronto Globe and Mail*, was at the Beijing Hotel later Sunday, when troops opened fire at the precise moment Tom Mintier and I were slipping our equipment away around the corner. "I saw troops firing at point-blank range into crowds as many tried to flee," she said. "I saw them shoot into their backs for three minutes. I stood there and timed the volleys."

Still, the total number of dead remained a vexing question, and in the many accounts published since then by eyewitnesses, participants, survivors, scholars, and journalists, there is no consensus on the number of casualties. This is not really surprising. In conditions of anarchy and martial law, it was almost impossible to visit all the hospitals or to get accurate information from terrified doctors or relatives. In the highly charged atmosphere immediately after the crackdown, wild rumors and speculation put the figure as high as several thousand, even while the Chinese insisted it was not more than three hundred. I tended to discount such extravagant claims and had consistently urged CNN to be cautious with any numbers. But it was true that Chinese Red Cross officials did initially use a figure of 2,600 dead when talking with some foreign journalists and diplomats. Soon after, however, the Red Cross retracted the claim, and then refused to speak with reporters. That was hardly the only challenge confronting those of us trying to put together a credible estimate. Very quickly, official pressure had prompted most doctors and hospital officials to refuse to answer reporters' questions, and the government itself refused to release the names of the dead. There were persistent rumors that the bodies of some of those killed had been secretly disposed of. Relatives of the victims were too frightened to speak out, and the anecdotal evidence—the friends who told us of the man whose head had been shattered by a stray bullet, the colleagues who'd visited a morgue where officials confirmed that many bodies had been brought but would not let reporters see for themselves—was insufficient to make an accurate calculation.

The fact is that we may never know the precise death toll, except that it was substantial. But in a sense, the exact number, and the question of whether the victims died inside the actual boundaries of Tiananmen or down the road, obscures the broader moral and political issues. The fact is that the Chinese army, on the orders of hard-liners in the leadership, was unleashed on crowds of largely unarmed and defenseless demonstrators, most of whom were committed to a campaign of nonviolent protest for political change. It was an episode that badly damaged the Chinese Communist Party's moral legitimacy, especially in the capital and among intellectuals and students, besmirched China's international reputation, and will forever tarnish Deng Xiaoping's legacy. The anniversary of June 4 is likely to haunt authoritarian rulers in China for decades.

Two weeks after the massacre, the Chinese Foreign Ministry

invited foreign reporters and TV crews for a look at the square, but I missed the story. Exhausted to the point of collapse, I had taken a long weekend to visit Lynne and Daniel in Hong Kong. My last act before leaving was to arrange for Sherlock's departure. With the exodus of foreigners now over, a friend at United Airlines was able to ship him to Lynne's parents in the U.S. When he left, there was nothing to do but cry.

In Hong Kong, I was disoriented and out of sorts as I walked through the territory's neon-lit streets, teeming with well-dressed crowds and overflowing shops. I was relieved to be out of Beijing and to see my family, but I couldn't get Beijing out of my mind. I tried to get my first good night's sleep in months, but found it hard to shake off the recurring nightmares. I hoped a brief break would help me to recover enough to resume work in China in the weeks ahead.

Meanwhile, Tom Mintier, nearing the end of a long stint in Beijing, and due to leave when I got back, took over reporting chores in my absence. As Cynde accompanied him on the official tour, the square was empty and quiet. Soldiers with rifles stood guard along the perimeter, while water trucks sprayed the pavement and workmen applied plaster to the damage on the Monument to the Heroes of the Revolution. "Our martial law troops did not kill one student or youth," intoned PLA spokesman Colonel Li Zhuyun in front of Cynde's camera. "Their vehicles did not crush one person. No massacre occurred."

"It's like a ghost town," Cynde wrote afterward in her diary. "They scrub away all signs of the democracy movement, but they cannot remove the faces from my memory."

Throughout the turbulent spring, Cynde had always carried a small Buddha from Tibet in her pocket as a good-luck charm, unconsciously reaching in to touch it at moments of acute tension or danger. "Today, remembering all those faces and listening to Colonel Li's smiling lies, I reached in to get my Buddha. It was in pieces, just broken to pieces. The lies were too strong."

CHAPTER TEN

A Tale of Two Chinas

China entered the last decade of the twentieth century enveloped in a suffocating cloud of propaganda and repression. Their anxieties heightened by the collapse of communism throughout the Soviet bloc, Party hard-liners stepped up a sweeping campaign to reimpose ideological orthodoxy. Liberal officials from the government and Communist Party were purged. Tiananmen Square activists who could not escape were searched out and punished. While Chai Ling and Wu'er Kaixi fled to the United States, Wang Dan was arrested and given a four-year term in jail. Other dissidents, like journalist Wang Juntao and social scientist Chen Ziming, were sentenced to thirteen years. Publishing houses, research institutes, and newspapers sympathetic to the now-disgraced former Party General-Secretary Zhao Ziyang came under intense political pressure. As the official media dished out a stultifying diet of turgid party tracts on the superiority of socialism, ordinary citizens were forced to show their loyalty to the new line by sitting through hours of "political study sessions," parroting the latest slogans. Daily life resumed its normal rhythm, but with little of the vibrancy and sense of movement that had marked the years before June 1989. The lid was back on.

For the foreign media, however, it was a different story. At a time when the government was tightening its control over information, successfully bullying the population into submission, making most Chinese too afraid to speak up, let alone talk to a Western reporter,

my colleagues and I in the Beijing press corps were left as virtually
the only people inside China still able to discuss publicly the sensitive issues the regime preferred to ignore. Our constant reporting
about arrests, trials, and purges, our frequent references to the
events of June 1989, the embarrassing questions we regularly posed
to the Foreign Ministry spokesman at his weekly news conferences,
and our unceasing, if often fruitless, efforts to contact the families
of imprisoned dissidents infuriated the regime. Always treated with
suspicion, we were now perceived as the enemy, a conduit for subversive information flowing into China and a source of constant
international embarrassment, further tarnishing a reputation the
Chinese leadership was desperately seeking to salvage.

The consequences were swift and unpleasant. Access to Chinese
units and officials, never easy for a TV crew even in the more relaxed
years prior to Tiananmen Square, virtually dried up, while police
surveillance and harassment intensified. Sometimes Cynde, Mitch,
and I could identify the men in their unmarked cars and motorcycles, sometimes not. But we knew we were being followed, that our
every move was charted by security agents. My life and work became
more circumscribed than ever. I lived in a state of perpetual tension,
my nerves rubbed raw by the oppressive weight of the Chinese state
and its insufferable, inescapable propaganda. I began to view my
reporting as a daily battle against the Chinese system, in which even
the smallest of victories—a stand-up or street scene successfully shot
before the police interfered, a Chinese person willing to say anything
to us on camera—became a source for celebration. Most of the time,
though, the victories were few and far between. My life in Beijing
became so stressful and dispiriting that I seriously considered leaving. My contract was up for renewal soon, and Lynne and I frequently
pondered other options. Western Europe, I thought, sounded just
about right.

Meanwhile, the skirmishes intensified during the spring of
1990, including a shouting and shoving match after local *waiban*
officials in the northeastern city of Benxi, where we were doing a
story on pollution, put their hands in front of the camera and tried
to physically prevent Cynde from taking shots of an innocuous vegetable market. We were expelled from Tiananmen every time we
showed up with the camera. Chinese journalist friends told me I
was near the top of a Foreign Ministry Information Department list

of reporters deemed "unfriendly" to China. My youthful romance with the People's Republic seemed an increasingly distant memory.

The battle between the press corps and the authorities reached a climax on the first anniversary of the crackdown. In the run-up to the night of June 3–4, heavily armed soldiers and police flooded the city, determined to prevent any outbreak of protest. Checkpoints were set up at every major intersection, and the government ordered work units to instruct their employees to keep off the streets and stay away from the square. Extra troops were deployed to cordon off the university district. Under the circumstances, my expectation was that nothing much would happen. But the local rumor mill was full of speculation that Beijing University students might hold a candlelight vigil or some other modest gesture of remembrance.

Sealed off to all but authorized visitors, the square was unnaturally quiet every time we drove by to check, as was the rest of the capital. It appeared as if we would spend this anniversary cruising for news that wasn't going to happen. In midevening, my crew and I set out for Beijing University, accompanied by my cousin, John Krich, a travel writer visiting from San Francisco who was eager to get a taste of the "exciting" life of a Beijing correspondent. Taking back roads, we eluded the checkpoints and circled the Beida campus. Guards stopped all reporters from entering the university, but a day earlier we had given a handycam to a young American woman student there who had promised to sneak some shots if anything happened.

Pulling up by Beida's west gate, we encountered what seemed to be half the Beijing press corps—TV crews, reporters, still photographers. All of us milled around under the street lamps. Just before midnight, we heard chants echoing from several of the dormitories on the other side of the wall. Within earshot, but out of view, a crowd of students gathered in protest around a bonfire. Aiming the camera at the dormitory windows, Cynde captured grainy images, the shadows of students moving about in the darkness. Soon after midnight, the demonstration died down. It was hardly dramatic television, but it was certainly enough to show our audience that the spirit of protest had not been totally extinguished. At least we would have a TV spot.

Leaving the camera with Mitch, Cynde and I entered a nearby guest house to telephone our student friend on campus and arrange to pick up the handycam tape from her. As we stepped inside, army trucks careened around the corner and dozens of rifle-toting troops ambushed the crowd of correspondents, most of whom were preparing to disperse anyway. Mitch swiftly placed the camera in the back of the bureau jeep, but before he could drive away, soldiers, cursing and shouting, ordered him and my cousin John out of the vehicle to join the other journalists held at gunpoint with their hands and legs apart against a wall. They could hear screams nearby as troops clubbed *Los Angeles Times* correspondent David Holley and his wife with their rifle butts, and beat a German TV reporter with truncheons while attempting to seize her camera. Mitch, a veteran at talking his way out of trouble on the streets of Beijing, apologized, groveled, pleaded, and cajoled. Abruptly, with a nod of his head, an officer motioned for Mitch and my cousin to leave. They accelerated out of the university district as fast as the bureau car could take them.

Unaware of the commotion, Cynde and I emerged from the guest house to discover the reporters gone and the street full of helmeted soldiers. We had no idea of what had happened and no desire to linger in order to find out. We began walking toward the nearest major hotel, where we hoped to contact the bureau and get a lift back, assuming our colleagues were not in custody. There was no guarantee two foreigners parading through a university district under virtual military occupation at one A.M. would make it safely to a hotel more than two miles away. We decided the best ruse was to pretend to be lovers out for an innocent late-night stroll, and play dumb if confronted by the omnipresent security forces. Holding hands, but feeling anything but romantic, Cynde and I set off for the Yanshan Hotel, wincing every time an army or police vehicle drove by. To our great relief, the scheme worked. When we telephoned, we found Mitch and John back at the bureau, badly shaken but unharmed. Miraculously, our video was intact. Bureau assistant Jessica Smith arranged a predawn rendezvous to collect the handycam material, and by daybreak our spot was done. There was no way the Chinese authorities would allow such a story to be fed via satellite from CCTV, so I sent Jessica to Hong Kong with the tape hidden in her purse. A few hours later, I saw it on the air.

The deliberate attacks on journalists became big news. I was uncomfortable that reporters had themselves become the story, but with so little actually happening on the streets, I was hardly surprised. The episode sent a tremor of anxiety through a press corps that already felt itself under siege. At the next Foreign Ministry press briefing, angry correspondents berated spokeswoman Li Jinhua.

"Are we correct in assuming that the Foreign Ministry endorses the attacks made against myself, my wife, and other foreigners in Beijing?" the normally mild-mannered David Holley of the *Los Angeles Times* asked angrily.

"Some correspondents violated relevant regulations by carrying out illegal press coverage," the dour, pinched-face spokeswoman replied in a monotone.

"They were using rifle butts!" shrieked another colleague. "When are they going to start using the law?"

The American, West German, Canadian, and Japanese embassies made formal diplomatic protests over the brutality, but their complaints fell on deaf ears. Relations between the foreign press and the Chinese government sank to their lowest level in years.

With China in a state of political deep freeze and conditions for reporters almost impossible, the year following Tiananmen was a good time to be on the road. The People's Republic was not the only Asian country struggling to cope with rebellion and repression, economic and political change, or the dreadful consequences of totalitarianism. In different ways, the whole region seemed to be in ferment. In late 1989, we went to Cambodia, from which Vietnam was withdrawing its army, ten years after invading its neighbor and toppling the bloodthirsty Khmer Rouge from power. It was a compelling drama—how a country reduced to primitive barbarism under the Chinese-backed Khmer Rouge had come to life again. Despite numerous logistical headaches, including having to carry large edit machines to the satellite feedpoint on a rickshaw in a monsoon downpour, we managed to file stories almost every day.

By the end of the trip, however, I found my emotions on overload. It was not simply the horrors I had seen: piles of bones, in one case a mountain of skulls twenty feet high, the Khmer Rouge torture chambers with dried blood still on the floor, the heart-wrenching stories of the survivors in a nation where almost everyone lost someone. Like Vietnam, the war in Cambodia had been one of the searing experiences of my youth, fueling my passion for Asia and my early sympathy for its revolutionary political movements. Now, looking at the consequences of one of the those movements run amok, I felt

confused and even ashamed of my earlier feelings. Was I so blind?
Or just young and naive? Were the circumstances so different then?
I suddenly felt weary and very cynical.

Two weeks later we were in Burma (present-day Myanmar), one
of the first Western TV crews allowed in the normally isolated country in over two decades. Here, it was not communist guerrillas but
power-hungry generals belonging to the SLORC—the State Law and
Order Restoration Council—who were the perpetrators of evil,
ruthlessly crushing a 1988 pro-democracy movement not unlike that
in Beijing, with the loss of thousands of lives. In contrast to China,
however, no TV cameras had recorded the slaughter in Rangoon
(today called Yangon). The upheaval caused little more than a blip
on the international conscience. Now its perpetrators were seeking
to present a more benign image by allowing a team from CNN to
visit. We were determined not to play along.

Burma was languid, lush, and tropical, but I found it to be as
repressive as it was beautiful. On the streets, people averted their
eyes when we approached them, and when we were taken to see a
tame and demoralized opposition politician, he was convinced our
two army escorts had come to arrest him. Foreign diplomats were
unanimous in denouncing the country's military dictatorship and
praising Aung San Suu Kyi, the leader of the democracy movement
who would eventually win the Nobel Peace Prize but who was now
under house arrest. We drove past her heavily guarded front gate,
and were able to sneak some video out of the car window. We
included it in a hard-hitting series that outraged the military authorities in Rangoon. They wrote a bitter letter of complaint to CNN
management, which I added to the growing list of denunciations
I had earned from Asia's authoritarian regimes.

Not all the news was bad. Mongolia, the vast, sparsely inhabited,
longtime Russian satellite on China's northern border, was the scene
of an astonishing bloodless revolution in early 1990. In a country of
windswept plains and merciless deserts, where half the population
of two million still eked out a living as nomadic herders inhabiting
felt-lined tents known as yurts, the idea of such a profound political
change seemed improbable. Yet the people of Mongolia, ignoring
winter temperatures of minus forty degrees, repeatedly took to the
vast, empty, streets of their capital city, Ulan Bator, demanding free-

dom and democracy after seven decades of Soviet-imposed one-party dictatorship. To almost everyone's amazement, the country's ruling Communist Party made one remarkable concession after another, inspired perhaps by *iltod* and *sunichlit*, Mongolian for glasnost and perestroika, the reform policies then being carried out by Mikhail Gorbachev in the rapidly changing Soviet Union. By the time Cynde, Mitch, and I arrived in April 1990, the Party had revamped its leadership, given up its constitutionally guaranteed monopoly on power, restored freedom of religion and the press, and had begun to lay the groundwork for a multiparty political system.

We found the reform movement to be surprisingly full of good humor, with none of the bitterness so evident in China. Its anthem was a rock ode to Mongolia's national hero, Genghis Khan, sung by a popular local band called Hongk, whose electrifying performance was one of the highlights of our trip. The song illustrated one of the most striking aspects of the political changes in Mongolia: the country's rediscovery of its long-suppressed cultural and historical heritage, After seventy years in which Mongolia's Soviet masters banned any mention of Genghis Khan from the history books, the great conqueror was appearing not only in songs, but in classrooms, cartoons, and movie theaters, heralding a resurgence of national pride. After so much despair and repression, I came away from Mongolia, with its vast spaces, friendly, plainspoken people, and inspiring moves toward democratization, convinced that somehow the grim days of repression in China would not last.

Watching Mongolia join its former Eastern-bloc allies in casting off the shackles of communism propelled me toward an important personal decision. In the bleak aftermath of Tiananmen Square, I had seriously contemplated leaving China when my contract with CNN came up for renewal. Lynne and I both worried that it was simply so grim and depressing that building a decent life, especially with Daniel, was almost impossible. What kind of childhood would it be for him to grow up in a society where his baby-sitter was forced by the government to spy on us and his parents were treated virtually as outlaws? We had already put in three years in Beijing. Perhaps it was time to move on. And yet, deep down, it was hard for me to believe that the freeze would last. Too much had changed in China since my first trip in 1973 for the forces of reform to be completely stifled.

If, almost unimaginably, communism was collapsing in Eastern Europe, surely something would have to happen in China. However unpleasant Beijing was now, we decided to stay on. I signed up for another stint with CNN, and Lynne became accredited as the *Business Week* Beijing reporter. We brought Sherlock back from his home in exile with Lynne's parents in the U.S.

We were not ready to abandon the China story. Not yet.

Still, for what seemed like an endless period after Tiananmen Square, I was on the road more than I was at home. I traveled not only to Burma, Cambodia, and Mongolia, but to half the countries of Asia: to Pakistan during a crisis with India over the disputed territory of Kashmir; to India following the assassination of Prime Minister Rajiv Gandhi—my second funeral of a murdered Gandhi broadcast live on television. Then I was on to Vietnam, which was embarking on its own halting, Chinese-style moves toward economic reform; to South Korea to interview President Roh Tae Woo about ongoing tensions on the Korean peninsula; to Hong Kong, covering the mounting local anxieties over the territory's 1997 return to Chinese sovereignty; to Taiwan, which was in the midst of building a new, more democratic system on the authoritarian foundation of the Kuomintang; to the Philippines, where President Corazón Aquino was preparing to leave office gracefully at the end of her six-year term, and hand over the government to a democratically elected successor. And there was a long stint in the Middle East during the Gulf War, when Mitch and I spent months in Saudi Arabia and Kuwait, while Cynde, predictably, volunteered to join Peter Arnett under the bombs in Baghdad—all of us part of the massive news machine that made CNN a household name across the globe.

Yet when we regrouped in Beijing, little appeared to have changed, at least on the surface. The Chinese Communist Party defiantly declared its allegiance to its brand of socialism; dissidents were still persecuted; human rights dominated and soured China's relations with the U.S. and other Western nations. The legacy of Tiananmen Square hung like a poisonous cloud over the capital. As I got back into the routine of daily journalism, however, I began to have a nagging feeling that I might be missing an important aspect of China's story: the fact that the market-style reforms of the pre-Tiananmen years had not been snuffed out. Foreign businessmen, now returning to the country in significant numbers, diplomats, travelers, Chinese economists, and others insisted there was more to the picture of China than just repression. The place to see it was the southern province of Guangdong. In early January 1992, Cynde, Mitch, and I set off to take a look.

Our first stop was Shenzhen, the once-tiny frontier village just across the border from Hong Kong through which I had passed when I first entered the People's Republic in 1973. I could hardly believe I was still in China. At the start of Deng's reforms in the late 1970s, Shenzhen had been designated one of several "Special Economic Zones," laboratories where China could open its doors to the outside world and begin to experiment with the ways of capitalism. Now Chinese-made Volkswagens, Cherokee Jeeps, and Peugeots, not to mention imported Mercedes and BMWs, clogged the streets. Shops, restaurants, and department stores lined the sidewalks, where, against the unceasing din of jackhammers reshaping the landscape, residents and visitors peered at imported fashions, appliances, cosmetics, and household goods. In the city center was China's pioneering stock exchange and its first McDonald's. At night, thousands of neon signs gave off an eerie glow, advertising Marlboro cigarettes, Hennessy cognac, karaoke bars, and massage parlors. In brightly lit restaurants and luxury hotel lobbies, well-dressed Chinese with pagers and cell phones planned the next big business deal.

My hunch was right. At a time when the West's image of China, and much of the energy of the Beijing press corps, remained focused on the bitter legacy of the 1989 crackdown and the repression that still enveloped the Chinese capital, Shenzhen, and all of Guangdong province, offered living proof that the process of reform in China was still very much alive.

While paying lip service to the hard-line rhetoric from the central government, Guangdong was obviously proceeding on a very different economic path. "In Beijing, they say 'if it's not approved, you can't do it,'" laughed the managing director of a canned beverage factory we visited outside the provincial capital, Canton, repeating a popular local saying. "Here, we say 'if it isn't prohibited, it's OK.' It's all a matter of names. The center lets us do pretty much what we want, as long as we don't call it capitalism."

Whatever the label, Guangdong's frenzied mix of free markets, private enterprise, and Sino-foreign joint ventures had generated a remarkable 20 percent economic growth rate for the province in 1991, far outstripping growth in the rest of the country. The difference was notable in how we were received too. Instead of treating us as enemies, the local authorities saw us as magnets to lure foreign investment. They took us everywhere we asked, and when the official schedule was finished, they left us on our own to wander with our camera without interference. After the pressures of Beijing, it was a bracing change. We drove across the province in a minibus, stopping at Hong Kong–funded factories where peasant girls from the rural provinces of western China carefully twisted on the heads and combed the hair of dolls destined for American toy stores. We stopped at the Avon training school, where the first of what would become tens of thousands of young women from the Canton area learned the art of door-to-door cosmetics sales; we toured construction sites for new bridges, roads, power plants, and other infrastructure projects; we visited bowling alleys, discos, new hotels, and nightclubs. The feeling of energy was overpowering. Of equal significance, I thought, was the irrelevance of communist ideology. The people of Guangdong appeared to be putting their faith not in Marx but the market. Over and over, when I asked people about their goals, I heard the same answer: "To get rich." The vast majority of Guangdong's citizens were not political. Canton was not a city one visited to interview dissidents. Yet the mere fact of their go-go, consumerist lifestyle seemed to me to be eroding the Chinese Communist Party's authority over their daily lives. There was more freedom of information, freedom of movement, greater job mobility, more Western influence. It was just what the hard-liners feared: "peaceful evolution."

Our five-part series, entitled A *Tale of Two Chinas*, aired in February 1992. It was one of the earliest Western TV reports to draw attention to the phenomenon of China's post-Tiananmen economic boom, and to challenge the one-dimensional, uniformly critical way the West still viewed the People's Republic. Soon after, Shanghai's *Wen Hui Daily* newspaper published an article hailing the reports and praising me by name. "This series," the paper declared, "shows that even American journalists can be objective about China." It was a classic Chinese experience. Three years after being denounced by the *Beijing Daily* as a "rumor-monger," it appeared that I was being officially "rehabilitated."

As it turned out, our travels in Guangdong coincided with a much more important journey to the same destination. Deng Xiaoping made his first public appearance in a year, visiting China's booming southeastern coast to call for a resumption of rapid, outward-looking economic growth. Following the collapse of communism in the Soviet Union, China's patriarch had concluded that only accelerated reform would save the Chinese Communist Party from a similar fate. Party hard-liners disagreed, urging tighter ideological controls. But Deng's *nanxun*, or southern tour, a term used to describe the travels of an emperor through the country in the days of imperial China, broke the nation's political deadlock and sparked a new wave of entrepreneurial energy and popular enthusiasm. The focus of the half-dozen stories we churned out for CNN every week shifted away from dissidents and human rights to documenting a country consumed by a gold rush. Most of the Chinese my crew and I now encountered were interested less in the rights and wrongs of 1989 than in how to buy shares on the new stock markets in Shanghai and Shenzhen, how to get a job in a Sino-foreign joint venture, or how to set up their own businesses.

The enthusiasm was shared by foreign and overseas Chinese investors. Charting the parade of Fortune 500 CEOs as they stumbled over themselves to get a piece of the action in the world's biggest market became a regular part of my beat. The bureau was inundated with faxes from foreign firms announcing press conferences, signing ceremonies, factory openings, and VIP visits. During the summer of 1992, we did several reports on Xiamen, the Chinese city closest to Taiwan, only 100 miles across the Taiwan Strait. Once a front line of Beijing's battle with the hated Chinese Nationalists, the steamy port town was now, like Shenzhen, a Special Economic Zone, and a magnet for Taiwan investors. Increasingly, the boundaries between Taiwan, Hong Kong, and China's freewheeling coastal provinces were fading, blurred by a wave of economic cooperation that had spawned a new term, "Greater China." Neither a political entity nor an organized trading bloc, it was nonetheless a reality, driven by a shared desire to make money. And it was a potent combination—uniting the marketing and managerial skills of Hong Kong, the technology and financial clout of Taiwan, and China's cheap labor and land. It was not impossible, I thought, that this combination could stimulate pressure for change in China that the Party hard-liners might find even harder to resist than the throngs of chanting students who had so frightened them in 1989.

Yet even as the economic and political consequences of the boom became a staple of my reporting, I found the West still had trouble shaking the violent images of Tiananmen Square. This became clear every spring when I covered the annual battle over whether the U.S. would renew China's most favored nation trading status, which gave Chinese goods the low tariffs the United States offers all its normal trading partners. China's many American critics wanted to use the threat of revoking MFN (most favored nation status) as a weapon to promote change and improve the human rights situation. The U.S. business community in Beijing, with billions of dollars tied up in the China trade, lobbied strongly to maintain the status quo. Often the battle was portrayed in the press as one between the forces of cynical corporate greed and those possessed of a high-minded concern for democracy. I was convinced that the picture was more complicated and that those calling for an end to MFN had profoundly misunderstood the nature of the dynamic changes under way in China. Every day I was filing stories on how the renewed spurt of entrepreneurial energy and accelerated inter-action with the West was itself generating important, if subtle, changes in China. The Communist Party's power and relevance was being eroded by the spread of Western ideas of doing business, indi-vidual responsibility, and profit and loss, all revolutionary concepts in an ossified socialist system. The booming China coast was the cutting edge of this process, the area most likely to be hurt by the termination of MFN. Even most dissidents I talked to acknowledged that revoking China's trade privileges would only strengthen the hard-liners and undercut the forces most responsible for generating change inside China.

I held myself, along with other TV broadcasters, partly responsi-ble for the misperception in the U.S. that not only fueled the calls to take MFN away from China, but perpetuated the notion of the People's Republic as a giant, monolithic, malevolent force. The images we beamed around the world in 1989 were so powerful that taking a more balanced view of China several years later was, for many citizens and politicians, still almost impossible. With their smug self-righteousness, intellectual hypocrisy, and all-too-eager willingness to lock up their critics, Li Peng, Jiang Zemin, and the rest of the Chinese leadership were easy to despise. It had taken a conscious act of will on my part to acknowledge the profound shift under way in China. My heart wanted to see the "butchers of Beijing" get their comeuppance, but my head told me that the best chance for such a change to take place was to keep the reform process alive. Most of my work was devoted to showing the way reform was transforming and generally improving and liberalizing the lives of China's citizens. It was a sobering illustration of the power of television that none of the images in my current stories could compete with the drama of the man confronting the tank.

As the climate in China changed, our tiny bureau faced a major change too. After five years, Cynde Strand decided she'd had enough of Beijing. In the wake of the Gulf War, CNN was opening a new Middle East bureau to cover crises in that part of the world, and she asked for the shooter's job there. I was terribly sad to see her go. There was a bond between us, forged through years of shared effort, deprivation, and success, solidified by the crucible of Tiananmen Square. We were, I felt, like soldiers who had fought and survived a war together. Now, though, Cynde was eager to cover other wars on other continents. I bade her a sad farewell, but was reassured by the fact that Mitch had been promoted to bureau shooter, and by the hiring of two new colleagues. Tim Schwarz was a quiet, even-tempered Englishman who, in an earlier time, would probably have been one of those explorers who paved the way for the empire. He spoke Mandarin, Cantonese, Russian, and Mongolian, and had lived in Moscow and Ulan Bator before becoming a producer for Britain's ITN network in Hong Kong. Rebecca MacKinnon, a recent Harvard graduate, had lived in Beijing as a child in the 1970s. With her flaw-less Chinese, she too proved a strong addition to our operation.

On the home front too, there was a major change. In mid-1992, Lynne gave birth to our second son, Benjamin. We quickly discov-ered that two fair-haired boys created a minor sensation everywhere we went in Beijing. Through the world's most restrictive population policy, enforced by a controversial system of rewards and punish-ments, China limited its citizens, especially those in the cities, to just one child per family. Most urban residents appeared to under-stand the logic of seeking to control the number of people in China. With 14 million new mouths to feed every year, the government certainly had every right to be concerned about population issues. Still, we knew many parents who desperately wanted a second child. This was especially true if the first one was a girl. Sons had always been more valued than daughters in China, and the tradition was still very much alive. The reaction we encountered was always friendly and curious, but frequently tinged with longing or downright envy. Lynne and I had decided, for our own reasons, to have two children. The people we met as we walked the streets with our boys were acutely aware that they were not allowed the freedom to make that choice. I had done many spots on China's restrictive family-planning policy, but only when Benjy was born did I fully understand how much the right to have a second child could mean.

Despite its suspicion of reporters, the Chinese leadership was beginning to understand, and seek to exploit, the power of television. In the spring of 1993, I was granted an interview with the man designated as Deng Xiaoping's new successor, President and Communist Party chief Jiang Zemin. I was only the second TV journalist to do so, following in the steps of ABC's Barbara Walters in 1990. My friend Liu, the Radio Beijing reporter who had been so helpful during the tumultuous days of Tiananmen Square, had urged me to apply for an interview early in the year. It was his last piece of helpful advice. Disillusioned and fed up with the Chinese political scene, Liu had applied and received a visa to go to the United States. He was giving up journalism and following the trend of many Chinese to *xia hai*, literally "jumping into the sea," the term used for people switching careers to go into business. Before long, he landed a job with a major multinational corporation and was soon back in Beijing, wearing well-cut suits and cutting deals across the country.

But Liu's sources had indicated to him that in China's more relaxed and outward-looking atmosphere, the leadership might be receptive to granting a TV interview to CNN. So I followed his parting advice and sent a detailed letter to the Foreign Ministry's Information Department requesting a meeting with Jiang. Five months of protracted and difficult negotiations ensued. The Chinese were interested, but they were clearly suspicious. Officials repeatedly mentioned Deng Xiaoping's 1986 interview with Mike Wallace of *60 Minutes*, in which CBS spent over half an hour with Deng but aired just eight minutes. "Chairman Deng was furious," one Information

Department official told me. "Since then, our leaders have been deeply skeptical of cooperating with any American TV network."

Typical CBS arrogance, I thought to myself. I recalled an episode in 1976, when I was a CBS stringer in Hong Kong, and the network's Southeast Asia correspondent, Peter Collins, managed to get an exclusive interview with the prime minister of Vietnam, which CBS never bothered to broadcast. I assured the Information Department that airtime was not a problem. The Chinese imposed other conditions. To preserve Jiang's "dignity," they insisted the interview not be interrupted by commercial breaks, a demand to which CNN readily agreed. And they wanted all the questions in advance, in writing, along with a commitment not to surprise the president by asking anything not previously agreed to by the Chinese side. This was a tougher call. Normally we refused to submit questions in advance. However, as long as the Chinese accepted my list of questions, I felt it was worth going ahead. Opportunities to engage Deng Xiaoping's designated successor were so few that I was convinced it would still be a valuable encounter. My editors agreed, and, somewhat to my surprise, the Chinese did not ask for a single change in any of the questions I submitted, which covered human rights, Tiananmen, Sino-U.S. relations, and a host of other controversial issues.

When, the day before the interview, the Information Department announced that Jiang Zemin would read his answers from a TelePrompTer, I understood why the Chinese seemed unworried by the toughness of my questions. The astonishing proposition was revealed as we set up our cameras and lights in a cavernous meeting room in the Great Hall of the People, where the interview was to take place. "I'm sorry," I replied. "With all due respect, that is unacceptable. This encounter is supposed to look on television at least something like a conversation with President Jiang. If he wants to bring notes, I have no objection. But he simply can't stare at the camera and read off a TelePrompTer." Foreign Ministry officials huddled anxiously, rushing in and out of the room to make a series of urgent phone calls, before telling us that they understood. Jiang would not use a TelePrompTer.

The former Party boss in Shanghai, Jiang Zemin had a reputation as an undistinguished apparatchik with conservative politics but some sympathy for Deng's market-style reforms. A compromise choice, he had been plucked from relative obscurity and promoted to

Communist Party general-secretary in June 1989, following the crackdown in Tiananmen Square. Since then, while his predecessor Zhao Ziyang remained in political oblivion, he had eclipsed Premier Li Peng and acquired the three most powerful jobs in China—head of the Party, head of the military, and state president. But many observers, both Chinese and foreigners, doubted he would last long once his patron, Deng Xiaoping, passed from the scene.

The "core" of the new generation of Chinese leaders was a stocky, broad-faced man with a surprisingly genial manner, resembling a kindly uncle more than a ruthless political operator. Diplomats had told me that he spoke English well and was fond of quoting passages from Abraham Lincoln's Gettysburg Address. He was also said to be an enthusiastic singer, often breaking into verses from Hollywood films he had seen as a child.

Seated opposite one another, I noticed that his trousers were hitched up almost to his ribcage, exposing his white socks. Despite the fuss over the TelePrompTer, the Information Department's concerns appeared unwarranted. Jiang spoke easily without notes, urging better ties with the U.S., hinting that some imprisoned Tiananmen dissidents might be freed, declaring that China's economic reforms were "irreversible," and insisting the country did not pose a threat to its neighbors. His comments were interesting, but Jiang lived up to his reputation as a cautious, colorless figure. He exuded none of the charisma I had witnessed in Deng Xiaoping or Zhao Ziyang. Yet I wondered if this was all there was to the man. His two predecessors, Zhao and Hu Yaobang, both outspoken, colorful characters, had been purged. While Deng and the other aging revolutionaries were still alive, it might be very good politics for Jiang to maintain a low profile, even if he had additional qualities of leadership. To survive in the job as long as he had without offending either his patron or his patron's rivals clearly took some degree of political dexterity. However underwhelming I found him, I came away convinced it was far too early to write off Jiang Zemin.

"To put it bluntly, we saw you as American devils. That's what we said: 'American devils.'" Yin Tianfu lit a cigarette, inhaled deeply, and smiled. "But now, we are studying your management methods." We both broke into laughter.

It had been twenty years since I had last seen Yin and his colleague Zhu Baochen. They wore stylish Western suits now, and signs of late middle age were evident in their faces and expanding waistlines. Otherwise they seemed little changed from our last meeting, when they'd acted as official guides on my first trip to China in 1973. Then their mission had been to show my group of antiwar American students the achievements of Mao's revolution, while simultaneously preventing our departure from rigidly controlled tours and events. They had been adept propagandists, spewing out party rhetoric and revolutionary clichés, but when they let down their political guard, they were also warm, friendly, and very human. I had no idea what had happened to them in the intervening twenty years, but when I tracked them down in the spring of 1993, they were delighted to hear from me and very eager to help with a project that had become an obsession—retracing my initial China journey.

My quest was motivated by more than just curiosity or a sentimental longing to relive one of the major turning points in my life. Despite the hundreds of TV spots I'd done since the boom took off over the previous eighteen months, I felt I was still not communicating adequately what I sensed was happening in China. The country was undergoing an immense, profound change. But it was a process, not a single, dramatic event. In a medium that was good at conveying emotion and action, process did not often make for riveting television. As I struggled to find a way to convey this slow-motion revolution to CNN's viewers, my thoughts turned to the fact that I had first set foot in China twenty years earlier. The changes now underway were inconceivable then. I became convinced that if I could retrace my initial journey and discover what had happened to the people and places I visited, I might do justice to the transformation unfolding around me.

It was a hugely ambitious undertaking to track down those with whom I had had absolutely no contact for two decades. In certain ways, however, China had not changed that much, and one of them was the continuing, although reduced, importance of the *danwei*, or work unit. As long as one had an individual's name and 1973 *danwei*, as well the cooperation of the local *waiban*, or foreign affairs office, locating someone was not impossible. Here, the Jiang Zemin interview proved to be a godsend. The day after it was broadcast on CNN, the government's account of what he said led every major Chinese newspaper, as well as CCTV's evening news broadcast. My post-

Tiananmen Square political rehabilitation appeared complete. Suddenly *waibans* from Shanghai to Shenyang were bending over backward to be helpful.

So were Zhu and Yin, whose own lives seemed to reflect the changes of the preceding two decades. With the advent of Deng Xiaoping's reforms, Zhu, who had been assigned by the government to work as a tour guide for the state-run China International Travel Service because of his excellent English, was able to return to his first love, academia. He joined the China Association for Science and Technology, traveled to the United States on scholarly exchanges, and eventually became vice president of a small college. "Such possibilities were hardly imaginable when you made your trip," he told me. "It was like a dream."

Still wiry, energetic, and witty, Yin Tianfu had moved in a different direction, leaving China International Travel Service, where we had first met, to set up his own travel agency. Constantly on the move, he now journeyed regularly to Europe, the U.S., and around Asia, drumming up business. "Does your office need a travel agent?" he asked, always the go-getter entrepreneur, "I'm ready to help."

In 1973, the strategic northeastern port city of Dalian had the feel of a front-line outpost in China's bitter struggle with the Soviet Union, whose border was just a few hundred miles away. Twenty years later, Yin Tianfu and I, with Tim and Mitch, returned to the Xigangchun Red Guard Elementary School, which I remembered most for its youthful students taking their daily target practice on what had been the school playground. Three teachers remained from that time, when I had also been shown the school's proudest achievement, the underground tunnel system built in response to Chairman Mao's instruction to "dig tunnels deep" to resist the Soviets.

"I was responsible for blasting the entrance," said one of the teachers with an embarrassed laugh. "We used picks and shovels and dynamite, working every day for two and a half years."

Above one dank doorway, I could barely make out three faded revolutionary slogans. A few yards away, totally oblivious to this decaying remnant of the Cultural Revolution, school children laughed, skipped, and played games.

"At that time," continued the old teacher, who retained vivid memories of my student group's visit, "we thought that what was being done was correct. But looking back on it later, we realized we were wrong. People's thinking was totally confused. We wanted to talk to you about it when you came then, but we weren't allowed." He sighed. "It was just the times."

In the city center, I remembered visiting another, much more elaborate underground tunnel system designed to provide shelter to tens of thousands of people in the event of a Soviet attack. Now enterprising city officials had turned it into an underground shopping mall. Tim, Mitch, Yin, and I wandered though corridor after corridor lined with stores offering jewelry, makeup, lingerie, pop-music recordings, cassette players, watches, T-shirts, leather jackets. We even encountered a onetime elementary schoolteacher who was running a roulette wheel to earn extra money. I was sure this was not what Chairman Mao had in mind when he said "dig tunnels deep."

For the people of Dalian, the growth of an entrepreneurial culture meant the return of a way of life violently disrupted by Mao's revolution. The city had always lived off its port. In the late-nineteenth century, when it was known as Port Arthur, Japan and Russia fought a war to control it. At the time of my first visit, during the Cultural Revolution, it had slipped into obscurity. Now, revived by Deng's reform program, it had become a booming entrepôt, the third largest foreign trade port in China.

For all the changes, the voyage from creaky, inefficient socialism to a dynamic, market-driven society was not proving to be an easy one. The rough edges were readily apparent as Yin, Mitch, Tim, and I retraced my 1973 itinerary. Northeast China had long been a center of heavy industry, whose state-run factories had been presented to me twenty years before as models of socialist enterprise. Now the over-staffed, inefficient state sector was bleeding the central government dry. Two-thirds of them were unprofitable, surviving only with huge cash infusions from Beijing. Unless they were made respon-sive to the forces of the market, China's economic reform drive would be in jeopardy. But state-run factories employed nearly a hun-dred million workers across China, providing not only jobs, but schools, clinics, apartments—the cradle-to-grave welfare system known as the "Iron Rice Bowl." Real reforms would require an end to this bastion of socialist economics, with the possibility that millions of workers might lose their jobs. For a Communist government worried about mass protest, the specter of an angry, unemployed working class taking to the streets was terrifying.

The huge statue of Chairman Mao still dominated the skyline in the industrial center of Shenyang, where I'd almost caused a riot by playing Frisbee twenty years earlier. Yet now I found the local authorities engaged in one of China's first experiments with bankruptcy, allowing a limited number of small- and medium-scale factories to go under. Some of those laid off had found new jobs in the expanding private economy, as street vendors, taxi drivers, shop assistants, car washers. But in a city where, in 1973, I was told by proud officials that unemployment did not exist, we were taken to an outdoor labor market, where groups of men in shabby clothes stood awkwardly on street corners, waiting for fast-talking agents to offer them ill-paid, often backbreaking work. With no Iron Rice Bowl, they had few alternatives. If the boom ever faltered, their numbers would likely increase dramatically, along with the prospect of unrest.

An hour's drive north of Shenyang was the city of Fushun, where in 1973 my student group had visited an open-pit coal mine, one of the largest in Asia. We had also stopped at an old-age home where an elderly coal miner proudly declared to us, "I may have retired, but my ideology has not retired!" Still dark, grimy, choked with coal dust and chemical fumes, Fushun turned out to be a good place to see how, in this era of reform, a Chinese Communist Party seeking to change the country's economic system was trying to keep its ideology from being retired as well.

Fushun was the site of the Lei Feng Memorial Hall, celebrating one of the party's most enduring, and least credible, revolutionary heroes. Ever since Chairman Mao had called on China to "Learn from Lei Feng" during the Cultural Revolution, the party had publicized the tale of this young soldier's selfless devotion to the Maoist cause. The story of how Lei Feng had lived an exemplary socialist life until his untimely death at age twenty-two, when a telephone pole fell on him, had been one of the clumsiest pieces of party propaganda. There were serious doubts as to whether he had even existed. But that did not deter the authorities.

In the wake of Tiananmen Square, the Lei Feng myth had been resurrected by hard-liners in an effort to instill in a cynical and increasingly materialistic population the virtues of total selflessness and unquestioning loyalty to the Communist Party. The Lei Feng museum in Fushun was its centerpiece. Dominated by a huge bust of the youthful hero in the foyer, its corridors were lined with blowup photos purporting to show Lei Feng playing with children, helping the peasants, washing his comrades' laundry, and, of course, reading the works of Chairman Mao. Also on display, under a protective glass covering suited to priceless ancient documents, were all his personal effects, including his wash basin, shoes, and tattered socks. The transparent falsity of it all was galling. As Mitch panned the camera around the room, we noticed the Memorial hall was now almost deserted. The story of Lei Feng was playing to an empty house.

The sleazy bar nearby, where Tanya and Tatiana earned their living, was not so empty. We met the two Russian women through an American engineer of Russian descent with whom we struck up a conversation over lunch in a nearby restaurant. The engineer, a consultant at a local chemical factory, had been in Fushun for months. Desperate for sociability, he had become friendly with virtually the only other foreigners living in the city—a group of Russian "hostesses," whose sad story read like a third-rate international police thriller. Giving Yin and our local *waiban* guide the slip, Tim, Mitch, and I made our way to the engineer's hotel room to interview the two women, taking advantage of Tim's Russian-language skills. Blonde, buxom, unsophisticated, and unemployed at home, Tanya and Tatiana told us they had been recruited in Moscow for what they had thought were waitressing jobs in booming China. Instead they found themselves in the clutches of a criminal gang, which had taken their passports, housed them in cramped rooms above the bar, and forced them to work as prostitutes, servicing local Chinese with money to spend. Tanya and Tatiana were effectively prisoners, and we could do nothing to help them. After leaving Fushun, we were never able to learn their fate. Their plight, I discovered, was not uncommon. Throughout China's urban centers, Russians were pouring in to take advantage of the boom. Just as White Russian bar girls were a feature of life in prerevolutionary Shanghai, now Russian whores were becoming part of a sleazy new urban scene in 1990s China.

In retracing my original footsteps, however, I was discovering that what had once been unthinkable was now almost predictable. I was beginning to feel like the man in the fable by the ancient Chinese philosopher Zhuangzi, who fell asleep and dreamed he was a butterfly, but after waking was never sure if he was a man who had dreamed he was a butterfly, or a butterfly dreaming he was a man. Still, nothing prepared me for what I learned when I returned to what had been the Chang Qing Production Brigade of the Wusan People's Commune. I had asked to visit Chang Qing, now called not a brigade but just a village, because I hoped to find Yu Kexin, the model Maoist peasant who in 1973 had introduced me to life in rural China. Local officials agreed to my request, but until I laid eyes on him in the village reception center, I had no idea whether Yu was even still alive, let alone able to see me. We recognized each other immediately.

"You haven't changed at all," I said as we exchanged warm greetings, to the surprise of the local guides. He laughed, took off his blue Mao cap, and pointed to his head. He was totally bald. Carrying his four-year-old granddaughter, Xiaotong, Yu, now fifty-eight, took me back to the house where we first met, and where we'd shared a memorable meal while he and his family talked of the commune's great achievements and their comfortable and happy life.

As soon as village officials were out of earshot, Yu began to pour out his story. As Mitch's camera rolled, Yu told me that almost everything I experienced during our first encounter had been an illusion. "I told you things were good when you visited," he said. "But when you foreigners came, we had to fix everything up first. We were just terrified we might say the wrong thing and upset the officials. Conditions were terrible then. Our income was tiny, and we had to feed six people. They didn't let us raise animals or grow anything for ourselves. We got that meal only because you came. It was trucked in from the city the day before. Back then, we were lucky to have a good meal once a week or even once a month."

For years, stripping away official fabrications and hypocrisy had been at the center of my continuing search for Chinese reality. Usually this took the form of catching party officials in blatant lies and distortion or pointing out the intellectual dishonesty of bureaucrats who piously proclaimed that they were building socialism while their policies allowed private business and free markets to flourish. Now, however, I had found an ordinary citizen—a blunt, plainspoken farmer—who was, with no prompting, revealing the official lies that had made up so much of my initial experience in China. Even after two decades of building up a shell of journalistic cynicism, I was sobered by what he told me.

For Yu Kexin, the turning point had come with Deng Xiaoping's reforms and the abolition of the communes in the 1980s. As family farming revived and peasants were allowed to go into business, Yu and his three sons set up a tire repair shop, where they now each earned 1,000 yuan, or $230, a month—six times his 1973 income.

"If I'd done this back then," he said as we toured the grimy workshop where Yu and his burly sons hammered, patched, and pumped up tires, "we'd have been condemned as counterrevolutionaries taking the capitalist road. Now our income is whatever we can earn. I'm an individual contractor. Whatever I earn, I keep."

Yu took me to the new, three-bedroom apartment, complete with color TV, which the good times the village was experiencing had made possible. To him, it seemed like an opulent mansion. "Now we can eat shrimp or fish or meat every day if we want. Back then—no way."

Yu's ramshackle old residence, where we had first met, was now home to a family of impoverished, imported farmhands, poor peasants from elsewhere in China, hired by the village to do the dirty work of growing fruits, vegetables, and grains. Farm officials proudly told me that three-quarters of the villagers had abandoned their fields for private business or to work in small-scale local factories. They were even considering declaring Chang Qing a Special Economic Zone in order to lure foreign investment. The notion was preposterous but indicative of the gold rush mentality so prevalent now in China. Yu Kexin didn't seem to mind that people like the imported laborers were missing out on the benefits of reform he was enjoying. As we parted, he said, in a burst of individualistic enthusiasm, "Life is ten times better now than it was before!"

Yu Kexin's transformation was so startling that I wondered if this too might be a fake. I thought it unlikely. The authorities had no way to know in advance that I would ask to meet Yu, and his story was totally consistent with the way millions of Chinese had benefited from Deng's reforms. I would put Yu on the air to illustrate the new, reformist China—a more credible symbol this time, I hoped, than when I first encountered him as a model Maoist peasant.

His hair almost completely white, his back slightly stooped, Professor Tong Shibai walked with me slowly through the campus of Qinghua University in Beijing. "There were two factions," he said.

"They attacked each other, first with big character posters, and then with weapons." Pointing toward a tree-lined pathway, he continued, "One time, a female student was killed just over there. Another time, it happened over here. There were a number of deaths, and many students were wounded."

Tong was describing the virtual civil war that tore the campus of China's most prestigious institution of scientific and technological learning apart at the height of the Cultural Revolution. In 1973, when my student group had toured Qinghua, the American-educated Tong was one of the university officials brought out to brief us. Then he had said nothing about the violence, portraying his own "reeducation" as an uplifting experience. Now he described it as a period of personal suffering and humiliation.

Tong told me the reform program enabled him to return to teaching and to revisit the U.S. where his son had later obtained a Ph.D. "When you came in 1973," he said, "I had lost hope of ever going to the U.S. again in my lifetime, let alone sending my son to study. It just didn't seem possible. I couldn't have imagined how swiftly things have changed for the better."

As we strolled the campus, the mood was quiet. Students pedaled by on bicycles, loaded down with books. Many had beepers clipped to their belts. The chaos of the Cultural Revolution seemed very far away. So too, did the fevered atmosphere of 1989, in which students from Qinghua had joined with those from other campuses in Beijing to protest in Tiananmen Square. My 1973 guide Zhu Baochen had been in the square, but not as a demonstrator. As head of the Beijing National Tourism College, he had gone to convince his students to leave.

"I believed there were problems that had to be corrected," he told me one afternoon as we chatted near the gates to the Forbidden City. "But you cannot achieve anything overnight, and I felt that going into the streets would not solve anything. So I urged my students to come back to school and stay quiet and reason things out. Some listened to me, but quite a few stayed in the square."

For my other guide, Yin Tianfu, the upheaval in Tiananmen represented something equally troubling—a throwback to the chaos of the Cultural Revolution. "We used to think that the Cultural Revolution, because it was led by Chairman Mao himself, was correct and represented the right path," he explained. "But now, I think it was wrong. China suffered much because of the Cultural Revolution. The country needs to be stable and united. So when the movement arose in 1989, I didn't really feel it was necessary. I felt we needed stability." Yin was hardly a doctrinaire Party hack, let alone someone who favored brutally attacking dissenters. Yet his words reflected a fear of *luan*, or chaos, that was deep-rooted among the Chinese. After a century and a half of almost continuous war, upheaval, and revolution, followed by the chaos of Mao's Cultural Revolution, many Chinese who had little sympathy for the Party desperately wanted to avoid another descent into anarchy. For those who had lived through the Cultural Revolution, it was a fear that, understandably, shaped their perceptions of the events in 1989.

Ren Yansheng shared this perception. In 1973, he had been a young professor at Qinghua University, briefing us on the glories of the Cultural Revolution along with Tong Shibai. Since I had last seen him, he had risen to become a senior Communist Party cadre, and after the Tiananmen Square crackdown, he was transferred to Beijing University, where the 1989 protests originated, to help oversee the Party's reassertion of authority. For a man who had been a Red Guard in his student days, it was an ironic turnabout, but, like Yin Tianfu, the emotional scars he carried from that time made his position understandable. "My generation participated in the Cultural Revolution, but we were also its victims," he told me. "No matter what, China must not allow further chaos. So I look at the unrest in 1989 as just a short interlude in the course of reform. And that interlude has already passed."

After my meeting with Ren, I walked through the tree-lined Beijing University campus, trying to piece together the many impressions of my retrospective journey, passing near the memorial to the 1930s China journalist Edgar Snow. I had to acknowledge that, in one sense, Ren Yansheng was right. However legitimate the grievances of the protestors, and however horrifying their bloody fate, reform in China did not die in Tiananmen Square. Everywhere Tim, Mitch, and I had traveled for this project—not only the Northeast, but Shanghai, Canton, and Foshan as well—the scale of China's economic, social, and psychological transformation was breathtaking. I was well aware that the process was uneven, with some areas, especially the rural hinterland, missing out on the boom. Still, I could understand why the party hard-liners worried about "peaceful evolution." With 1973 notions of class struggle being replaced by the struggle to get rich, the Communist Party's inclination and ability to micro-manage the lives of China's citizens was unquestionably being eroded.

But I also continued to find echoes of the China I first visited. Back then, Chairman Mao had but three years to live. There was a sense that an era was coming to an end. The battle to succeed him was already under way. In mid-1993, Deng Xiaoping was eighty-nine and ailing. However long he lived, another potentially destabilizing succession struggle was looming in a political system, which, despite the economic reforms, remained one of the most secretive in the world. In some ways, it was as hard for China watchers to figure out what was going on now as it had been then. Moreover, when it came to overtly political matters, fear still stalked the country. For those like Professor Tong, who might harbor doubts about the 1989 crackdown, it was still safer to express no opinion. When I asked for his views of the student movement, he would only reply, "I believe that history will be the judge of those events."

But what verdict would history render, not simply on Tiananmen but on China's entire experience of the preceding two decades? At the end of our travels, Tim, Mitch, and I produced an hour-long program on our journey entitled *China: The Quiet Revolution*. I ended it by noting that, "in the twenty years since I first came to China, the Chinese have reversed the verdict on almost everything. The Cultural Revolution, once glorified, is now condemned. Chairman Mao, once deified, is now a mere mortal. Deng Xiaoping, once vilified, is now paramount leader. Western influence, once scorned, is now welcome. Trade and investment, once spurned, is now coveted. All of which raises the question: What is the real China? Is it the China that has opened the door and made farmer Yu Kexin prosperous, or the one that puts dissidents in jail to help a small group of old men hang on to power? Will the changes today be judged by history as creating a new, enduring Chinese reality, or will they be just another Chinese illusion?"

Deep down, I had to admit I still wasn't sure of the answer.

CHAPTER ELEVEN

Inside the Hermit Kingdom

The huge circular table was elegantly set and groaned with delicacies. As the midday sun poured through the large picture windows, waiters in starched white jackets and black bow ties glided silently from guest to guest, offering choice morsels of lobster, vegetables delicately carved into the shapes of flowers, quail-egg soup, chicken, turkey, and the spicy pickled cabbage known as *kimchi*. Ever attentive, they promptly refilled our crystal goblets with wine or beer. It was Saturday, April 16, 1994, and I was having lunch with a man widely viewed as one of the most dangerous leaders in the world.

Across the table, Kim Il Sung rose to make a toast. This contemporary of Josef Stalin and Mao Zedong, the man who had started the Korean War in 1950 and was now the center of a growing international crisis over suspicions that he was developing nuclear weapons, had celebrated his eighty-second birthday the day before. Mysterious and reclusive, the president of North Korea was described in his own country as the "Great Leader," "sun of the nation," "peerless patriot," "ever-victorious," "iron-willed," "brilliant commander," "hero of the international communist movement," and "the genius of mankind," but the twinkle in his eyes gave him the air of a benevolent grandfather rather than a ruthless megalomaniac whose nuclear ambitions had raised fears of a second bloody conflict on the Korean peninsula. The only disconcerting feature was an enormous lump or tumor protruding from the right side of the Great

Leader's neck. It was the size of a large grapefruit and gave his otherwise sturdy frame a slightly distorted quality, as if something in his perfectly ordered world was out of sync.

His hand steady despite his advanced years, Kim lifted a wineglass and looked around the table before offering a toast. His "distinguished guests" were, by any standard, a strange lot—a delegation of obscure former politicians from Costa Rica, Egypt, Canada, and France, and a tiny handful of journalists. Not for the first time this day, I wondered what Mitch Farkas, Tim Schwarz, my longtime foreign editor, Eason Jordan, and I were doing here. As Kim began to speak, the rays of the sun flooding the room seemed to burn brighter, bathing him in a golden glow that created an aura of divinity. In his deep, gravelly voice, he thanked us for visiting Pyongyang on the occasion of his birthday, expressed a hope for peace, and wished us good health and long life.

Sitting down to resume our lunch, Mitch Farkas leaned over and whispered excitedly, "Did you notice the lights?"

I looked up and didn't see a thing.

"The whole room is lined with them," Mitch went on. "They're so tiny and well-disguised you don't even notice them. But when Kim began to speak, someone faded them up, and faded them back down when he was done. It was an incredible effect," he marveled. "I'd love to meet their lighting technicians." Although Mitch had been the only one who noticed, the subtle rosy glow around the Great Leader contributed to a brilliantly manufactured illusion— one we would struggle to penetrate on each of our extraordinary visits to North Korea.

Like China in the 1950s and 1960s, the country Kim Il Sung ruled had long been out-of-bounds to Westerners. The United States and the Soviet Union had created what was intended to be a temporary demarcation line dividing the Korean peninsula along the 38th parallel at the end of World War II in 1945. Following the defeat of the Japanese, who had colonized Korea in 1910, Washington and Moscow failed to agree on a formula for reunifying the country. The line dividing Soviet and American troops stationed in Korea was frozen into a boundary separating two new Korean states. In the North, the Russians installed Kim, a little-known former guerrilla leader who had fought under communist tutelage against the

Japanese in Korea and Manchuria, as head of the Democratic People's Republic of Korea (DPRK). In the South, the Americans supported Syngman Rhee, an eccentric right-wing nationalist, as head of the Republic of Korea (ROK). The two despised each other. Both leaders were despots, both ruthlessly cracked down on internal opposition, and both dreamed of ruling a united Korea. In June of 1950, Kim Il Sung, with Stalin's blessing and Mao's tacit acquiescence, launched a massive invasion of South Korea to topple Rhee's unpopular and corrupt regime and reunify the country under his sole authority. Under a U.N. mandate, the United States led a multinational army to repel the invaders. Millions on both sides died in the three-year war, one of the most brutal of this century, which ended with the border unchanged. A still-divided Korea remained one of the Cold War's most volatile flashpoints.

While committed to socialism and firmly allied with his patrons in both Moscow and Beijing, Kim Il Sung carved out a unique ideology in North Korea called *juche*. Its central ingredient was an extreme form of self-reliance, which drew on the country's historical role as the "hermit kingdom," one that had fiercely resisted contact with the West since the arrival of the earliest traders and missionaries the century before. Kim cut the DPRK off from the outside world, sustaining his system and rule by a militant, xenophobic Korean nationalism. Special venom was reserved for the United States and the pro-American "puppets" in South Korea, but *juche* also allowed Kim to avoid an entangling dependence on his quarreling socialist allies in Moscow and Beijing, helping North Korea to stay afloat when the Soviet bloc collapsed. He achieved some early economic successes, rebuilding through mass mobilization a society literally flattened into rubble by American bombing and, in the years just after the war, outstripping South Korea's economic growth rate. By the 1970s, however, the North Korean economy began to sink, burdened by socialist inefficiency and the buildup of a large and increasingly costly military machine. Kim also presided over the creation of the world's most extreme personality cult. From within the country's sealed borders came astonishing stories that its twenty-two million people had turned into regimented robots, wearing Kim Il Sung buttons as they slavishly worshiped the "Great Leader" and his son, the "Dear Leader," Kim Jong Il, as virtual deities. At the same time, North Korea displayed a truculent face to the international community, its rhetoric invariably harsh and provocative, its million-strong army deployed menacingly close to the demilitarized zone (DMZ) separating the North and South. Its agents staged terrorist attacks on South Korean political leaders, raiding the presidential residence in Seoul, assassinating the wife of President Park Chung Hee, murdering four members of the country's cabinet in a bombing in Rangoon, Burma in 1983, and blowing up a South Korean airliner the year before the 1988 Seoul Olympics. Rumors abounded that Pyongyang was secretly developing nuclear weapons. To most of the world, Kim Il Sung seemed to be a Stalinist megalomaniac presiding over a nation as bizarre as it was sinister.

That had certainly been my impression on my first visit to North Korea in August 1989. The sensation of traveling through the looking glass began even before I left Beijing with Cynde Strand and bureau assistant Tan Yadong, who was filling in as soundman for the vacationing Mitch Farkas.

"Don't worry. Korean airlines perfect," declared the wiry man with the reassuring grin, halting English, and the Kim Il Sung button pinned to his chest. "Please to board the plane. We take off soon for Pyongyang." Standing on the steaming tarmac at Beijing airport, gazing uneasily at the ancient twin-propeller Russian-made Antonov-24 of the North Korean airline, Air Koryo, I wasn't so sure. I'd flown Antonovs around China, and they always felt like they were held together with glue and rubber bands. Nervously, we clambered on board. Inside, I gasped in amazement. Like so many other aspects of North Korea, the interior of the plane challenged my preconceptions. The small cabin was divided into two compartments, each featuring a bed, plush seats with their own tables, and a bevy of attractive, fresh-faced flight attendants, all wearing buttons bearing the face of the Great Leader. It was North Korea's version of an executive aircraft, used most of the time, the ever-smiling Air Koryo representative hinted, by Kim Il Sung's son and designated heir, the "Dear Leader," Kim Jong Il. Now, in early August 1989, the plane had been sent to Beijing to ferry a small group of specially invited Western reporters to North Korea. The world's most secretive and closed society was opening its door just a crack.

With slogans evocative of Newspeak and the image of Big Brother, in the person of Kim Il Sung, peering down from all public places, Pyongyang seemed like a giant set for George Orwell's famous novel *1984*. Tall, modern-looking, surprisingly attractive buildings lined vast boulevards, which stretched past carefully manicured parks and gardens glistening in the hot August sun. But although the North Korean capital reportedly had a population of two million, the boulevards were virtually empty. Apart from the convoy of official Mercedes cars for our small group of reporters, I saw almost no shops, no markets, no advertisements, no restaurants, and virtually no other vehicles, not even the bicycles so common in China. Policewomen in smart white uniforms and jaunty caps stood on candy-cane colored stands at major intersections, waving batons like automatons, directing traffic that didn't exist. I wondered: Where are the people?

But there was no shortage of monuments to the glory of Kim Il Sung. On every street were posters and billboards extolling the Great Leader and the Dear Leader. On Mansudae Hill, overlooking the city, we came upon a colossal bronze statue of Kim, his right arm outstretched, wearing a trench coat, and staring fearlessly ahead. Built to commemorate Kim's sixtieth birthday, it was twenty meters high and dominated the Pyongyang skyline, which also featured an Arch of Triumph (built for the Great Leader's seventieth birthday celebration and similar to the one in Paris but even bigger) and the Tower of the Juche Idea (a 170-meter obelisk in praise of Kim's contribution to political theory). It was taller than the Washington Monument, and the flame on the top glowed bright revolutionary red at night.

The North Koreans had not invited us to visit because of a sudden desire to open up their long-closed society. They had a specific propaganda goal in mind. A week earlier, a South Korean college student named Im Su Kyong had arrived in Pyongyang with a group of fellow dissidents. Visiting the North in defiance of South Korean regulations was intended to demonstrate their longing for a reunified Korea. In a dramatic final gesture, Im Su Kyong announced plans to travel back to Seoul by crossing the DMZ on foot. The North Koreans, eager to stir up South Korea's radical students while seeking to shift responsibility for the country's division onto the U.S. and South Korea, wanted us to witness the brilliantly staged event, complete with weeping, hysterical crowds organized to cheer her on, and a sobbing farewell when she walked across the demarcation line to face certain arrest at the hands of South Korean soldiers.

Back in Pyongyang, we were allowed to spend a couple of additional days in the country before returning to Beijing to edit our material, since the North Koreans made clear that feeding spots via satellite from their capital was out of the question. Although Im Su Kyong's theatrics had provided us with a colorful story, I disliked the sensation of being manipulated by the North Koreans. The experience was an extreme version of the carefully stage-managed events that had characterized my early trips to China in the 1970s. I was determined to use the remaining time to shoot interviews and pictures for a broader report on life in the country, but we remained virtual prisoners in the forty-story Koryo Hotel, where we were awakened every morning at six o'clock by loudspeakers outside that exhorted, "Wake up, citizens, and go to socialist construction work under the beautiful leadership of the Great Leader." We, however, were never allowed to go more than one hundred yards from the hotel on our own. The government guides who had arranged every detail of our itinerary from the moment of our arrival saw to that. It was far more restrictive than any of my China trips. We were physically present in one of the world's most unusual societies in the world, but we saw so little of North Korean reality that we felt we were in a hermetically sealed cage.

We were escorted to pay our respects at Mangyongdae, Kim Il Sung's birthplace. The thatch-roofed hut on the outskirts of Pyongyang had long ago been turned into a religious shrine, where our guides told us 1.7 million people—a twentieth of the entire population—visited every year. We watched long lines of North Koreans staring worshipfully at the room where Kim had allegedly been born, at the utensils with which he supposedly ate as a child, at photographs of his parents. After much prodding, our guides finally agreed to let us interview a few of the visitors on camera.

"The Great Leader President Kim Il Sung achieved the liberation of the fatherland and led our people to build a new and happy life," intoned seventeen-year-old student Hyong Un Kyi. "We have high respect and reverence for him, and we are determined always to be faithful to the call of the Great Leader."

"That was spontaneous," I growled to Cynde in frustration. "Let's ask someone about the "Dear Leader" and see if we do any better."

"The Dear Leader Kim Jong Il is doing his best to put into practice the ideas and intentions of the Great Leader President Kim Il Sung," eighteen-year-old student Han Yong Mi replied to my question. "He is looking after the well-being of the people. Therefore, people hold him in high esteem. The people are determined to carry out his teachings."

I tried patiently to explain to our guides why we needed to take pictures of ordinary people doing something other than worshiping Kim Il Sung. We meant no disrespect toward President Kim, but surely, I argued, the Great Leader would want the world to see how the citizens of North Korea were happily engaged in building socialism. Finally they agreed to let us visit the Pyongyang Fruit Farm, located in rolling fields a few miles from the capital, where we were ushered into a rectangular building with a huge portrait of Kim on the wall. "This museum commemorates the six visits to our farm by the Great Leader President Kim Il Sung" farm director Chang Yong Man declared. "He gave important on-the-spot guidance on how to grow fruit."

"But where are the farmers?" I asked.

"They are busy studying the works of the Great Leader," Chang replied.

Our guides quickly interrupted, saying it was time to leave.

Protesting vigorously, we pointed out that we couldn't do our story without at least one shot of a farmer engaged in farming. TV, after all, was a visual medium. After a huddled conference between the guides and Director Chang, we were allowed to walk back to the apple orchard and turn the camera on as the farm leader was joined by two other people. Mounting ladders, they each pulled a handful of apples from a tree, and, as Cynde rolled, placed them in straw baskets, climbed down, and walked away.

"There," said the guide in a satisfied tone. "You have seen what you wanted. Now we will return to the hotel." In the car on the way back to Pyongyang, Cynde labeled the tape "Apple Zombies."

The next evening, without telling the guides, I arranged to meet one of the few foreign diplomats residing in Pyongyang for coffee in the Koryo Hotel bar, a dimly lit corner off the lobby that was virtually only hangout for Pyongyang's tiny and very unhappy foreign community. The diplomat had been there for three years, and my conversation with him helped to answer some of the many questions I had about what I had seen in the past several days.

He confirmed my impression that Pyongyang was a capital city designed almost exclusively as a showcase to impress visitors. The population was screened by the government every three years in order systematically to evict and send to the countryside the elderly, the disabled and, above all, the politically unreliable. The city was for the political elite, the most senior of whom lived two blocks from my hotel in a neighborhood that was gated and patrolled by rifle-toting guards. "That's Pyongyang's 'Forbidden City,'" the diplomat said. "It is home to several thousand top party and state cadres, the people who drive around in Mercedes while the average citizens are forbidden to ride bicycles." The degree to which people were graded by their political loyalty was evident even in the small Kim Il Sung badges every citizen was required to wear. The diplomat told me the pins differed in shape, color, and size, according to a person's rank in society. Buttons with Kim Il Sung's visage on a small red flag, for example, were worn by members of the ruling Korean Workers Party. Those with a large red flag designated members of the Communist Youth League.

The Kims, of course, had special privileges, including the third lane in the middle of most major highways, which was reserved for their exclusive use. "Sometimes, diplomats have seen a two-seat sports Mercedes racing along one of those lanes in downtown Pyongyang at 100 kilometers an hour," he said. "We assume that is Kim Jong Il." His description of the Dear Leader was hardly flattering. "Kim Jong Il is said to have three passions," he told me, "Movies, women, and sports cars." This assessment echoed U.S. intelligence reports depicting Kim Jong Il as a binge drinker with a taste for Hennessy Cognac, imported Swedish prostitutes, and reckless driving. "His father, the Great Leader, whom I have met, is very sharp," this diplomat continued. "He is charming and has great charisma. But the son, he is so strange, he must either be mad or on drugs."

There was no way to confirm anything the diplomat said, of course. His comments seemed to me to have the ring of truth, although, after three years in the strange world of North Korea, it was possible that his own judgment was as distorted as the society in which he was required to live. Irritated at the mere fact of my meeting with him, our guides refused even to discuss the diplomat's comments. I was left to compare North Korea with the Soviet Union under Stalin, which Winston Churchill had described as

"A riddle wrapped in a mystery cloaked in an enigma."

Still, CNN expected me to produce a story explaining the country. On our last afternoon in Pyongyang, we were taken to the local amusement park, where we finally got a brief sense of the ordinary people of North Korea. Young couples laughed and played with their children, who excitedly clambered aboard the merry-go-round and other rides. For once, the Kim cult was briefly put aside. Cynde and I searched desperately for images that might convey the flavor of the place. As we watched the youngsters spin through the air, Cynde grabbed her camera, climbed aboard the fastest of the rides, and, squeezing herself into a plastic seat resembling a North Korean fighter jet, struggled to hold the camera steady as she was whipped around and around. When we looked at the video, we saw the skyline of Pyongyang, with its elaborate monuments spinning by in a barely discernible blur. At last we had found our image.

"This is a nation," I said in my story, "where the line between reality and fantasy is so blurred no one seems able to tell the difference."

The next day, following another nerve-racking voyage on Air Koryo, we returned to Beijing. Two months after the crackdown in Tiananmen Square, the capital was still under martial law. Armed, helmeted troops patrolled all key intersections. The government was in the midst of hunting down leading student activists. But, after North Korea, I was actually glad to get back.

On my next Air Koryo flight, I was not as nervous. God, I thought, might be looking out for me. My fellow passenger was the Reverend Billy Graham, who, with a half dozen associates, had chartered a North Korean plane from Beijing to make his first visit to Kim Il Sung's forbidden kingdom. I found it more than a little strange that the world's most famous Christian evangelist, a longtime confidante and spiritual advisor to American presidents from Eisenhower to Nixon to Bush, would secure an invitation to Pyongyang. Then again, Kim Il Sung had given himself near-divine status. He would probably enjoy speaking with someone else who, although in a very different way, felt close to God.

The Graham trip in April 1992 was a big story. It came at a time of growing tension between North Korea and the United States, sparked by renewed indications that Pyongyang was seeking to develop nuclear weapons. The evangelist's impending arrival set off widespread speculation that Kim Il Sung wanted to signal his desire to resolve the nuclear crisis and establish better relations with Washington. Despite intense press interest, however, Graham invited only a CNN crew—Mitch Farkas and myself—to accompany him. It was another sign of the network's growing international prestige and credibility. However, the North Koreans initially balked at giving me a visa. Unhappy at my tough reporting in 1989, they urged CNN's management to send another correspondent. CNN President Tom Johnson stood firm. North Korea was part of my beat. Either I covered Graham, he insisted, or no one from CNN did. Following complicated negotiations among the network, Pyongyang, and the Graham organization, the North Koreans relented, on condition that my reporting be confined to the evangelist's trip. My editors and I reluctantly agreed, but made it clear to Graham's staff and the North Korean Foreign Ministry that, for us, covering the visit required putting it into the broader context of North Korea's internal development and its relations with the U.S. and the international community. It was a definition that would allow me to discuss such sensitive questions as the succession from Kim Il Sung to Kim Jong Il, the nuclear issue, and the peculiarities of the North Korean regime. Grudgingly, the North Koreans went along.

I had seen Billy Graham in action once before, when he made his first trip to China in 1988, preaching his unique brand of the gospel to a packed congregation at Beijing's leading Protestant church. His charismatic presence seemed to me to be both a symbol and a catalyst for a growing official tolerance of religion in post-Mao China. The People's Republic was not the first socialist nation Graham had visited. In forty years he had preached in over eighty countries, on several occasions taking his evangelical crusade to the Soviet Union and Eastern Europe. The North Koreans, however, had always rebuffed his overtures.

Although Graham's Christian proselytizing was remote from my beliefs, I was delighted to find him warm and friendly, a man of genuine integrity, and surprisingly approachable, despite his fame. On the plane, as he and his colleagues spelled out their goals for the trip, my respect for him grew. Earlier in the century, they told me, Pyongyang had been a center of Christianity in Korea, with a large and vibrant Protestant community. In the 1930s, it boasted a church-run school, where many Asia-based Western missionaries educated their children. Among the students had been Graham's wife, Ruth, the daughter of missionaries in China, and James Lilley, the U.S. ambassador to Beijing, also the child of a missionary family. In the wake of the Korean War, however, the Christian community in the North, because of its long-standing links to the West, came under a cloud, and many members were accused of being American spies or collaborators. Churches were closed and believers persecuted as the worship of Kim Il Sung replaced all other organized religions. Now, in what appeared to be a sign of at least modest relaxation, one Protestant and one Catholic church had been allowed to open in Pyongyang. After several years of trying, Graham had at last been granted permission to visit. He hoped to generate goodwill that might secure more breathing space for North Korea's ten thousand practicing Christians, and perhaps contribute to a thaw in the DPRK's relations with the United States. "There's been no religion in North Korea, no praying, no Bibles printed, no Bibles distributed," Graham told me. "For them to allow me to come and preach is a step in the right direction."

Set on a small hillside in a Pyongyang suburb, the newly built Bongsu Church was packed. The mostly middle-aged or elderly congregation had arrived early, waiting impatiently to hear the first foreigner to preach the gospel in North Korea in half a century. As Graham stepped toward the flower-lined altar, the crowd burst into prolonged, rhythmic clapping, while Mitch and I scurried around the austere church recording the unlikely encounter. With Dwight Linton, a longtime American missionary in South Korea, acting as interpreter, Graham launched into a sermon on the theme of love, peace, and devotion. The audience sat in rapt silence, hanging onto every word, as Graham subtly sought to bolster the religious devotion of the North Korean believers whose faith had clearly been sorely tried over the years.

"We are not robots," he declared. "Everyone worships something. For Christians, we call him God, and the Bible tells us to celebrate this God." At the conclusion of the sermon, the congregation sang hymns in Korean with a fervor that left Mitch and me deeply moved. The display further eroded my image of North Koreans as brainwashed automatons without feelings or beliefs of their own. Afterward, with the permission of our guides, I spoke with one of the worshipers, a sixty-year-old man named Kok Ho Un.

"Have you ever heard a foreigner preach before?" I asked.

"Yes," he replied with a faraway look in his eyes. "In the 1930s, my father took me to church when I was little boy, and one time we listened to an American missionary. I am so glad to have had the chance to hear Reverend Graham. It has been such a long time." In a nation where people routinely talked in political slogans, these words were the closest I had yet come to hearing an ordinary North Korean imply that he was not absolutely content in Kim Il Sung's socialist paradise.

"Wake up," my guide Mr. Nam said urgently when he phoned my hotel room at 6:45 A.M. "You must get ready. You will have an important meeting today."

"With whom?" I asked.

"You will see," he replied. "It is important. Wear your best attire."

In the hotel lobby, Mitch and I were thoroughly frisked by muscular security agents who rummaged through our gear and declared that we must leave our tripod behind. Our guides were in a state of high excitement. It was obvious that we were going to meet the Great Leader himself.

"You must have a gift to present," said one of them. "Did you bring a gift?"

I had not anticipated the need to make such an offering to the President. Frantic, I rummaged through my bag. What could I possibly give that the Great Leader did not already have? Finally, I found a souvenir pen, still in its box, with the letters "CNN" engraved on the side.

"Will this do?" I asked anxiously. "The Great Leader could use it when he writes important works of political theory."

"Yes, yes. That is appropriate."

Later I learned that a special museum existed at Mount Myohyang outside Pyongyang, whose sole purpose was to house the presents brought by visitors granted the privilege of an audience with Kim Il Sung. The CNN pen soon took its place there.

We set off in a shiny Mercedes on an hour-long drive through the countryside, passing barren fields under a thin spring sun where a handful of farmers squatted, doing apparently nothing. The road was empty, and the overwhelming impression was of stillness and inactivity. Twenty miles farther, our vehicle made a left turn onto a small mountain road, where it was quickly stopped at a roadblock of rifle-toting soldiers who scrutinized our papers and then let us through. Two more roadblocks followed before we reached an enormous villa set against a hillside and surrounded by more sentries. We had arrived at the official residence of Kim Il Sung, where the Great Leader would meet Billy Graham and his entourage. Ushered into a large lobby, we encountered a half dozen Korean photographers and cameramen. The far wall was completely covered with a huge painting depicting Mount Paektu, the sacred mountain of Korea. Our guides shooed us to the right-hand side of the room. "You may take pictures of the Great Leader," one said, "but only from this angle. You may not move."

Suddenly Kim Il Sung walked into the room. The Korean journalists bowed reverently. I was swept by a wave of excitement. As far as I knew, Mitch and I were the first American television journalists ever to have this opportunity. The political symbolism of even the briefest of audiences with Kim was immense. North Korea's irritation at my 1989 reporting appeared to have been put aside. Apparently, by virtue of my association with Billy Graham, I was being rehabilitated. The Great Leader wore a black suit and moved stiffly, his hands clasped behind his back as he stood in front of the Mount Paektu picture. We had been positioned so we that could take pictures only from an angle where we could not see the huge lump protruding beneath Kim's right ear. Security men stood in the center of the room to ensure we could not get a shot from any other vantage point.

A moment later, Billy Graham was announced. His voice a deep rumble, Kim grunted a hello and the two men shook hands. As Mitch rolled, I took in a scene as bizarre as it was historic: the world's most reclusive dictator meeting the world's most famous evangelist. The formalities over, Kim prepared to escort Graham into a meeting room. First, however, Mitch and I were summoned to shake hands and offer our gift. "On behalf of CNN," I declared as solemnly as I could as I handed over the cheap ball-point pen, "I would like to present you with this small token of our esteem. I hope in the future CNN will be able to return to your country." Kim grunted a response and beckoned us to join him for a photograph, again arching his head so his lump would not appear in the picture.

"We are having sunny spring weather today," Kim remarked to Graham during a brief photo opportunity, which Mitch and I attended before the two men began their private discussions in a large, airy meeting room. "I hope this means that a new spring will come in relations between my country and the United States." Graham agreed, handing Kim a personal letter from President George Bush, which he later described to me as a broad statement of goodwill, containing no specifics, but expressing a similar hope of improved ties, with the unspoken implication that the nuclear issue must be resolved first.

From Kim Il Sung's point of view, there was a strong incentive to seek a new relationship with Washington. By all accounts, the situation inside North Korea had grown sharply worse since my last visit three years earlier, with reports of slumping agricultural production, growing food and fuel shortages, and factories operating at minimal capacity. As evidence of the scale of the problems, the North Korean press had recently issued a call for citizens to eat only two meals a day, and, for the first time, Pyongyang residents had been allowed to ride bicycles, not as a sign of liberalization, but because there wasn't enough fuel to keep buses and trams running. The sharp domestic decline coincided with the collapse of communism in the Soviet Union and Eastern Europe and with China's adoption of market-style economic reforms. These events not only disrupted Pyongyang's crucial economic links with its giant socialist neighbors, but also sent a clear message: Kim Il Sung had to do something to avoid meeting the same fate as his old Communist comrades, such as East German leader Erich Honecker, deposed and in exile, or Romania's Nicolae Ceausescu, who was executed in cold blood along with his wife. Better treatment from the United States and American gestures that would legitimize his regime and bolster his economy might well be the key to North Korea's survival in the post–Cold War world.

Graham and Kim seemed to get on well, continuing their discussions over a lavish lunch after a private three-hour meeting. The notion of two men from such different worlds meeting, let alone hitting it off, seemed utterly implausible. What sort of common ground could they possibly find? As I struggled to understand the dynamics of the political and social system that Kim Il Sung had created, I came to realize that it was not productive to view North Korea as merely just another slightly more eccentric communist state. The best analogy, it seemed to me, was to a religious camp grafted onto a very conservative, inward-looking society steeped in Confucian traditions, where the purpose of life was to glorify the reigning deity, namely the Great Leader. There were, in fact, some striking parallels—not with the substance but with the trappings— of primitive Christianity. Kim's birthplace at Mangyongdae resembled the nativity scene, to the point that, among themselves, members of Graham's entourage jokingly called it Bethlehem. There was a father (Kim Il Sung), a son (Kim Jong Il), and a holy ideology, *juche*. People displayed their faith by wearing not crucifixes, but the ubiquitous Kim Il Sung buttons. And, as in medieval Christian societies, heretics were condemned to terribly brutal punishments. When we asked one guide what would happen if he ever said anything uncomplimentary about the Great Leader, he first appeared shocked and offended that we would even raise the possibility. Then he slowly lifted his index finger to his temple and said, quietly, "*bang*," evidence of how harshly Kim Il Sung dealt with dissent. Even at the height of its Maoist madness, China had pockets of at least passive resistance, but there were no such signs in North Korea. The country appeared to deserve its reputation as one of the worst violators of human rights in the world. Yet North Korea's living God was portrayed as all-knowing and benevolent, and those who believed in him would certainly be redeemed. No wonder Kim and Graham appeared to have much to discuss.

However strange and repressive I found it, I was beginning to see that North Korea did have its own internal logic, an impression buttressed by a long conversation in my room at the Koryo Hotel the next evening with Steven Linton. Steve was a thin, intense, Korea scholar at Columbia University who served as Graham's interpreter for nonreligious events, including his long conversation with Kim Il Sung. Like his uncle Dwight, Steve had been born and raised in a missionary family in South Korea. His deep understanding of Korean culture and history enabled him to offer me insights about the Confucian veneration of the traditional Korean sage-king, which added a unique psychological dimension to the Kim cult. This deeply held belief was intensified by the Koreans' sense that they had been mistreated by bigger powers throughout their history.

It was the feeling of being under continual siege, Linton argued, rather than any intention to start a second Korean war, that explained Pyongyang's often truculent posture toward the South and the U.S. I asked Steve if he'd be willing to go on camera to share some of his thoughts. As Mitch set up the gear, our North Korean minders burst in the door. Making no secret of the fact that my room was bugged and that they had just listened to our entire conversation, they strongly objected to Steve's doing an interview, on the grounds that the topics were not directly related to the Graham visit. We argued for almost half an hour, until I made clear that Mitch and I would go ahead unless they physically stopped us. Eventually the guides backed off.

This episode was hardly the only problem we encountered in getting video and background information. In addition to objecting to the Linton interview, our minders actively tried to prevent me from meeting resident foreign diplomats, even threatening that if I did so I would not be allowed back into the country. I ignored their warnings. In addition, the guides pushed us to take pictures only of buildings, not people. This was especially frustrating since, this time, the streets of Pyongyang were filled with dancing people. According to the minders, the masses were rehearsing for a giant "soiree," a huge festival of song and dance, to celebrate Kim Il Sung's eightieth birthday on April 15. "Could we shoot them?" we asked. "No, they were only rehearsing." The dances were not yet "perfect." Neither, under the circumstances, were the three stories that Mitch and I edited upon our return to Beijing. Despite our frustrations, though, I felt we did manage to put the Graham visit into its broader context—that Kim Il Sung was signaling a desire for an accommodation with his longtime enemies in Washington.

The explosions reverberated across the frozen hillside near the demilitarized zone. Puffs of smoke filled the winter air as the American GIs in full battle gear fired their rifles, ran forward, dove for cover, and opened fire again. Hugging the ground for protection, the 120 men of Alpha Company slowly worked their way up the hill toward the unseen North Korean enemy. It was late November, 1993, and the promising talk of a thaw on the Korean peninsula had been replaced by mounting fears of war.

As Mitch Farkas, Tim Schwarz, and I watched this unit of the U.S. Army's Second Infantry Division engage in live-fire exercises just south of the DMZ during an assignment in South Korea, tensions over North Korea's nuclear program were reaching a crisis point. In late 1992, soon after the Graham trip, the International Atomic Energy Agency (IAEA) turned up evidence that the North Koreans had secretly reprocessed plutonium, the key ingredient for building atomic bombs, and had hidden their effort from international inspectors. In early 1993, faced with IAEA demands to allow inspections, the North Koreans took the unprecedented step of announcing their withdrawal from the Non-Proliferation Treaty (NPT), the international agreement designed to prevent the spread of nuclear weapons. Although Pyongyang declared three months later, in response to an intense American diplomatic effort, that it was "suspending" its withdrawal, it continued to rebuff international pressure, especially from the U.S. and South Korea, to come clean on its nuclear program. By the fall of 1993, the film and the batteries in the cameras used by the IAEA to record activity at North Korea's Yongbyon nuclear facility sixty miles north of Pyongyang, part of the standard monitoring procedure to ensure NPT compliance, were about to run out. This raised the question of what was termed "continuity of safeguards." American and South Korean officials warned that if continuity was broken, creating a period of time in which North Korea's nuclear facilities were unmonitored and more bomb-making plutonium might be reprocessed, they would seek U.N. sanctions against Pyongyang. The North Koreans countered that they would view such a move as an act of war.

It was a dangerous moment, made worse by what seemed to me to be an outbreak of war hysteria among my colleagues in the media. The tension was fueled by a bitter, behind-the-scenes debate in the U.S. government between those who viewed North Korea as an implacable adversary rushing to acquire a bomb, and those who argued that Pyongyang's posture could be moderated through sensitive and patient negotiations. Throughout the fall and winter, a barrage of selective, inflammatory leaks from senior officials, especially in the Pentagon and the intelligence community, where the hard line was most prevalent, made the headlines. The goal was clear: to push the Clinton administration to get even tougher with North Korea. It began in November 1993, when, following a visit to South Korea, officials on U.S. Defense Secretary Les Aspin's plane told reporters of what they described as an alarming new North

Korean military buildup near the DMZ. Soon after, two highly classified Pentagon computer simulations were leaked to *Newsweek*.
Published as the magazine's cover story, they showed that North
Korea would win a new Korean war. Just before New Year, the CIA
leaked a study to the *New York Times* asserting that the North
Koreans "probably" had at least one atomic bomb. A chorus of editorials, Op-Ed pieces, and other leaks followed. All had the same
theme: that the danger from a bellicose, potentially nuclear-armed
Pyongyang was growing, and that tough measures—U.N. sanctions,
possibly even American military action—were required to reverse
the situation. The tense atmosphere was not helped by the cascade
of inflammatory rhetoric and dire warnings of impending confrontation coming from the North Korean media. Picked up and
repeated in Western news reports, usually without any background
explanation of North Korea's political culture, anxieties over its
long-term survival, or negotiating tactics, such stories reinforced
the deep-seated Cold War image of North Korea as a wholly irra-
tional rogue state and international bad guy. Events seemed to be
spiraling out of control.

Among those caught in the middle was Danny Russel. A New
York native with a sardonic sense of humor, Russel was a longtime
Foreign Service Asia hand now working as the chief North Korea
watcher at the U.S. Embassy in Seoul. At our first meeting, over
kimchi and barbecued beef at a traditional Korean restaurant in the
South Korean capital, where we left our shoes at the door and sat on
the floor, he spelled out the multiple layers of confusion and uncertainty involved in assessing the North and its nuclear program. But
Russel, a soft-spoken, bespectacled man with the air of someone
who had watched politicians behave like fools for too many years,
argued that there was a method to North Korea's madness. I found
his bluntness refreshing. "It is easy to forget to what extent North
Korea has been treated like a caricature," he told me. "But I believe
this is a system that does operate according to discernible laws. It is
not simply a whacked-out fantasyland that begins every day on the
basis of some crazy new edict from the Great Leader. It does have its
own political dynamic. What we are watching is the continuing saga
of North Korea's attempts to trade its nuclear card for international
assistance and engagement."

Russel's arguments impressed me. Increasingly, as I canvassed opinions while in Seoul and by phone from experts in Washington and Beijing, I found that his perceptions and analytical framework made sense, crystallizing my own understanding of North Korea as a more complex and nuanced place than it initially appeared. Convinced that many of my colleagues were in danger of being manipulated in the battle of the leaks over control of the Clinton administration's Korea policy—especially the vast majority of reporters and editors with no firsthand exposure to the North—I redoubled my efforts not to let the conventional wisdom cloud my own judgment. It was a conviction buttressed by the fact that during my month-long stint in South Korea at the end of 1993, I had found the overall situation on the ground to be sharply at variance with the alarmist headlines coming out of Washington.

"Stop scaring our families," U.S. military spokesman Jim Coles said to me as I walked into his office in Seoul to request permission for to my crew to shoot American troops in the field. "There has been no significant change in North Korea's military deployment near the DMZ. The reports of a major new North Korean buildup are just plain wrong, and by hyping them, you press guys are making the problem worse." Leaning on his rifle as his men carried out live-fire exercises near the DMZ a few days later, Alpha Company's Captain Charles Hodges made the same point. "We train 365 days a year. We continue to be prepared to go to war. But nothing has changed on the ground. We are doing the exact same thing today that we do every day." I used our pictures of Alpha Company for a story Mitch, Tim, and I transmitted to CNN headquarters that evening. Its main point was that, for all the alarmist talk, war did not appear imminent.

The next evening I ran into ABC's Beijing correspondent Deborah Wang and her crew at O'Kim's, a boisterous, Irish-style pub with miniskirted waitresses in the basement of the Chosun Hotel, favored by visiting reporters in Seoul. Deborah and her crew had just flown into the South Korean capital. They told me their bosses at ABC New York had seen my spot the night before, with its dramatic pictures of GIs in combat gear, and had concluded, in stark contrast to the actual substance of my story, that the danger of war was increasing. Now ABC executives ordered them to Seoul on a few hours' notice with the assignment to do a "war clouds over Korea" story using similar pictures. Although the story Deborah did turned out to be more balanced than her excited bosses anticipated, the entire episode confirmed my suspicion that among the most frightening of the war clouds, many were media-generated—which nevertheless made them no less worrisome. I was concerned that exaggerated or sensational press reports could take on a life of their own. In an atmosphere as highly charged as that of Korea, with all sides burdened by a legacy of suspicion and mistrust dating back to the Korean War, news stories that led to angrier rhetoric or a hardening of public positions of all the governments involved could easily spark a dangerous escalation.

As the winter of 1994 gave way to spring, however, it appeared as if the media was no longer exaggerating. Frantic diplomatic efforts to resolve the nuclear crisis foundered, and tension reached a frightening new level. As the U.S. and South Korea began to move ahead with plans to introduce a resolution at the U.N. imposing sanctions on North Korea, Pyongyang again warned that such a step would be viewed as a declaration of war, with one North Korean official proclaiming that in the event of conflict, Seoul would be "turned into a sea of fire." Soon after, Secretary of Defense William Perry responded that the United States would risk war, if necessary, to see that sanctions were enforced. The U.S. announced plans to send Patriot antimissile batteries, anti-artillery weapons, and Apache helicopters to beef up its forces in South Korea. Danny Russel, deeply involved in U.S. diplomatic moves, remained a beacon of calm insight as the crisis mounted, and I spoke to him regularly on the phone. In late winter, he confessed to me, "I am considerably more worried now than I have ever been. I fear the groundwork is being laid for a giant step in the wrong direction."

With the confrontation intensifying, the country now widely described as the most dangerous in the world remained wholly inaccessible to Western journalists. Repeated attempts by CNN to obtain visas for North Korea met with no response, and other news organizations had no better luck. Information and insights about the country's leaders and intentions remained at a premium. In their isolated Stalinist fortress, the North Koreans appeared to the world to be more menacing and difficult to deal with than ever.

The Colombian man with the slicked-back hair, expensive cologne, and finely pressed suit seemed an unlikely intermediary.

But as he sat across from Tim, Mitch, and me at a hotel coffee shop in Beijing in late March 1994, Antonio Betancourt insisted he could get CNN into North Korea. On the face of it, the idea seemed far-fetched. Betancourt was the executive secretary of the Summit Council for World Peace, a front organization for the Korean-born Reverend Sun Myung Moon, whose Reunification Church, an eccentric and lavishly funded religious cult, had long been a source of controversy. But in 1991, Moon, who had once been a political prisoner in North Korea in the late 1940s before his liberation at the hands of American soldiers during the Korean War, had returned to Pyongyang. There, in yet another example of Kim Il Sung's apparent soft spot for messianic religious leaders, Moon established a cordial understanding with the North Korean president. As a result, a team from the Moonie-subsidized newspaper, the *Washington Times*, was visiting Pyongyang while Mitch and I were there with Billy Graham in 1992. Now Betancourt, apparently eager to bolster his organization's clout and prestige by acting as a power broker, was dangling the possibility that the Moonie connection could open the door to North Korea for us at a moment of great international tension. Eason Jordan and I were dubious, but with the drumbeat of war growing steadily louder, we were willing to pursue all conceivable options.

Betancourt's proposal was simple. The North Koreans had asked him to organize a goodwill delegation of international VIPs to visit Pyongyang to mark Kim Il Sung's eighty-second birthday on April 15. He would try to convince the North Koreans to permit a CNN team, along with a crew from the Japanese network NHK-TV, to enter the country for the ostensible purpose of covering the visit.

A few days before Kim's birthday, Betancourt sent an urgent fax to Eason. Despite the Moonie connection, the plan was in trouble. Granting permission for CNN to visit was viewed as so politically significant that no North Korean official wanted to take the responsibility for making the decision. "They attach so much importance to the coming of the world media to their country," Betancourt wrote, "that they feel this is a responsibility that should rest only on the Great Leader's approval." It was a fascinating insight into the nature of decision-making in Pyongyang. As a compromise, however, Betancourt had convinced the North Koreans to extend an invitation to Eason alone. The idea was that he and Betancourt would negotiate directly with the North Koreans, and, hopefully, secure an invitation for me and my crew.

Late in the afternoon of Wednesday, April 13, 1994, Eason called from Pyongyang, where he had arrived with Betancourt and the other "VIPs" the day before. He had met with the secretary of the ruling Korean Workers' Party, Kim Young Sun, an extremely powerful figure believed to be related to Kim Il Sung. Soon after, Kim Young Sun, who had conducted earlier rounds of nuclear negotiations with U.S. officials in New York, told Eason that our trip was on. The decision to grant us permission, he said, had been taken personally by Kim Jong Il. CNN would charter an Air Koryo jet to fly us to Pyongyang early Thursday. I should await a call from the North Korean Embassy in Beijing to collect our visas. I telephoned Danny Russel in Seoul to get his reaction. "I am very glad they are letting you guys in," he said. "The fact that the North Koreans are issuing visas is important in and of itself. When they are feeling beleaguered, they usually close the doors. When they invite visitors, it suggests a more international frame of mind, indicating they may be receptive to a new round of diplomacy."

At midnight, when the call came from the North Korean embassy, I raced through the darkened streets of Beijing to the embassy's visa section, where a pock-faced assistant sat alone in a small room behind a long counter and slowly copied out our visa applications. He handed me a blue piece of paper with the precious permission stamped on it. I noticed the North Koreans never stamped their visas directly into a visitor's passport, presumably because they did not want to risk contaminating their approval with any stamp from the "illegitimate" South Korean authorities.

Moments after I got home, the phone rang again. It was Assistant Secretary of State Robert Gallucci, the U.S. diplomat in charge of nuclear negotiations with North Korea. He had just arrived in Beijing as part of an Asian tour to discuss the crisis with concerned governments. Danny Russel, believing, as he put it, that "the U.S. needed to communicate with North Korea by means other than telepathy," had urged Gallucci to call me.

"I know that journalists are not supposed to carry messages, and I am not explicitly giving you a message for the North Koreans," Gallucci told me carefully, " but I hope you will keep some things in mind when you talk to them. If they ask your understanding of

American policy, you should know, and they should know, that the U.S. wants to continue discussions. We are continuing to look for ways to get back to the negotiating table. We are not trying to derail their regime. We are trying to get the nuclear issue behind us. We need them to understand that."

Gallucci's decision to take me into his confidence underscored that the highest levels of the U.S. government felt their own lines of communication with the North Koreans were inadequate at this time of crisis. In a climate where mutual distrust and suspicion made it almost impossible for these two adversaries to deal rationally with each other, CNN's global access and coverage put me in a unique, if somewhat awkward, position. The fact that I was going to the normally inaccessible Pyongyang made this more than just another assignment. In a dangerous diplomatic drama, with all the talk of war, I was suddenly one of the very few people with high-level access to both sides. If the two governments were exploiting CNN for their own purposes in order to halt the slide toward confrontation, it seemed to me to be one more instance of journalists and politicians using each other. And I was certainly happy to exploit the apparent willingness of the Americans and North Koreans to share their private thoughts with me. Probing both sides, I felt, was part of my job, and gave me an unparalleled sense of how policy on such a high-stakes issue was being made in both capitals. I was not entirely comfortable being put in a position of conveying Gallucci's message to the North Koreans, but I decided to take advantage of the situation. I would tell officials in Pyongyang what Gallucci said, gauge their reaction, and put everything I learned from both sides on the air.

Moments after arriving in Pyongyang and informing Eason and Antonio Betancourt of my conversation the night before with Gallucci, I was ushered into a hurried meeting with Kim Young Sun, the influential secretary of North Korea's ruling party. Kim was a stocky, well-built man with thick glasses, wavy hair, and a long mouth that appeared frozen in a perpetual sneer until it broke into a surprisingly warm smile. In the late April chill, his long underwear stuck out below the cuffs of his well-tailored brown suit. He listened intently, thanked me profusely, and promised to convey what I had said directly to Kim Jong Il and Kim Il Sung. As for Pyongyang's position, he replied, "What are the prospects for U.S.–DPRK talks? This question should be addressed to the U.S. A clap cannot be sounded by one hand." Like Gallucci, Kim seemed to be taking a relatively moderate tone.

Two hours later, Kim summoned Eason and me for a more extended discussion in a sun-filled room at the Koryo Hotel. Leaning forward in his overstuffed armchair, with a portrait of the Great Leader and the Dear Leader peering down from the wall, Kim smiled, lit a cigarette, and said through an interpreter, "You won't believe this, but I am a big fan of CNN. When I was conducting negotiations with the U.S. side in New York, I became addicted to CNN. Your visit could be the beginning of an excellent relationship between us." To our delight, Kim indicated we would be allowed to book satellite feeds from North Korean Television and transmit edited stories each night of our stay. Eason asked whether we would be able to do live shots as well. Kim was noncommittal. With edited spots, the North Koreans evidently felt that they could retain some degree of control. Allowing me to speak extemporaneously would be, for them, a huge political gamble. Our entire visit was such a new experience, he indicated, that things would have to be taken one step at a time.

As we struggled to make our first feed work that night, I began to wonder whether we would be able to put anything from Pyongyang on the air. First, we had to contend with our minders, who, despite Kim Young Sun's assurances of a free editorial hand, had hovered in the hotel room while we put our story together. The piece combined my initial impressions of Pyongyang, which I found to be remarkably tranquil and undisturbed, despite the heightened tension with Washington, and the conciliatory signals from Gallucci and Kim Young Sun. I made the point that, from my understanding of the situation, war did not appear imminent and renewed negotiations were not inconceivable. Although our guides made no attempt to change our language or content, they insisted on reading my script in advance, and standing inches away from Tim as he frantically edited the package, while I tried to explain to them the interplay of narration and video that made up a TV story. After a lifetime of watching only North Korean TV's carefully orchestrated propaganda, they did not appear to understand.

Then we discovered that North Korean TV did not have a single international telephone line. The only way to coordinate the satellite feed was for Eason to remain in the Koryo Hotel, talking to Atlanta on one phone in our three-room suite and to us at the TV station on the other. Tim would then verbally relay to Mitch the instructions Eason was receiving from Atlanta. Mitch then twiddled dials and pushed the appropriate buttons while I stood nervously in a corner worrying that the logistical obstacles would prevent all our hard work from ever being seen. Miraculously, everything went smoothly. Twelve hours after stepping off the plane from Beijing, my first spot from Pyongyang went on the air. "This does not look like the capital of a country preparing for war," I reported. "On the contrary, for all the bellicose rhetoric, Pyongyang appears remarkably relaxed."

In the days that followed, that impression, so sharply at odds with what most of the world believed and what, despite Danny Russel's prediction, I had half expected to see, was only reinforced, suggesting a more complex picture of a country the world feared but still knew remarkably little about. On Kim Il Sung's birthday, for example, ten thousand people gathered in Kim Il Sung Square in the center of Pyongyang for what the North Koreans called a "soiree." It was the same kind of birthday festival for which the people had been rehearsing, but which Mitch and I had not been allowed to shoot up close in 1992. As I stood on the balcony of the Great Study House of the People, the national library, overlooking the square ringed by giant billboards of Marx, Lenin, and Kim, the mass dance looked like all the other regimented exercises that were a North Korean trademark. Yet as we wandered through the crowds at ground level, where some of the locals even asked us to dance, I got a very different sense. I saw individuals, dressed in their best, smiling and laughing, enjoying a break in their usually drab lives; the North Korean equivalent, I thought to myself, of New Year's Eve in New York's Times Square.

The same absence of tension in Pyongyang was also evident on a visit to the demilitarized zone, the most heavily fortified front line on earth. Our guides first took us to a museum depicting "U.S. atrocities," where among the displays was the axe used by North Korean troops to kill two GIs in a notorious 1976 incident at the Panmunjom Truce Village. But we then became the first Americans to visit a small farm within sight of the South Korean side of the DMZ. The South Koreans had long dubbed it "propaganda village," and I had no doubt the local residents were fully briefed on what to say and do during our brief stop. But as we wandered through simple but clean

341

farmhouses, asking questions about daily life, diet (rice and *kimchi* three times a day, meat only on special occasions), and conditions along the border, I found the atmosphere to be one of absolute calm. My stay in North Korea was both short and very strictly controlled—the North Koreans were obviously not going to show us any significant military installations or preparations, and they were not beyond creating an elaborate facade to deceive a visiting foreigner. But from what I could see, North Korea did not appear to be a country either mobilizing for war or on the brink of collapse.

A day after his eighty-second birthday, Kim Il Sung appeared as if he didn't have a care in the world. On a sunny Saturday morning, my crew and I accompanied Antonio Betancourt and his group of VIPs to meet the Great Leader, not at the countryside residence where he received Billy Graham, but at the Kumsunsang Palace on the outskirts of Pyongyang. Here, amid carefully manicured grounds, surrounded by extremely tight security, under fifty-foot-high ceilings and brilliantly polished marble columns and floors, Kim entertained us for over three hours. In a handsome, wood-paneled meeting room, we were allowed to shoot most of a ninety-minute discussion, the first time the Great Leader had ever appeared at length before Western TV cameras. Gesturing forcefully, his moonlike face often breaking into a chuckle or laugh, Kim spoke in a deep, rumbling voice as he moved from history to philosophy to ideology to homespun Korean folklore. It was a masterful performance, confident and vigorous, revealing a man who, however bloody and ruthless his past, seemed far more interesting and lively than the cardboard caricatures and even his own scarcely credible cult suggested.

Focusing on broad themes and issues rather than details, he made it clear that North Korea's survival in the post–Cold War world was his central preoccupation. "The reason why Eastern Europe collapsed," he declared, "was that they followed exactly what the Soviet Union did. They created a bureaucracy, which led to a great gap with the masses. We did not copy mechanically the ingredients, principles, or mechanisms of Marxism-Leninism. That is the reason why we are standing firmly while the others collapsed. People thought that when other parties collapsed that our party would follow suit. But they were mistaken."

With the camera rolling, Kim was vague when asked about the nuclear issue. But he expressed a desire for better relations with the United States, and hinted that he might be prepared to cooperate with IAEA inspectors. "We are keeping no secrets, except some military ones," he said. "That is a common practice. Apart from those, we are ready to open to the outside."

The formal discussion over, Kim's staff motioned us to put our equipment away and join the Great Leader for lunch. We weren't the only journalists present. Betancourt's Moonie connection had enabled the same team from the *Washington Times* that Mitch and I had encountered in 1992 to return to Pyongyang. A crew from Japan's NHK-TV had been allowed in as well. All of us followed the small group of visiting former politicians into one of the palace's large, spotless dining rooms. Here, during a lavish and elegantly served meal, highlighted by the special effects Kim's lighting technicians produced when he made his toast, the conversation continued.

While we ate, I finally managed to slip in a question, pressing Kim again on the nuclear issue. Gesturing forcefully, he raised his voice and categorically declared that North Korea did not have and would never develop nuclear weapons. "In some cases," he said, "the world is calling on our country to show the nuclear weapons we don't have. I have just about had enough. There is nothing for me to do when they say we have nuclear weapons and we don't." Looking straight at me, he continued, "I promise you. We have no weapons, no delivery systems, no technology to build them, no reason for a bomb, and no secrets to conceal." And he made it clear he did not want war. "We have built so many monuments and apartments. Why would we destroy them? Those who want war are out of their minds." But his denials were coupled with a forceful statement of what seemed to be at the heart of many of North Korea's anxieties — Korea's long and unhappy history as a small nation surrounded by bigger, often hostile ones. "We will never have nuclear weapons in the future." he emphasized. "We don't want to become a big power. But we don't want to be subjugated by others. We are surrounded by big countries — China, Japan, the Soviet Union, the U.S. We will never become a satellite of any country. We will never be anyone's lackeys. We will maintain our independence and sovereignty."

To me, Kim's words underscored what seemed to be a central reason for the belligerence and truculence North Korea so often showed to the world, as well as for the all-pervasive cult he had imposed on his people. Without that kind of harsh discipline, patriotic fervor, and national unity, without a willingness to endure hardship and sacrifice for the nation, Kim obviously believed his small and isolated North Korea stood no chance of surviving, especially in the post–Cold War era.

Kim ate heartily as the conversation rambled from topic to topic. At one point, in an effort both to impress and inform the Great Leader, Eason Jordan displayed a map showing all the satellites through which CNN was distributed. The leader of Betancourt's delegation, former Costa Rican president Rodrigo Carazo, chimed in: "This TV network, Mr. President, is how the president of the United States can sit in his home and watch you." Kim's eyes widened slightly as he grunted his approval. He then began to regale us with stories of his recent bear-hunting exploits.

A special unit of soldiers had been given the responsibility for raising the bears, Kim told us, and making sure they reached their full weight and height before the Great Leader took out his hunting rifle. "They lay out some food so the bears won't run away," he told us with obvious delight, "and then I shoot them. I shot two recently. Each weighed 250 kilos. The most recent one heard a car and climbed up a tree. While it was sitting there, I shot it." I wondered what happened to the soldiers if the bear turned out to be uncooperative, and the Great Leader missed his shot. Kim made it clear he loved to hunt and fish, even framing an expression of interest in visiting the United States in terms of an outdoor holiday. In reply to a question from Antonio Betancourt asking if he would be interested in visiting New York to speak at the United Nations, Kim said, "Thank you, but I think I would rather go fishing. I would like to go someplace in the U.S. where I could fish and shoot animals and make new friends."

At the end of the meal, prompted by a question from Josette Shiner of the Washington Times, Kim talked about his health and his son and heir, Kim Jong Il. "Mr. President, I think you look younger and more handsome than the last time I saw you in 1992," Shiner noted flirtatiously. "Can you tell us your secret of good health?" Kim laughed and clapped his hands. "There is nothing special," he replied, "only the same optimistic feeling I have always had. In fact, there are some things I cannot do now because of aches and pains. For instance, I can no longer play tennis, But my son, he is such a good son. He is very concerned for my health and looks after me very well. He always tells me to be careful in case I catch a cold when I tour the countryside. He worried I would have eye problems from reading too much, so he recorded many documents on tape. I listen to them when I go hunting or fishing. I am proud to have such a good son. I even wrote a poem about him."

As we left the Palace, Eason, Tim, Mitch, and I all realized that we had a huge story on our hands. Not only had Kim Il Sung spoken out publicly on the nuclear issue for the first time, but he had provided us with an unprecedented glimpse of him as a person as well as a leader. Like my earlier and much briefer contact two years before, this longer encounter further undermined the one-dimensional image I had held of the Great Leader as either crazy or senile. Instead I thought he had something of the aura I imagined had surrounded the other giants of the communist world, such as Stalin or Mao. Clearly accustomed to total control, Kim struck me as cunning, astute, and determined to do whatever was necessary to ensure the continuation of the dynasty he had created. This clearly included playing a dangerous game of nuclear brinkmanship. Yet after listening to him, I was willing to countenance the possibility that his goal was not conflict or conquest. Instead he seemed to be seeking to trade the one card in his deck—the ambiguity over the exact status of his nuclear program—for a deal with the United States that would help ensure North Korea's survival. At the dark and nearly deserted TV station where we fed our edited package later that night, I concluded my report with this observation: "By emerging publicly to deny reports of a nuclear weapons program, by declaring his desire for peace, President Kim appears to be seeking to defuse the current crisis. But he did not answer the question of whether international inspectors would be allowed back into North Korea's nuclear sites. And without an answer to this question, the nuclear issue is unlikely to go away."

Our broadcasts of Kim Il Sung created a sensation, providing the world with its first real glimpse of the mysterious and much-feared North Korean leader. The international wire services and newspapers from Tokyo to Seoul to New York picked up our story, but the reaction was mixed. Uncomfortable at having their own long-held preconceptions of North Korea challenged, some South Korean politicians and newspapers attacked me for being Pyongyang's "dupe." I had been aware that merely going to North Korea at such a highly charged moment would open me to criticism. But I had gone to great lengths, I felt, to make sure my reporting was careful and responsible. If it didn't fit someone's ideological agenda, that was their problem. When I returned to Beijing, I found an army of South Korean reporters waiting for me at the airport. Some were skeptical, but others gave me the flattering but undeserved compliment of comparing my work to that of Edgar Snow, the first American journalist to interview Mao Zedong in the 1930s. However controversial, my reports had unquestionably had an impact, especially in the corridors of power in Washington.

"We imagined the North Koreans were lusting for war," recalled one senior State Department Korea expert in Washington, who favored pursuing the path of negotiations. "Yet CNN gave us an insight into the other side's fears. We thought we were looking at a bunch of bombastic SOBs. But when you looked at them on CNN, they sounded frightened, anxious, almost human. The North Koreans were no longer communist lemmings."

Ten days after leaving Pyongyang, I was in Atlanta, attending the CNN World Report Conference, at which President Bill Clinton had agreed to spend ninety minutes on the air answering the questions of the international broadcasters gathered there. Before speaking, the president toured CNN's facilities with Eason Jordan and network President Tom Johnson. As they made their rounds, Johnson, eager for me to share my Korean insights with Mr. Clinton, went out of his way to introduce me. For all my years as a foreign correspondent, I still felt slightly ill at ease hobnobbing with presidents and prime ministers. Demonstrating students or Third World peasants were my usual beat. But apart from Eason, I was the only person in the world who had, in the span of two weeks, met both Kim Il Sung and Bill Clinton. Slightly intimidated, I shook Mr. Clinton's hand and tried to summarize my impressions for him. "Mr. President, my colleagues and I spent three hours with Kim Il Sung last week, during which he answered many of our questions. He left me with the clear impression his government would like to talk to you—that the North Koreans really are interested in a negotiated solution to the nuclear crisis."

Looking slightly startled, the president responded, "Thank you.

We're working on this issue as hard as we can," and walked away.

In Washington a few days later to touch base with North Korea and China watchers, I stopped in to see Robert Gallucci. It was early in the evening, and the Assistant Secretary of State looked tired and discouraged. "I just came from a meeting at the White House on North Korea, where a lot of people were sitting around and saying 'What does it all mean?' That place is so murky, even the simplest models of their behavior are open to question." Gallucci listened eagerly as I spelled out my own impression that the North Koreans were not mobilizing for war and that Kim Il Sung genuinely wanted a deal, if he could find a face-saving way of achieving one. The problem, it seemed to me, was that the North Koreans were looking for what they called a "package solution," explicitly linking a freeze in their nuclear program to gestures from the United States. However, the Clinton administration, fearful of setting a dangerous precedent in the area of nonproliferation, was insisting that it would not even open talks on other issues until Pyongyang complied with Washington's nuclear inspection demands. Making the mere fact of negotiations a prize offered to the North Koreans in return for con- cessions, instead of a tool to be used to secure those concessions, seemed to me to be an unproductive strategy. But Gallucci saw things differently, expressing concern that the North Koreans would use talks over a "package deal" as a delaying tactic while proceeding with their nuclear program. For all the conciliatory signals, the diplomatic process had stalled again.

In the meantime, tension rose sharply. The catalyst was North Korea's decision in early May to begin removing 8,000 spent fuel rods from its main Yongbyon reactor. U.S. and IAEA experts believed the rods, if reprocessed, would provide North Korea with enough plutonium for four or five atomic bombs. Throughout May the IAEA and the North Koreans squabbled over terms for agency inspectors to monitor the process of unloading the fuel. At the end of the month, talks between the two sides broke down in acrimony, with the North Koreans threatening to expel the two inspectors still in the country, and the IAEA declaring it could no longer confirm that North Korea was not diverting plutonium for weapons purposes. In response, North Korea announced plans to withdraw from the nuclear watchdog body. Under the circumstances, the U.S. and South Korea accelerated their drive for United Nations sanctions against

Pyongyang. The talk of war reached a dangerous new crescendo. Amid a series of strident threats and counterthreats, the U.S. began beefing up its military posture in the South. Preparations were made to send additional troops. The State Department actively considered ordering the evacuation of all U.S. civilians from South Korea. In Seoul, President Kim Young Sam's government announced plans to mobilize millions of reservists for a daylong war-preparedness drill. Panic buying swept the city, while in Washington, Pentagon planners examined the military options for taking out the North's nuclear capabilities. In early June, the *Washington Post* published an article outlining what might happen if a second Korean war broke out. It would begin with "the heaviest artillery barrage since World War One," the paper speculated, followed by the use of chemical weapons and nerve gas, and, if the North did indeed possess and sought to use its own crude nuclear devices, could lead to limited nuclear war. It seemed inconceivable, but such a horrible conflagration was now a frighteningly real possibility.

On June 15, 1994, the air raid sirens sounded in Seoul, stopping traffic and forcing people off the streets. Convinced that armed conflict with the North might be imminent, the South Korean government was staging the country's biggest civil-defense exercises in years. On the South side of the Panmunjom Truce Village at the DMZ, two hundred reporters and cameramen gathered, waiting anxiously within sight of the demarcation line. A moment later, beaming his famous toothy grin, Jimmy Carter, his wife Rosalynn, and a handful of aides crossed the world's most volatile frontier. In a half century of tortured relations between Washington and Pyongyang, there had never been a scene like this: a former president of the United States setting foot in North Korea on a mission of peace against a backdrop of growing fears of war.

Along with North Korea's Foreign Minister, a solitary Western TV crew was there to greet the small delegation. For the second time in less than two months, Eason Jordan, Mitch Farkas, Tim Schwarz, and I were back in Kim Il Sung's mysterious kingdom. The government in Pyongyang had granted CNN exclusive permission to cover Mr. Carter's visit. Giddy from elation and exhaustion, feeling like kids who'd been given the last piece of candy, we waved and grinned at the crews from ABC, NBC, CBS, and our other envious competitors a few yards away across the demarcation line. Tom Mintier, covering the South side of the story, gave us a thumbs up. Savoring the moment, Eason turned to me with a huge grin and said, "You live for days like this."

When he had made his decision a week earlier to go to North Korea, Mr. Carter, a Georgia native, had called Eason at CNN headquarters in Atlanta to pick his brains about our April visit and our meeting with Kim Il Sung. But while Mr. Carter indicated that he would welcome having a CNN team in Pyongyang with him as he sought to reverse the growing momentum toward war, he made no special effort on our behalf. Instead, in the days before his departure, Eason and I frantically lobbied every North Korean contact we could, including a mysterious Mr. Lee. He had sidled up to us during the Pyongyang "soiree" on Kim Il Sung's birthday and whispered, "I am Lee. I am in Vienna. I wish to work closely with you," and slipped back into the crowd, leaving us only a Vienna cell-phone number, and the impression that he was a key North Korean operative overseas. Now we appealed to him, to Party Secretary Kim Young Sun's office, to Antonio Betancourt, to the North Korean Embassy in Beijing, its mission at the UN, and anyone else we could think of. As usual, final approval didn't come through until a few hours before the departure of the twice-weekly Air Koryo flight from Beijing to Pyongyang. Upon our arrival in the North Korean capital, we were told that over three hundred news organizations had applied to cover the Carter trip and that the North Korean Foreign Ministry had opposed granting visas to any journalists. Our influential friend, Secretary Kim Young Sun, representing the ruling party, disagreed and put the case to Kim Jong Il. According to Kim Young Sun, the Dear Leader himself, pleased by the impact of our broadcasts of his father two months earlier, made the decision to let CNN in.

Whatever the internal politics, once we were on the ground, the North Koreans went out of their way to be helpful, giving us virtually unfettered access to Mr. Carter and permission not only to transmit taped reports, but to do live shots from DPRK-TV as well. On the last night of our April visit, we had tried a live shot, the first ever done from North Korea. The arrangements were so primitive, it was a miracle the feed worked at all; and any discussion back and forth with CNN's anchors was out of the question. Now we discovered that by booking a special satellite communications link called a four-wire through Tokyo, where our Japanese affiliate TV Asahi could patch the signal through to Atlanta, we could have two-way voice communication during any feed. Daily live reports were back on the agenda.

"My old friends!" Kim Il Sung's gravelly voice boomed out across the vast reception hall of the Kumsunsang Palace. Striding toward Eason, he held out his hand, then greeted the rest of us with equal warmth. The Great Leader was in good humor, laughing and joking as Mitch took pictures. Eason used the opportunity to pop a question on the nuclear issue while requesting a formal TV interview for a later time. As Kim started to reply, his aides interrupted to announce that President Carter had arrived. In frustration, we stepped back to record the scene.

The night before, in a banquet hall so brightly lit it resembled a television studio, Foreign Minister Kim Young Nam had hosted a dinner for Mr. Carter in which he said, "We believe if the United States renounces its concept of confrontation with us, respects our natural sovereignty, and treats our country on a equal footing, the nuclear issue will be resolved satisfactorily." For his part, Mr. Carter called for friendship and understanding, and for full transparency on nuclear matters. Afterward, an all-female North Korean rock band with frilly dresses, electric guitars, and robotic movements serenaded the Carters with "Oh Susannah," "My Darling Clementine," and such local hits as "My Country Is the Best" and "Stay, Night of Pyongyang." We dubbed them "the Kim-ettes."

The cordial mood carried over to the first Carter-Kim meeting, where the Great Leader declared, "What is important between us is trust, understanding each other." Afterward, the former president would say little to us about what had transpired, except that the two men had spent three hours in detailed discussions on the nuclear question. Later that afternoon, in an astonishing scene, my crew and I watched Mr. Carter and his aides huddling for a strategy session on a Pyongyang sidewalk. It was the only way they could escape their bugged rooms at the Presidential Guest House.

It was one A.M. on Friday, June 17. Tim and I had just finished a live shot in which I had pointed out that, "North Korea for years has sought recognition and legitimacy from the United States. To have a former American president here is precisely the kind of gesture the

North Koreans have been seeking, so they've gone out of their way to lay on a very, very warm welcome. Whether that will translate into substantive progress on the nuts and bolts of the nuclear issue is another question."

We returned to the hotel, hoping it was not too late to order a pizza from the bar. Earlier in the day two secret-service agents, who had stayed in the Koryo Hotel for two days ahead of Mr. Carter's arrival, had fallen violently ill, requiring an emergency visit from Kim Il Sung's doctor at the Presidential Palace. We assumed the hotel's barely edible fare was the cause, although having been served donkey pâté at a farewell banquet in April, we realized there could be many possible culinary suspects. In any case, we were determined to avoid the same fate by eating the only item on the menu we felt was safe—frozen pizzas imported from Hong Kong and served in the lobby bar, where an automated piano played "Those Were the Days" over and over again as foreign guests and resident diplomats, all with the same disoriented, Pyongyang look, gathered to socialize. As we arrived, we found an urgent message from Eason, who, along with Mitch, had accompanied Mr. Carter to a cultural performance while Tim and I did the feed. Now they insisted we join them immediately at the Presidential Guest House. Racing through the darkened streets, past multiple checkpoints, we arrived at the luxurious compound where Mr. Carter and his party were staying. Like all official buildings in North Korea, its monumental rooms and corridors dwarfed all who entered. Eason was in a state of high excitement. "Carter has apparently achieved a breakthrough," he said breathlessly. "Mitch and I have got him on tape, and he's about to announce the news in a live phone interview on CNN."

Moments later, Mr. Carter walked in looking pale and tired, and, after greeting us, got on the phone with Atlanta, where he told White House correspondent Wolf Blitzer that Kim Il Sung had pledged not to eject international inspectors from North Korea's nuclear facilities, and to allow continuous monitoring of the complex as long as "good-faith efforts" were being made to resolve the crisis. Describing the move as a positive step, Mr. Carter called on the Clinton administration to pull back from its sanctions drive and immediately open high-level talks with Pyongyang.

As we stood silently in the vast guest house watching Mr. Carter announce the breakthrough via telephone on CNN, President Bill

Clinton and his top national-security aides were in the midst of a council of war, discussing the possibility of sending more troops, planes, and ships to South Korea, even considering a U.S. air raid on the Yongbyon facility, much as Israel had destroyed Iraq's nuclear reactor in a similar attack in 1981. Alerted by a call thirty minutes earlier from the former president, the senior officials gathered around a TV set. They watched Mr. Carter's announcement with rage and embarrassment. Many members of the administration had been uncomfortable with the Carter mission from the start, doubting the wisdom of any self-appointed American emissary trying to engage Kim Il Sung while the U.S. was seeking to mobilize world opinion for sanctions, and questioning in particular the suitability of a man who, as president, had often been labeled a weak and ineffectual figure. Now here he was, not only negotiating in public but apparently securing concessions the administration had itself been unable to achieve. "It was humble pie in living color for Clinton," one senior State Department official recalled later. "Through CNN, Carter had jammed the bureaucracy, and gave those who'd been arguing for restraint the ammunition they needed."

For us, it was another huge North Korea scoop, and we raced back to the TV station, forcing our minders to awaken the staff there at 3 A.M. to feed an updated story. Meanwhile, Jimmy Carter remained at the guest house, where through the night he held a series of extended, sometimes heated phone discussions with U.S. National Security Advisor Anthony Lake. The calls were not easy, not least because the telephone operator at the guest house spoke almost no English and seemed to take forever to get through to Washington. Moreover, the former president had no secure means of communication. His every word was uttered on what was obviously a tapped phone line.

Early in the morning, having had no sleep, Tim and I returned to DPRK-TV, where another feed was booked for me to appear on *Larry King Live* jointly with Tom Mintier in Seoul. It was a TV first. Reporters in the two hostile capitals had never appeared on the same screen at the same time. The North Koreans were so excited by all the live reports I had been doing that they provided a backdrop for my appearances—a painted screen depicting the Pyongyang skyline with the red flame of the Juche Tower burning brightly. It was tacky beyond words, but I thought it looked wonderful. Standing in front of it, heavily made up to disguise my fatigue, I discussed Mr. Carter's apparent breakthrough, observing that Kim Il Sung may have been prompted to offer his concession because the former president had given him the kind of respect he had never before received from an American official. Mintier provided an update of the cautious reaction in Seoul, and King played a clip of a sober President Clinton saying that a genuine North Korean nuclear freeze could lead to new bilateral talks, but in the meantime, the push for U.N. sanctions would continue. Originally the show had scheduled a longer appearance for us, but there was other major news that day. After ten minutes, Larry King interrupted. "Thanks, guys. Thanks for making a little history. Now," he told CNN's audience. "is O. J. a suspect or not? We'll be back to talk about the O. J. Simpson story, right after this."

While I was answering Larry King's questions, Eason and Mitch went boating with Mr. Carter and Kim Il Sung. The North Korean leader offered the presidential yacht, an opulent vessel with huge picture windows and an all-glass elevator, as the venue for the next round of talks. At midday, after the two men had spoken for more than three hours, my colleagues returned to the Koryo Hotel, where Tim and I had finally ordered our pizzas. I could sense Eason's excitement. "You won't believe what Carter told Kim!" he exclaimed. "He announced that the Americans had agreed to stop the sanctions push now. And we have the whole exchange on tape. We're going to book a feed as soon as possible."

Looking at the tape, I understood Eason's astonishment. The tape showed Jimmy Carter stating, "I would like to inform you that they [the U.S. government] have stopped the sanctions activity in the United Nations." Mr. Carter added that if the North Koreans froze their nuclear program, it was his understanding that the U.S. was also willing to discuss helping North Korea acquire a light-water reactor, which produced much less plutonium than the old, Soviet-model graphite-based reactors the North Koreans were currently using, and begin new, high-level bilateral talks. All the elements of a compromise were there. The former president appeared on the brink of a dramatic diplomatic breakthrough—possibly, I observed in my on-camera stand-up, the beginning of the end of the Korean nuclear crisis.

The firestorm of controversy erupted just moments after our

story with the Carter sound bite went on the air. Angry and embarrassed, administration officials insisted that Mr. Carter was wrong, that the U.S. had *not* dropped its sanctions bid. Presidential press secretary Dee Dee Myers immediately issued a statement to that effect, and a flustered-looking President Clinton, traveling in Chicago, reiterated the point on camera several hours later. Meanwhile, other White House aides, speaking on background, denounced Mr. Carter for engaging in freelance diplomacy and undermining U.S. foreign policy. One of them was quoted in the *Washington Post* as saying, "Carter is hearing what he wants to hear, both from Kim Il Sung and the administration. He is creating his own reality."

Wholly unaware of the reaction, we returned to the Presidential Guest House after feeding our story for a farewell chat with Mr. Carter, who was scheduled to leave Pyongyang early the next morning for Seoul. The former president was in a good mood, confident he had made major progress. He repeated his belief that U.S. sanctions could lead to war because, in North Korea's unique society, the formal branding of the man revered as the Great Leader as an international outlaw could not be tolerated. And he reiterated the importance of direct dealings with Kim Il Sung: "You have to have direct communication with the only man in the country who can make a decision," he insisted. In discussing his meetings with Kim, Mr. Carter was at pains to stress how important language and phrasing were in such a volatile situation, how careful he'd tried to be. If I had any thoughts that the former president had misspoken earlier in the day, they now disappeared.

The North Koreans were pleased too. Before we left to return to the TV station for our final feed, a senior official on Kim Il Sung's staff, with great solemnity, gave each member of the CNN team a button of the Great Leader.

"I'd better not wear this on the air," I joked to Eason. "There are probably a lot of people who already think we're dupes of the North Koreans just for being here."

The next day, Jimmy Carter arrived in Seoul, where he delivered another bombshell—a proposal from Kim Il Sung for a face-to-face meeting with his arch rival, South Korean President Kim Young Sam. Had Mr. Carter not been able to convince the South Korean leader to agree, his whole mission risked failure. But the former president, using the same combination of sincerity, persistence, and respect that he had employed in Pyongyang, was able to transform a suspicious and alarmed Kim Young Sam into a receptive and cooperative partner. Immediately after the two met in Seoul, the South Korean president accepted Kim Il Sung's offer of talks. But confronted with a barrage of criticism for his on-air comments in Pyongyang, Mr. Carter backtracked about what he'd said in our presence on the sanctions issue, telling reporters at a news conference before leaving Seoul, and again upon returning to the U.S., that he had failed to make clear he was expressing only a personal opinion that the sanctions bid would be stopped. "I regret the misunderstanding," he announced. "It was my fault."

Back in Beijing reviewing Mr. Carter's role, I was not so sure. The former president was playing a complicated game on this trip, seeking to circumvent what he viewed as a mistaken and dangerous U.S. policy by pulling the elements of a nuclear deal together himself. He may well have misspoken. But I think it is equally possible that he was indeed trying to "create his own reality," deliberately exceeding administration guidelines to elicit more concessions from Kim Il Sung and buttress his case for a compromise solution. It was here that CNN's role—the fact that Mr. Carter's statements were captured on camera and transmitted and broadcast almost instantaneously changed the entire dynamic of diplomacy. The whole world knew what Mr. Carter had said and done at the same time that the key policy-makers in Washington and other capitals became aware of his actions. Detailed consultations and internal analysis were no longer possible before senior American and South Korean officials were forced to respond. The result was that in the forty-eight hours immediately after our controversial broadcast, it was possible to see an almost hour-by-hour evolution of U.S. policy toward North Korea taking place on CNN's air. As the impact of the concessions Mr. Carter had secured in Pyongyang sank in, the tone of officials from the president on down shifted from calling for U.N. sanctions to welcoming new, high-level negotiations with Pyongyang. For all the criticisms of Carter's role, it quickly became clear that the former president's intervention had halted a dangerous slide toward confrontation. The shadows of war over the Korean peninsula abruptly disappeared.

Shortly after returning to Beijing, I called Danny Russel in

Seoul. "We were right at the edge of the cliff," he said. "We were really close to a war. Jimmy Carter saved us from that." The emotion in his voice clearly audible, Danny continued. " I don't quite know how to say this, but I believe with all my heart that you were a participant in a miracle." Four months later, Assistant Secretary of State Robert Gallucci and North Korea's First Vice Foreign Minister Kang Sok Ju signed an agreement in Geneva paving the way for a peaceful resolution of the nuclear crisis.

CHAPTER TWELVE

End of the Dynasty

The last time I saw Kim Il Sung, at his meeting with former President Jimmy Carter in Pyongyang on June 16, 1994, he looked terrific—alert, vigorous, and bursting with energy. The contrast with Deng Xiaoping, Kim's fellow communist patriarch in Beijing, was striking. The previous February, Deng had appeared on Chinese television to mark the Lunar New Year, an annual ritual. The brief flim clip showed China's paramount leader with his mouth slack, his eyes vacant, tottering precariously as he was supported by his daughters. His weakened condition was shocking to me and to the millions of Chinese who watched. Now, four months later, I turned to Eason Jordan as we left Kim's palace in Pyongyang. "Boy, the Great Leader seems in great shape," I marveled. "I bet he'll outlive Deng Xiaoping by a decade."

Three weeks later, Kim Il Sung was dead.

I heard the news in Geneva, where I had gone to cover the new round of U.S.–North Korean nuclear negotiations that had been set in motion by the success of the Carter visit. When the CNN International Desk awakened me to report the North Korean announcement at 5 A.M. on July 8, I was stunned. The aura of near-divinity that surrounded Kim, and the fact that I had just seen him, in apparently excellent condition, made it almost inconceivable that the Great Leader could simply keel over and die of a heart attack. It was a huge story, with potentially ominous implications—not just for the nuclear talks, which were immediately suspended, but for the future of the entire Korean peninsula. In totalitarian states like China or North Korea, the succession to a departed strongman is always the most dangerous time and was one reason I had been trying in Beijing to keep such close tabs on Deng Xiaoping's deteriorating health. But in the North Korean system, where Kim Il Sung was the foundation of the entire system, the prospect for a major convulsion seemed even greater. I wondered how the people of North Korea would react to the news that their god-king had turned out to be a mere mortal. The conventional wisdom was that, without the Great Leader to hold it together, the North Korean system would soon collapse. Few analysts expected the Dear Leader, Kim Jong Il, to survive long in his father's absence. There seemed good reason to worry.

Eason asked me to fly from Geneva to CNN headquarters in Atlanta to help coordinate our coverage of Kim's funeral. The North Koreans politely turned down our request to travel to Pyongyang for the event, but they did agree to make North Korean TV's coverage of the ceremonies available to CNN. Over two successive nights, I sat in the studio, joined by North Korea expert Steve Linton, my traveling companion from the Billy Graham visit two years earlier, as CNN aired more than six hours of some of the most astonishing images I had even seen: endless streams of weeping mourners prostrating themselves before the towering statue of the Great Leader on Mansudae Hill; crowds lining the normally empty streets of Pyongyang, almost hysterical with grief as the motorcade bearing Kim's body drove past; North Korean TV reporters weeping uncontrollably as they conducted interviews or read official declarations; and, most intriguing of all, the reclusive Kim Jong Il, his face pale and puffy, grimly receiving the condolences of senior officials beside his father's bier. Among those officials was our main contact, Party Secretary Kim Young Sun. It was all broadcast live on CNN, providing our international audience with a remarkable glimpse into a normally secretive society.

The rumors and speculation that Kim Jr. wouldn't last and that North Korea would collapse intensified, fueled in part by a harsh wave of anti-Pyongyang diatribes from South Korea. Even though President Kim Young Sam had been due to meet Kim Il Sung in a historic North-South summit at the end of July, the government in Seoul not only refused to express condolences on Kim's death, it barred any South Korean citizen from doing so, and sharply escalated its denunciations of the North. In such a highly charged environment, with the whole world watching anxiously to see whether North Korea would follow its fellow East-bloc allies into oblivion, getting to Pyongyang became a top priority. Yet again, Eason and I worked all our contacts, lobbying, pleading, and cajoling. A few days after Kim's funeral, the mysterious Mr. Lee called from Vienna to say that Eason and I were welcome in Pyongyang the following week. We would be the first Americans and the first journalists to visit since the death of Kim Il Sung.

When we arrived, an exhausted Secretary Kim Young Sun told us that our extensive coverage of Kim's death had been greatly appreciated by Kim Jong Il, who had been able to watch CNN on his personal satellite dish. To our astonishment, we learned that the Dear Leader had ordered North Korean TV to rebroadcast *our* coverage of *their* coverage. It was an unprecedented gesture. North Korean television never broadcast foreign news, let alone any other material from overseas. Its staple fare, which we watched in our hotel room many evenings, since we had nowhere else to go, consisted of endlessly repeated pictures of the Great Leader and the Dear Leader touring the country, interspersed with dramas glorifying the Kims' revolution. One Pyongyang-based diplomat had once joked to me that the only way the North Korean people would learn that the queen of England or the president of the United States had died would be if the North Korean media published a letter of condolence from Kim Il Sung. Still, for a country whose thirst for international respect and recognition had been so evident on all my visits, showing CNN's funeral coverage was not an altogether surprising gesture, although the North Koreans had never asked permission or informed us beforehand, and we never discovered whether the critical on-air observations and comments from me and other analysts were actually translated into Korean. What we at CNN had viewed as a major TV coup was being presented to the North Korean people as a major propaganda triumph.

Eason and I found the country in a state of shock, with enormous throngs still pouring into Pyongyang to pay their respects and the official propaganda exhorting the masses to turn their grief into loyalty to Kim Jong Il, who, after appearing during the funeral activities, had again slipped from public view. But contrary to much of the speculation outside North Korea, I detected no sense of unusual tension or impending collapse. The resident diplomats with whom I spoke confirmed my impression that the succession so far appeared to be going smoothly, and that Kim Jong Il, by his dignified, grieving demeanor during the funeral, had acted in a manner entirely appropriate to North Korea's traditional, Confucian culture. Of course, over the long term, it was impossible to judge what would happen. But as I traveled around the country—the North Koreans, apparently as a gesture of gratitude for CNN's extensive coverage of the Kim funeral, arranged for us to spend three days driving over five hundred miles from east to west and north to south—I came away convinced that reports of the system's impending implosion were, at best, premature.

Our journey was a study in contrasts. In an aging but well-maintained Mercedes, we were driven along virtually deserted highways carved through jagged, rock-strewn mountains, thick forests, and rushing rivers. I had no idea how beautiful and unspoiled North Korea was. If they ever started a tourist industry, I thought to myself, it would swiftly become one of the most spectacular destinations in Asia. Yet, underscoring the country's economic woes, we passed more disabled trucks and jeeps by the side of the road than vehicles on the move. There appeared to be no public transport. Anyone who wanted to go anywhere had to walk; we frequently passed people trudging by the side of the road. Periodically we drove by villages where I could see farmers at work in the fields. Their dwellings were plain, even spartan, as was the clothing they wore.

The base for our excursion was a luxurious government guest house surrounded by high walls with armed guards at the gate in the Kumgang Mountains, not far from the demilitarized zone. Eason and I were each given an enormous suite full of books by Kim Il Sung and were treated to lavish meals with our hosts, who included senior North Korean officials, former diplomats, and even the mysterious Mr. Lee, who flew in from Vienna especially to see us. There was much political discussion as Eason and I lobbied intensively for an interview with Kim Jong Il. At one point, I produced a collection of the most damaging Western newspaper clips about the Dear Leader that I had been able to find before leaving for North Korea, articles describing him as a terrorist, a drunkard, a womanizer, a sadist, and a psycho. "If you want to rebut such allegations," I said to our hosts, "then you should allow us to interview the Dear Leader."

To my surprise, our hosts were not angry that I had made such a sacrilegious suggestion, but as always, they remained noncommittal about whether we would be able to see Kim Jong Il on this trip.

While I was unable to talk to ordinary people, and although all my observations were made from inside my luxurious bubble, I did come away with the clear impression that, while life for the ordinary citizens of North Korea was grim, the lack of transport and communication, the intensive propaganda, and the all-pervasive security apparatus made a Soviet-style collapse highly unlikely. Whatever outsiders thought of Kim Il Sung and Kim Jong Il, the North Koreans, having known nothing else, appeared to accept them. I was reminded of a comment my American diplomat friend Danny Russel had made to me on the phone from the U.S. Embassy in Seoul right after Kim Jong Il's appearance at his father's funeral. "This is a time of reckoning for all North Korea experts. Those who predicted the Dear Leader wouldn't last a week," he said sardonically, "have to leave the room. Next it will be the turn of those who thought he wouldn't last a month."

"It was the Dear Leader General Kim Jong Il himself who instructed me to take you sailing today," Party Secretary Kim Young Sun said. "This is his personal boat, and these sailors are his personal staff."

Eason and I were sitting in the stateroom of a sleek, fifty-foot yacht, with spotless, polished decks, and plush chairs and couches. We were waited on by a dozen North Korean navy sailors, immaculately turned out in their blue-and-white uniforms. The rest of the world may have believed that North Korea was on the brink of collapse, but the secretary of the country's ruling party was taking us fishing. The yacht plowed through the swells off the eastern Korean coast near Wonsan. We were in the same area where North Korean gunboats had captured the U.S. Navy spy ship U.S.S. *Pueblo* in 1968, setting off a major confrontation between Pyongyang and Washington. We, however, were being treated not as hostile intruders but as honored guests. After years of being viewed as a virtual spy by the Chinese government, it was a strange sensation to be feted as if I were the head of a fraternal socialist party. But the whole atmosphere underscored how little the North Koreans knew of the ways of Western journalists. We had been annointed "old friends" by Kim Il Sung himself during our final encounter, and our North Korean hosts apparently believed that they were not only carrying out the Great Leader's wishes by laying on such a lavish reception for us, but also ensuring good CNN coverage. I was gleaning fascinating insights about the lifestyle as well as the thinking of the North Korean elite. Our luxurious treatment didn't altogether surprise me, but I did not feel comfortable at the obvious way the North Koreans were trying to woo us. Yet to be deliberately rude or scornful of their hospitality to prove our journalistic independence seemed pointless, if not churlish. In their own awkward, unsubtle way, the North Koreans were opening up to us, even as they were trying to manipulate us. I was well aware of their game, but I felt that if playing along was the price for access to a country still widely viewed as one of the most menacing and least understood on earth, it was worth it. If any questions were raised about my fairness or objectivity, I was confident that my reports, which were totally under my control, would speak for themselves.

Secretary Kim escorted us onto the main deck, where our ever-helpful attendants handed us each a fishing rod, the bait already attached. Sitting in comfortable chairs, we dropped the lines overboard. Moments later, the fish began biting. As we reeled in our catch, the sailors took our rods and handed us more. I had never been a successful fisherman, having neither the inclination, luck, nor the necessary patience. Here, however, I was landing a fish with almost every drop of the line, and so was Eason. I ended up with seventeen catches, and he with twenty-nine, almost as many as our host. It was, like so much else in North Korea, almost miraculous. Secretary Kim laughed uproariously at our amazed exclamations. I suddenly remembered Kim Il Sung's hunting tale, how his soldiers chased bears into trees for him to shoot. For a fleeting moment, I had an image of North Korean frogmen floating beneath our ship, energetically pulling live fish from a container and attaching them to our hooks. Nothing else, it seemed, could explain our phenomenal success.

Soon after, we transferred to an even bigger vessel for lunch. A hundred feet long, it was the most luxurious yacht I had ever seen. Here, over Iranian caviar, foil-wrapped clams, lobster, and the fish we had caught, Kim Young Sun spoke with astonishing frankness about the current political situation. His central point was not only that the country remained stable, but that Kim Jong Il was determined to carry on his father's policy of seeking a rapprochement with the United States, including a nuclear deal. We pressed for a chance to meet the Dear Leader, but were told that he was observing a three-year mourning period for his father. "In Korea, we do not have the saying, 'The King is Dead, Long Live the King.'" he explained. "That is considered unseemly. But when the time is right, you will meet the Dear Leader."

At a time of tension and uncertainty, Secretary Kim's comments were major news; and despite the absence of a crew, with Eason using a handycam and acting as cameraman, we were able to send several stories from North Korean TV. Our videotape looked a little rough, but it was better than nothing. On our final night, officials from North Korean TV dropped a bombshell that epitomized the pitfalls and possibilities of dealing with the North Koreans. In a sign that their motives may have been financial as much as ideological, they announced that they were billing CNN $80,000 for the Kim Il Sung funeral coverage. We were speechless. Was that how the North Koreans handled their negotiations, even with Kim Il Sung's "old friends?" No wonder Assistant Secretary of State Robert Gallucci and his American negotiators were so consistently frustrated. And we had no U.N. sanctions to threaten, either. Eason, however, quickly came up with a response, declaring that CNN would bill them $80,000 for their rebroadcast of our funeral broadcast. The North Koreans realized they had been outwitted. They laughed and let the matter drop.

In Beijing, the Deng Xiaoping deathwatch now began in earnest. The CCTV pictures from the Chinese New Year celebrations of 1994 had made his declining health visible for all to see. Deng had survived far longer than I could have ever imagined, but his legendary toughness and resilience could not last forever. His passing promised to be the biggest China story since Tiananmen Square. He was the architect of the country's reforms, and through his southern tour, or *nanxun*—an act of extraordinary physical stamina for an eighty-eight-year-old—had saved his program from a concerted attempt by party ideologues to roll back the clock following the collapse of the Soviet Union. How long he lived, and the nature and timing of his death, would in many ways determine the fate of the remarkable process of change he had set in motion.

Among my press colleagues, Chinese friends and associates, as well as diplomatic and business contacts, speculation about the state of Deng's health began to overshadow other topics of conversation. For me, such contemplation was mixed with very practical concerns. As a reporter for a twenty-four-hour-a-day television service that now billed itself as "the world's most important network," I could not afford to be unreachable or unprepared for his passing. Like the wire services, where competitive success was measured in minutes and even seconds, I lived with the chronic anxiety that Deng might die when I was not in a position to go on the air almost immediately. I remembered hearing a story, when I first moved to Hong Kong, about a Beijing-based European reporter who decided to take a vacation in January 1976, and thus missed Zhou Enlai's death on January 8 of that tumultuous year. Cutting short his holiday, he raced back to Beijing and attempted to resume his break in April, only to be away during the first Tiananmen Square riot on April 5, which resulted in the ouster of Deng Xiaoping. Returning again, he attempted another vacation in midsummer, and this time managed to miss the Tangshan earthquake in late July, which killed hundreds of thousands of people. After interrupting his holiday for the third time, he made a final attempt in September, and was thus out of China for the biggest story of all, Mao's death. The tale may have beeen exaggerated in the retelling, but I was haunted by fears of suffering a similar fate. I tried never to leave home without my beeper and became obsessive about checking the Xinhua News Agency ticker and the Western wire services throughout the day

I knew as well that CNN headquarters would want saturation coverage from the moment Deng died, prompting me to put together in advance a series of feature and analysis pieces for feeding to Atlanta that would be available for air within minutes of the announcement. Like all reporters, I had long ago written and edited an obituary of the Chinese leader, which sat on the International Desk's HFR—"hold for release"—shelf in Atlanta. My only frustration was that, since Deng refused to die, every few months I was compelled to rewrite the ending. My colleagues and I began to joke that Deng himself was on the HFR shelf, but the Politburo would not allow him to be released. The other Western TV correspondents in Beijing faced similar concerns, and together we devised an elaborate "Deng death-pool coverage plan." This included prebooking, and paying for, shared transmission facilities to be on permanent standby at CCTV, and an elaborate system for sharing rotations on satellite feeds so that all of us would have an opportunity to do live shots once the news broke.

None of this would be of any use, of course, unless we could figure out what was actually happening to Deng, and here the job was much harder. Periodically rumors of a deterioration in his condition would sweep through Beijing, with some of them ending up in print, the stories usually citing "reliable Chinese sources," "Chinese military sources," "medical sources," "senior Chinese sources," and so on. A Japanese newspaper reported Deng hospitalized in such bad shape that doctors would not allow his designated heir, Jiang Zemin, to visit. A South Korean paper also claimed he was in the hospital. The Asian *Wall Street Journal* declared that Deng was in a coma and confidently predicted he would not live past March 1995. Invariably such reports produced a series of anxious phone calls from my editors in Atlanta demanding immediate verification or clarification. I remained deeply skeptical about all such "exclusives." Every foreign journalist in Beijing had Chinese sources and contacts, some with high-level connections, possibly even with accurate insights into Deng's condition. But there was simply no way to be certain. I decided that unless I felt comfortable that a person offering inside information on Deng's health had actually seen Deng or had meaningful access to those taking care of him, I would not give such reports the worldwide credibility that came with an airing on CNN. I urged the company's newswriters to ignore or downplay similar stories on the wires: the risk was too great, not only of being wrong but of being manipulated. Floating rumors about Deng's health to depress share prices, for example, was a common ploy of speculators in the volatile Hong Kong and Taipei stock markets. Based on my experience as a fledgling China watcher at the time of the death of Zhou Enlai and Chairman Mao, I remained convinced that it would be impossible to cover up Deng's death: an official announcement would come quickly. When it did, I told Atlanta, I would report it. Until then, I vowed to stay away from specific rumors, although I would not hesitate to report on the impact all the rumors were having on the country's political situation.

The more the Deng deathwatch consumed me, the more I thought back to 1976. For all of China's much-vaunted openness in the intervening years, I was struck by how little hard, credible information about Deng's condition was actually available to reporters. The health and internal maneuverings of China's most senior leaders remained cloaked in as much secrecy now as they had been when I first started my career that year in Hong Kong. The crisis sparked by Chairman Mao's death that September, which, I recalled with anxiety, I had missed because I was on vacation (hardly a comforting omen), had produced intense political infighting which went on for two years, until Deng Xiaoping eclipsed Mao's designated heir. When he became paramount leader in 1978, Deng had been well aware of the dangers of the succession process. Much of his energy since then had been devoted to arranging for a smooth succession when he left the scene: he designated an heir, eased conservative members of the old guard out of their leadership positions, and sought to institutionalize the most important of his economic reforms. But even before Tiananmen, Deng had been forced by the hard-liners to dump his first annointed successor, Hu Yaobang. The upheaval in 1989 led to the ouster of his second protégé, Zhao Ziyang, and the third choice, Jiang Zemin, remained an uninspiring figure, utterly lacking Deng's prestige and national political base. Like all Leninist parties, the Chinese Communist Party did not have an institutionalized mechanism for a legal and orderly succession. From Liu Shaoqi and Lin Biao, purged by Chairman Mao, to Hua Guofeng, pushed out by Deng himself after Mao's death, to Hu and Zhao, the history of the People's Republic was littered—figuratively, and sometimes literally—with the bodies of unsuccessful successors. How ironic that the plans of Deng Xiaoping, the great reformer, should meet a similar fate.

It was ironic, too, that I had begun my career as a China hand by chronicling the demise of Chairman Mao, and now found myself living through an eerily similar experience. Events seemed to have come full circle. I had devoted virtually my entire adult life to China. It had been a romance, often unrequited, but which had often inspired, always stimulated, frequently puzzled, and sometimes even horrified me. Now, two decades later, older, wiser, and shorn of illusions, I discovered that my passion was fading. Deng Xiaoping was the last of the old revolutionaries whose exploits a half century earlier had drawn me to China. With his departure from the scene, China would be a very different place. It was, perhaps, time to consider moving on.

The last time I saw my friend Dave Schweisberg, UPI's Beijing bureau chief, was in November 1993, when Chinese Foreign Minister Qian Qichen held a news conference at the Great Hall of the People. Dave was in his usual good form, cynical and wisecracking. As we left, we exchanged the latest Deng death rumors and agreed to get together for lunch soon. Two days later, Dave collapsed and died of a massive heart attack. He was thirty-nine years old, and his death shook me to the core. Of all the reporters in Beijing, he was my oldest friend, a soulmate and collaborator. He was a larger-than-life figure, pounding out the news all day and playing rock 'n' roll with his Chinese musician friends all night, drink and cigarette in hand. That he should die before reaching forty, while Deng Xiaoping and the other octogenarian leaders we so despised lived on, seemed horribly unjust.

"It's typical Schweisberg," one friend consoled me, as we reminisced afterward. "Deng Xiaoping must have died, and Dave, true to form, has just beaten everyone else to the story." It was the kind of comment Schweisberg would have enjoyed.

With Dave's death, I found myself thinking more and more about leaving China. For me, his passing was not only a terrible shock, an almost inconceivable tragedy, it also came to symbolize in some way the changing of the guard already under way in the Beijing press corps. Like me, Dave had been drawn to China before it opened up, captivated by the romance and mystery of penetrating a distant and closed society. Both of us, I felt, were part of a pioneering generation of journalists for whom China was not merely a story but a calling, a state of mind, sometimes even an obsession. Now a new crop of reporters was arriving. They were undeniably talented, but they seemed to me products of a later and different time. China was now less an exotic, often unfathomable destination than simply another assignment for an aspiring foreign correspondent on the way up the career ladder. I was hardly old, but among this new wave, I occasionally felt like a holdover from a vanishing era—one of the few reporters still around who had been through the ordeal of setting up a China bureau from scratch, in a time when resident journalists were still something of a rarity and in a country that, less than a dozen years removed from Mao's death, was more suspicious of foreigners than it was now. I decided that I would see the story through to Deng's death, and then I would leave. I was not prepared to stay on endlessly, so I hoped the old man would cooperate.

A few days after Dave's death, friends and colleagues gathered in a small, seedy bar—of the kind he so enjoyed—to mourn his passing and celebrate his life. The place was packed with reporters, diplomats, rockers, and dissidents—the full range of his very varied world. At the table next to me, I noticed someone with a familiar face. Looking closely, I realized it was Wei Jingsheng, the leading figure of the 1978–79 Democracy Wall movement, recently released after fourteen and a half years in prison for "counterrevolutionary activities." I had been planning to look him up, but Dave, as usual, had beaten me to the punch. At one of our last meetings, he had laughed uproariously as he described taking Wei, just out of prison, for lunch at McDonald's. Now I walked over, introduced myself to Wei, and exchanged phone numbers. We agreed to meet soon. Going home that night, I murmured a final thanks to Dave. Even from the grave, he was still sharing his sources with me.

After two long meals and an extended conversation on camera, I understood why the government was afraid of Wei Jingsheng. He was unlike any other Chinese dissident I had encountered. I had only seen photographs of him, plus the grainy Chinese TV film of his 1979 trial, which I had narrated for an NBC News spot. Then he had seemed a tall, gangly youth. It was hard to imagine that while I had traveled the world, switched jobs, married, started a family, moved to Beijing, lived through Tiananmen Square, and entered middle age, Wei had sat alone in a squalid Chinese prison cell. Now his hair was gray and his body bore the scars of more than a decade of suffering and deprivation—no sunlight, no vegetables, rotten food, and, above all, no human contact. For fourteen and a half years, he had been held in solitary confinement. Yet his mind remained clear, his spirit unbroken, his commitment to promoting democratic change in China and his courageous willingness to continue to defy the government, as well as his sense of humor, intact. Wei was no ivory-tower intellectual. A former soldier and electrician, he seemed to have an instinctive feel for ordinary people in China and a way of expressing himself that would, I suspected, be very compelling if he were ever to find a public platform in China. If he were allowed to organize, I suspected Wei Jingsheng would make a formidable adversary.

Over dinner at an Indian restaurant and a subsequent lunch at a Scandinavian-run joint-venture hotel, both carefully watched by plainclothes security agents, we talked at length about his prison experiences and his views on the future of China. Despite the vastly different courses our lives had taken, I found him uninhibited and much easier to relate to than most Chinese officials I had encountered. Wei was well aware that after the repression at Tiananmen Square, a mass movement in the streets to demand political change would be almost impossible. Instead, acknowledging that the economic reforms that had occurred during his prison years were themselves helping to open up Chinese society, he hoped to establish links with other activists while articulating more modest, short-term goals, such as free speech and a freer press. Between sips of red wine, which he clearly enjoyed, he was scathing about the government's claim that Western concepts of human rights did not apply to China. "There is no such thing as Asian human rights or Western human rights, or human rights for black-haired people and human rights for blond people," he told me. "That way of talking merely reinforces racist ideology that classifies Chinese people as an inferior race. This kind of dogma is ridiculous. It makes no sense."

With his easy grin and quiet manner, Wei hardly looked like a man who'd just emerged from a decade and a half in the Chinese Gulag. As he described the suffering he had undergone, I tried to imagine how I would react in a similar situation. It was beyond comprehension. Wei said that many other inmates had cracked under the strain, but that he had remained defiant, although not bitter, to the end. "I thought it was worth it. At least I could let the government know that not all the Chinese people are soft and weak and easy to bully, and also let the people know that there are still some of us who are not afraid of any hardship or pain who are trying to do something. So China still has hope."

Despite intense police surveillance and warnings to cease contact with foreign reporters, Wei continued to speak out, apparently unconcerned about the possibility of being sent back to jail. In March of 1994, he held an unannounced meeting with John Shattuck, the U.S. Assistant Secretary of State for Human Rights, in advance of a visit to Beijing by Secretary of State Warren Christopher. Within a month, he was rearrested. For over a year and a half, he was held without charge by a government that evidently felt no obligation to make his whereabouts, state of health, or legal circumstances known either to his family or the rest of the world. The disappearance of China's most famous dissident was a big story. Like most of my colleagues in the Beijing press corps, I was angry and upset at his fate and in no mood to let the government get away with acting as if he had disappeared from the face of the earth. Every few weeks, I did another spot on his plight, hoping that continual public pressure would prompt the authorities to reveal Wei's fate. Eventually, after being held for twenty months without charges, he was sentenced in a closed trial to fourteen years in prison for sedition. It was shocking to imagine Wei going through the same ordeal again. It was a terrible indictment of the Chinese system that such a man could spend virtually his entire adult life behind bars.

With Wei's arrest, a government campaign against dissidents, many of whom had begun testing the limits of official tolerance again in early 1994, shifted into high gear. Hardly a week went by without a phone call to CNN or another news organization from agitated friends or family members of newly detained activists. One of the most prominent targets was Wang Dan, the Tiananmen Square student leader who had been sentenced to four years in jail for his role in the 1989 demonstrations. Released in early 1993 as part of China's failed effort to improve its international image and win the rights to stage the 2000 Olympic Games in Beijing, Wang Dan had immediately resumed his political activity, working with other dissidents and speaking out. I had always found him the most thoughtful and intelligent of the protest leaders, an impression that did not change when we met again following his release. Jail had aged him, but he remained unrepentant about the movement he had helped to create five years earlier. When he handed me his name card, I noticed that in the place of a job description were the Chinese characters for "Free Man." However, Wang, like Wei Jingsheng, now recognized that the times had changed. Taking to the streets was no longer an option. Instead he called on the government to allow open political debate in order to give a rapidly changing Chinese society a safety valve that would reduce the chances of a future explosion.

"I openly admit that I am part of the political opposition," he told me. "But I operate openly within the bounds of the law. People definitely hold diverse views within China. The first thing the government should do is to allow these different political views to exist, and give them space to operate, because there are now a lot of social contradictions that can only be brought out by an opposition group. If people's concerns cannot be openly raised and redressed, they might resort to irresponsible tactics that are harmful to the society."

It was a message that the government did not want to hear. Preventing dissidents from speaking to reporters became a top police priority. Wang was followed constantly, his movements were restricted, and he found himself regularly hauled in for interrogation by public-security officers. Frequently police cut off access to the dingy apartment block where he lived, making it impossible for journalists like us to visit him. Depriving dissidents of the oxygen of publicity proved to be a very effective way of muzzling those whose opinions the government didn't like, without actually having to put someone behind bars. My print colleagues were still occasionally able to talk to dissidents on the phone. But for TV reporters, lack of physical access meant no pictures, and no pictures usually meant no story—the always daunting limitations of the medium.

The effectiveness of this government tactic was brought home to me in the spring of 1994, when I tried repeatedly to arrange an on-camera interview with Ding Zilin, a professor of philosophy at the People's University in Beijing. Her seventeen-year-old son had been killed by the army on the night of June 3, 1989, and she had emerged as an outspoken defender of the interests of families who had lost loved ones during the massacre. Aware that her phone was tapped and her apartment was closely watched, my friend Bob Benjamin, a *Baltimore Sun* correspondent, asked a young student from Singapore who was working part-time for him as an unofficial translator to make a discreet visit to Ding and ask her on our behalf if she would be willing to do a joint interview. Ding readily agreed, and in a cloak-and-dagger arrangement straight from a B-movie, she and her husband arranged to meet the student, who was herself ethnic Chinese and thus able, we thought, to mingle unobtrusively with the locals at a store outside the campus a few days later. The plan was for the three of them to take a taxi to a Pizza Hut near the compound where we lived, and then switch to my car. I would drive them into the compound's underground parking lot, take them straight into the elevator, and up to Mitch's flat, where the camera would be ready to roll. On the morning of the rendezvous, I waited for them outside Pizza Hut, but to my steadily growing anxiety, no one showed up. Some hours later, the Singaporean student returned alone. Even though Bob, the student, and I had never discussed it on the phone, the police had known of the entire plan. When the student arrived at the store, Ding's husband walked by her, motioned to several plainclothes security men, and walked on. A moment later, a burly young man sidled over to the student and roughly ordered her to get lost. So intense was the police surveillance of Ding that they had become aware of our efforts from the moment the Singaporean student made contact with her. The interview never happened.

The government's campaign against Beijing's tiny community of dissidents was a reflection of its extreme sensitivity toward anything it perceived as a threat to the Communist Party's authority or legitimacy, not only in domestic terms but in foreign affairs as well. It was no coincidence that Wei Jingsheng's detention and the stepped-up measures to silence other critics—a drive that effectively neutralized virtually all prominent dissidents for the rest of my stay in China—came close on the heels of a visit to Beijing by Secretary of State Warren Christopher.

Christopher's three-day trip in March of 1994 was intended to press China for concessions on human rights in the run-up to the annual debate in Washington over renewing China's most favored nation trading status. Instead I watched in astonishment as Chinese leaders lectured the secretary as if he were an errant schoolboy. It was an extraordinary spectacle, which Christopher later described to associates as his worst experience as Secretary of State. But it underscored the increasingly belligerent and intransigent tone that China was adopting on a host of issues affecting its relations with the rest of the world, a prickly and truculent attitude driven largely by a rising tide of Chinese nationalism. In part, the phenomenon was the product of an understandable desire among many Chinese for their dynamic, economically vibrant nation to take its rightful place in the world, and resentment that foreign pressure, especially from the United States, was denying China the international respect and dignity to which they believed it was entitled. U.S. opposition to Beijing's bid to host the 2000 Olympics (China lost) and to China's swift admission to the newly established World Trade Organization were seen by many people as evidence of an American policy to thwart China's emergence on the international stage. Christopher's sanctimonious tone—in his stops in Asia prior to arriving in Beijing, he had declared his intention to lecture the Chinese on human rights and demand concessions—didn't help the situation.

But there was a more volatile and sinister element at work too. The global collapse of communism had left the Chinese regime with no credible ideology to justify its continued hold on power. Increasingly the leaders in Beijing were turning to nationalism to shore up their rule. In public statements, in the mass media, in educational institutions, the government lost no opportunity to contrast China's past humiliations at the hands of foreigners with its present achievements, deliberately fostering a siege mentality, in which all problems could be blamed on sinister outside forces. The struggle within the leadership to succeed the failing Deng Xiaoping exacerbated the phenomenon. "In the midst of succession politics," one Chinese journalist friend told me over lunch, "no leader can afford to look weak in dealing with domestic challenges or foreign governments, especially the U.S. They all have to wave the flag."

Lynne and I noticed the changed mood on the streets, which now bubbled with an undercurrent of assertive, in-your-face nationalism. Some episodes were petty, such as when a Canadian friend asked a taxi driver to put out a cigarette, only to be greeted with a torrent of abuse and the declaration that "This is China. I am Chinese. You foreigners can't tell me what to do!"

Increasingly, the government began to describe all international criticism or pressure on human rights, or most other issues, for that matter, as a devious ploy to weaken China, and denounced political dissent at home for undermining China's unity and opening the door to new humiliations at the hands of foreigners. It was an ugly atmosphere. Strident nationalism translated into a harder line on a host of thorny issues: from deliberately provocative Chinese responses to U.S. calls for the release of dissidents; to stalling, obfuscation, nonenforcement, or blatant noncompliance on agreements governing copyright protection, market access, prison-labor exports, and other trade issues; to continuing violations of international arms-control agreements, to hard-line attitudes on Tibet, Taiwan, and Hong Kong. The ultimate symbol of this new attitude was the erection of a huge digital clock in Tiananmen Square to count off the hours, minutes, and even seconds until the return of Hong Kong to Chinese sovereignty on July 1, 1997—a gesture of triumphalism designed to stir up patriotic fervor as well as remind the Chinese people of the wrongs done to China by the British imperialists who colonized Hong Kong a century and a half earlier.

Brandishing a BB gun and a knife, Feng Huimin stood on an apartment balcony in Shanghai, making his last stand. His neighbors had long ago disappeared. With its gaping holes, cracked masonry, broken glass, and fraying wires, the building, the only one left in what was once a small neighborhood, looked as if it had taken a direct artillery hit. But Feng Huimin intended to remain in his tiny apartment, determined not to become the latest victim of a construction boom that was forcing hundreds of thousands of Shanghai residents to leave their homes.

My crew and I encountered Feng on a walk through the center of Shanghai in late 1994. We had gone there to do a series of reports on the city's ambitious plans to make itself the financial center of Asia, the engine that would pull the Chinese heartland, the Yangzi River Delta, toward modernization. Central to the plan was a massive redevelopment scheme, in which real-estate companies, mainly from Hong Kong, were paying the local government billions of dollars for the right to bulldoze the old colonial-style neighborhoods in the city center and replace them with shopping malls, apartment houses, luxury hotels, and offices.

For Feng Huimin and a half million other longtime Shanghai residents, however, the city's ambitions had produced only heartache. "They want to sell this piece of land to some foreign company and move us to the outskirts of the city," he said with bitterness. "It's unfair. My family has been here for generations. Now they're just moving us out without a word of explanation." Even in a society that was used to arbitrary decisions by the state, the evictions were generating intense anger and bitterness. "The situation now in China," Feng continued, "is that a small group of people are getting rich, and the rest of us suffer."

Feng Huimin had put his finger on what was becoming a new theme in my own reporting: the dark side of China's economic miracle. The gap between those benefiting from the reforms and those being left behind was growing, and no amount of consciously stoked nationalist ardor could disguise it. I could see it not only in the plight of people like Feng Huimin and the vast number of city dwellers uprooted by urban renewal, but also in the growing numbers of vagrants and beggars on the streets. Many of these were peasants and migrant workers from the countryside who were fleeing poverty, high-handed local officials, arbitrary tax levies, and increasing instability, in search of jobs and a better life in the cities. Some estimates put the total number of this floating population at over 100 million. Enough were absorbed into construction or factory jobs spawned by the boom to prevent a widespread social explosion, but many others became part of a vast, restive urban underclass, forced to eke out a living in sweatshops or to resort to crime, which now surged to epidemic proportions.

Criminal gangs, kidnapping, drug use, and prostitution—unheard of at the time of my first visit in 1973—became a common feature of the Chinese landscape. The newspapers, now competing for readers, were full of lurid, sensational reports of serial killers, depraved cops, vice dens, and fraud schemes. Occasionally such stories were juxtaposed with announcements about new campaigns against crime and corruption. All I had to do, however, was talk to Chinese friends forced to pay bribes to get a new apartment, or foreign business executives trapped in a nightmare of red tape and grasping local officials, or walk through the lobby of a major hotel and notice the attractive, single Chinese women crowding the lobby, or drive past the profusion of "barber shops" featuring young, miniskirted masseuses that had opened for business just two blocks from my apartment in Beijing, to see that the talk of a crackdown was empty.

Every day, it seemed, brought a new scandal to light. The most controversial revolved around the suicide of Beijing Deputy Mayor Wang Baosen, who shot himself in April 1995. I first heard of the suicide from one of my oldest Chinese friends in Hong Kong, a longtime senior official in the Xinhua News Agency. My friend had grown increasingly disillusioned with the direction the system he had served for so many years was taking. He was strongly in favor of the reforms, but sickened by the abuses they had spawned, and fed up with the uninspired apparatchiks and technocrats now presiding over the government. "This is definitely connected to some kind of corruption case," he told me as he pointed out the story of Wang's death in a Hong Kong newspaper. "I am sure of it."

My friend was right. Although the Beijing press almost completely ignored the story, rumors and leaks floating around the capital made clear that Wang's suicide was connected to a huge corruption scandal. It involved massive payoffs from Hong Kong real-estate developers to members of the Beijing city government and the Communist Party organization that had authority to approve many of the construction projects that were, in this time of explosive economic growth, transforming the city's skyline. So egregious was the corruption that the central government, led by President and Communist Party General-Secretary Jiang Zemin, ordered the ouster and detention of Beijing Party chief Chen Xitong, one of the most prominent supporters of the army crackdown in Tiananmen Square in 1989. At the time, Chen had railed against so-called "decadence" from the West. To me and to many Beijing citizens, there was a certain satisfying irony in the fact that Chen met his political end because, for all his ideological pretensions, he had been exposed as just another corrupt Chinese official. But the case underlined how extensively the rot had permeated China's power structure, exacerbating the Communist Party's already severe crisis of identity and legitimacy. Even as the boom continued, the question of what kind of China was being created became increasingly disturbing.

His shoulder-length hair flying back and forth, sweat pouring off his face, He Yong pounded his guitar and leaned into the microphone. "We live in a garbage dump," he howled. "People live like insects, with everyone struggling and stealing. We swallow our consciences and shit ideology."

In the auditorium in Tianjin, sixty miles east of Beijing, ten thousand young people, many of them dancing in the aisles, roared their approval, while the police looked on benignly. If this had been a protest rally, the security forces would have never let it happen, but it was only a rock concert. In the paradox that was mid-1990s China, what would just a few years earlier have been regarded by both the authorities and the foreign press corps as a dramatic sign of youthful rebellion occurred almost without notice.

A new CNN Beijing bureau cameraman shot the He Yong concert. Wenchun Fan, a tall, quiet, extremely capable Chinese-American who had grown up in Beijing and earned a degree from Beijing University, had joined the bureau to replace Mitch Farkas. After seven years, Mitch had decided to follow the Chinese fad and *xia hai*, or "jump into the sea." He purchased his own camera gear and went into business for himself as a Beijing-based freelancer. It was the right move for him: he would be his own boss and would make much more money than CNN could ever offer, but I was very sorry to see him go. We had been through a lot together. Now I was the only one left of the trio that started CNN Beijing and put the bureau on the map. But I, too, would soon be gone. I was already among the longest-serving Western correspondents in Beijing. Around the time of Mitch's departure, I told Eason Jordan that I wanted to leave for good in mid-1995. That would make eight years as CNN's Beijing bureau chief. It was, I felt, long enough. I couldn't wait forever for Deng Xiaoping to die.

One of my final projects was an in-depth look at the state of Chinese culture as the twentieth century drew to a close. It was a topic that had long intrigued me, and one I was convinced might provide a more revealing glimpse at China's future direction than any number of stories about the pecking order in the Politburo. Over the course of several months, Tim Schwarz, Wenchun, Rebecca MacKinnon, bureau assistant Miranda Kuo, and I sought out writers, rock stars, directors, painters, actors, playwrights, and filmmakers. Unlike in our attempts to interview the dissidents, we encountered almost no official obstacles, even though we made all the arrangements ourselves without informing a single *waiban*. What we found was a cultural scene in the midst of change so profound that it challenged the West's conventional image of China as a country of brutal dictators, beleaguered dissidents, and corrupt deal-makers.

For decades, Chinese culture had been shaped by Chairman Mao's dictum that there was no such thing as art for art's sake, that all art must serve politics. That explained why every cultural event I witnessed on my earliest trips to China—the model revolutionary operas, the movies extolling the heroic Communist Party guerrillas, the children in their classrooms singing the praises of the Chairman—were devoted to furthering the Maoist cause. It had not been an accident that Mao called his last great attempt to transform the very essence of China the Cultural Revolution. Now, though, it seemed to me that the country was in the midst of another cultural revolution, this one driven not by ideology but by money and consumerism on the one hand and a deep sense of social alienation on the other.

The cultural commissars had not, however, entirely disappeared. Many artists still found it neccessary to walk a tightrope between the conflicting pressures of money, politics, and personal vision. One of those was Zhang Yimou, China's most acclaimed film director, whose films *Red Sorghum, Raise the Red Lantern, To Live,* and *Judou* had garnered kudos around the world, with two of them being nominated for Academy Awards. His romance with his long-time leading lady, the beautiful actress Gong Li, had captured the imagination of tabloids across Asia. We caught up with Zhang on the set of *Shanghai Triad*, a gangster epic set in the corrupt and free-wheeling 1930s. Wearing a padded green Chinese army greatcoat to protect him against the chill of the unheated studio, Zhang spelled out the theme of his new film.

"I feel that the reality of that time actually resembles China now," he told me. "In China today, Beijing, Shanghai, Canton, Shenzhen, and other cities resemble 1930s Shanghai, where everybody was flocking to make money, thinking only of how to get rich. This film explores what's behind this kind of condition." But Zhang insisted it was wrong to see his films in purely political terms. "Chinese society has been a political society, so if a film is going to realistically discuss the lives of people, you can't possibly omit the political backdrop. But I don't make films for political reasons. I believe that art and politics are different. Art should not serve politics. Art is a reflection of humanity, a reflection of a person's inner emotions, character, and heart. The individual is the primary focus of my films."

Climbing through the rafters of the cavernous and drafty set, Wenchun and Tim took pictures as Zhang painstakingly shot and reshot a scene of a gangster bathing in his luxurious mansion. Assistants sprayed mist, through which we could see the naked bodies of a hoodlum and his servant boy sitting on the edge of a brilliant orange hot tub. In a quiet voice, Zhang coached the shivering actors after each take, doing the scene over and over again until his finely honed cinematic vision was satisfied. The film was in its final stages, but there had been a point a few months earlier when it was not certain if it would be made at all. Initially a Sino-French co-production, work came to a halt when the Chinese Film Bureau banned Zhang from making any films with foreign partners, in retaliation for his decision a year earlier to release without first submitting to government censors the film *To Live*, a bleak picture of Chinese life that, despite Zhang's denials, some officials interpreted as a veiled criticism of contemporary Chinese society. By apologizing, obtaining funds from a domestic film studio, and confining himself to a gangster epic, Zhang Yimou was able to win official blessing for *Shanghai Triad*. It was the kind of balancing act that he and other directors had to pull off with virtually every project.

For Zhang Yuan, though, there had never been an official blessing. Operating on a shoestring budget from a small, cramped basement apartment in Beijing, the thirty-one-year-old Zhang was one of a new breed of wholly independent Chinese filmmakers who continued to produce movies despite an official ban on their work. A stocky man with a shock of curly hair, Zhang smoked continuously as we spoke one chilly morning. "Our working conditions are very difficult," he conceded, pointing to piles of film cans and editing equipment that mingled with teacups, ash trays, and cheap plastic chairs in the scruffy room. "But through my films, I like to reflect the living conditions of the people today, to show the kind of place we are really living in." Zhang earned the ire of the government with his film *Beijing Bastards*, a semi-documentary film about alienated Chinese youth full of drinking, swearing, and anger.

"*Beijing Bastards* doesn't really have a story or complete plot," Zhang explained. "It's about the pain and suffering most young people have while seeking meaning and purpose in their lives. But I am not a politician. I am not using this film to incite rebellion or achieve a political goal. I am using film simply to express my reactions to the world." Although it was banned in China, Zhang managed to have *Beijing Bastards* shown abroad, where the film acquired something of a cult following. That overseas connection, along with private screenings inside the country, had enabled Zhang to continue his work, which involved plans for a rock video, a documentary on Tiananmen Square, and a gay love story.

From underground filmmakers, we moved on to avant-garde theater companies. In a small warehouse, the Beijing Experimental

Theatre Troupe was producing a play called *I Love You XXX*, in which for two hours the cast repeated the words "I love" against a bewildering array of backdrops and sound effects. Among them were film clips of Mao Zedong greeting hysterical Red Guards in Tiananmen Square during the Cultural Revolution, and a tape of the Beatles song "Revolution," in which John Lennon sings, "You say you want a revolution, well, we all want to change the world. But if you go carrying pictures of Chairman Mao, you ain't gonna make it with anyone anyhow." Organized, funded, and performed outside official channels, productions like *I Love You XXX* or the equally controversial *Related to AIDS*, in which the entire cast, dressed up in chef's costumes, made traditional Chinese dumplings on stage while never once mentioning the word AIDS, were as far removed from the revolutionary epics I saw on my first China trip as it was possible to get. I had no doubt that a vibrant, independent culture increasingly detached from Communist Party control was emerging. But in a country where people now seemed far more interested in money and personal fulfillment than politics, it was not explicitly a culture of protest either, which was why the authorities allowed it to exist in a gray area, not officially sanctioned, but not the target of a crackdown either.

The rock scene epitomized these contradictory reactions. The music of punk singer He Yong and other rockers represented China's post–Tiananmen Square generation. Disillusioned with politics and the corruption, greed, and ugliness around them, they were no longer seeking to transform society but simply trying to find meaning and direction in their own lives. One afternoon, I went to talk about the phenomenon with disc jockey Zhang Youdai, a soft-spoken young man with shoulder-length hair who hosted his own show on a government-run radio station in Beijing, introducing both Chinese and Western rock to audiences numbering in the millions. "The uniqueness of rock 'n' roll is that it expresses young people's thinking," he said, sitting in his small apartment with shelf after shelf of CDs lining the wall. "It talks about their emotions, their culture, their livelihoods, their relations with their parents. That's most important—not social and political issues."

It was a far cry from the spring of 1989, when He Yong and Cui Jian (China's best-known rocker) lent their voices to the protesting students in Tiananmen Square. Six years later, Cui Jian, whose song

"Nothing to My Name" had been something of an anthem for the demonstrators, was still the most political of China's rockers. "Rock 'n' roll must confront reality," he told Tim Schwarz while taking a break from rehearsing with his band. "It must confront society and reflect the dissatisfactions of young people. This is not a job. It is a duty." In the title song from his just-released album *Eggs Under the Red Flag*, Cui sang, "We are wholly submissive, like eggs under the red flag. The revolution continues. The old men are still in power." Such angry, almost bizarre lyrics continued to pose problems for Cui, making it difficult, although not impossible, for him to secure permission to perform. But rock 'n' roll was now becoming increasingly accepted, because, with the exception of Cui Jian, in China's new consumer culture, most rock singers were staying away from politics. Instead, many were rushing to sign contracts with Hong Kong and Taiwan record companies, becoming slicker and more professional, and in the process, losing their edge. "All these bands are part of the commercial culture," Zhang Youdai told me as he slipped a CD into his expensive Japanese player. "Most rock bands are looking for a way to make a living. They have to sign with labels. And then China won't have any underground bands."

That Chinese society no longer confined such art forms to the underground and was now able to tolerate an astonishingly wide variety of music, film, and writing, marked an important step foward. Yet with government subsidies for traditional arts such as classical Beijing Opera or the ballet shrinking as the state raced to embrace the market, with pop singers signing lucrative contracts, and writers abandoning serious literature to compose TV ads or soap-opera scripts, the commercial co-option of Chinese culture was a mixed blessing. One afternoon, I spent several hours talking with the well-known writer Dai Qing, who had spent ten months in jail after the June 1989 crackdown. "Right now, I think there is a kind of sickness of heart in China," she told me. "Many of my friends and colleagues who, in the past, would have done serious work are now just money-happy. They do something that has no value but pays well, such as writing commercials. We didn't like the restrictions of the Communist Party, but we don't like the restrictions of commercialization either."

Still, what was most striking for me as I wrote the scripts for a documentary I called *China's Cultural Revolution* was the extent to which Chinese culture was no longer evolving in response to the dictates of the Party commissars, but instead to broader trends in Chinese society—a desire among people to find meaning in their own lives, a yearning for self-expression, a search for answers to the moral, spiritual, and intellectual questions that arose side by side with the country's economic success, but for which the Communist Party offered no answers. The Party had made it clear that searching for those answers in overt, public political activity would be met by fierce repression, as Wei Jingsheng had discovered—to his sorrow. But in private, there were almost no limits on what Chinese could say to each other or to foreigners, and if the search were channeled into cultural expression, as long as it stayed away from explicit challenges to Party rule, it was, increasingly, tolerated by the authorities. In Wenchun's videotape of the He Yong concert for our project, there was one scene where a young man writhed ecstatically in his seat while waving his fingers in the V-for-victory sign, and the singer concluded his number by raising a clenched-fist salute. I had not seen such a gesture from a Chinese youth since Tiananmen Square. But even stripped of its political meaning, at a concert dominated by commercialism, I still felt the music and the passionate response to it represented a challenge to the established order. A whole generation of young people were proclaiming their right to be themselves, the core of an enormous, hugely popular counterculture, in which the Chinese Communist Party appeared to be condemned to eventual irrelevance.

In mid-May of 1995, forty-five well-known Chinese scientists and intellectuals issued a public appeal to the government, asking that it lift the "counterrevolutionary verdict" on those who had taken part in the Tiananmen Square protests six years earlier. In a climate of political repression and social ferment, sharpened by the approaching death of Deng Xiaoping and the continuing jockeying for power among his potential successors, it was a daring and provocative gesture of protest. The signatories included the designer of China's first atomic bomb, members of the Chinese Academy of Sciences, the country's most prestigious research institute, former university presidents, former editors of the *People's Daily*, and leading dissidents like Wang Dan. Representing the tip of the iceberg of disillusionment with the country's political structure, it was the most important act of protest since the pro-democracy demonstrations of 1989.

The petition was faxed to several Western news bureaus in Beijing. I was working at my desk on the script about avant-garde art for my culture project when I learned about it. For my print colleagues, a copy of the document and a brief telephone conversation with some of those who had signed it was enough to write a story. TV, however, required pictures. I was certain that the security services would move against the petition organizers as soon as the appeal was made public, at a minimum cutting off their phones, preventing them from meeting with journalists, and possibly even placing them in detention. If we wanted to do a spot, we had to move at once. Although Wenchun, the new bureau shooter, was six feet, six inches tall, as an ethnic Chinese, he was less conspicuous than anyone else in the office. I asked him to drive out to the university district in northwest Beijing in the hope of contacting the man who had drafted the petition, a retired professor of physics named Xu Liangying. An hour later, the phone rang. "The weather is clear right now," Wenchun said obliquely, "but it is expected to cloud over very quickly. Let's do this right away."

Tim and I grabbed the gear and raced across the city to meet Wenchun at the Yanshan Hotel opposite the People's University. It was here that I had fled with Cynde after police broke up the crowd of journalists covering the first anniversary of Tiananmen Square at Beijing University in 1990. It seemed to be a good spot for a clandestine rendezvous. Picking up Wenchun, we drove to a nearby residential compound, constantly looking through the rearview mirror to see if we were being followed. Quickly carrying the camera into a dilapidated building, we walked up seven flights of stairs and knocked on the door. It was opened by a frail, bespectacled man with a shock of white hair and a deeply lined face.

Xu Liangying was a distinguished scholar, best known for translating the collected works of Albert Einstein into Chinese. The project had sustained him during twenty years of internal exile that began in 1957, when he spoke out against Chairman Mao's "anti-rightist campaign" in which hundreds of thousands of intellectuals were persecuted. Rehabilitated after Mao's death, Xu continued to call for a more open society. In 1994, he had been placed briefly under house arrest and faced intensive police surveillance after he and a half dozen other intellectuals had urged the government to end its harassment of dissidents. Now Xu had drafted a petition not only demanding that the "verdict" of June 4 be overturned, but that all Chinese imprisoned for their beliefs or speech be freed, and that the government abandon "the ignominious tradition of literary inquisition that has persisted in our country since ancient times."

Xu led us into his study, lined with books on physics, science, and human rights. Two posters of Einstein dominated the walls, one adorned with the renowned physicist's famous quotation: "Great spirits have always encountered violent opposition from mediocre minds." Sitting behind a wooden desk on which a small picture of the Statue of Liberty was mounted, he outlined his reasons for organizing the petition.

"Our main point is that China needs tolerance. China is now trying to modernize. But without tolerance, modernization will not be successful. Simply focusing on the economy is not modernization. People, by nature, have ideas and reason and aspire to freedom. People aren't animals. Filling your stomach is not enough. If that's the case, we're no different than pigs or dogs. People need human rights like freedom of thought, freedom of speech, and freedom of publication. You can't just allow one way of thinking, one ideology."

His eyes burning with passion in his wrinkled face, Xu continued. "The top leaders still lack a basic spirit of tolerance, which is why the tragedy of June 4 occurred. The government insists on calling this a counterrevolutionary revolt. We common people cannot accept this. The students' demonstrations were originally just peaceful appeals for democracy and freedom, and an end to corruption. But the government could not tolerate this and used the military to suppress it. But we say the government must seek truth from facts and reverse the verdict."

As the camera rolled, I expected the police to burst in the door at any moment. When Xu finally finished, we packed up the camera and tripod and exited as swiftly as possible. To my intense relief, we were not tailed back to the office. We had moved quickly enough to be in and out before the security services were able to react to the fact that the petition was being distributed to the media. In deliberately vague language, I advised the CNN International Desk to expect a strong story. The next morning, I sent Rebecca MacKinnon, with the videotape hidden in her bag, down to Hong Kong. From there, the story was transmitted back to the Atlanta studios. On this day, we had outscored the government.

But in the run-up to the sixth anniversary of the massacre, the mood in Beijing became notably more tense. We could see a significant increase in the number of police patrolling the streets and the square. Intent on prohibiting gatherings of any size, numerous popular restaurants and discos were closed for the weekend of the anniversary. Even the guards at the gate to our residential compound heightened their harassment of local Chinese who were trying to visit, on one occasion denying entry to a carload of Chinese army officers arriving for a formal diplomatic dinner at the home of the U.S. Air Force attaché. Lynne and I began picking Chinese friends up a block or two away from the compound and driving them through the gates. The guards, we thought, were unlikely to physically stop a car driven by a foreigner, and once inside, we could escort our friends upstairs without much trouble.

We also felt the ability of the state to make life unpleasant in another way. In what appeared to be a crude attempt to make money, the Beijing city government, already embroiled in a major corruption scandal, issued a new set of regulations governing dog ownership. The economic boom of the past few years had begun to produce a Chinese middle class with money to spend, and having a pet dog was a popular new fad. When we arrived in 1987, Sherlock was one of only a handful of dogs in Beijing, almost all belonging to foreigners; but now the city's nouveaux riches were spending big bucks for the joy (and, no doubt, the status) of owning a dog. Ostensibly concerned to prevent rabies and eliminate the fouling of Beijing's streets, the new rules required dog owners to pay a registration fee of over $700, plus an annual fee of nearly $300, a fortune for ordinary Chinese—and no mean sum for us. In addition, the public security bureau announced that only dogs under thirteen inches in height— the size of the average Pekingese—were permitted. Any bigger pets would have to go. Chinese dog owners were outraged, and the regulations sent a tremor of anxiety through the foreign community too, many of whom had, like us, brought their pets with them to China. The impending crackdown produced a strongly worded letter of protest signed by several Western ambassadors, which the Chinese Foreign Ministry refused to accept.

Although reluctant to see me leave Beijing, CNN had finally agreed to let me wind up my China assignment and head for a new post in mid-June of 1995. I would take a year off to write this book, and then become bureau chief in Hong Kong in time to cover the territory's historic return to Chinese rule in 1997. As we prepared for our departure, Lynne and I worried about ensuring that Sherlock, old, arthritic, and a Tiananmen evacuee, could leave with us. For days, in the midst of both packing and trying to monitor the mounting political tension as the anniversary approached, we talked of little else. In the grand scheme of things, the fate of one dog was of minor importance. But the distress the new rules created for us was a blunt reminder of the arbitrary power of the Chinese state, even during this time of reform.

On the morning of June 4, 1995, I took a taxi and returned to Tiananmen Square for a last look before my departure. The weather was the same as on the day of the massacre: hot, sunny, and muggy. Driving along Changan Street, I passed the corner at Wangfujing where the young man had so bravely stopped the tank. It was now the site of the largest McDonald's in the world. Another sign of the changing times: across from the Beijing Hotel was a huge billboard promoting an anticorruption conference. I got out near the East Gate of the Great Hall of the People, where the protesting students had gathered on the day of Hu Yaobang's funeral in 1989 to demand dialogue with the government. Walking onto the square, I passed scores of plainclothes policemen whose identity was obvious from their walkie-talkies, earpieces, and handycams. One of them was surreptitiously taking pictures of me. At the base of the Monument to the Heroes of the Revolution, I saw five teenagers dressed in white shirts and red pants, two of them solemnly holding a red flag. The crowds were sparse this day. Most people had apparently heeded the by-now annual warnings from the government to stay away from the square. It was unnaturally quiet. Yet when I shut my eyes, my mind was swept by images from that magical, terrible time. I could almost feel the crush of bodies, the exitement, the tension, and I could hear echoes of the chants and songs. I could also feel the ghosts from the night of June 4, an almost palpable presence.

I walked to the north end of Tiananmen, past the place where the Goddess of Democracy had stood, toward the CNN live-shot location. I felt a pang of nostalgia. If they ever reversed the verdict on June 4—the day of the crackdown and, incidentally, my birthday—

I mused, maybe they would erect a small monument to CNN there. I stared across the street at the Tiananmen rostrum, with its giant portrait of Chairman Mao. Even now, the Gate of Heavenly Peace, so imposing and full of history, a potent symbol of my own long China journey, held the power to move me. I had been drawn to China because, at a time of tumult in my own country, I believed the Chinese revolution offered hope and inspiration to a troubled world. That had been one of the first of my youthful illusions to go. Yet as I prepared to return to the United States twenty-two years after I first set foot in the People's Republic, I had to admit I still found it hard to get a handle on a country I had learned was far more complicated and difficult to understand than I had ever imagined. In 1973, the veneer of Maoist political conformity and the all-pervasive sense of revolutionary mission had masked the tensions, conflicts, and human dramas just below the surface of Chinese society. In the partly open China of the mid-1990s, it was possible to identify and even to report on many of these once-hidden complexities. But I remained unsure what to make of them.

From a nation of certainties, China now seemed to me a country of paradoxes, which could not be reduced either to the ideological simplicities of my youth or the journalistic simplicities that so often characterized foreign reporting from Beijing. There were so many questions. How did one reconcile a society bursting with new forms of wealth and entrepreneurial energy, in which tens of millions of people had been lifted out of poverty in perhaps the greatest economic miracle of modern times, with one rotted by corruption and despotism, where those who dared to speak out were ruthlessly suppressed? In spite of the repression, was the Chinese Communist Party really in charge? Or was it like a hard crust clamped over a seething, boiling mass that threatened to crack its authority—to the point that it could well become a marginalized force in the China of the next century? Was the nation spinning out of control, veering toward the chaos, or *luan*, that my 1973 tour guides so greatly feared?

I did not know the answers, and there were times I still felt like the character in Zhuangzi's fable—not sure if I was a man dreaming he was a butterfly, or a butterfly dreaming he was a man. But I did know that watching the Chinese come alive in the years after Mao, living through and telling the world about their achievements and disasters for the better part of a decade, taught me more about heroism and cruelty, wisdom and folly, truth and falsehood—in short, the human condition—than anything else I could have ever imagined. China was a hard school, and none of what I learned there came easily. But I had no regrets that this ancient, tumultuous country had consumed almost a quarter-century of my life.

As I turned to leave the square, a man walked by me. When I saw his T-shirt, I did a double take. It read LIVE FREE OR DIE. I looked more closely. It was the motto of New Hampshire, emblazoned on the state's license plate. In smaller letters, I read: SOUVENIR OF USA.

A few days later, Lynne, Daniel, Benjamin, and I boarded a Finnair jet bound for Helsinki and New York. My old Radio Beijing friend Liu, now a senior China executive for a U.S.-based multinational, came to see us off. As we embraced, I brushed back tears. Then Lynne and I steeled ourselves for what we feared would be a final nerve-racking encounter with the Chinese bureaucracy. We had come prepared with every available document and letter of authorization we could secure, all of them full of official chops, or seals. But in the prevailing climate, we knew things could still go wrong. The Finnair station manager, a friend of ours, came to our preemptive rescue. Wearing so many ID cards, badges, and airport-security clearances that he resembled a decorated war veteran, he took our most precious piece of "luggage" and loaded it onto a small baggage cart. Without stopping to explain himself, he wheeled the heroic but aging Sherlock past openmouthed customs and immigration officials and onto the open-mouthed plane for a new life and freedom.

international tensions, 317, 320, 325–26,
326, 333–56, 363
religion in, 327–28
satellite feed from, 340–41, 349–50, 352
North Korean Television, 340
"Nothing to My Name," 380–81
Nuclear Non-Proliferation Treaty, 333

P

Pacific News Service, 65, 71
Pakistan, 108, 298
Afghan refugees in, 109
Palace Hotel, Beijing, 260–61
Palestine Liberation Organization (PLO), 120
Pathet Lao, 61
Peace Café, 98–99
People Power, 136, 141, 144, 267–68
People's Daily, 14, 43, 70, 82, 149, 192, 198, 203,
206, 213, 214, 235, 245, 382
People's Liberation Army (PLA), 33–34, 35
27th Group Army, 225, 270, 271
38th Group Army, 225, 270, 271
anniversary of Tiananmen Square crackdown,
293–95
crackdown in Tiananmen Square, *see*
Tiananmen Square protests of 1989, the
crackdown
interaction with protesters, 21, 200, 220, 221,
226, 247–48, 278
people's belief in, 270–71
People's Republic of China:
children in, 153, 303–304
Chinoy's idealistic attraction to, 11, 27, 36, 87,
95, 293, 387
commune system, 43–44, 312, 313
Communist Party of, *see* Chinese Communist
Party
connections (*guanxi*) in, 162, 175, 196
Cultural Revolution, 27, 30, 35, 36, 39, 48–49,
67, 68, 75, 85, 89, 95, 99, 158, 314–15,
316
investigation of unjust persecution during,
96–97
culture of, 376–82
dissidents, *see* Human rights, in China; *names
of individuals*; Tiananmen Square protests
of 1989
earthquakes in, 79–80, 364
economy of, *see* Economy of China
foreigners, treatment of, 13, 41, 45, 159–64,
368
founding of, 19, 39, 177
human rights in, *see* Human rights, in China
labor camps, 95
media and, 13, 69, 70, 87, 106, 145–46,
291–95, 304–306
opened to, 115–16

Tiananmen Square protests and, *see*
Tiananmen Square protests of 1989
nationalism in, 373–74
Northeast provinces, *see* Manchuria
opening of, 12, 29–31, 88, 94, 99–100
population policy, 303–304
religious expression in, 95, 126–27, 158–59
secrecy of, 13, 43, 316
Sino-Soviet relations, *see* Soviet Union,
Sino-Soviet relations
Tibet and, 166–74, 181, 236
–U.S. relations, 29–30, 106, 125, 205,
275–76, 298, 372–73
most favored nation trading status, 302, 372
Vietnam and, 100–102, 106–107, 114
Perry, William, 336
Pessin, Al, 283
Philippines, 136–44, 267–68, 298
Phoenix, 56
Pixelator, 233, 255
Pol Pot, 101
Pomfret, John, 283
Pramoj, Kukrit, 72
Pratt, Bud, 90, 106, 115
Provisional Beijing Students' Union, 195, 198, 202,
203
Pyongyang, North Korea, 318, 320–32, 337–63
passim

Q

Qaddafi, Muammar, 127, 128–29
Qian Qichen, 367
Qinghua University, 48, 197, 313–15
Qiu Shi, 159
Quiet American, The (Greene), 62, 78

R

Radio Beijing, friend at, 218, 263–64, 276, 280, 282,
304, 388
Raise the Red Lantern, 378
Ramos, Ferdinand, 144
Ramos, Fidel, 137, 139
Rather, Dan, 64, 204, 212
Reagan, Ronald, China trip of, 125–27
Red Cross, Chinese, 288
Red Flag, 159
Red Guards, 35, 39, 48
Red Sorghum, 378
Reform the Armed Forces Movement (RAM), 139,
140
Register, Larry, 212, 221–22
Reinhardt, Burt, 24, 118, 123
Related to AIDS, 380
Ren Wanding, 177
Ren Yansheng, 48–49, 315
Republic of China, *see* Taiwan
Republic of Korea (ROK), *see* South Korea

A NOTE ON THE TYPE

The text of *China Live* was composed using the Electra family. Designed in 1935 by William Addison Dwiggins, Electra was conceived with the idea of modern, streamlined precision in a face "for setting down warm, human ideas." Today, it is admired for its even color and ideal legibility. In addition, we have also used the companion set of Caravan Borders, also by Dwiggins.

Printed and bound by Quebecor,
Martinsburg, West Virginia